VICHY IN THE TROPICS

Vichy in the Tropics

PÉTAIN'S NATIONAL REVOLUTION IN
MADAGASCAR, GUADELOUPE, AND
INDOCHINA, 1940-1944

Eric T. Jennings

STANFORD UNIVERSITY PRESS
STANFORD, CALIFORNIA 2001

Stanford University Press
Stanford, California
© 2001 by the Board of Trustees of the
Leland Stanford Junior University
Printed in the United States of America

Library of Congress Cataloging-in-Publication Data

Jennings, Eric Thomas.
    Vichy in the tropics : Pétain's national revolution in Madagascar,
Guadeloupe, and Indochina, 1940–1944 / Eric T. Jennings.
       p.   cm.
    Includes bibliographical references and index.
ISBN: 978-0-8047-4179-8 (alk. paper)
ISBN: 978-0-8047-5047-9

    1. France—History—German occupation, 1940–1945.
2. France—Colonies—History—20th century. 3. Guadeloupe—
Colonial influence.   4. Guadeloupe—History—20th century.
5. Madagascar—Colonial influence.   6. Madagascar—History—
1885–1960.   7. Indochina—Colonial influence.   8. Indochina—
History—20th century.   I. Title.

DC397.J45   2001
909'09712440824—dc21   2001042866

This book is printed on acid-free, archival-quality paper.

Original printing 2001

Last figure below indicates year of this printing:
10   09   08   07   06   05   04   03   02   01

Typeset at Stanford University Press in 10/13 Galliard

Acknowledgments

This book would not have been completed without the generous support of several organizations. The Social Science and Humanities Research Council of Canada funded three years of graduate study at the University of California at Berkeley, during which time this project took shape. A Mellon Foundation dissertation prospectus fellowship and a Jeanne Marandon predissertation fellowship from the Société des professeurs français et francophones d'Amérique permitted preliminary trips to Aix-en-Provence's Archives d'Outre-mer. A generous Franco-American Foundation Bicentennial Fellowship allowed me to pursue research over an entire year at these same archives. A subsequent research trip to Guadeloupe was made possible by a University of California at Berkeley Humanities Research Grant. Grants from the University of Toronto's Connaught Fund, the Social Science and Humanities Research Council of Canada, and the University of Toronto's History Department enabled me to conduct further work in Hanoi, Bordeaux, Paris, London, and Antananarivo. A fellowship from the Mabel McLeod Lewis Memorial Fund proved invaluable during the writing stage.

I also wish to recognize my friends and colleagues for their many insights. I am deeply indebted to Susanna Barrows, who supervised my dissertation at U.C. Berkeley, for her scrupulous reading of a great many drafts. Her encouragement, enthusiasm, advice, and friendship were instrumental in shaping this work from start to finish. Also at Berkeley, I wish to thank Anthony Adamthwaite for his helpful suggestions at every stage of this project. At the University of Toronto, David Higgs has provided encouragement and sound, practical guidance from the very beginning of my graduate studies.

Among the many readers who have improved this manuscript through their suggestions, I must extend my heartfelt thanks to Alice Conklin, William B. Cohen, and Bertram Gordon for their very detailed and constructive comments. Martin Klein, Ann Smock, Clifford Rosenberg, Tina Freris, Chantal Bertrand-Jennings, and Lawrence Jennings also read complete drafts, providing helpful advice. The Berkeley French History Dissertation Group and the European Studies Seminar at Cornell University offered engaging feedback on chapters relating to Indochina under Vichy. These same sections were also improved by careful readings from Peter Zinoman, Michael Vann, Bruce Lockhart, and David Del Testa.

At Stanford University Press, Norris Pope, Laura Comay, John Feneron, and Martin Hanft saw this project through to fruition. My sincere thanks for their assistance throughout the editing process.

In France, I wish to recognize a community of archivists and historians around the Archives d'Outre-mer. Messieurs Dion and Villon and Madame Vachier shared their archival expertise on Guadeloupe, Madagascar, and Indochina, respectively. Also in Aix, I benefited from the company of an exceptional circle of researchers, including Olivier Vergniot, Jean-Louis Pretini, Clifford Rosenberg, Jacques Cantier, Ruthie Ginio, Mike Vann, David Del Testa, and Florence Camel. I would also like to thank Monsieur and Madame Guillaume of the Université de Bordeaux for telling me in 1997 about the still unsorted Decoux papers at the Bordeaux Municipal Archives; without their tip, I would have missed a rich and unique resource.

At the University of Toronto Libraries, Jane Lynch of interlibrary loan tracked down one-of-a-kind monographs as far away as Martinique and Japan. Graham Bradshaw helped acquire many valuable newspapers on microfilm, which proved helpful for this project. I am grateful to my colleagues Hy Van Luong, Michael Lambek, and Andrew Walsh at the University of Toronto's Anthropology Department for having helped pave my research trips to Vietnam and Madagascar, respectively.

On location in Vietnam, Professor Phan Huy Le, director of the Center for Vietnamese Studies at Hanoi University, greatly facilitated archival access in my behalf. My cousin Franck Bénard at the Alliance Française de Hanoi proved a wonderful guide and companion in all things gastronomic. In Guadeloupe, Madame Ghislaine Bouchet, directrice des Archives départementales, and her family were at once generous hosts and incomparable guides to the archives. In Madagascar, Madame Razoharinoro, directrice des Archives nationales, not only expedited my research formalities but also kindly familiarized me with archival holdings and the intricacies of local classifying. Closer to home, Tina Freris shaped this project in countless ways. She also endured more lengthy ruminations, distant travels, and wild goose chases around *Vichy in the Tropics* than one could imagine.

E.T.J.

Contents

(photographs follow pages 78 and 198)

Maps

VICHY IN THE TROPICS

Introduction

[handwritten margin note: time of social darwinism]

This book is not only about an empire at war. ~~It is about an empire on the verge of a cataclysm.~~ Even at first glance, the importance of the Vichy period in the colonies is apparent. The years 1940 to 1944 preceded a sea change within the French colonial empire, with Indochina erupting in war in 1945, and Madagascar in 1947. Upheavals of another sort occurred in Guadeloupe, which took an opposite course, becoming territorially part of France in 1946. Vichy's imperial episode represents at once the coming to power and the last spasm of essentialist French colonialism—a form of colonialism steeped in social-Darwinist determinism and rooted in a reductionist, organic understanding of other, usually "primitive," societies and "races." After Marshal Pétain's brand of colonialism, there would be no turning back. In this sense, the Vichy moment lies at the very crossroads of colonialism and postcolonialism.

That Marshal Philippe Pétain's collaborationist regime ruled over an empire from 1940 to 1944 is often overlooked by historians. That it spelled changes in the colonial realm is even less acknowledged.[1] One of the most comprehensive texts on French colonialism holds that Vichy leaders did not possess a colonial policy of their own, and stood instead for "the political status quo."[2] Similarly, studies of the Vichy regime itself make little mention of what took place in the overwhelming majority of colonies that remained loyal to Pétain until 1942.[3] Historians of decolonization for their part, though they have generally recognized the Second World War—and the First World War—as decisive turning points,[4] have nonetheless failed

[handwritten margin note: ppl often forget that Vichy was an empirical power]

to discern significant ideological shifts in French colonialism between 1939 and 1944. In this way, the Second World War is often presented as an agent of change in the colonial sphere only insofar as it engendered a "loss of prestige" for the colonizer,[5] or an increased reliance upon colonial troops to liberate the motherland. This book suggests that in the French case at least, the years 1940 to 1944 contributed to decolonization in a much more tangible way, by ushering in a reductionist ideology and a new, harsher brand of colonialism, which both directly and indirectly fueled indigenous nationalism.

Any study of colonial Pétainism must first tackle the myth—propagated by such films as *Casablanca*—that Nazi pressure lurked behind the Vichy government's colonial actions. Such an approach strips the Vichy regime of any agency in colonial affairs. In reality, far from allowing the Germans to run French colonies from behind the scenes, Vichy French leaders followed a much more duplicitous course. On the surface, they elaborated a strategy of imperial neutrality.[6] Officially at least, "loyal colonies" would be off limits to both the Allies and the Axis. This is not to suggest that Vichy officials somehow forgot the empire. On the contrary, a steady stream of telegrams and radio messages from Vichy attests that the colonies were very much a prime focus of the regime until 1943. Vichy directives to its imperial proconsuls reveal that the regime sought far more than neutrality from its colonies. It actually cloned itself overseas. This was not limited to disseminating the "spirit of defeatism across the sea,"[7] as General Charles de Gaulle had feared in 1940. In reality, the Vichy regime, of its own volition and without Nazi prompting, projected its ideology throughout the French empire between 1940 and 1944. That Vichy officials extended an undiluted form of their ultraconservative ideology to distant colonies clearly demonstrates to what extent Pétain's politics of "National Revolution" were internally generated.

But the colonies under Vichy reveal much more than merely a German absence. Vichy, I will argue, delivered to its empire not only an authoritarianism that was bound to elicit opposition but also the seeds of nationalist resurgence. That Pétainists exported such potential time-bombs to distant colonies is striking enough in its own right. That they did so in the face of an almost permanent Allied threat to their colonies verges on the incomprehensible. For Vichy's empire, in the throes of an imperial civil war, shrank on an annual basis. And Pétain's entourage convinced itself quite readily that successive British, Gaullist, or joint attacks—first on the French fleet at Mers-el-Kébir (Oran) on July 3, 1940; then on Dakar Senegal in September 1940; Syria in June–July 1941; St. Pierre and Miquelon in December 1941; and Madagascar in May 1942—constituted a pattern of imperial revenge and pillage on the part of an old imperial rival at the expense of a now vulnerable and truncated France. Pétain thus grew obsessed with the empire's loyalty. One source recounts that he kept near him a map of Africa, outlining the advance of Gaullist "dissidence." Not a day passed without Pétain's mentioning the empire.[8]

The marshal had every reason for concern. The trickle of imperial defections to Charles de Gaulle's Free French—and hence to the Allies—in 1940 turned to a steady stream by 1942. In July 1941, Syria was conquered by the Allies. November 1942 marked a major turning point, with Vichy losing control over all of its remaining African possessions. By August 1943, the Vichy camp was left with only one colony, Indochina. Pétain even revamped the suddenly underworked Colonial Secretariat into a joint Ministry of the Navy and the Colonies—an administrative tandem that had last existed a century earlier under King Louis-Philippe.[9] From 1940 to 1943, the loss of colony upon colony sent colonial and diplomatic experts at Vichy into frenetic quests to protect the empire, to recapture lost territories, or even to invade British ones.[10] Beleaguered on every side, as indeed they were, Vichyites nonetheless persevered in adapting their ideology of "National Revolution" to the tropics.

My archival research has focused largely on changes in French colonial ideology and practices, and on interactions between Pétainist ideology and indigenous cultures. Through this approach, I have pondered whether Vichy ideology proved unpopular enough to foment revolt, or whether it stirred nationalist sentiments by striking resonant notes of traditionalism and *völkism*. One should not of course overstate the impact of the Vichy era, or of the war as a whole, upon the *longue-durée* of decolonization.[11] Nonetheless, this book suggests that the Vichy regime quite unwittingly set in motion several forms of opposition in its "loyal colonies." It did so on two levels; first by hardening an already ruthless colonialism; second, and more ironically, by introducing to the empire Pétain's cherished themes of authenticity, tradition, and folklore. In this way, Pétainist ideology interacted with a nexus of indigenous nationalist themes. The result was a curious coexistence, or even, in the case of Indochina, an outright symbiosis between Pétainism and local nationalisms between 1940 and 1944. It would appear that Vichy officials inadvertently created a setting in which their own reductionist ideologies, folkloric nostalgia, and language of particularism were actually turned against them.

What rendered possible this curious interaction of French and indigenous notions of "authenticity" was of course the political turn that took place in France in 1940. Marshal Philippe Pétain's new authoritarian Vichy regime reneged on the admittedly faltering promises of egalitarianism and universalism, advocating in their place order, tradition, and a notion of difference embedded in inequality. The new regime's ideology of "National Revolution" was encapsulated in its motto "Work, Family, Fatherland." Vichy's repudiation of universalism should be understood as a reaction against the Third Republic, and the French revolutionary legacy of "Liberty, Equality, Fraternity." Although colonial historians have rightly pointed out that across the French empire the promise of republican universalism had in reality proven illusory and hollow,[12] this was not the interpretation of Vichy rulers. Decrying the "false equalities" of the Republic, they based their reductionist turn on hyperbole and caricature. The assimilation they so vilified was largely a product of their imaginations. But its role as a straw man explains much of the new regime's avowedly antiuniversalistic and antiassimilationist colonial discourse.[13]

In this respect, as in many others, the parallels with the modern-day French political universe are striking. Over the past two decades, the far right in France has raised the specter of immigration to the same heights as Vichy had elevated the alleged evils of assimilation, egalitarianism, and universalism. More apparent yet, the present-day virtual monopoly of the French far right over the language of difference in France finds its origins in the Vichy era. To be sure, the prime "other" under Vichy had been the Jew. But as the enemy of the French far right has shifted from the Jew to the postcolonial immigrant, so our attention might turn to the Vichy regime's perceptions of the "colonial"—then an *indigène,* now an *immigré.*[14] That no one has heretofore systematically broached this topic is curious, for it holds the key to understanding how the politics of difference in France got a bad name. Although this book is about the early 1940s, it finds resonance in contemporary French politics and society.

Overall, this text lies at the crossroads of three fields. It contributes to a larger debate on decolonization that has for too long overlooked the role of colonial ideologies; to Vichy studies, which have ignored nonmilitary events in the empire; and finally to the study of French epistemological models, arguably divided since the Enlightenment between enshrining the universal or the particular. This said, I must caution that the following chapters are more concerned with the ironies inherent in unplanned readings of Vichy's ideology of National Revolution in the colonies than they are with the history of indigenous peoples, indigenous resistance, or for that matter the actual unfolding of decolonization. In other words, rather than provide a comprehensive domestic history of the colonies themselves, or of resistance movements proper, I have focused on what archives yield for the period: an analysis of Vichy's volition, its opportunism, its colonial vision, and how the latter was actually applied overseas. I would not presume to recount or compare the rise and the course of nationalism in Madagascar, Guadeloupe, and Indochina. Nor do I claim to focus on the diplomatic, military, or international intricacies surrounding Vichy in the tropics: these have been thoroughly studied by Martin Thomas, Paul-Marie de la Gorce, Kim Munholland, and Desmond Dinan, to name only a few.[15] Rather, I have chosen to examine how Vichy's ultraconservative ideology played itself out in a colonial context.

Three Case Studies

Although I first imagined this project as approaching the issue of Vichy in the tropics from the "center" rather than the "periphery," it soon became apparent that a Vichy-centric approach would reveal little more than imperial projects. Moreover, I soon noticed a sizable discrepancy between Vichy's imperial rhetoric—already studied by Charles-Robert Ageron and Pascal Blanchard[16]—and much more overlooked and revealing colonial practices. This gap between colonial discourses and practices could be addressed only by studying the most regional records (thus, wherever possible, I have utilized local sources, down to municipal documents). Nor did I want to follow the other extreme by examining Vichy in one colonial subregion alone.[17]

The question then arose of which colonies to study. Only a comparative approach, it seemed, could illuminate the remarkable consistency and malleability of Vichy ideology in vastly different settings, as well as the patterns of adaptation and opportunism by all parties during this period. Here, Gwendolyn Wright's *The Politics of Design in French Colonial Urbanism* proved a fruitful model.[18] Wright compared and contrasted, albeit on quite another register, Indochina, Morocco, and Madagascar from the turn of the century to the 1930s. She succeeded at once in providing sufficient local context and in extrapolating broad, empirewide observations. A host of other factors also informed my choices. It is quite clear that some former French colonies are much better represented in the archives than others. In all three cases, I have been able to consult archives in both France and in the former colonies themselves. I chose my case studies, then, both for reasons of archival availability and diversity of colonial models.

Other considerations also governed my decision. The colonies I chose ought to be devoid of a possible Nazi presence. Indeed, the territories I examined should be well out of reach of direct Nazi influence for any litmus test on the nature of Vichy to be effective. This immediately eliminated French North Africa as a whole. Moreover, the fascinating case of Algeria, where the 1870 Crémieux decree enfranchising North African Jews was repealed under Vichy (on October 7, 1940), is one that archival lacunae and restrictions still render difficult to piece together.[19] In addition, these case studies should be representative of the diversity of the French colonial wartime experience, both administratively and chronologically. Hence, for a representative "sampling," I chose Guadeloupe, an *ancienne colonie* that had been French longer than Corsica or Savoy, and which had previously benefited from full-fledged republican rule; then Indochina, a vast and diverse region conquered by the French as of the mid-nineteenth century; finally, Madagascar, a highly centralized "recent" colony. Indeed, on the Indian Ocean island, only forty-five years of French domination had preceded the Vichy episode. There, the tensions between assimilation and association, colonial "liberalism" and repression, had been concentrated and heightened over a short lapse of time. There too, the French administration had plainly sought to replace the island's previous rulers, the Merina, and had quite transparently attempted to anchor its authority and root its legitimacy in terms of centralized Merina rule (sometimes taking advantage of it, sometimes playing upon coastal opposition to perceived highland/Merina hegemony).

Chronologically too, these choices represented a broad spectrum: Madagascar remained loyal to Vichy for a relatively short time, as British troops expelled the Vichy administration in September 1942. In contrast, Guadeloupe stayed under Vichy control until July 1943, and Indochina maintained its allegiance to Pétain even after the regime fell into oblivion in the summer of 1944. These three colonies also presented a gamut of political and administrative systems. Guadeloupeans, through a long process begun in 1789, were considered full-fledged citizens, although their island would become a French department only in 1946. A number of representative bodies, elected by universal male suffrage, made this colony virtually no different from the metropole institutionally (save for the fact that a governor, rather than a prefect, represented Paris in Guadeloupe's capital of

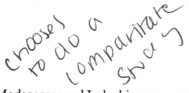

[handwritten marginalia: chooses to do a comparitate study]

Basse-Terre). Madagascar and Indochina were quite another matter. In the former, the French replaced the void left by their toppling of the Merina monarchy with authoritarian colonial rule. In Indochina, the colonizers allowed monarchies to remain in place in Annam, Laos, and Cambodia, although their influence was kept in check, and often reduced to naught. In the words of Bao Dai, emperor of Annam: "[In] Indochina the monarchs may rule, but the [French] Admiral governs."[20]

Finally, these case studies provide three quite different trajectories, from the standpoint of resistance and decolonization. In Madagascar before 1940, a budding dissident movement had largely been confined to demands for assimilation and equal rights. After the advent of Vichy in 1940, opposition would take an increasingly nationalistic turn.[21] This path would eventually culminate in the insurrection of 1947, which was brutally suppressed on orders from Marcel de Coppet, who returned to crush the rebellion, long after having first acted as the island's governor in 1939.

In Indochina, meanwhile, the Second World War marked an important watershed in Communist resistance. By 1941, Communists assumed the mantle of nationalism, rejecting class struggle for a "national liberation revolution."[22] That a complex interrelationship linked Vietnamese nationalists with the National Revolution's rhetoric of difference will be suggested in later chapters.

Finally, in Guadeloupe, the Vichy period bore equally significant although altogether different consequences. There, Vichy's antirepublicanism was equated with a return to prerepublican autocratic rule. Vichy was in fact understood as part of a cycle of reaction whose manifestations had included the reinstatement of slavery in 1802, the abolition of universal male suffrage under Louis Napoleon, and the abrogation of political freedom in 1940. Rather than pushing most Guadeloupean dissidents toward secession, the Vichy experience led most to seek guarantees of future republicanism.

Before considering the implementation and adaptation of the National Revolution to these individual colonies, one must first explain the dynamics of its dissemination overseas. After the Vichy government retained most French colonies in July 1940, it was no foregone conclusion that it would propagate its ideology to these territories (after all, full-fledged republicanism had never been exported to the empire). Even Hitler initially suspected that Pétain would play a double game in the empire.[23] But he did not. The year 1940, the "terrible year" in the metropole, marked a clean slate for the empire. Opportunists on all sides would try to put their stamp on the emerging new French colonial order. And opportunities would indeed abound, made possible by the change of regime and accompanying ideological shifts, as well as by the power vacuum that followed in the wake of the French military defeat of June 1940.

Vichy's Empire in 1940: A New Colonial Vision

> The Crime of this Armistice is to have capitulated as if France did not have an Empire.
>
> —Charles de Gaulle, July 30, 1940

> One of the first consequences of these abominable Armistices will be the disaffection and probable revolt of the natives of the Empire.
>
> —Charles de Gaulle, Aug. 29, 1940[1]

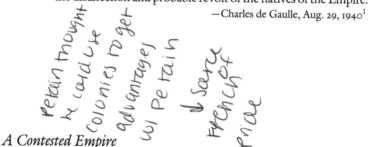

A Contested Empire

Both of these statements, pronounced over the BBC by the maverick Free French general Charles de Gaulle after France's June 17, 1940, armistice with Germany, underscore the importance of the French colonial empire in 1940. After the fall of France, all eyes turned to the colonies. To the emerging collaborationist Vichy regime under the leadership of Marshal Philippe Pétain, the colonies represented a distant and therefore much coveted prize with which to entice—and perhaps extract concessions from—Nazi Germany.[2] For Vichy propaganda agencies, the empire was presented as a "trump card" to be played against Hitler, should Germany try to impose too harsh a peace. Vichy-endorsed film reels also used the colonies as a much needed source of French pride after the successive humiliations of 1940. To de Gaulle, and his handful of Free French supporters who vowed to continue the war against Hitler in 1940, the French colonies promised an elusive reward: territorial and political legitimacy for a marginalized movement operating out of London. And yet de Gaulle would wait mostly in vain, as only one governor of a major colony voluntarily joined the Free French in 1940; that was Chad, which under the leadership of its black Guianese governor, Félix Eboué, officially rallied to the general on August 26, 1940.

Interestingly, in his 1940 statements, de Gaulle reserved his greatest critique for Vichy's refusal to consider the empire as a possible bastion for resistance. Why, might one ask, would remote colonies join the camp of the Vichy regime, instead of continuing the war alongside the British empire? After all, Belgian and Dutch colonies had stayed out of the sphere of the Axis powers, despite the defeat of their respective "mother countries."[3] As both de Gaulle and Pétain recognized, the French empire, too, was completely out of German reach, and colonials were consequently "entirely free."[4] The cover of the British navy alone seemed to guarantee immunity and material security for the French empire, had it rallied to the Free French. De Gaulle therefore had cause to hope that his proclamations would sway to his side if not entire colonies, then at least a great many colonial officials.

And yet only a handful of top-ranking colonial officials, never mind entire colonies, ventured to join a general then considered a renegade. In fact, few colonizers were ever swayed to the Free French of their own accord. The historian Marc Michel, directly challenging the Gaullist myth of an empire immediately rallying behind the general, has argued that only Chad ever joined de Gaulle of the free will of its administrators—let alone of its indigenous populations.[5] Even after all of French Equatorial Africa followed Chad's lead later in 1940 (buckling to strong military pressure from the Free French), Vichy's total colonial losses still represented only one-sixteenth of all French colonial territory.[6] Moreover, some rallyings to the Free French, such as those of the tiny French outposts in India on September 9, 1940, or the New Hebrides on July 23, 1940, were entirely determined by British proximity. Later "rallyings," as in Syria in July 1941, Madagascar, and North and West Africa from May to November 1942, should all properly be referred to as conquests.

How could de Gaulle have been so unsuccessful in 1940? Were indigenous populations indifferent to the Free French message? Or were colonial administrators somehow not as free as he surmised? One should not be altogether surprised by this outcome. In reality, indigenous populations had no say whatsoever in determining loyalty or resistance in 1940, as they were never consulted.

Colonial officials for their part were driven to Pétain's camp for a num-

anti-eng sentiments in colonies

ber of reasons: loyalty to what seemed the sole and unquestionably legitimate government of Vichy (after all, Pétain had been granted full powers
by the National Assembly),[7] a belief in Pétain's claim that the empire constituted France's trump card, an ideological sympathy for the political direction promised by the new paternalist regime, and a latent anglophobia,
exacerbated by the tragedy of Mers-el-Kébir. The British sinking of the
French fleet at the Algerian port of Mers-el-Kébir in early July 1940 heightened anti-English sentiments, which already ran higher in French colonial
circles than perhaps anywhere else. Though one could not consider colonial officials predisposed to Pétainism on antirepublican grounds—many,
if not most, hailed from staunchly republican families[8]—they were certainly sympathetic to the new regime's anglophobia. Indeed, resentment
over the Franco-British colonial crisis at Fashoda in 1898 was still strong,
even by 1940. So too was the idea of an English conspiracy to steal French
colonies, a notion supported by pointing to a "pattern" of previous English
"thefts" of French colonies, from Acadia and Québec to Mauritius.[9]
Though often seduced by Kipling,[10] French colonial administrators were
also taught to meditate the lessons of Marchand and Gallieni, who had
come into conflict with the English at the turn of the century in East Africa
and Madagascar. In this sense, de Gaulle fundamentally misjudged his
audience; to most colonials, joining the Free French in London was as un-
appealing as a political risk as it was inconceivable on anglophobic
grounds.[11]

Ideological complicity with the emerging Vichy regime represented
perhaps the deciding factor for French colonizers confronted with a divided France, and soon with a pan-imperial civil war. The Third Republic,
although in many ways responsible for the colonial élan of the New Imperialism (circa 1871), had by the late 1930s grown especially unpopular in
colonial circles.[12] Many colonizers now reviled it for its purported weakness, corruption, and attachment to "false ideals" of Liberty, Equality, and
Fraternity. Most *colons* (colonial settlers) had long considered these principles irreconcilable with colonialism; now colonial administrators seemed
at last to concur, and countenanced a less hypocritical form of exploitation
and domination. In such circles, the advent of Vichy seemed a divine surprise indeed—to borrow Charles Maurras's oft misquoted expression.[13]
Among such colonizers the Vichy regime promised "the golden age of
[French] colonialism, for it eliminated all of the ambiguities of the policy
of assimilation."[14] In this way, the defeat of 1940 was opportunistically
seized upon to usher in unabashedly inegalitarian colonial schemes, ges-

finally realized it was hypocritical to claim liberty as a settler

tating for decades in colonial minds but repressed under the republican regime. In the process, the long contested republican and universalistic ideal of assimilation was finally repudiated, in favor of transparent antiegalitarianism.

This evolution mirrored—and in fact exaggerated—that of the metropole. In mainland France, the 1930s had been rife with xenophobia and antirepublicanism. Though such beliefs gained in popularity, they were nonetheless largely kept out of power until 1940. So too in the colonies did 1940 signal the triumph of antirepublican extremists. In remote Madagascar, for example, the colonial administration—officials, functionaries, and governors—had long been considered something of a safeguard against the excesses of intractable *colons*—be they planters or industrialists. When in 1940 administrators themselves embraced Vichy's antirepublican ideals, the floodgates of antirepublicanism were opened. Throughout the empire, reprisals were exacted on the advocates of a long detested "liberal colonialism." As in the metropole, the tide had turned in a protracted French civil war. The history of this civil war was instantly rewritten by the victors. As early as July 1940 (at a time when Nazi-Soviet collusion should have spelled restraint), a pro-Vichy pamphlet lashed out at Communism, a prime enemy of the French far right. The 1930s were now presented as the heyday of Communism. Nowhere had Marxism supposedly been more virulent than in the colonies, where it had "reared its head" most visibly at the 1930 Yen Bay rebellion in Indochina.[15] Such rewritings of the 1930s signaled more than an about-face of political fortunes. The revision of the colonial history of the past decade was also part and parcel of a newfound 1940 fascination with all things imperial, itself building upon the less positive legacy of the 1938 *repli impérial*, a form of colonial isolationism.

1870–71 *Revisited?*

With French attention in 1940 riveted on the empire, parallels with the colonial élan of the 1870s seemed inevitable. Just as the vanquished France of 1871 had turned to colonial expansion, so too was the humiliated France of 1940 expected to pursue an imperial resurgence. The parallels did not end there. According to this reasoning, French colonial zeal after 1870 stemmed more precisely from the loss of Alsace and Lorraine; an even more truncated France in 1940 should therefore find all the greater salvation in the empire. Marius Leblond—a Réunionais of Greek origin, whose adopted name might betray an identification with a certain kind of

France—succinctly elaborated this theory:

> The defeat is not only a trial but also a lesson and a school—one of reflection, of determination, of wisdom and of flourishing. Our wonderful colonial empire of today sprang up from our defeat in 1871. The latter left the French shocked, crushed, full of self-doubt, intimidated, limited in Europe: out of a profound and ancestral instinct, they turned to colonial expansion. ... The colonies became a school of breathing, aspiration, and freedom, as well as laboratories of hope.[16]

Such ideas were widely shared. A journalist in 1942 Toulouse commented upon the broader manifestations of the "1871 syndrome": "There has been a profusion of colonial literature since the Armistice. It really seems that the French have rediscovered the importance of their empire."[17] Of course, with metropolitan newspapers proclaiming in their headlines that "France is an Empire,"[18] from 1940 to 1942 the colonies were difficult to overlook. A *Comité France Empire* was created in early 1941 so as "better [to] explain to the French the notion of empire and the fact that they are members of a community of 110 million inhabitants."[19] Some projected Vichy's colonial enthusiasm to quite unrealistic ends. In January 1941, a journalist for the collaborationist metropolitan daily *Les Nouveaux Temps* professed that "tomorrow's France will be maritime, colonial and corporative,"[20] no doubt forgetting that even at Germany's military height in 1941, neither Vichy nor the Axis was in a position to control the high seas.

The image of the colonies as "laboratories of hope" was not the only factor propelling Vichy's colonial renaissance. One must not forget that from its very inception, Vichy was in the throes of an imperial civil war against the Free French; any imaginable occasion was therefore used to stress colonial loyalty and to deride Gaullist dissidence overseas. The famous royalist Charles Maurras became one of many specialists at slandering the Free French. Maurras claimed that their true colors were revealed when de Gaulle supposedly held the bishop of Libreville at ransom during the Gaullist takeover of Equatorial Africa in 1940.[21] Meanwhile, "positive" colonial propaganda was provided by metropolitan Vichy newspapers, as they chronicled "the loyalty of the Guianese" and the "fidelity and gratitude of Réunion."[22] Similar although much more insistent and widespread propaganda was being delivered to the colonies themselves. On September 3, 1940, Pétain gave his first speech directed at the empire. He seized the opportunity to proclaim his cardinal colonial principle—that the empire represented his trump card, and that its unity was therefore indispensable. The marshal declared:

I wanted this first message addressed to overseas populations, to the governors, the *colons,* to French citizens, subjects and those under protectorates. I wanted this message to be from the Head of State himself. France has lost the war. Three-fifths of its territory are occupied. It is bracing itself for a cruel winter. ... But its unity, a unity forged by a thousand years of sacrifice, remains intact. It cannot be compromised. No encroachments, from any side, no matter what ideals they might claim, can overcome our unity. The first task today is to obey.[23]

By August 1941, the message of obedience and unity could be transmitted to the empire on a daily basis, thanks to the establishing of the empirewide Vichy colonial radio station, "Allouis."[24]

Another, more obscure factor played a role in the Vichy regime's fascination with the empire. Ever since the rise of the New Imperialism, the spas of the town of Vichy proper had attracted thousands of colonial administrators. Vichy's waters had earned a reputation for curing colonial ailments. In this sense, Vichy had been a de facto capital of the colonizers[25] long before 1940, because of the constant stream of colonials traveling there for *ressourcement.* A "Missionary House" had been founded there in 1930, in light of the number of missionaries and colonial functionaries present.[26] This colonial connection carried over into the Pétainist era. In the town of Vichy, from 1940 to 1944, colonial conferences were organized, colonial folklore was showcased, and indigenous notables delivered speeches on "the Annamite soul" and "Malagasy evolution."[27] Surely this atmosphere of colonial euphoria could not fail to influence the political climate in such a tight-knit and provincial surrounding as the town of Vichy—suddenly projected into the capital of nonoccupied France.

Colonial Collaboration

While the Vichy regime's colonial enthusiasm was professed far and wide, Pétain's government gave much less publicity to another use of empire in 1940. Vichy France, the only pre-existing European government to cooperate with Hitler rather than choose exile, would also present imperial booty to the Third Reich. It included Vichy's enforced colonial neutrality, which could only benefit Hitler, and an especially advantageous supplying of colonial products to the Nazi German war effort. One French source had no qualms about advocating such a course of action in 1940. In a November 1940 article in the *Revue des deux mondes,* Edmond Vivier de Streel, a colonial industrialist, prominent member of the *Union coloniale,* and former cabinet chief at the French colonial ministry, elaborated a new imperial blueprint. Vivier de Streel envisioned a future Europe under Nazi leadership, in which France would wear the colonial helmet. Combining colonial enthusiasm with a collaborationism no doubt stoked by the Hitler-Pétain interview of October 24, 1940, at Montoire-sur-Le-Loir, Vivier de Streel stated that

> by intensifying its colonial activity, our country can orchestrate a material turnaround under the aegis of a noble ideal that will vivify the flame of its patriotism; it can also, with the help of other European states, ensure others their supply in raw materials, and a parallel increase in exports which will liberate them from their own geographical servitude.[28]

At one level, this colonial expert formulated a vision of a Vichy France fitting in to a new German-dominated Europe, by offering it a window to the world. On quite another score, he also unwittingly acknowledged that France was so infirm that it need rely upon its empire for revivification.

October–November 1940 also witnessed more concrete discussions on how French colonies could benefit Germany materially. On October 21, 1940, shortly before the much-publicized Hitler-Pétain encounter at Montoire, French and German armistice authorities at Wiesbaden negotiated "the handing over to the Reich of a percentage of certain colonial products."[29] By November 19, 1940, specifics had been arranged. Germany would be granted half of French West African industrial diamond output, while undetermined percentages of Malagasy graphite and Indochinese rubber would be delivered to Germany via Vladivostok and the trans-Siberian railroad.[30] Only should this itinerary prove ineffective or should it be cut off would the riskier all-maritime route be utilized.

Overall, the course of negotiations on colonial goods confirms the historian Robert Paxton's argument that "Pétain wanted collaboration; Hitler wanted only booty."[31] Indeed, on November 19, 1940, the German representative Schone requested seventy thousand tons of French colonial palm oil, twice the French colonial annual output.[32] When discussions turned to banana imports, Tupiner, the French delegate and head of economic affairs at Vichy's colonial ministry, protested, "You cannot ignore that the rations of meat allocated to the French are much lower than those of the Germans, and that we need bananas as a substitute product." Thereupon, his German counterpart retorted, "You always talk of the French rations. They are a consequence of the war and the defeat!" An indignant Tupiner concluded, "This is a far cry from collaboration!"[33]

In spite of Tupiner's moment of revelation, French colonial products continued to reach the Reich, in accordance with Vichy's policy of achieving collaboration by enticing Germany with colonial "loyalty" and booty. The neglected question of Vichy's imperial collaboration warrants a study of its own (economic historians have concentrated upon Vichy's colonial modernization projects, rather than examining the final destination of colonial goods between 1940 and 1944). Suffice it to say here that British officials were correct in suspecting that Vichy's colonial shipping supplied the Third Reich. After a French cargo ship moving from Madagascar to Marseilles was intercepted by the Royal Navy in November 1941, the British concluded that the mica, graphite, and raffia on board were destined for Germany. Vichy naval authorities, far from contesting the charge, conceded that France needed to barter colonial goods in exchange for basic foodstuffs from Germany, such as potatoes and sugar.[34] They neglected to add that France had been self-sufficient in, and in fact an exporter of, sugar and potatoes before Germany began funneling them eastward in 1940.

The French empire was on the minds of the highest Vichy and German officials in 1940. At the Wiesbaden armistice talks in July of that year, the head German economic negotiator, Richard Hemmen, gladly accepted "the idea of a Franco-German collaboration in the colonial sphere." He then enumerated German priorities in the French empire, as if drawing up a global shopping list: "oils, textiles, iron ore, phosphates, cereals and other foodstuffs."[35]

On the French side, Vichy's second most important leader and *vice-président du Conseil*, Pierre Laval, brushed up on his knowledge of the colonies, the better to entice the Germans with them. In November 1940, he received colonial advice from Jules Brévié, former governor of Indochina and soon to become Vichy's colonial secretary in April 1942.[36] Realizing that German officials wanted to avoid running French colonies themselves "because of the administrative costs involved," Brévié counseled a policy of imperial economic reform aimed at satisfying German economic demand.[37] Brévié's proposed colonial reform was further intended to stave off impending economic misery in formerly stable French colonies, now deprived of European capital. Advocating a Napoleonic policy of *grands travaux*, and the injection of German investment, Brévié became one of the first to elaborate an imperial vision informed by both collaborationist and colonial concerns.

Colonial Administrators and the Advent of Vichy

Jules Brévié encapsulates some of the contradictions of colonial Pétainism. Those who have seen him described in pre-1940 literature are often startled to discover that Brévié would later hold a high office under Vichy. He had been renowned early in his career for his "liberal" ideals.[38] He had served as governor general of West Africa between 1930 and 1936, where he had proposed to increase the powers of colonial councils. As the proconsul of French West Africa, he had demonstrated a clear interest in local cultures, founding the Institut Français sur l'Afrique noire in Dakar.[39] Brévié's case further belies any systematic and simplistic conflation of association with reaction; prior to 1940 he had championed a British-style association, while being widely recognized as "progressive." In fact, in 1936 the Socialist-led Popular Front Government named him to the crucial post of governor general of Indochina.[40] There he declared an amnesty for political prisoners and liberalized previously draconian press laws. By the time he reached Indochina, Panivong Norindr has argued, Brévié was renowned for "his integrity and for his opposition to colonial abuses."[41]

How then could such an administrator have become an ardent supporter of collaboration with Nazi Germany? Of course, one must recognize that many former Socialists of the interwar era—among them Pierre Laval—later joined, and played crucial roles in, Pétain's administration.[42] In many ways, Brévié resists facile classification, having served by necessity under a variety of colonial ministers and adapting to the changing times. No doubt the political upheaval of 1940 smacked of déja vu to administrators who had learned long before the chameleonic art of compromise, adaptation, and steering the course under vastly different governments. Brévié's case, then, exemplifies how important it is to anchor Vichy's colonial vision into the continuum of French colonialism—for it was almost always the same personnel that implemented first republican, then later Vichy, directives in the colonies.

The National Revolution Overseas: Subversion in the Making, or Imperial Climax?

As Pétainism began to show its true colors—those of an explicitly anti-democratic, ultraconservative, xenophobic, and essentialist regime—a fundamental question arose: should Vichy's ideology be exported to the colonies? Bona fide republicanism had never been exported to the colonies, after all. To some, the very name "National Revolution," used to designate Pétainist ideology, seemed inherently problematic in a colonial context. Were the words "National Revolution" not potentially subversive when transferred to Indochina or Madagascar? Indeed, were they not more subversive even than illusory notions of "Liberty, Equality, and Fraternity"?

Two colonial experts stepped forward early on to denounce any attempt at introducing Vichy ideology to the tropics. The first was Pierre Lyautey, nephew of the famous colonial administrator Marshal Louis Hubert Lyautey (Pierre Lyautey was a specialist of colonial affairs himself, and would later join de Gaulle's Fighting French forces in 1943). In 1940, Pierre Lyautey cautioned:

> The effort of French national renovation is, admittedly, closely watched overseas, but each colony, each protectorate, each mandate is an edifice ordered on delicate and scientific terms. Much as a fire can ruin one of our greatest cathedrals in a few hours, all that would be required to destroy our masterpiece of an empire would be a few inopportune measures. Let us not export too hastily measures which make sense here, but which over there would give rise to all sorts of difficulties. Should we apply over there, and without any modalities, texts which have been judged appropriate here? We think not.[43]

Lyautey clearly foresaw the potential danger of bringing to the colonies an ideology steeped in ultranationalism, regionalism, folklore, nostalgia, and a merciless condemnation of the preceding French regime. The last thing Lyautey wanted was to introduce to the empire the "mood of self-flagellation"[44] that reigned in France after the defeat of 1940. Vichy's conjuring up of an idealized nationalistic rebirth seemed an even more dangerous export to regions where the French had until recently sought to erase the local past.

Robert Poulain, a journalist for the respectable conservative French newspaper *Le Temps*, echoed Pierre Lyautey's beliefs. According to Poulain, exporting the National Revolution to the colonies amounted to providing "natives" ammunition with which to oust the French later. Poulain, however, borrowed a much more revealing image to convey this message. He wrote in a June 1941 article entitled simply "The National Revolution and the Colonies":

> One does not serve with impunity a glass of alcohol to a newborn, or even to an adolescent, and we very much fear any infringements on this basic truth. The natives of our colonies, no matter what their degree of evolution or of "primitiveness," are above all strict logicians, much like children.[45]

Poulain used pre-existing French colonial paternalism for new ends. Portraying infantilized "natives" as fine imitators and deducers, he warned that one could not run the risk of imbuing them with an ideology that vaunted integral nationalism. The journalist for *Le Temps* went further still. He advocated a continuation of the pre-1940 colonial status quo, asserting that

> because our colonial methods have proven fruitful, I do not see how the National Revolution could bring anything new to the relationship between whites and natives, except, for ill-intentioned spirits, the opportunity to further their own causes.[46]

Here Poulain captured some of the ironies inherent in the Pétainism's colonial forays. First, Poulain warned, the National Revolution could be reinscribed and used for altogether different ends by nationalists all too ready to exploit imperial ambiguities. Second, Poulain implied, how could Pétainism in any way harden or alter an already rigid, hierarchical, and antiegalitarian ordering of colonizer and colonized?

Such fears were well founded. Poulain's remarks found special resonance after Vichy began exporting its ideology overseas in the fall of 1940. Nationalists in the colonies would indeed turn the National Revolution on its head, by using it to undermine French colonial dominance. They would do so on a number of registers, from direct appropriations and adaptations of Vichy's cultural policies to more subtle and convoluted *tournures d'esprit* that played upon Vichy's exaltations of difference and custom.

Poulain's first observation, on the futility of Pétainism in an already hierarchical framework, proved somewhat less accurate. Admittedly, as Poulain suggested, on the surface the advent of Pétainism in the colonies did usher in slighter changes than in the metropole. France's much vaunted assimilationism, and its "enlightened, humanist colonialism" under the ideals of "Liberty, Equality, and Fraternity," had been more myths than colonial realities long before 1940.[47] Hence, their elimination in 1940 caused less of a stir in areas where they had always been dead letters. Even as official myths, though, they had provided a modicum of restraint that administrators could impose on *colons,* and an albeit modest safeguard against outright fascist and avowedly discriminatory ideologies. Both these restraints and safeguards were lifted with the advent of Vichy in the colonies.

Exporting the National Revolution

In spite of repeated warnings from colonial Cassandras, the National Revolution did reach the empire in 1940. Vichy's colonial ministry orchestrated the systematic duplication and adaptation of Pétainism overseas. The ministry of the colonies, like all other government agencies, had been forced to abandon its Paris headquarters for a modest hotel at Vichy during the debacle of May–June 1940. The ill-fittingly named Hôtel Britannique became the cramped home for the transposed ministry. There, four to eight functionaries shared hotel rooms hastily converted into offices. To add to the confusion, by March 1941 only 120 colonial ministry officials had been able to reach Vichy from Paris, out of a total of 500.[48] Undeterred by this serious lack of personnel and resources, successive colonial ministers set about plotting the dissemination of the National Revolution to the colonies from their overcrowded hotel in central Vichy.

Vichy's first colonial minister, the Martiniquais mulatto Henry Lémery, established the precedent for keeping colonial governors abreast of Vichy reforms. Lémery, a renowned Antillais conservative, was a close personal friend of Marshal Pétain. Although undoubtedly more moderate than his successor, Admiral René-Charles Platon, Lémery nonetheless laid the groundwork for future Pétainist reforms. First, he fought diligently to keep the empire out of Gaullist hands. On July 15, 1940, Lémery sent all "loyal" colonial governors a call for unity, in which he personally thanked them for "their touching unanimity." To his death, Lémery failed to understand why his "loyalty" had earned him prison time, while Governor Félix Eboué's "infidelity" secured him a place in the Panthéon.[49] Before his dismissal in September 1940, Lémery had also become a pioneer at injecting Pétainist dogma into colonial directives. On August 16, 1940, he sent the following orders to the West African city of Dakar, which would be the site of an Anglo-Gaullist attack only a month later:

> I ask you to ensure that in Dakar a strong discipline and rigorous order be maintained, as well as a respect of leaders. You are to prevent the all too frequent and unnecessary desertion of the village, undertaken out of a desire to escape obligations. The net effect has been the swelling of urban centers.[50]

Only two months after France had requested an armistice, its colonial minister was projecting overseas Pétain's demonizing of urbanism, his "return to the soil," as well as his cherished notions of hierarchy, order, and obedience. More revealingly still, Lémery extended to the empire the metropolitan laws of August 18 and 29, 1940, preventing elected councils from convening in "extraordinary sessions" and banning "secret societies"[51] — one of Vichy's many scapegoats.

Lémery's stint as colonial minister would be short-lived; he was dismissed as part of a cabinet shuffle on September 6, 1940. Lémery later claimed, no doubt correctly, to have been the victim of German pressure to remove him from office because of his "colonial origins."[52] His successor, the fanatically Vichyite and rabidly Anglophobic Rear-Admiral Platon, had come strongly recommended by Fleet Admiral François Darlan.[53] Platon, a survivor of the debacle at Dunkirk, soon won the esteem of the marshal himself.[54] He held close ties to the notorious antirepublican Charles Maurras, whom he frequently consulted on colonial matters (Platon took advice often, as he had little if any previous training in colonial affairs).[55] Platon's orthodoxy soon repelled Vichy moderates. His tenure as head of Vichy's ministry of the colonies would be longer than any other; he was installed at the Hôtel Britannique in September 1940, only to depart on April 18, 1942. He would also hold the dubious honor as the greatest propagator of Vichy institutions and doctrines to the colonies.

Platon proved zealous on many scores. First, he waged the imperial civil war against Gaullism with dogged determination, castigating the Free French as "a bunch of renegades made up of volunteers of the Universal Jewish Empire."[56] (It was for this zealousness that Platon was later executed as part of the *épuration* in March 1945.)[57] Second, Platon fought for the piecemeal, then later the wholesale exporting of the National Revolution to the colonies. Perhaps the most striking demonstration of his resolve in this matter came after the August 29, 1940, creation of a single party and veterans' organization, known as the Légion française des combattants. On September 21, 1940, Platon complained in the following terms to the head of the newly founded Légion:

> I must call your attention to the fact that the new [Légion] ... seems to have been conceived entirely for metropolitan France, to the exclusion of overseas territories. It would be extremely regrettable, especially under the current circumstances, to give to our colonial possessions the impression of having been ... kept out of an organization of this sort. ... The dissident propaganda of ex-General de Gaulle could only gain from it.[58]

In this way, Platon constantly quipped to Vichy agencies "not to forget the empire." While Lyautey and Poulain presaged disaster if the National Revolution were exported to the colonies, Platon foretold precisely the reverse. Convinced that colonizers and colonized alike would feel slighted if they were denied the "fruits" of the National Revolution, Platon pressed for its extension to the colonies on every possible occasion. In this manner, Platon would ensure the introduction to the colonies of most of Vichy's anti-Semitic and anti-Masonic legislation, as well as its regimentation of youth, its violent antiparliamentarism, its cult of the leader, and its exaltations of the soil and of an idealized past. By 1942, the colonial expert René Maunier could rightly declare that "the same wind, the same spirit, now blows [in the colonies] as does here [in the metropole]."[59]

On March 10, 1942, Henri Brenier, the former head of economic affairs in Indochina, advised Pétain on a number of colonial matters. Writing from Marseilles, Brenier urged the marshal to consider first the complete extension of the National Revolution to Indochina, and second, a plan providing greater autonomy for Laos, Cambodia, and Annam, all provinces of the French Indochinese federation. Vichy's colonial secretary, René-Charles Platon, offered a telling response to Brenier's suggestions. To the first proposal, Platon countered: "Of course the National Revolution is transposable locally. This is a government matter—and we are already hard at work on it."[60] But Platon was intransigent on the second recommendation: "[U]nder current conditions, the preparation, no matter how long term, of plans for eventual independence is not to be contemplated."[61] Platon correctly claimed to have already extended the National Revolution to Indochina. As for Brenier's schemes for Indochinese autonomy, these ran fundamentally contrary to a ministry that championed an inflexible form of colonialism. Most disturbingly for Platon, Brenier seemed to be confirming Poulain's and Lyautey's worst fears. If even colonizers could equate the introduction of the National Revolution with notions of rebirth and independence, then surely indigenous resisters would do the same.

Theories of Colonialism

Brenier's proposals were not the only grand imperial reforms advanced under Vichy. As William Cohen has shown, in January 1942 the Académie des sciences d'outre-mer put forward a plan for imperial citizenship. Cohen stresses, however, that the project was eventually aborted, and had in fact been deceptively hierarchical and manipulative from the outset.[62] Though Vichy certainly conceived of an alternative vision of "imperial citizenship," one must of course measure the directions of such projected reforms. One must not take at face value Vichy's self-portrayal as a regime bent upon lofty colonial idealism and bold innovation. Nevertheless, some historians have accepted the cliché that Pétain's colonial administration was visionary, and its colonial theories far more daring than those advanced at the Gaullist conference on future French colonial doctrines at Brazzaville in 1944.[63]

In reality, Vichy's colonial visions—like the regime itself—had been shaped by a myriad of forces from previous decades. In the "domestic" sphere, these influences ranged from corporatism to the beliefs of Charles Maurras, Edouard Drumont, and Salazar on the one hand, to the cult of the former Dreyfusard Charles Péguy on the other. In the colonial realm, the hodgepodge of ideological antecedents was equally complex. While Vichy was at pains to establish its ideological lineage, it encountered no such difficulty in listing its enemies. Domestically, these were identified as Jews, Freemasons, Communists, and democrats. Institutional enemies included parliament, democracy, republicanism, and the specter of international capitalism. Grouped together in a vast conspiracy theory, these "antinational forces" were dubbed *"l'anti-France."*

In the colonial sphere as well, a handful of these same enemies emerged; thus Vichy's *milice* persecuted and eventually assassinated the Jewish former colonial minister Georges Mandel in 1944. But in the colonial realm, where few of Vichy's scapegoats were to be found (save perhaps Freemasons, who did indeed enjoy a certain following in some colonial circles), others needed to be invented—if only to conjure up an antithetical antecedent to Vichy's brand of colonialism. This colonial straw man would supposedly have shown weakness toward Communism, placed indigenous interests above those of settlers, and decadence over labor. Vichy's colonial authorities, responding no doubt to long-standing *colon* sentiments (the *colon,* or settler, is to be distinguished from the colonial administrator), vilified colonial assemblies, "liberal colonialism," and the doctrine of assimilation. They concentrated their attacks on the very timid, and in fact largely nonexistent, colonial reforms of the Popular Front. What mattered in 1940 were perceptions of decadence and degeneration, themselves interconnected with a new spirit of scapegoating. When wanting to condemn colonial reforms, or colonial "softness" in general, between 1940 and 1944 one had only to make them up. For the reality was that the suddenly proscribed values of Liberty, Equality, and Fraternity had never penetrated far into the French colonial universe.

In order to understand the violence of Vichy's attacks on such largely imagined phenomena as "liberal colonialism," colonial assemblies, and assimilation, one must examine both mainstream and marginalized colonial ideologies of the previous decades. Vichy's brand of colonialism, like its domestic politics, had been informed by a set of Social Darwinist and integral nationalist theorists from the fin-de-siècle. As early as 1901, the notorious anti-Semite, anti-Dreyfusard, and antirepublican Edouard Drumont had plainly condemned colonial assimilation, advocating instead the British model of indirect rule. He did so for economic reasons, arguing as the journalist Raymond Cartier and the extreme-rightist politician Jean-Marie Le Pen would long after him (the first in the 1950s, the second in the 1980s and 1990s) that overseas France had become a financial burden. Surely the colonies could simply be pilfered for economic gain, Drumont argued. Already at the turn of the century, in the colonial sphere, fiscal and ideological conservatives alike were drawn to a new vision, known as "association." Responding to Drumont's allegations, the leading colonialist newspaper, *La Dépêche coloniale,* defended the republican colonial record with lofty, if clearly misguided, republican universalism: "We the French try to civilize, to facilitate the accession of natives to our civilization which we take to be more advanced. This is the French method. ... It may be more expensive, but it is worthier of our great nation."[64] As Alice Conklin points out, both assimilationists and associationists shared the language of, and a belief in, a so-called Civilizing Mission. But it is important to note that in the protracted battles of the Third Republic, "assimilationist colonialism" was largely the preserve of the French republican left (though the matter is far from black and white: indeed "socialist universalism" bears resemblance to that of a distinctly nonrepublican force, the equally evangelizing universalism of missionaries). This is not to suggest that association was somehow inherently unrepublican, that advocates of association were necessarily more racist than their assimilationist detractors, nor to deny that association and assimilation could coexist, for that matter. Nonetheless, after 1895 a certain strain of colonial thought did begin to lean toward an increasingly cynical, racist, segregationist, and avowedly exploitative reading of association—one already sketched out around the turn of the century by Edouard Drumont, Léopold de Saussure, and Jules Harmand, to name only a few.

Historians Raymond Betts, Alice Conklin, and Gwendolyn Wright have shown how the colonial doctrine of association, though an extremely old concept to be sure, began to gain currency after the First World War. Betts gives the French prime minister Waldeck-Rousseau's definition of the doctrine: "[To] develop the natives in the framework of their own civilization."[65] This compact definition contains the seeds of the major differences within associationist thought. The ambiguities inherent in it are glaring: as Alice Conklin has suggested, association could spell a greater knowledge of, and even a fascination for, indigenous cultures, though certainly one with political ramifications of its own. It was, at its origin, a way of achieving an entente between French colonizers and indigenous populations, by respecting local societies in exchange for greater cooperation from them. But on the uneven colonial playing field, it could also make for a thinly disguised basis for exploitation and racism, predicated on an integralist understanding of "cultural differences." Finally, as Conklin has noted, association was also largely a response to new and more vigorous forms of indigenous resistance. According to Conklin, the enemy in colonial thought had changed: while pre-1914 assimilationists had chastised the "feudalism" of indigenous cultures, associationists now condemned any "premature demands for freedom."[66] Association, in this sense, was a most malleable "compromise" solution. In this way too, one can deduce how elusive association became as a concept. In fact, as Betts suggests, it was often reduced to a catchword.[67] Little wonder, then, that the concept could be borrowed and entirely revamped by colonial theorists under Vichy.

Naturally then, post–World War I association was by no means the monopoly of ultraconservatives and illiberals. On the contrary, as both Conklin and Betts show, its origins are demonstrably republican, and its initial intentions quite "liberal." First of all, association rested upon the recognition, rather than the denial of, indigenous cultures. Thus, Conklin demonstrates that early associationists in French West Africa "embraced a much more positive image of traditional West African social and political organization than had existed in the past. Federal authorities now insisted that their subjects had institutions, such as the chieftancy, which were not nearly so exploitative as the French had once thought."[68] Secondly, association often signified a certain devolution of power and responsibility back to indigenous leaders. Thus Conklin shows how the colonial minister Albert Sarraut (1921–25), vaunted by some for his colonial liberalism at the time, accompanied his proclamations on association with assurances of greater representation for indigenous populations.[69]

However, in counterpoint to these "liberal" readings of association, one finds a host of more pragmatic adherents to the doctrine, who contributed to its eventual ultraconservative turn. Association, it should be stressed, lent itself to as many permutations as readings of indigenous cultures would allow; to the reform-minded it could signify the respect for local customs, but to conservatives it could be employed to justify discrimination and to exacerbate inequalities. Two of the doctrine's main exponents, Marshal Gallieni and Hubert Lyautey, had already demonstrated before the turn of the century in Tonkin and Madagascar how it could be employed pragmatically to cloak the colonizer in the mantle of indigenous custom. Much later, Vichy would seize upon this conservative reading of association—one previously developed and refined by colonial specialists like Léopold de Saussure and Louis Vignon.

The French naval officer Léopold de Saussure figures among the most influential proponents of the ultraconservative branch of association. His 1899 *Psychologie de la colonisation française* was inspired by the elitist and racist writings of the famous crowd psychologist Gustave le Bon. As historian Michael Adas has observed, de Saussure couched his racism entirely in "scientific" terms, clearly influenced by the writings of Gobineau as well. De Saussure, like other conservative associationists, embedded the adaptive dimension of association within a framework of scientific racism, concluding that education, for example, need be "geared to the level of evolutionary development of each culture in question."[70] Little wonder, then, that de Saussure, like Le Bon, would later receive praise under Vichy for promoting racial supremacism.

Louis Vignon was another ideological forerunner of Vichy's brand of colonialism. His 1919 *Programme de politique coloniale* provided an alternative to Arthur Girault's earlier republican assimilationist colonial model, outlined in his 1894 *Principes de la colonisation et de législation coloniale.*[71] What de Saussure had argued in the field of colonial theory, Vignon applied to colonial law. Hubert Deschamps, a former French colonial administrator in the Ivory Coast, Madagascar, and Djibouti, recalls that Vignon's *Programme de politique coloniale* was especially despised in Socialist colonial circles, since the book came to incarnate new, hierarchical readings of association. In Deschamps's words:

> Vignon represented a more recent and reactionary tendency, which had flourished before 1914 among some rightist intellectuals: Gustave Le Bon, Léopold de Saussure and Jules Harmand. While the assimilationists, in the tradition of the French Cartesians, deemed that "Reason is ... a global concept," this school, known as "Association," emphasized the differences between men.[72]

Deschamps's case, however, should also serve as a caution against drawing too close a connection between conservative associationism and Vichy. Indeed, Deschamps, as a staunch Socialist enemy of association (cum postwar Sorbonne professor), would nonetheless remain in office under Vichy, playing a crucial role in 1940, by maintaining Pétainist control over the North-East African colony of Djibouti, besieged by the British.

While Vignon, De Saussure, and certainly Lyautey and Gallieni were well-respected members of the French colonial establishment (or national heroes, in the case of the latter two), more radical rightist thinkers on the margins of colonial power also began to thrive in the interwar period. Indeed, it is hardly surprising that a large number of colonial officials should have joined the ranks of fascist and other extremist veterans' leagues in the 1930s, as these movements saw a meteoric rise in overall popularity. One such figure, Jean Paillard, had served as a journalist for the colonial section of the royalist and anti-Semitic newspaper *l'Action française* between 1935 and 1939.[73] In a book ominously entitled *La fin des Français en Afrique noire* (the end of the French presence in black Africa), Paillard had already in the 1930s expressed his fears of miscegenation and degeneration, fears that bridge the gap between de Saussure's and Vichy's colonial visions. This 1935 book advanced the idea that whites would gradually be evicted from Africa by the Syrian-Lebanese merchant classes, intent on "mongrelizing" Africa through intermarriage and assimilation.[74] Marginal figures like Paillard, in tandem with more respected conservative associationist thinkers, all served in different ways as ideological precursors to Pétain's brand of colonialism. Though Vichy might not have invented its reductionist brand of colonialism, it did bring the phenomenon to an unmistakable paroxysm. In the words of Pascal Blanchard, a specialist on the colonial outlook of the French far right: "[T]he colonial ideology of the far right would find both its pinnacle and its application in the regime of Marshal Pétain."[75]

In this way, two of the most influential colonial theorists under Vichy, René Maunier and Jean Paillard, drew heavily from the experience of the preceding decades.[76] Maunier clearly established in his 1942 volume *Sociologie coloniale* that "we are inventing identities in the colonies."[77] When Maunier did pay lip service to "assimilation," it was to the assimilation of National Revolutionary legislation by French colonies—a far cry from the revolutionary egalitarian ideal that first bore the name.[78]

This confusion around "assimilating Pétainism to the empire" is actually revealing, if one places it against a backdrop of associationist thought. When one considers that association rested upon the belief that one could not introduce to the colonies "preconceived formulas [and] imported principles,"[79] then Vichy's own actions seem to fly in the face of associationist tenets. And yet, this is precisely what Vichy's colonial minister Charles-René Platon set out to do—save that he exported a different set of "preconceived formulas" than those envisaged by earlier antiassimilationists. But in this sense, the associationist critique of assimilation could be, and indeed was, turned against Vichy's administration to condemn the wholesale dissemination of Pétainism to the French overseas empire (hence how Lyautey's nephew could remain faithful to his uncle's philosophy, by rejecting any hasty "exporting" of domestic remedies overseas).

Setting aside such contradictions inherent in Vichy's colonial views, one could argue that Vichy's hard-line colonialism reached a climax in 1943, with the publication of Paillard's *L'Empire français de demain*, prefaced by Marshal Pétain himself. Under Vichy, the former *Action française* journalist became head of Pétain's *Bureau des corporations,* an important government agency dedicated to propagating the doctrine of corporatism.[80] His 1943 work advocated much more than the total rejection of assimilation. Paillard recommended the introduction of racial segregation, so as to protect France from "dangerous foreign influences."[81] Fearful of the supposed inroads achieved by the Chinese community in Indochina, and Syrians in French West Africa, Paillard dreaded miscegenation above all.[82] Hence he recommended that "the title of French citizen can belong only ... to a son of a Frenchman, carrier of the blood representative of the genius of his race."[83] Paillard applied this pseudo-scientific racism to his analysis of *"anciennes colonies."* There he deplored that "granting the ballot to natives who represent a constant majority, amounts to withdrawing the same right from the *colons,* who will be in a perpetual minority." Paillard maintained that Third Republican colonialism would ultimately have led to an empire in which, "due to universal suffrage, and the implacable law of numbers, the colonizers would eventually come under the domination of the [majority of] colonized."[84] Paillard's fears of "native domination," his professed desire to safeguard the "French race," and indeed to maintain the "purity of races" in the French empire, made him the champion of a sinister reductionism that held greater sway under Vichy than under any previous twentieth-century French regime.

Interestingly, the apex of radical essentialism came after Vichy had lost the vast majority of its colonies. As the metropolitan regime veered toward outright fascism in 1943–44,[85] the doctrines concocted by some of its colonial experts followed suit. A May 1944 study commissioned by the ministry of the colonies on the "Condition of detribalized natives" illustrates this point. The study, authored by four colonial functionaries, went a step further than Paillard's, by calling for "the systematic and immediate expulsion of any native illegally entering metropolitan France."[86] This proposed measure, so eerily prefiguring those of the late-twentieth-century French far right, hinged on a reductionist vision of "the native." Of course, these arguments were certainly not new—they had been informed by a host of reductionist thinkers from Gustave Le Bon to Edouard Drumont or Alexis Carrel. Neither was xenophobia in France in any sense a recent invention, but rather an ongoing phenomenon manifested in 1893 by the massacre of Italians at Aigues-Mortes, the systematic supervision and control of North African immigrants in Paris, or the forced expulsion of Chinese students in 1921.[87] But this particular proposal to expel all "natives" was raised under a regime bent upon denaturalizing its perceived enemies and relegating nonwhite French citizens in the colonies to the rank of subjects. The authors of the report maintained that "the detribalized native becomes an immoral creature as soon as he reaches the city."[88] In this respect, the authors expanded upon the antiurbanism first expressed by Lémery in his August 16, 1940, directive to Dakar. The "Condition of detribalized natives" then enumerated methods of alleviating the effects of "detribalization." "Detribalization" was to be avoided at all costs; however, when it became unavoidable, it should be accompanied by a strict regimen. In this regard, sports were perceived as beneficial in "avoiding the rupture of balance so common among the detribalized." Left to their own devices, the "detribalized" allegedly ended up in "bars and other *débits de boisson* ... [as a result of] their desire for contact with Europeans."[89] This piece, so clearly aimed at inventing a "retribalization" and hence an inherently subservient position for "natives," represented the climax of years of essentialist thinking. All of these theories, be they related to "detribalization, mongrelization, or authenticity," hinged upon apocalyptic fears of a world dominated by unruly and debauched "natives," uprooted from their "natural environments."[90] This was Maurice Barrès's *Les déracinés* ("The Uprooted"), transposed to the tropics.

Vichy had shown its true colonial face long before its spiral toward outright fascism. Indeed, 1940, the *année terrible* as far as the war was concerned, was seen as an *annus mirabilis* by the colonial far right. Vichyites could console themselves over the defeat at the hands of Germany by fending off most Allied designs on "their" empire—including a hard-fought military victory over the English and Free French at Dakar between September 23 and 25, 1940. Moreover, colonial administrators could boast of having generated an imperial élan of their own. Indeed, they had developed such confidence as to export the National Revolution to the tropics. This had been accomplished in defiance of all colonial logic, and over cries for restraint from some colonial experts. Vichy's colonial ministry had initiated the process of introducing the National Revolution to the empire. On location, this ultraconservative ideology would take on a dynamic of its own, presenting unexpected opportunities for both colonizers and colonized. For the colonizers it seemed a vindication of their *Weltanschauung,* and an open mandate for unabashed inegalitarianism and untempered exploitation. For the colonized it would amount to a mixed bag—at once a step toward unflinching, harsher colonialism, and a complex catalyst for national liberation struggles. In many ways, the National Revolution carried with it the seeds of French colonial undoing. In the exaggerated and distorted universe of colonial domination, Vichy ideology would be subjected to tortured twists of the imagination from many different quarters. Its malleability was put to the test, in settings where interpretations of "the return to the soil" and "national renovation" proved at once so similar and so removed from those of Pétain.

CHAPTER 2

The French in Madagascar and the National Revolution

Until I came to Madagascar, I had always found it a little difficult to take the statement seriously that Vichy had instituted in unoccupied France a very fair replica of the Nazi machine. I had always believed subconsciously that the French character could not possibly stand for it. One month in the island was enough to change my views.

—Gandar Dower, 1943[1]

Such were the impressions left on the British war correspondent Gandar Dower a year after his foray into Madagascar. His testimony appears all the more remarkable because Madagascar was not merely "unoccupied" by Germany: it was removed from mainland France by 10,200 kilometers, and its sole Germanic element consisted of a handful of anti-Nazi exiles. Nevertheless, in an environment clearly unfettered from Nazism, French administrators and *colons* had, in the span of two years, from July 1940 to September 1942, espoused Vichy ideology, implemented Pétainist legislation, and finally rejected a pro forma republicanism long considered the guiding principle of French imperialism. Indeed, Madagascar had been conquered by the French in the first place at least nominally in the name of "republicanism" under the pretext of abolishing slavery, and hence "liberating" Madagascar's coastal peoples from the highland Merina.

Colonial Madagascar

The French conquered Madagascar, the world's third largest island, in 1895. Actual conquest had been preceded by a jostling for influence between

Map I. Madagascar, 1942

French and English governments, and Norwegian, English, and French missionaries. The royal family of Madagascar had attempted in vain to play English against French and even German colonial ambitions, but negotiations between colonizing nations in 1890 placed Madagascar in the French zone of control, dashing the hopes of continued Malagasy independence.[2] For Madagascar, unlike many other French colonies, had been an independent and unified, though certainly not homogeneous, state prior to the French invasion of 1895. It had been ruled from the highland capital Antananarivo (which became "Tananarive" in colonial times) by a royal family of Merina—or central highland—descent. Historian Pier Larson has shown that the very term "Merina" is more recent an invention than one might imagine. The French erroneously used it and the term *Hova* interchangeably to designate Madagascar's central highland peoples, whom they believed to be of Southeast Asian descent and "more advanced" than the lowland coastal peoples, to whom they ascribed an African ancestry. The term *Hova* is a clear misnomer, as it designates in reality a "middle class" within the Merina social system that included *Andriana* (highest rank), *Hova* (middle rank), and *Andevo* (lowest).[3] After the conquest, the French quite naturally interpreted to their liking what they considered an extremely hierarchical caste society, ushering in what the "pacifier" of Madagascar, Joseph Gallieni, dubbed a *"politique des races."* This was a Machiavellian policy of dividing and conquering by exploiting rifts between highland and coastal peoples to the colonizer's advantage.

Conquest in the name of French republicanism proved harder than expected. French casualties were high in 1895—largely on account of malaria. Moreover, a vast movement of resistance launched in the south, the rural Menalamba rebellion that began in November 1895, proved a formidable challenge to French rule.[4] This uprising centered at once on a reaction against the French invasion, and against Merina royalty—perceived as now collaborating with the French. It also assumed a religious dimension, with Menalamba rebels attacking the Christianization of Merina sovereigns, most notably by Protestant missionaries.[5]

Historian Yvan-Georges Paillard has argued that the Menalamba movement curtailed initial French hopes to turn Madagascar into a Tunisia-like protectorate.[6] From that point onward, French indigenous policy in Madagascar would involve an almost schizophrenic combination of calculated and highly selective applications of republican assimilationism on the one hand and pragmatic associationism on the other. Indeed, Joseph Gallieni, the first French governor of Madagascar, and his military collaborator, Louis Hubert Lyautey, willfully grafted a centralized French colonial administration upon an already centralized Merina one. Direct rule, rather than British-style association, became the hallmark of French colonial Madagascar. If centralization was part of French revolutionary ideology, so too was the eradication of perceived despots. Hence, on February 27, 1897, Gallieni dissolved the Malagasy monarchy in the name of republican assimilation, sending Queen Ranavalona III into exile. Invoking French revolutionary values, Marshal Gallieni further banned slavery in September 1896. He abolished the ritual of the Royal Bath, making July 14 the national holiday in its stead.[7] More ruthlessly, Gallieni selected two prominent members of Ranavalona's court and had them summarily executed on October 15, 1896.[8] Gallieni's republican anticlericalism brought him into conflict with missionaries, both Protestant and Catholic, who had been operating in Madagascar long before the French takeover. Finally, Gallieni's undiluted assimilationism introduced French as the official language of Madagascar. Such a policy gained widespread support in colonial circles. An indignant letter to the editor of a mainstream colonial review asked in 1901:

> Is it tolerable to allow [city and place] names that are anathema to the French mind: Manjakandriana, Ambohidrahino, Maevatanana, Andrangokoaka, etc.? ... Why do we not replace them with French names ... like *"Belle Fontaine"* ... or the names of [great] men? The following advantages would result [from such a change]: 1) it would render it easier for French people to learn about their colonial empire; 2) it would give our conquest an aura of definitiveness; 3) it would force natives to pronounce French words; 4) it would affirm "greater France"—Imagine that in twenty years Madagascar ... escapes our control; there would not be the slightest trace of our time there.[9]

Such was the state of mind of Madagascar's conquerors, who initially sought nothing short of total gallicization for the island. In this same way, Gallieni's curious colonial positivism involved misapplied adaptations of French republican precepts, practiced *à outrance* in an inegalitarian and exploitative colonial context.

But at the same time, Gallieni also sought to drape himself in the legitimacy of Merina monarchs. On March 14, 1897, he oversaw the transferal of the bodies of past Merina kings to Tananarive and orchestrated what he considered to be a meticulous replica of ritual Malagasy reburials.[10] As part of the "politique des races," he proclaimed the independence of Madagascar's non-Merina ethnic minorities—within the context of the charade of "liberation." Between misguided assimilationist republicanism and pragmatic associationism, in 1896–97 the Malagasy were arguably left with the worst of both French colonial doctrines.

Still, by the early twentieth century, Gallieni's ruthless practices had been challenged even within the French colonial system. Victor Augagneur, the Socialist governor of Madagascar between 1905 and 1910, though every bit as much an anticlerical and republican, proved more conciliatory and understanding toward indigenous elites in particular. In an important and damning condemnation of colonial excesses published in 1927, Augagneur vehemently denounced colonial abuses while at the same time outlining a policy of "liberal colonial reform."[11] More than in other colonies, Madagascar's post-1900 colonial school system bore some of the hallmarks of republican universalism; a French colonial administrator noted how much more widespread schooling was in interwar Madagascar than in French West Africa.[12] By the 1930s, in fact, republicans broadly defined had emerged as the most moderate of colonial alternatives. By 1940, those preaching authenticity, "retribalization," and difference were the very lobby advocating widespread forced labor and rejecting albeit timid proposals for partial indigenous political representation. Colonial intransigence, once a trademark of republican zealots, had become the preserve of their antirepublican counterparts.

Madagascar during the Second World War

On the eve of the Second World War, Madagascar's ethno-demographic makeup was the following: 3,600,000 Malagasy, some 20,000 French (roughly as many as today!), 10,500 Africans and Asians (including Indian and Chinese traders and shopkeepers), approximately 3,000 "other Europeans" (most notably Norwegian missionaries and Greek expatriates), and some 2,000 "métis."[13] Of the 20,000 to 25,000 French, approximately half were civil servants, and the other half "colonists, industrialists and merchants."[14]

Strategically, Madagascar was in no way predisposed to falling into the hands of Vichy. On the contrary, the island's remoteness from all other French territories save the Comoros and Réunion, and its proximity to British East Africa, might logically have led Madagascar to join de Gaulle's Free French in 1940.[15] The anglophilia of many Malagasy—especially in Protestant Merina circles—also might have prompted the island to join the

Allies, had indigenous populations ever been consulted on such matters. Most important, perhaps, gradual internal reforms in the late 1930s had in no way foreshadowed any kind of return to unyielding colonialism.

However, over the course of three months, from June to August 1940, Madagascar's French administration opted to proclaim its allegiance to the government of Marshal Philippe Pétain and to embrace the ideology of National Revolution. This decision was motivated by a number of factors: the apparent legitimacy of Vichy in 1940, which it would be gravely anachronistic to overlook, and the international situation, but also a shared belief in the political agenda of the "pacifier of Morocco" and "savior of Verdun," Philippe Pétain. Indeed, if Madagascar's indigenous populations were seen as generally favorably disposed toward Great Britain, the same cannot be said of its colonizers. Many of these continued to suffer from the "Fashoda syndrome" of Anglo-French colonial rivalry. Many had also come to embrace the antirepublican extreme right[16] — and hence welcomed the fall of the republic.

Madagascar's tragic notoriety in the Second World War is associated with a failed scheme to create a settlement colony for Europe's Jews — a project put forward by Poles, French, and Germans in the 1930s;[17] the plan was in keeping with numerous earlier proposals to colonize an island that was considered grossly underpopulated, with fewer than four million inhabitants (in 1926, this worked out to an average of five inhabitants per square kilometer).[18] However, surprisingly few histories have examined the island in its own right during this war, which by all accounts represented a watershed period in the history of colonialism.[19]

In Madagascar, the Second World War began much as had the previous global conflict: with staged shows of loyalty on the part of Malagasy notables, pronouncing their "entire submission" to "France their beloved mother," soon followed by recruitment of Malagasy into the French military.[20] The Third Republic governor of Madagascar, the newly appointed socialist Marcel de Coppet, who had previously served as governor of French West Africa under the Popular Front, attempted to present the war as a communion of Franco-Malagasy friendship. An anticlerical himself, he nonetheless sought to appeal to Madagascar's many Catholics by organizing a religious procession and public prayer for the victory of the Allies on May 26, 1940, in the Mahamasina quarter of Tananarive.[21] A proclamation issued by de Coppet on September 2, 1939, had already called for displays of "patriotism from the great isle at a time when France, faithful to its civilizing mission and to its generous traditions, readies herself to defend liberty once more." Finally, de Coppet, after appealing to the Malagasy on religious, patriotic, and ideological grounds, ordered local authorities to "exercise greater liberalism" when it came to applying the harsh judicial system for "natives" known as the *indigénat*.[22]

When news reached Madagascar of France's calamitous military collapse at the hands of the Third Reich in June 1940, initial reaction was one of panic. A political report from the port city of Tamatave on the island's east coast reveals a persistent and obviously unfounded rumor that "Germans might be disembarking any day in Tamatave."[23] Nevertheless, some French and Malagasy alike expressed early vows to fight on. On June 20, 1940, three days after Pétain had asked for an armistice in France, the France–Great Britain association of Madagascar addressed letters to France, London, and Tananarive,[24] "protesting energetically against German conditions for peace" and calling for a continuation of the struggle.[25] De Coppet himself vacillated at first, only to resign after the July 3, 1940, British sinking of the French fleet at Mers-el-Kébir. Madagascar's largely antiassimilationist, antirepublican, and anglophobic colonizers—still suffering from the "Fashoda syndrome," whose symptoms were only accentuated by Mers-el-Kébir—resented, in their majority, not only de Coppet but also the leaders of the France–Great Britain group. Many of Madagascar's French (essentially meaning French whites,[26] for only an insignificant number of Malagasy were ever naturalized) therefore delighted in the news that Léon Cayla, former authoritarian governor of Madagascar, had been nominated by Vichy to run the island. Cayla was described respectively by American and British sources as a "table-thumping, garrulous ... dictator"[27] and "an arriviste and opportunist [who] appears to enjoy the role of dictator in Madagascar; he is more pro-Vichy than Pétain."[28] Cayla was a *pied-noir,* a French Algerian who had governed Madagascar in the 1930s, including under the Popular Front, which he served grudgingly and whose prime minister, Léon Blum, he disliked for anti-Semitic motives.[29] Upon his return to Madagascar on August 2, 1940, Cayla declared that he would "associate Madagascar to the redressment which the new government is conducting." He added: "Thinking French means to think of France only."[30] In the span of three months, the French in Madagascar had thus been won over to the National Revolution, which, local administrators soon concurred, suited and simplified the colonial mission.

As in metropolitan France, the Vichy period in Madagascar saw "terrible avengings of internal politics."[31] A Gaullist "plot" to seize power on September 3, 1940, was crushed, its leaders jailed and castigated as anti-

French.[32] Thereafter, scores of prominent European figures, such as the lawyer Don Ignace Albertini,[33] as well as notable Malagasy dissidents and members of the Franco-British association, were preventively incarcerated. Sentencing proved unusually harsh for Europeans in French colonies, as even hints of anglophilia were taken for sedition. Thus an administrator by the name of Ficheterre was sentenced to two months in prison simply for expressing Gaullist sentiments.[34] The methods employed by Cayla and his successor, Annet, likewise shocked the colonizers. In addition to regular police forces, Vichy's governors were said to rely upon some three hundred plainclothes Malagasy spies.[35] The use of indigenous spies appears to have been resented as an especially pernicious violation of colonial power relations. To Europeans in Madagascar, it now seemed that politics had come to supersede race.

By November 1940, Cayla reported to Vichy that "public opinion has evolved in a favorable direction, thanks not only to repressive sanctions, but also to active propaganda which we have been waging since early August by radio, press and bulletins."[36] But the advent of the National Revolution brought with it far more than repression. It ushered in a variety of authoritarian, far-rightist schemes, be they economic, social, or cultural. It also spelled the adoption of metropolitan policies, such as the persecution of Jews and Freemasons, and, as far as the Malagasy were concerned, the use of forced labor on an unprecedented scale, as well as the fostering of a cult of Pétain. When Cayla was replaced by an even more convinced Pétainist, Armand Annet, on April 15, 1941, these trends were only exacerbated.

Vichy's rule of the island would be cut short, however, by British military interventions in May, then September 1942. No sooner had Madagascar's authorities declared their loyalty to Vichy in July 1940 than Britain had mounted an economic blockade of the island, in hopes of pressuring its rulers to rally to the Allied cause, but also so as to ensure that the colony would not contribute its resources to the industrial production of a France now collaborating with Hitler. The blockade had an important impact on the island by dramatically reducing imports. This brought further misery and sometimes famine for the Malagasy,[37] who saw their standard of living drop astronomically. The war, a Malagasy historian has written, "was the primary cause of the impoverishment of the rural masses."[38] The colonizers, for their part, were faced with the less trying prospect of producing baguettes from rice, cheeses and butter from zebus, and wine in the Betsileo region.[39] More ominously, autarky was invoked as a motive for implementing new forms of forced labor, and for converting standard elementary schools into technical or agricultural institutions. As for the main British goal of bringing trade from Madagascar to the metropole to a standstill, it clearly failed. Annual customs reports from the year 1941 reveal that while imports to Madagascar had been halved, total exports to France still amounted to 75,051 tons, only 22 percent less than before the blockade.[40] As Armand Annet, Vichy's second governor of the island, suspected, Germany was no doubt the final destination for Madagascar's valuable mineral and metal exports.[41]

Compounding the issue of trade was the even more significant strategic importance that Madagascar assumed as the war progressed. The fall of Singapore to the Japanese on February 15, 1942, and potential German threats to the Suez Canal that same year, suddenly propelled Madagascar onto the center stage of a strategic battle for the control of the Indian Ocean. The British, fearing that the island was imminently threatened by Japan, launched a preventive attack on the northern port city of Diego-Suarez in May 1942 and invaded the rest of the island in September. The entire campaign was carried out primarily by South African and East African soldiers under British officers.

Far from negotiating, Vichy forces fought to the bitter end, waging a scorched earth campaign that included the sabotaging of fifty-eight bridges as they retreated southward on a fifty-six-day guerrilla campaign.[42] After the initial raid on Diego-Suarez, Winston Churchill, trying to mend the irreparable, declared before the House of Commons on May 7, 1942: "[We] grieve that bloodshed has occurred between troops of our two countries whose peoples are united against the common foe."[43] Seeking tactfully to minimize the impact of the greatest Franco-British land battle since Waterloo, Churchill added that at Diego-Suarez "the French fought with great gallantry and discipline."[44] Henri Grapin, a French participant in the campaign, was less generous. In his memoirs, he contended that the military and civil leaders of Madagascar, General Guillemet and Governor Armand Annet, "placed their pledge of allegiance to Marshal Pétain above their colonial mission," going so far as to wage pitched battles against the British at Diego-Suarez and Ambositra, and ambushing British forces throughout the campaign. The battle of Diego-Suarez alone cost the French 171 lives, and the British nearly 400 casualties.[45] In refusing to surrender, Annet, his immediate entourage, and his administration down to the most subaltern clerk demonstrated their loyalty to Pétain personally, and in some cases their adherence to the National Revolution.[46]

The seeming metamorphosis in two years of colonial officials once offi-cially loyal to the Third Republic into staunchly anglophobic and fiercely loyal Pétainists can be explained on several levels. One should not overlook the fact that Vichy, and not the Free French, doubtless seemed most le-gitimate to French people as a whole from 1940 to 1942. Another plausible hypothesis is that Vichy had appeared in 1940 not merely as a logical le-gitimate choice but actually as a self-validating "divine surprise" for many colonial officials who perceived themselves as models for the metropole— inasmuch as they presented themselves as virile, self-abnegating, and de-void of decadence in their "glorious mission." In short, it will be argued, many colonials saw themselves as Vichyites before the letter.

Decadence and the Identities of
Colonizer and Colonized

The Vichy expert Robert Paxton has argued convincingly that "everything done at Vichy was in some sense a response to fears of decadence."[47] This statement finds special meaning in colonies in which the very identity of the colonizer was constructed as a reaction to "decadence." Indeed, the new regime vaunted the *colon* and the missionary as "representative of the French genius,"[48] even presenting them as supermen of sorts. Having been stationed overseas during and often long before France's dark hour of de-feat in May–June 1940, they were generally exempt from criticisms of decadence that befell their metropolitan counterparts. A 1942 article in the metropolitan Vichy review *Idées* went a step further, contending:

> The ethic of the National Revolution, like its politics, requires an effort of unity and excess. The new and necessary man whom we still await will be drawn from the monk and the warrior, the missionary and the colonial, the militant of the far right and that of the far left.[49]

The colonial, then, by nature and by occupation, was not merely uncon-taminated by decadence but could actually contribute to the piecemeal construction of a "regenerated Frenchman" in a characteristically fascist in-vention of an *Übermensch.*

The identity of the colonizer was—and had long been—determined as a function of perceived French racial superiority. In a 1942 New Year's mes-sage to Madagascar's French "Volunteers of the National Revolution," a youth indoctrination and regimentation organization reminiscent of the *Compagnons* in metropolitan France, Ponvienne, the secretary general and commissioner to youth in Madagascar, exalted "[t]he immaculate whiteness of your uniform symbolizing the honor and force of our race."[50] To be sure, the colonizer had long relied upon racism to rationalize colonialism; here, however, an explicit correlation is drawn between the trappings of a movement associated with the new ideology, and racial purity and strength.

The colonizer was further imagined to be virile and healthy, in contrast to his supposed antitheses, be they the Popular Front, the Third Republic, the "natives," Freemasons, or Jews. These, accordingly, incarnated "effeminacy and sickness." An article published in the metropolitan French newspaper *l'Oeuvre* in 1942 underscored the gendering of Madagascar in the colonial fantasy, by referring to the island as "a splendid girl, worrying, fascinating, multiple and fantastic like a woman. … It was almost by force that her father, Gallieni, had made her French."[51] According to this remarkable article, Léon Cayla, following Gallieni's initial act of incest, had tamed and embellished the island. Here one observes a variation on the theory outlined by Frantz Fanon in his *Black Skin, White Masks*; the black is indeed "reduced to the genital" and presented as a "biological threat," but is feminized rather than masculinized as Fanon asserts.[52] Far from instilling a fear of incest in the white as Fanon postulates, the Malagasy, through the "sexuality" of "their sorcery" and their mysterious "Malaysian origins," actually embodied the femme fatale—at once "devilish," "passionate," devious, and passive in the collective colonial imagination.[53] As incarnations of effeminacy, the Malagasy were portrayed as the antithesis of the virile colonial. They were to be dominated, yet perhaps emulated in one respect—for their fertility (this point seems ironic inasmuch as Madagascar was also presented as underpopulated). Indeed, Armand Annet reported the Malagasy reputation for "proliferation," fertility, and "honoring the family" to Vichy's colonial secretary on April 18, 1942, and an article in Madagascar's government-run *Bulletin d'Information et de documentation* could hardly contain its admiration for "the proliferation of the Malagasy race."[54]

As for the related metaphor of health vs. sickness, nowhere is it more apparent than in a speech by Olivier Leroy, the fanatically Vichyite director of education in Madagascar, who declared in 1941:

> The National Revolution will succeed because it is real and vital; [it is] a psychological necessity akin to that which drives a living body to seek health in the laws of hygiene. It will succeed because France was guilty of a poor political hygiene, but thankfully she carried within her reserves of strength and health. [However,] the need to pierce certain abscesses and to cauterize them must not

lead us to believe that France was sicker than she was. One can say on the contrary that the French organism showed a marvelous resistance to the parasites which afflicted it, and ridden of these parasites, it will find a new vitality.[55]

This trope betrays many of the main rhetorical tenets of fascism: the designation and dehumanization of a "parasitic" scapegoat, the stark contrast of virility and decadence, the notion of purging the body as a sanitizing of the state, and a pseudo-scientific rationalization of the political. Although historians generally acknowledge that Vichy was more ultraconservative than fascist,[56] certain discernibly fascist strands certainly permeate elements of Vichy's domestic, and a fortiori colonial ideology (one might point to the cult of the leader; or to corporatist schemes; the cult and regimentation of youth; the construction of an *Übermensch;* the extolling of earthy, rural, and *völkisch* values; a belief in innate "natural" hierarchies; and a fascination with order and virility).

Also evident in Leroy's speech is a reluctance to sully the icon of metropolitan France. This typified what the colonial critic Albert Memmi later termed "the dialectic of exaltation-resentment"[57] toward the metropole, a fundamental ambivalence that was only exacerbated by the traumatic defeat of France in May–June 1940. To many colonizers, the military debacle of 1940 only accentuated contradictory feelings of communion with and disdain for a metropole alternately presented as utopian or decadent.

This obsession with decadence was formulated in slightly different terms in Madagascar than in the metropole, but it assumed similar manifestations. Colonials found in the new regime's glorification of sports at once a remedy to combat the supposedly nefarious effects of the tropics and a recipe for the rejuvenation of the French "race." In February 1942, a civil servants' recreational athletic federation petitioned the governor for early dismissals from office duties twice weekly so as to conduct rugby and soccer practices.[58] *Hébertisme* for its part, the French navy's so-called natural method of physical education, seemed to offer a "collective discipline"[59] so dear to the new order. While boys were to be invigorated and regimented by physical exercise, a balanced sports regimen could prove beneficial for girls in quite another respect, by "preparing them for their feminine role by favoring the normal development of their organs."[60] Convinced of the salvational qualities of sports, Vichy officials encouraged their promotion by all possible means: athletic associations were invited to perform *mouvements d'ensemble* before virtually every official ceremony, and more concretely, Vichy officials planned the creation of a physical education school, the *École Supérieure d'Éducation Physique de Madagascar* at Fianarantsoa. It was imagined that sports could provide a remedy for countless social afflictions, from idleness to infertility and *laisser-aller*, associated respectively with the "native," the Third Republic, and the tropics. Sports seemed to offer an antidote for a decadence itself allegedly derived from modernity; Olivier Leroy admonished, in a flourish of mixed metaphors:

> The principal fault of our modern life, of our colonial existence is of depriving ourselves of movement, of preventing our muscles from developing themselves, and our lungs from breathing. ... Decadence is the final plight of a people who abandon physical exercise. We are entering on a new path, let us not miss the boat.[61]

Here Leroy contrasted on the one hand the decadence associated with immobility and suffocation with, on the other hand, the action inherent in a "new path." In so doing, he also interlaced notions of modernity and colonialism. Furthermore, the author betrayed his belief—widely shared at the time, to be sure—that Vichy was not to have been an ephemeral parenthesis of history, but was rather destined to have participated in a "new dawn." From July 1940 to May–September 1942—the extreme dates of Vichy's rule on the island—with the Allies on the defensive on virtually all fronts of the war, rare were the signs auguring the eventual defeat of the Axis and the disgrace of Vichy.

The National Revolution and the Colonizers

Fears of decadence, compounded by anglophobia, and of course a belief that the Vichy regime was legitimate and there to stay, were by no means the only factors that drove the French in distant Madagascar to adhere to Vichy. The main explanation lies elsewhere, in the fact that many of Madagascar's administrators and *colons* had already come to repudiate the Third Republic. As in metropolitan France, the republic and the Popular Front in particular were blamed for all imaginable, and often imaginary, ills: from the alleged increase in "insolence" among Malagasy teachers; to the rise of Communism on the island; to inebriation among the Malagasy; to a drop in productivity, imputed to the Popular Front's abolition in 1936 of the forced labor program known as SMOTIG (*Service de la Main d'Oeuvre des Travaux d'Intérêt Général*). The years 1937 to 1940 were considered, in short, to have marked a period of "vacuum in authority," whereas 1940 signaled "a return of authoritarian power."[62] It was hoped that the new regime would pay less attention to "natives"—toward whom too much benevolence had already been shown, it was argued—and more to the industrious *colons*, through the creation of "a new regime, the Protection of *Colons*."[63] And indeed, this rhetoric made its way into official correspondence and practice, to the delight of long-frustrated *colons,* who had seen in the likes of Governor Augagneur weak Socialist humanists inclined to support the Malagasy in disputes with settlers. In the summer of 1941, Governor Annet tackled the delicate "problem" posed by the difficulties for whites in obtaining rural properties, given the "land claims of natives." The long-term solution adopted by Annet was to commence registering all Malagasy claims and estates, in an effort to inventory all "remaining areas," which could then be allotted to *colons,* or to the colony.[64]

The National Revolution's appeal to *colons* ran deeper still: politically, it promised "authoritarianism" through a "traditional revolution" that abolished "the lie that was universal suffrage."[65] Naturally, in Madagascar there was very little of a "lie" to abolish; colonial rule on the island had always been measured in degrees of authoritarianism, and only a single token election had been held under the French. To colonials, this merely confirmed that the metropole had found salvation in the empire, "the sign of [France's] revival."[66] The empire's lead was one of paternalism, authoritarianism, tradition, and hierarchy. Vichy's motto, *Travail, Famille, Patrie,* or "work, family, homeland," thus found more fertile ground on the Red Island than had the republic's "Liberty, Equality, Fraternity," deemed fundamentally incompatible with colonialism. In some respects, exporting the National Revolution to Madagascar's French was like preaching to the converted. What has been said of Algeria under Vichy applies to Madagascar as well: had the National Revolution not been sent to Madagascar, it would have had to have been invented.[67]

But was a prepackaged National Revolution exported en bloc from the metropole to Madagascar? In reality, much of the impetus for the new ideology emerged locally. At a time when means of communication—even radio links—with the metropole were unprecedentedly strained by the war and the blockade, the Red Island was, to some extent, left to its own devices. As early as July 1940 certain patriotic organizations were founded that clearly prefigured Vichy institutions, and would in fact later be integrated under the umbrella movement Légion Française des Combattants et des Volontaires de la Révolution Nationale. The latter served at once as a veterans' association and as Vichy's approximation of a single party.[68] The island's governors formulated countless other initiatives in line with the National Revolution. Far from merely obeying orders from Vichy's colonial secretariat, these veritable proconsuls zealously devised new tools of repression and sought to fix loopholes in the implementation of the National Revolution. To cite only one example, in a November 1941 telegram to Vichy's colonial secretary, Admiral Platon, Armand Annet drew his superior's attention to the fact that in Madagascar some minor functionaries were still not required by law to sign an affidavit swearing that they had never belonged to a Masonic lodge. This situation, Annet pleaded, needed to be remedied immediately, through a reformulating of existing legislation.[69] The spirit of denunciation and the dynamics inherent in demonstrating unconditional allegiance to the new regime, both so prevalent in metropolitan France under Vichy, were manifestly also present in Madagascar. There, in the hands of virtually omnipotent governors, they became arbitrary tools of repression.

Irrespective of its local or metropolitan origins, one point seems certain: the National Revolution thrived in Madagascar. As in France, where Philippe Pétain, "the prime signifier ... was displayed everywhere like an icon,"[70] the marshal's image soon became ubiquitous in Madagascar. In a ritual reminiscent of Hitler's loyalty oaths, all functionaries in Madagascar, be they magistrates or librarians, were to "swear fidelity to the person of the Head of State."[71] To the surprise of the head of France's Protestant Church, Philippe Boegner, even Protestant chaplains in Madagascar were to "declare absolute fidelity to the Marshal ... and his local representatives."[72] Meanwhile, school children were encouraged to write a 1941 Christmas letter to father Pétain. The winner of the contest for the best letter had written on this occasion:

> I [wish to] assure you that across the seas, in my great Island, there are children, young people and men ready to sacrifice everything to the sacred cause, even death if need be. ... I swear that as a French girl I will accomplish my duty to the end.[73]

Finally, as in metropolitan France, not just children—and girls specifically—tokens of the country's rebirth, but cities themselves paid tribute to Pétain. In an act steeped in the symbolism of a radical change of regimes and ideology unparalleled in Madagascar since Gallieni's conquest of the island in 1896, the towns of Tamatave and Antalaha rebaptized their *Boulevards de la République* into *Boulevards du Maréchal Pétain*.[74] It was into this bizarre arena that the British irrupted in May and then September 1942, leaving Gandar Dower to contemplate posters "declaring that the National Revolution was *en marche*—which indeed it was. ... Others informed you ... : *Your name is French, your party French, your password France*."[75]

As this tautological slogan suggests, the violent rejection of pluralism constituted an important facet of the new ideology in both metropolitan France and Madagascar. On the Red Island, Léon Cayla set the tone of repression early. On September 10, 1940, he took the initiative of cabling Vichy, asking whether he had the authority to ban de Gaulle's symbol of resistance, the Croix de Lorraine. The latter was being worn by "sympathizers of the dissident movement ... in Tananarive."[76] By November 1940, Cayla moved from denouncing resistance to threatening it, and vowed to "crush mercilessly" any dissent.[77] By then, the successive rallying of French Equatorial Africa and the French South Pacific to de Gaulle from August to September 1940 had crystallized fears that Madagascar might rally to the Free French. On September 10, 1940, Vichy had accordingly extended to its colonies wartime legislation for the internment of individuals considered "dangerous to national defense."[78] Eight days later, by virtue of this new law, Cayla established a political prison in Antsirabe, in which suspected Gaullists and leftists were immediately detained.[79] In this field as well, Gandar Dower's testimony proved perspicacious: "In addition to penalties for listening to the BBC, the employment of political spies, including native spies, coupled with savage sentences not merely for political crimes but even political opinions, made life in Madagascar no joke at all."[80] Vichy's political witch-hunts in Madagascar had in fact been even more thorough and virulent than Gandar Dower suspected: they had targeted all of the alleged enemies of the National Revolution, from suspected "antinational" films,[81] and perceived *laisser-aller,* to Gaullists, Communists, Socialists, and Jews. Witch-hunts of this sort were the product of two discrete dynamics: they emanated from colonial ministry directives at Vichy, and were rendered possible locally by zealous enthusiasm on the imperial "periphery."

Conversely, responsibility for the extension of anti-Semitic legislation to "loyal" colonies falls squarely upon the shoulders of authorities at Vichy. Already on March 15, 1941, Vichy's Jewish statute of October 3, 1940, defining Jews and listing professions prohibited to them, had been extended to the colonies by decree.[82] In May 1941, Admiral Platon, Vichy's longest running *Secrétaire d'Etat aux Colonies,* agreed to a proposal by Xavier Vallat, the *Commissaire Général aux Questions Juives,* to include the colonies in another anti-Jewish law (passed on June 2, 1941). By the following month, Platon advanced a series of suggestions intended to clear glitches in the application of Vichy's anti-Semitic laws to individual colonies.[83] On December 31 of the same year, Xavier Vallat besought Admiral Platon no longer to consider the application of anti-Semitic legislation to the colonies simply on a case-by-case basis. Instead, Platon was to "prepare ... as a general rule ... for the extension to our overseas territories of metropolitan legislation concerning the Jews."[84]

In Madagascar, the law of June 2, 1941, requiring the census of all Jews—a centerpiece of Vichy's anti-Semitic apparatus[85]—was adopted on July 5, 1941. The press announced that Jews had one month in which to come forward to register and declare their wealth.[86] These measures also triggered a litany of affidavits by colonial administrators and entrepreneurs, certifying their appurtenance to the "French race" and Catholic religion. Although exhaustive investigations revealed the presence of only twenty-six "Israélites" on the entire island,[87] the handful of Jews serving in the administration were nonetheless dismissed on August 15, 1941.[88] As in metropolitan France, letters of denunciation followed the adoption of discriminatory measures. One such letter, emanating no doubt from a business competitor or personal rival, denounced "the Jew Alexander Dreyfus" in Antanimena for continuing his job as a rice merchant in defiance of the law of November 17, 1941, banning Jews from a series of professions including the selling of cereals and grains. Since rice constituted a grain, this predictably anonymous logician concluded, the said Alexander Dreyfus should immediately be prevented from continuing in his line of work, lest the administration seem lax or even "ridiculed by a common Jew."[89] Action ensued swiftly; four days after the writing of the letter of denunciation, the head of the region of Tananarive ordered his police chief to see that "Dreyfus ... immediately cease his activities in the grain sector."[90] Surely, even Pétain had not foreseen his criminal persecution of French Jews ending up firing a rice seller in Madagascar. Thus, anti-Semitism under Vichy in Madagascar clearly illustrated the projection of metropolitan demonizations onto the colonies. That Vichy should have persecuted the twenty-six Jews on this remote island, where the only Nazi pressures had involved prewar suggestions of Jewish emigration, is perhaps more telling of the metropolitan regime than of its colonial authorities. It underscores the extent to which Vichy actively generated French-bred anti-Semitism.

Freemasons, unlike Jews, were regarded by French colonial officials in Madagascar as scapegoats indigenous to the island. Since the turn of the century, Madagascar's European population had been broadly split into three camps: the largely conservative Catholic majority, a minority of Protestants who had succeeded in converting many Merina, and some self-proclaimed "free-thinkers," leftist anticlericals such as governors general Victor Augagneur (1905–10) and de Coppet.[91] The advent of Vichy was accompanied in Madagascar by the revenge of the majority on the minorities: Protestants were suspected of anglophilia, while "free-thinkers" were stigmatized as Freemasons. To be sure, there were bona fide Freemasons on the island, but the secretive nature of Freemasonry, and Vichy's demonization of it as an Anglo-Bolshevik, anti-Catholic plot, made for a facile mental amalgam of leftist and Freemason. Many French inhabitants of the Red Island were therefore favorably predisposed toward Vichy's anti-Masonry. Vichyites in Madagascar echoed Pétain's belief that "a Jew is never responsible for his origins; a Freemason is mason by choice."[92] In this department Annet proved far more *engagé* than his predecessor, Cayla. Indeed, armed with Vichy's discriminatory legislation on Freemasonry, most notably the law of August 11, 1941 (adapted to the colonies on August 18, 1941), Madagascar's second governor under Vichy left no stones unturned in his hunt for Freemasons. He fired schoolteachers and police officers alike, and even investigated allegations that Freemasons had infiltrated two of the linchpins of the National Revolution in Madagascar: the youth indoctrination camps at Manjakandriana and the Légion Française des Combattants et Volontaires de la Révolution Nationale (hereafter referred to as the Legion).[93]

This last organization represented the vanguard of the National Revolution in Madagascar.[94] Its goals, declared its local branch in the town of Majunga, on the northwest of the island, were to implement "[t]he National Revolution, which you should make your own. We must strive to rediscover the high virtues of the French race which 79 years of democracy have made us lose."[95] The broad extension of the Legion to all of Vichy's colonies can be traced to Admiral Platon's September 21, 1940, request that it not "neglect" the empire.[96] After having served essentially as a veterans' group and as a propaganda agent since its inception in August 1940, the Legion was officially revamped on November 18, 1941. The reformed Legion would admit not only First World War veterans but also civilian "volunteers for the National Revolution"—a tandem of old and new emblematic of Vichy duality.

In Madagascar, the Legion possessed its own tribunal, a youth organization and social and economic planning commissions.[97] By April 1942, it counted 2,563 members, of whom 870 were "European veterans," 919 "Malagasy veterans," and 774 volunteers—all "European."[98] Local leaders of the organization included missionaries, entrepreneurs, scientists, engineers, *colons,* and administrators. Throughout the island, the Legion offered speeches on the theme of *Travail, Famille, Patrie,*[99] collected funds to assist the beleaguered metropole, and prepared elaborate ceremonies. For the celebration of the Legion's first anniversary, on September 1, 1941, Tananarive witnessed the following spectacle:

> In the huge stadium of Mahamasina, in front of 2000 spectators ... the Legionaries, some of whom had come especially from the *brousse* [bush], repeated the loyalty oath in unison of voice and heart. ... In front of a gigantic portrait of the Head of State, surrounded by panels depicting the *francisque* [Vichy's symbol and equivalent of the fasces] and the hero of Verdun, the flame was brought in by an athlete of the gymnastic society who lit it. ... The flame which rose like incense symbolized the rising hopes in the country's resurrection.[100]

This ceremony, marked at once by a cult of the leader, a religious apotheosis, and an exaltation of youth, regimentation, and unity, epitomized the new regime's iconologies and hagiographies.

The most groundbreaking project hatched by the Legion in Madagascar was a proposal to adopt the new metropolitan Labor Charter, as part of a broader corporatist experiment.[101] In April 1942, Colonel Besse, the newly nominated head of the Legion in Madagascar, assigned the task of conducting a feasibility study for this idea to the Legion's regional branch in Tamatave.[102] In concert with the town's chamber of commerce, Tamatave's Legion devised a scheme that would at once resolve the island's supposed labor shortage and answer the new regime's corporatist aspirations (see Figs. 1–2). For rural Madagascar, they recommended the reintroduction of the *Fokonolona*—or village councils—to re-establish structure, authority, hierarchy, and tradition.[103] The urban Malagasy, conversely, were to be divided into guilds. As for foreigners, Chinese and Indian immigrants in particular, they were to have their businesses strictly regulated, because of their supposed domination of certain sectors, such as housing.[104] Finally, prewar trade unions, only recently legalized under the Popular Front and immediately abolished by Vichy, were to be replaced by a new corporatist order. This veritable caste system conferred absolute power upon "European merchants" over Malagasy and Asians.[105] Tamatave's Legion justified this scheme by arguing that it was in no way racist but simply reflected and accounted for "profound differences in mentalities, customs, language and lifestyle." They further maintained:

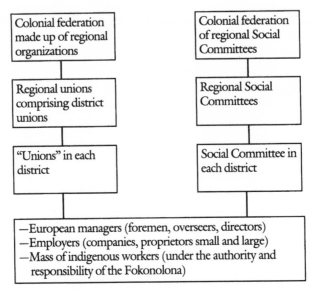

FIG. 1. General Organization—rural: *Agriculture* (Source: CAOM, Madagascar 6[2]D 49).

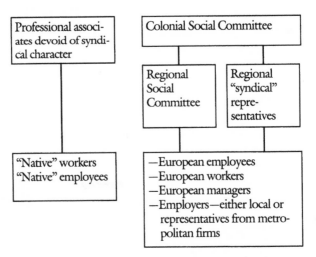

FIG. 2. General Organization—urban: *Commerce and Industry* (Source: CAOM, Madagascar 6[2]D 49).

Far from disdaining the native—any more than placing a metropolitan shoe-maker in a separate assembly from a bookkeeper constitutes disdain ...—it is on the contrary a mark of respect for the workers ... to let them be experts in what they know. That is the very essence of the corporatist system that is [the basis of] tomorrow's France.[106]

Under this mantle of "difference" Tamatave's Legion sought to consecrate, codify, and indeed deepen inequalities. The example of the cobbler and the bookkeeper is especially telling: much as Pétain believed in a "natural hier-archy" of professions for the metropole, so Tamatave's Legion proposed a "natural hierarchy" of race for Madagascar.[107] Nor were such Mussolinian utopian projects foreign to the island's governors. Already in May 1941, Armand Annet had informed the prewar Malagasy labor leaders Randriambeloma and Rakotomanga that the abolished unions might soon be replaced by "professional associations." These, along with the family nucleus, were to constitute the cornerstones of the new order in Madagascar.[108]

Extremists in the Brousse

Vichy's rule in Madagascar witnessed the reproduction and adoption of many such far-rightist institutions and currents from the metropole, ranging from the Legion, which in France later branched into the notorious *milice,* to anti-Semitic and anti-Masonic legislation, and finally to corporatist schemes. In Madagascar, as in the metropole, internal rows emerged over precise readings of Pétainist "orthodoxy," with various currents drawing vastly different interpretations from Pétain's sometimes cryptic declarations. Similarly, in Madagascar as in metropolitan France, some assumed a holier than thou attitude, claiming a monopoly on Pétainist loyalty and orthodoxy.

One such stalwart of a "true" National Revolution disembarked at Tamatave on July 18, 1941, claiming to be the personal envoy of Marshal Pétain, charged with the mission of overseeing the new ideology's adoption in Madagascar. Lieutenant Gresset, who "presented himself as racist, anti-Mason, anti-Jewish and anti-English,"[109] rapidly garnered the support of local authorities, which became willing sycophants to this would-be representative of the marshal. Gresset grew especially influential in French military circles, which found Annet's policies to be too lax. According to Annet, these *frondeurs* even went so far as to plot a coup, which was aborted once it was revealed that Gresset had come to Madagascar entirely on his own initiative.[110] Gresset's subterfuge illustrates to what extent the new regime relied upon personal authority—upon a literal embodiment of power not seen in French politics since Napoleon III.

Gresset's was by no means the only organization calling for a radicalization of Vichy ideology on the Red Island. Marc Chaumet, the editor of the ultrareactionary *Servir, Hebdomadaire Chrétien*, stands as a model of colonial collaborationism. On September 11, 1942, twelve days before Tananarive fell to the British, Chaumet echoed Pierre Laval's infamous phrase of June 22, 1942: "Yes, I am for a German victory." Chaumet added for good measure: "Long live Pétain! And above him, eternally, Christ."[111]

The ranks of the Legion, for their part, were rife with royalists. In March 1941, the pamphleteer Gaétan Brunet led a revolt within Madagascar's Legion against its first leader, Colonel Forgeot. Brunet (whose nom de plume, Brugaët, besides constituting a contraction of his two names, may betray an assumed Breton or Chouan identity) did not mince words when he declared: "You are betrayed by Forgeot, the former supporter of the Popular Front who went to France at our expense to celebrate the 150th anniversary of Marianne [symbol of the republic], the old slut whom he fondled all his life."[112] This vitriolic ad hominem attack appropriates many of the techniques of contestation from French revolutionary and counterrevolutionary traditions—including the engendering and sexualization of the political, the disempowering of the libertine enemy[113]—and uses them to subvert the Third Republic. Equally instructive are the tropes of Brunet's political ravings. He asked in a March 1941 pamphlet:

> Why are we legionnaires? To defend the National Revolution. ... Against what? Against the former regime, the Third Republic. Against the return of the 900 kings produced by the electoral quagmire, against the socio-communists, against Freemasonry. ... The National Revolution lies to the Right. It signals the return to the Monarchy. King Pétain reigns absolute and can designate his successor. ... [He] will resurrect eternal France ... that of the Sun King, Louis XIV. Legionnaires must be anti–Third Republic, therefore anti-socio-communist and anti-*mpakafou*. We will no longer tolerate being led by the *mpakafou-ing* Forgeot.[114]

The borrowing of the Malagasy expression *mpakafou* seems especially noteworthy. It was used by the Malagasy to designate "heart-thieves." The widespread belief in the countryside of Imerina—that Europeans (*vazaha*) were heart-snatchers—seemingly stemmed from an important cultural difference: the European practice of removing and embalming the hearts of saints or prominent figures. (This rumor and belief could be fruitfully compared with East and Southern African fears of colonial administrators—firemen and doctors especially—as vampires.)[115] Organ removal, or any other perceived desecration of bodies, ran fundamentally contrary to Malagasy burial rites and religious beliefs. Between 1890 and 1893, Madagascar's Catholic clergy had attempted to use the mounting fear of *mpakafous* for its own ends by labeling Freemasons as heart-thieves.[116] The idea stuck, and Brunet appropriated this Malagasy fear, itself reinvented by the Church, and utilized it to decry his supposedly vampiristic enemies: Freemasons, leftists, and the Third Republic.[117] The *mpakafou* constitutes in a sense a more overarching, vivid, and Malagasied variant of the fascist image of parasitic scapegoats cited earlier. In fact, Brunet asserted, those calling themselves "free-thinkers" were by definition *mpakafous*. Brunet and his followers thus constructed a curious colonial hybrid ideology: at once "creolized"—to the extent that they couched their theories in Malagasy beliefs—Catholic, violently anti-Masonic, and more royalist than the king, to use a fitting French expression.

Épuration

When the British overran Vichy's troops in Madagascar in September 1942, they began the process of purging the island's administration before handing it over to the Free French. The Madagascar Proclamation, issued by the British Military Administration in Madagascar, represented the centerpiece of this policy. Article 5, dated December 4, 1942, stipulated that the Légion Française des Combattants et Volontaires de la Révolution Nationale was to be disbanded and outlawed.[118]

Did the National Revolution then vanish as quickly as it had come? Charles de Gaulle suggested as much in 1943, referring not to Madagascar specifically but to all territories reclaimed from Vichy:

> Why is it that all these portraits, symbols, and slogans have made way in a wink to the heroic Croix de Lorraine, national symbol of deliverance and pride if ever there was one? All that was required for this pathetic scaffolding to crumble instantaneously was for the enemy to withdraw.[119]

The answer for Madagascar, at least, is that Vichy was not as easily forgotten as Gaullist mythology would have posterity believe. First of all, Vichy's trappings in Madagascar had never relied upon the support of "the enemy," since no Nazi ever set foot on the island under Vichy. Here Vichy had existed, and indeed thrived, without any German proximity. Secondly, Vichy's pervasive iconography proved difficult to efface: in some Malagasy villages, every dwelling possessed a picture of Pétain.[120] The French, moreover, were extremely wary of announcing yet another change of regimes to the Malagasy (three had already occurred: the Third Republic to Vichy, Vichy to the English, the English to the Free French), for fear that it might constitute a further display of discord and weakness. In addition, the sheer volume of Vichy's propaganda rendered its annihilation difficult. Thus, for official correspondence, Gaullist administrators in Madagascar in 1943 used the reverse side of Pétainist propaganda posters vaunting: "One leader, three colors. Long live France! Long live Pétain!"[121] This was done ostensibly so as to recycle scarce paper, but also in an effort to obliterate the memory of Vichy through a literal reinscribing, by using Pétainist tracts as palimpsests.

The cult of Pétain, however, proved more profoundly engrained than Gaullists had expected. The Free French representative to Majunga drew his superior's attention to the fact that in April 1943 two French women and a captain leaving Mass had refused a Gaullist leaflet entitled: "There Is No More Marshal." The captain in particular had logically objected: "[W]hether they like it or not, there is still a Marshal." Nor was the Croix de Lorraine the overnight success de Gaulle described. Also in Majunga, in May 1943, a captain having raised the Croix de Lorraine in front of his troops was promptly ordered by his superior to take it down. In a curious inversion, oppositional practices most often associated with the French Resistance became the preserve of Vichyites in 1943 Madagascar. In the capital Tananarive, Gaullist posters were immediately covered by pro-Vichy graffiti "hostile to the Free French and the Allies."[122] All of these cases point to the enduring success of Vichy's ideology among the French in Madagascar, and suggest that in 1943 at least, official Gaullist ideology, iconography, and memory were still far from triumphant on the island.

In the final analysis, the success of the National Revolution among Madagascar's French community raises a number of considerations. The fact that an ultra-right-wing ideology should have thrived at such a distance from the metropole suggests that National Revolutionary politics were not imported overnight. In this sense, the 1930s in Madagascar, as in France, can be seen as something of a period of undeclared civil war between increasingly polarized factions. On the Great Isle, these tensions finally came into the open after the advent of Vichy, when the likes of Leroy and Brugaët, no longer restrained by a modicum of republicanism, unleashed their hostilities upon Malagasy, Jews, Freemasons, and other scapegoats. Still, there can be little doubt that directives emanating from Vichy's colonial secretariat also played a decisive role in steering Madagascar in the direction of Pétainism. Admiral Platon, convinced that exporting the National Revolution would somehow secure the loyalty of the colonies, almost single-handedly pressured the French veterans' ministry to establish branches of the Légion Française des Combattants et Volontaires de la Révolution Nationale overseas. The ministry in question had never even considered such a possibility, and colonial governors themselves were none too enthused by a scheme that seemed to divest them of some of their powers. The reproduction of such Vichy institutions, as well as the persecution of the handful of Jews on Madagascar, speak volumes on the nature of Vichy rule overseas.

CHAPTER 3

Travail, Famille, Patrie, and the Malagasy

The words of the Marshal, made real by his large portrait seen everywhere—even in the most humble huts—have as profound an impact on the Malagasy as on the Europeans. The principles of authority and discipline that are now in a place of honor have also contributed to an excellent new atmosphere.

—Political Report on Madagascar, 1941[1]

This 1941 report stands as a testimony to the pervasion of Vichy ideology in Madagascar. And yet, historians of Madagascar have tended either to ignore the Vichy era altogether or to minimize its impact. Francis Koerner, a specialist on the colonial era in Madagascar, has stated that "the period from 1940 to 1942 has been totally overlooked in the historiography of Madagascar."[2] For his part, Solofo Ranrianja, an expert on Communist resistance in Madagascar, has suggested that Vichy actually changed very little for the Malagasy.[3] Others studying the insurrection of 1947 on the east coast of Madagascar, which cost the life of approximately seventy-five thousand Malagasy (the precise number of casualties remains uncertain, however, and the figure of seventy-five thousand has been contested by some), have glossed over the period of 1940 to 1942, contending that the root causes of the revolt should be traced back no further than 1944.[4] As will be seen, the Vichy years actually marked the most radical shift in colonial ideology ever witnessed on the Red Island, while also contributing at least indirectly to the 1947 rebellion by representing a watershed period for Malagasy nationalism. However, before turning to the Vichy period proper, one must first survey the evolution of the rapports between colonizers and colonized on the Red Island prior to the Second World War.

Madagascar had been dominated by the Merina people of the high central plateaux and governed by a powerful monarchy from roughly 1787—when the great king Andrianampoinimerina first launched Merina expansion—until 1895, when a French military force under Joseph Gallieni conquered and then annexed Madagascar and exiled the last queen, Ranavalona III.[5] The French invaders presented themselves as "liberators" of Madagascar, sent to rid the island of its absolute monarchs in the name of the French Republic. In this same vein, the new rulers of Madagascar abolished slavery and proclaimed their intention to "free" the island's coastal peoples from the yoke of the Merina monarchy.[6]

Between roughly 1900 and the Second World War, French colonial experts were broadly divided between those on the one hand in favor of taking republican propaganda to its logical conclusion by assimilating the Malagasy, and those on the other hand resolved to strengthen the colonialist hierarchy. A book released on April 25, 1940, only weeks before the fall of France in May–June 1940, and coauthored by none other than the French novelist Marguerite Duras seems to indicate that the assimilationist ideal was still very much alive on the eve of the Second World War. (Duras later repudiated her first book, which reads as an apology for, and an aggrandizement of, empire. She wrote it, one should keep in mind, after having worked several years at the Colonial Information Services of the French Colonial Ministry in Paris.)[7] Duras and Roques contended that the Malagasy were: "clever and endowed with an exceptional faculty at assimilation and imitation."[8] It was therefore thought by some that Madagascar and the High Plateaux especially could serve as a fine laboratory for the application of full-fledged republican assimilationism.

Politically, postconquest Madagascar thus came to epitomize the contradictions of French colonialism. Albert Memmi's maxim, "It is the colonized who, at first, desires assimilation, and the colonizer who refuses it,"[9] finds special resonance in colonial Madagascar. Indeed, from 1896 to 1940, even Malagasy Marxists demanded not independence nor even autonomy but full assimilation,[10] arguing that when Madagascar had been annexed in 1896, its inhabitants should have become ipso facto French citizens. The fact that, in governing circles, colonial theories of associationism were beginning to gain favor over assimilationist discourse,[11] failed to change the appeal of assimilation for many Malagasy (indeed, it may even have increased the popularity of assimilationism). One of the island's most important interwar protests, on May 19, 1929, was staged under the banner of equality through assimilation.[12]

It was, true to Memmi's theory, the colonizers who refused assimilation after having promised it. Specifically, decades of tension between on the one hand a handful of administrators and the Malagasy elite, intent upon assimilation, and on the other hand *colons* determined to view the Malagasy as "human cattle ... and a source of cheap labor,"[13] had long rendered illusory the promise of assimilation. Moreover, during much of the interwar period, Madagascar's governors had favored a policy of association, which, under the guise of respecting difference and traditional hierarchies, often amounted concretely to either "authoritarian paternalism"[14] or a thinly veiled rationale and tool for conducting exploitative *mise en valeur* campaigns.[15] Only after the election of the Socialist government under Léon Blum in France in June 1936 did French colonial authorities begin, extremely timidly and half-heartedly, to accede to Malagasy demands. On October 14, 1936, a decree was passed in Madagascar granting citizenship to any Malagasy having culturally "demonstrated total assimilation." Later legislation in April 1938 further simplified the nationalization process.[16] Even though French citizenship was actually accorded to only a token two thousand or so Malagasy by 1939 (although some estimates run as high as seven thousand),[17] it nonetheless remained a powerful ideal for many, and for the Merina elite in particular.

The immediate prewar period brought other limited but nonetheless significant concessions on the part of the colonizers. Amid much pomp and ceremony, an election was held on May 14, 1939, to designate a Malagasy representative to the Conseil supérieur de la France d'Outre-mer. Although only nineteen thousand were actually enfranchised, French newspapers proclaimed that generous France had written the final chapter in the liberation of Madagascar from "the absolutism of its kings," adding:

> [T]he former subjects of Andrianampoinimerina have resolutely set foot into European civilization. One need not be a psychologist to understand, as one watches them approach the ballot box, symbol of republican government, the transformation that their minds have undergone since the rigid era of the Hova monarchy.[18]

Evidently, in 1939 assimilationist and republican discourse were not yet extinguished; France was still at least officially bent upon a "civilizing mission" akin to a crusade, whose avowed goals included republicanization through education.[19] However symbolic and paternalistic the elections of

May 1939 may have been, they would be reviled as decadent and unnatural a year and a half later under Vichy, for which even show-elections were anathema.

The overall situation in Madagascar on the eve of the Second World War was perhaps best summarized by one of the island's few American residents, who reported privately to the U.S. intelligence agency, OSS.: "Until 1940 ... the government was strong and paternalistic, but the native share in governmental affairs was being slowly and steadily increased."[20] Vichy would mark a brutal rupture with this admittedly gradual liberalization inaugurated in 1936.

The Advent of the New Order

Although the Vichy authorities in Madagascar never articulated an indigenous policy per se, it seems nonetheless apparent that Vichy French officials systematically reacted against the reforms of the Popular Front, be they in the realm of forced labor, symbolic enfranchisement, or assimilation. The initiative for such reactions often emerged locally, from all-powerful French administrators—or *rois de la brousse*—who quite simply associated the National Revolution with unabashed exploitation. However, two fundamental political trends devised by the colonizers for the colonized do emerge for the entire island under Vichy: first a growing antiassimilationist sentiment, and second a desire to turn the clock back to a bygone era. If in France Vichyites constructed an imaginary lineage back to Joan of Arc,[21] so in Madagascar they conjured up the heyday of preconquest Madagascar, the days of the eighteenth-century expansionist absolutist sovereign Andrianampoinimerina—precisely the era stigmatized in 1939 as absolutist, un-European, "uncivilized," and nonrepublican.[22] The case of the town of Soavinandriana under Vichy serves to illustrate how antiassimilationist and Procrustean colonialism—nothing new to Madagascar, to be sure—reached new heights in the hands of local French administrators who took the fall of the Third Republic to signal the advent of pure exploitation and repression.

Soavinandriana under Vichy

The town of Soavinandriana, some sixty miles southwest of the capital, Tananarive, had long been headed by the *chef de district*, André Costantini, a Corsican veteran of the First World War who had already earned a reputation for tyranny in the interwar years. With the advent of Vichy in Madagascar in July 1940, Costantini shed all pretense of restraint he might have shown under the republic. Claiming to be the island's only true adept of the National Revolution, he denounced Soavinandriana's English pastor on the unlikely charge of spreading Communism and for possessing works of André Gide in his library.[23] Costantini's principal victims, though, were the Merina who inhabited the district. The National Revolution, he affirmed, should spell a return to hard-line colonialism. He especially reviled the Merina elite, symbols of assimilation: "[L]iking luxury, dressing like Europeans ... their guide is idleness, the mother of all vices. The administrator's responsibility is to place them back on the right track. After an exemplary punishment, one usually gets them to re-enter their shell."[24] Asserting that "God was thinking well when he made rattan [for caning] and Malagasy grow in the same regions," Costantini sought, in effect, to invent a retribalization of sorts for the Malagasy by forcing them to "re-enter their shell." This they were to accomplish through a return to "native costumes," or *lamba*, to the village structures of the *Fokonolona*, and to a subservient status.[25] Here Costantini merely reflected the prevailing wisdom of Vichy ideology: "unnatural elites," be they Jews, Freemasons, or Europeanized Africans, were to be replaced by "natural leaders"—youthful men from the *terroir* or, in the colonies, by traditional chieftains. This "Revolution" was not ordered from above: it appeared simultaneously and spontaneously in all corners of France and its empire.

Costantini followed up his theories of discipline and social engineering with actions. Correspondence from Soavinandriana to Cayla and Annet attests to the ruthless persecution of Malagasy notables. One letter to Annet pleads in Malagasy: "[We] implore you for your immediate paternal intervention, Sir, for in his hands we will end up dying." Another, dated March 17, 1941, from a prominent villager whose husband was jailed seemingly at random, read: "[C]ome to our rescue, for we and all the inhabitants of Soavinandriana are being oppressed."[26] Costantini utilized both old and new tools in his quest to "redress the character"[27] of the Malagasy elite, employing both the *indigénat* and new wartime legislation to dispense penalties of incarceration and forced labor. Costantini pronounced his policies an unmitigated success, especially in light of the fact that "three years earlier Communism had passed through the town."[28] In this hinterland of Tananarive, the Vichy years manifestly signaled a discernible hardening of colonialism—one clearly formulated as a reaction to an imagined "laxism" and Communism.

"Transforming the Native": The Rejection of Assimilation

Perhaps the most interesting facets of Costantini's political outlook involve his rejection of assimilation—manifested through his persecution of the Malagasy elite—and his schemes to drive the Malagasy back into their "shell." The two are undoubtedly related, the first marking a reaction to republican assimilationist discourse, and the second constituting a fanciful effort of "retribalization" as part of an active struggle to combat the effects of Europeanization on the Malagasy—a struggle akin to the desire to stave off the "nativization" of the colonizers. The fact that assimilation had never actually become a reality in Madagascar was of little importance to Costantini and to other Vichyites, who imagined it at work everywhere, acting as a supposedly unnatural underpinning of pre-1940 colonialism.

Vichy's repudiation of the very idea of assimilation is perhaps best illustrated by the educational reforms and youth camps devised by Vichy officials on the island. Their objective was to "transform the native"[29] by replacing general education curricula, long considered the cornerstones of republican education, with technical and agricultural programs, and by concurrently establishing youth movements to regiment and inculcate Malagasy children.[30] This answered at once the need to increase local industrial and commercial output imposed by the British blockade, the new regime's desire to foster agricultural and artisanal skills so dear to the traditionalist Pétain, and the will to ruralize and de-Europeanize the Malagasy. These last two considerations were articulated by the head of the southern region of Fort-Dauphin when he stated in his political report on 1941: "We have too many bad intellectuals and not enough good artisans. Everyone agrees on the need for this reform."[31] Other officials invoked more pragmatic motives for promoting regimentation and technical education over a republican curriculum long ridiculed for supposedly teaching African children about "their ancestors the Gauls."[32] One such administrator commented: "Young generations must be turned away as much as possible from certain liberal careers among which most political agitators are recruited."[33] In this way, education in Madagascar under Vichy was openly rationalized as a tool for social control.

Vichy's educational reforms were carried out with remarkable celerity. Traditional schools were transformed into *écoles fermes,* and workshops soon became the center of school activity.[34] Meanwhile, Vichyite youth camps were founded as early as December 1940. The first such institution for Malagasy youngsters, established in Tananarive, was geared toward industrial apprenticeship. However, this camp was relocated to the countryside in Angavokely on May 20, 1942, Armand Annet deeming a "return to the soil"[35] to be the sine qua non of the implementation of the National Revolution in Madagascar.[36] Another camp for Malagasy youngsters, in Antsirabe, aimed to "specialize native children in agriculture and cattle raising."[37] In the span of two years, Cayla and Annet, assisted by the head of education, Olivier Leroy, had sought to refashion Malagasy youth—and hence shape what then promised to be the future of Madagascar—through ruralization and degallicization.

This educational overhaul notwithstanding, it would be misleading to suggest that all of the traces of pro forma republicanism vanished overnight with the advent of Vichy in Madagascar. Olivier Leroy employed the term "assimilation" in 1942, although to designate something quite different from what it had meant under the republic. According to Leroy, the National Revolution could be considered assimilationist because, like ancient Rome, it incorporated ideals from a variety of origins, presumably even Malagasy.[38] Perhaps the most convincing evidence of the retention of vestiges of assimilationism under Vichy lies in the fact that some Malagasy continued to be naturalized from 1940 to 1942, although admittedly far fewer than under the republic (only twenty-three were even considered in 1941).[39] The initiative for decreasing the number of naturalizations emanated from Vichy itself, whose colonial secretary instructed: "[to] send dossiers of naturalization only when they present a definite national interest."[40]

More significant still, although a handful of Malagasy were naturalized from 1940 to 1942, others were actually denaturalized. A law of April 17, 1942, called for the revocation of French citizenship for "formerly native *(indigène)* French citizens" who had been imprisoned or found guilty of "anti-French activities."[41] This denaturalization was further extended to the family of the person in question. By virtue of this legislation, one of the fathers of Malagasy nationalism, Jules Ranaivo, naturalized in 1922, was stripped of his French citizenship on July 2, 1942.[42] The law of April 17, 1942, which has gone largely unnoticed by historians, might be situated somewhere between Vichy's stripping of nationality from Gaullists and its denaturalization of Jews—inasmuch as it was at once politically and racially motivated. This retroactive stripping of citizenship from the recently naturalized further betrays a belief in a racial rather than cultural construction of Frenchness—Ranaivo, having had to prove cultural assimilation so as to be naturalized in 1922, was denaturalized two decades later on account of his "native" origins. In this sense, the impetus for Ranaivo's denaturalization as an "anti-French activist" but also as "a former indigène" may have found its broader origins in Vichy's reductionist xenophobia and in its racialization of the political.

As Robert Paxton and Michael Marrus have observed, the treatment of blacks under Vichy was "lenient"[43] compared with that of Jews. Robert Paxton concludes from this indisputable fact, however, that Vichy's contrasting attitudes toward blacks and Jews are imputable to the regime's retention of assimilationist ideals, arguing that "Vichy xenophobia was more cultural and national than racial, in a French assimilationist tradition."[44] Vichy's educational reforms in Madagascar, its orders on limiting the number of Malagasy naturalizations, and especially the law of April 17, 1942, may point to a more general antiassimilationist current inherent in the xenophobic nationalism of the French far right. In this sense, the rise of the antiassimilationist far right in Vichy's colonies might best be understood as an ideological forerunner of the antirepublican colonial phalanges—most notably the OAS (Organisation de l'Armée secrète)—which waged war on the French Fourth and Fifth Republics in the 1950s and 1960s, and which themselves served as breeding grounds for Le Pen's National Front. These same phalanges had prompted Albert Memmi to argue in 1966: "Any colonial nation carries in it ... the seeds of a fascist temptation. ... Colonial fascism ... represents a permanent danger, a pocket of venom constantly threatening the Metropolitan organism."[45]

Pétain as Ray-Aman-Dreny: Rooting the National Revolution into Malagasy Culture

Vichy's efforts to deassimilate the Malagasy were accompanied by an attempt to forge a new Malagasy identity and indeed to recast Malagasy society. Vichy officials invoked the heyday of the Merina past—the reign of Andrianampoinimerina—as a blueprint for the new Madagascar. They had certainly not invented the idea of utilizing indigenous traditions to the advantage of the colonizer. Ever since Gallieni's conquest of the island, the French had promoted, in the words of Gwendolyn Wright, "historical preservation" as a way of exploiting "the hierarchy of authority associated with the island's premodern culture."[46] Under Vichy this prewar trend was to reach an unmistakable apogee.

The rule of Andrianampoinimerina, a contemporary and admirer of Napoleon Bonaparte, has been described as follows by the historian of

Madagascar, Mervyn Brown:

> While consolidating the last of the old customs, he imposed a new organiza-
> tion which resembled in many ways the feudal society of medieval Europe. At
> the center was an all-powerful, semi-divine figure of the king; the link with
> God and the ancestors, the source of all authority and the owner of all the land.
> ... In each village the people grouped in an assembly known as the *fokono'òlona*
> ... were made responsible for law and order, the settlement of petty disputes,
> the organization of unpaid labor for public works. ... There was a rigid class
> structure with strict rules about intermarriage.[47]

Between 1940 and 1942, Vichy officials, through their promotion of
"tradition," encouraged a return to the Madagascar of the late eighteenth to
early nineteenth centuries, which corresponded to a metropolitan Vichyite
nostalgia for a bygone era. At the crux of this "return to one's roots" in
Madagascar were notions of authoritarianism and social hierarchy, rituals
of tribute and allegiance, as well as forced labor.

French colonial experts, bureaucrats, and high-ranking officials in
Madagascar under Vichy pointed time and again to the surprising congruence between traditional Malagasy hierarchies and the National Revolution. Interestingly, such interpretations were also elaborated in metropolitan France. In the opinion of one colonial specialist in the metropole under
Vichy, F. H. Lem: "The communal principles of the National Revolution
found, in Madagascar, eminently favorable circumstances in terms of the
administration of native communities."[48] In postulating that Malagasy society was somehow suited to the National Revolution, Lem advanced a
dual argument: not only did the National Revolution fit Madagascar like a
glove, he contended, but the supposed stratification, simplicity, primitiv-
ism, and inegalitarian communalism of Madagascar could serve as useful
models for the metropole. Hence, Lem asserted: "[M]ost indigenous societies ... had, in the context of their tribe, their clan, their village or their
family unit, organized coherent groups where the interest of the individual
was subordinated to that of the community."[49] And later: "This conception
of reciprocal duties became so rooted into Malagasy mores that the community in all its forms had achieved in Madagascar, lengths undreamed of
in Europe."[50] To Lem, Malagasy history, culture, and village councils, or
Fokonolona, in particular, were so much in tune with the National Revolution as to provide possible blueprints for a future France.

Although officials in Madagascar do not appear to have taken the argument to these lengths, they did report unforeseen affinities between the
National Revolution and Malagasy culture. According to one district head:

"In the minds of the natives, the Marshal is not a king, not a dictator, but a *ray-aman-d'reny* (a father and a mother). They have always so designated their traditional chiefs."[51] The head of the region of Majunga, in the northwest of the island, corroborated the claim, stating in his 1941 annual report: "One can find the picture of the head of state in even the humblest dwellings. The Marshal is truly the *Ray-Aman-Dreny* for our Malagasy."[52] The head of the district of Tamatave on the east coast asserted, in a similar vein:

> Marshal Pétain constitutes in their eyes the *mpanjaka* of the French, in the literal sense of the term, in other words not exactly the "king" but the supreme French administrator. For the Malagasy, Marshal Pétain assumes the role of a true *ray-aman-dreny,* which they long ago attributed to their own sovereigns.[53]

Pétain earned yet another traditional Malagasy epithet, that of *Vovonana iadian'ny lohany,* or "summit upon which rests the rafters of the roof."[54] Perhaps the most explicit correlation between the cult of Pétain and traditional Malagasy culture was spelled out by the head of the region of Diego-Suarez in 1940: "The idea of the Supreme Chief, father of his subjects, is profoundly rooted in ancestral traditions which are now fortunately being resurrected."[55] Vichy officials actively promoted the grafting of the National Revolution onto Malagasy society by sending orders, even to remote regions of Madagascar once resentful of Merina influence, to propagate the image of Pétain as *Ray-Aman-Dreny.*[56] Vichy manifestly sought to foster in the same breath the cult of Pétain and a return to premodern, non-European traditions in a Madagascar whose new sovereign, Philippe Pétain, was reinvented as a successor of Andrianampoinimerina.

The concordance of Merina tradition with the National Revolution was further presented as a welcome change from a Third Republic considered incongruous with Malagasy concepts of government. Hence, the head of the region of Diego-Suarez commented in 1940: "The name of Marshal Pétain is becoming known to natives who see in him the natural Chief, or *Mpanjaka Lehibe,* personifying the state which thereby becomes real and tangible to them."[57] The theory that the new authoritarian French state was better suited to the Malagasy than the republic was couched in racial as well as historical terms. As one administrator argued: "The Malagasy gladly sees the necessity of the New Order. His character demands authority."[58] Regardless of its rationale, the notion that the Malagasy were somehow predisposed for Pétainism gained common currency. The district chief of Marovaya wrote to his superior, the head of the region of Majunga, on December 16, 1941:

> To the native the Marshal is the *mpanjaka* of the whites and this crystallizes much better in his eyes the authority of the administrator than had the republic, of which he obviously had only the faintest and most confused notions.[59]

The head of the region of Fort-Dauphin, in the far south of Madagascar, echoed such sentiments in his 1941 political report:

> As for the French Government, it has ceased to be an abstract idea. In the minds of the natives a single man now personifies government: Marshal Pétain. The confusion which reigned in the minds of natives on the nature and quality of the authority that commands us has disappeared. From now on, they envision the Marshal in the image of their former *Mpanjaka*, who embodied absolute power. Things are much better so.[60]

Marshal Pétain thus donned the status of absolutist monarch once conferred upon Merina royalty. Whether or not this proved beneficial in the deep south of the island, longtime hotbed of resistance to the Merina, is quite another question. Irrespective of regional ramifications, however, Vichy officials, playing on the supposed incompatibility of Malagasy society with republicanism, clearly sought to anchor the cult of Pétain and indeed the entire National Revolution in Malagasy's history and cultures.

A further reinscribing of the National Revolution onto Malagasy culture involved rituals of homage to the new regime. Philippe Pétain's new-found status as *Ray-aman-dreny*—at once father and mother—derived from more than mere paternalism. His Malagasy subjects were instructed to pay tribute, often pecuniary, to the ailing motherland France, and to Pétain himself, the magnanimous father who had offered the "gift of his person" to the nation. If in the metropole the antecedents for fidelity oaths to Pétain might be traced back to early modern France, whose language of fidelity was itself informed by "a traditional Christian view of the value of political and social action,"[61] so in Madagascar under Vichy did authorities rely upon two traditions of fidelity: one Christian, the other Merina. It was under Andrianampoinimerina that Merina rituals of royal homage had first taken shape. In the *hasina* rite, the "homage rendered by inferiors to superiors," or *hasina 1*, was exchanged for "blessings of fertility and efficacy," or *hasina 2*.[62] This rite, in conjunction with the rigid tax system elaborated by the Merina monarchy, provided important legacies of fidelity and tribute, respectively.

Armand Annet employed one ceremony in particular, the *Santa-bary,* to root the new regime's authority and even legitimacy explicitly in Merina custom. A February 2, 1942, report from Annet to the secretary general to the colonies in Vichy, Admiral Platon, chronicled this remarkable event:

On December 19 [1941] a ceremony that dates back to King Andrianam-poinimerina, the best Malagasy sovereign, was renewed in the park of the General Residency. The said ceremony, known as *Santa-bary,* involves the offering of the first sheaf of rice to the head of the colony. Rural notables, preceded by sheaf bearers, paraded while music played. The representative of the notables pronounced the traditional speech, to which I responded that the call to work was one of the precepts of the Marshal. Then, still in keeping with ancestral custom, I handed a symbolic *angady* [spade] to each of the sheaf carriers.[63]

Here Annet amalgamated Vichy's return to the soil and to tradition, its exaltation of the symbolic virtues of manual labor, with a Merina *hasina* ritual. By recasting himself as the successor to Andrianampoinimerina, Annet accepted homage from Merina notables while promoting the ideology of the marshal and concomitantly "renewing" ancestral Merina traditions. This staged performance reveals vast stretches of the imagination on the part of Vichy administrators intent upon amalgamating the ultranationalist and authoritarian National Revolution with a distant Malagasy past.

In addition to grafting the National Revolution onto Malagasy rituals, Vichy officials endeavored to invest Vichy ideology and programs with Malagasy meaning. The new regime's motto of *Travail, Famille, Patrie* was explained as follows to the Malagasy during speeches *(kabarys)*:

> The new state's motto is *Travail, Famille, Patrie*. You must therefore respect the family, and care for it. ... Everyone must work, for the more you work the better you can clothe and nourish yourselves. ... Finally ... we must remain united around our leaders. You know that a family in which discord reigns finishes in misery, whereas one that is united prospers.[64]

Vichy functionaries also relied upon written propaganda to indoctrinate the Malagasy. In the Majunga region, a large panel bearing the words "The Marshal Says" displayed various proverbs of Philippe Pétain. French administrators expressly tailored this propaganda to a culture that ascribed a special importance to aphorisms.[65]

Like Lyautey before them, Cayla and Annet were also careful to pursue a *politique des races*—a strategy of dividing and conquering that now took on new National Revolutionary dimensions. Thus in August 1942, Governor Annet reproached his subordinates for never volunteering coastal peoples for honorary distinctions. The medals of the new order in France, he bemoaned, had been awarded almost exclusively to Merina, and that even within coastal areas with hardly any Merina presence to speak of. This phenomenon, of course, reflected the fact that Merina held the vast majority of administrative posts across the island—itself a carryover from the

Merina conquest of Madagascar under King Radama I. To remedy this state of affairs, Annet advised that medals be awarded in future to "non–civil servants," most notably "in the field of agriculture, commerce and industry."[66] Here, the values of "Work, Family, Fatherland" were no doubt wedded to an effort to favor the supposedly "simpler" coastal peoples over "duplicitous" and "Europeanized" Merina. In fact, Annet threatened to disregard any subsequent request for medals, distinctions, or awards that did not sufficiently reflect ethnic diversity—read a coastal candidate who embodied the ideal of "the return to the soil." Such an effort to curry the favor of coastal populations was as old as the colonial enterprise in Madagascar; but under Vichy it took on new ideological meanings.

Vichy officials promoted not only the new regime's ideology but also its institutions. In Madagascar under Vichy, contribution to the Secours National—a charity fund to assist the poor in metropolitan France—soon became the quintessential mark of fidelity. Some Malagasy viewed the Secours as a form of taxation akin to that once paid to the Merina state; in March 1942, a Protestant pastor claimed to have been coerced by Malagasy functionaries into collecting funds in Temple for the Secours National.[67] Similarly in the district of Saboty-Namehana, near Tananarive, a Malagasy functionary allegedly "forced the inhabitants to contribute to the Secours National—20 Francs per person for men and 10 Francs per woman."[68] Vichy officials seem to have consciously encouraged the Malagasy to raise such sums through traditional methods and channels, most notably via the *Fokonolona*. In the Soalala district of the Majunga province, for instance, a local French administrator reported on July 1, 1942:

> The *Fokonolona* of the villages of Ambohipoky and Bevoay each handed me 350 Francs for the Secours National ... I stress these gestures because they came on the heels of an earlier donation by these same villages of moneys intended for the Quinzaine impériale.[69]

Irrespective of methods of collection, the contribution of the impoverished island of Madagascar to metropolitan France seems significant in its own right. In late 1941 the head of the district of Ambato-Boéni (modern-day spelling: Ambato-Boeny) reported to his headquarters in Majunga:

> The adhesion of the population to the government of Marshal Pétain is complete and knows no exception. Propaganda conducted by local authorities, by missionaries, by teachers, have reaped their rewards, and in December 1941 the Asian and native population of the District donated 117,000 Francs to the Secours National, while in 1940 they had offered only 40,000F.[70]

"Donations" to the Secours thus constituted a yardstick by which to gauge fidelity. On the occasion of the Quinzaine coloniale in 1942, Armand Annet asked for donations as "a duty of solidarity, a confident reply to the calls of the Marshal."[71] That allegiance was paid personally to Pétain further reflects the French administration's effort to model itself according to almost feudal Merina ties.

Tribute to Pétain was sometimes neither rhetorical nor pecuniary but material. In May of 1942, Vichy received crates full of jewels destined for the Secours National from colonies determined to demonstrate their fidelity.[72] Then too, with Diego-Suarez already in the hands of the British, Annet sent a gift to Pétain on behalf of the Red Island—a mohair and silk "landikeley" fabric, token of Madagascar's artisanal rebirth and resistance to the British blockade (at the Liberation, another "gift from Madagascar," a seashell from Tuléar engraved with a portrait of the marshal, was found among Pétain's private belongings).[73] This gift was based upon similar shows of allegiance from French metropolitan workers who had likewise offered Pétain products of their labor. It further constituted a show of "affection and respect"—a form of *hasina 1*—from the populations of Madagascar to their leader.[74] A month earlier Pétain had sent an airplane from France to Madagascar to bring his "message of paternal affection," declaring that in the wake of the first British attack on the island, "the Nation is proud of your fidelity."[75] The military conjuncture of the Second World War, as well as Vichy's reliance upon a personalized language of fidelity, thus combined for highly symbolic displays of homage and fidelity, couched in both French and Malagasy cultures.

Vichy authorities in Madagascar found forced labor, like shows of loyalty, to be doubly beneficial, providing at once a return to tradition and a step in the direction of the National Revolution. Indeed, Vichyites on the Red Island never tired of repeating that "work" represented the first commandment of the new regime.[76] Vichy officials in Madagascar rationalized forced labor on other bases as well: as an adoption of Vichy metropolitan legislation to curb unemployment, and as a measure supposedly requested by Malagasy notables themselves in a November 26, 1940, meeting on economics and finance.[77] Finally, the recrudescence of forced labor in 1940 was justified as a remedy to combat the "economic asphyxia"[78] of the British blockade.

Vichy officials, however, did not invent forced labor so much as perfect it. The French in Madagascar had long sought to profit from cultures in which almost feudal corvées to royalty had played an important role. To the

Sakalava people of the west coast, a kingdom once mightier than that of the Merina, there existed two kinds of work: "*asa,* their own domestic work, and *fanompoana,* the royal work or service which is part of their political, religious and economic obligation to the monarchy."[79] The French, argues the anthropologist Gillian Feeley-Harnik, "borrowed the word *fanompoana* ... to refer to statute labor, presumably as part of their effort to transfer the prestige and influence of Sakalava sovereignty to the colonial administration."[80] The use of forced labor, extremely commonplace in the interwar years, had earned Madagascar a reputation as "a country of slavery" in the pages of the Paris-based newspaper *Le Cri des Nègres,* whose many Malagasy contributors emphasized time and again the "enslaving" nature of the French regime on the island.[81] Forced labor, however, dwindled after 1936 when the Popular Front abolished its chief institution, the SMOTIG, or Service de la Main d'Oeuvre des Travaux d'Intérêt Général, first established in 1925. However, statute labor was firmly re-established on the eve of the Second World War, and under Vichy it reached a heretofore unparalleled pervasiveness.

Although archival lacunae currently render impossible a systematic statistical analysis of forced labor for the entire island, it nonetheless seems apparent that *colons* became increasingly dependent upon statute labor under Vichy. Dox F. Ratrematsialonina has shown that in the regions of Tananarive, Diego-Suarez, Majunga, Tamatave, Fianarantsoa, and Morondava, individuals combined for 716,604 days of forced labor in 1941 alone. Moreover, Ratrematsialonina suggests, forced labor and repression went hand in hand, the administration handing out on average twice as many sentences of forced labor under the *indigénat* in 1941 than in 1939.[82] The case of the district of Mahabo in the region of Morondava seems typical of the general increase in forced labor. The head of the district observed in his 1941 report:

> As for the execution of the services of forced labor, an extremely strict controlling mechanism has spelled marked progress. Over the course of 1941, 102,450 days of forced labor were executed compared with only 64,650 in 1940.[83]

Locally, the owners of Madagascar's latifundia delighted in "the current regime of requisitioned labor."[84] One such *colon* wrote to the administration on April 16, 1942:

> I am happy to inform you that the 200 statute laborers currently present at my estate in Mahajamba have fully satisfied my expectations. There has been real progress in both discipline and regularity of work when compared with years

past. This is unquestionably the result of the current policy of redressment, and I gladly tip my hat to the administration for it.[85]

An anonymous *colon* from the *brousse* reported similar "improvements" to the newspaper *Servir, Hebdomadaire Chrétien* in October 1941: "In 1940 I suffered from a serious shortage of labor, but things are already improving, thanks to the requisitioning of lazy Malagasy for private companies. Those who worked very poorly in 1940 are working better today."[86] Forced labor became such a staple of Madagascar's economy under Vichy that the head of the Majunga region warned in his 1941 final report that if it were one day to be abolished, it would be essential to do so gradually, "if one does not want to see the doors of every factory in the region close abruptly."[87]

Not content with the already phenomenal spread of forced labor, *colons* and administrators alike elaborated a wealth of reforms intended to extend its scope even further. In an October 1941 report, Armand Annet sought to codify statute labor: "It would be prudent to seek a rationalization which, while taking into account the habits and customs of certain races on the island, would also effectively protect the organization of labor."[88] On March 30, 1942, Annet took a step toward this "rationalization" by instructing his subordinates to draw up lists of potential workers. The *Fokonolona* would be placed in charge of the actual convoking of workers.[89] This measure answered at least one *colon* proposal. An anonymous *colon* writing to *Servir, Hebdomadaire Chrétien* had already suggested as much in October 1941: "Could we not, as in the past, make the *fokonolona* entirely responsible for the policing of their members? There are enough good elements desiring work who would not hesitate to denounce parasitic rascals."[90] Local *rois de la brousse* also put forward schemes to improve the application of forced labor. Some *chefs de district* sought to combat a form of resistance to forced labor that consisted of simply moving when requisitioned. In September 1941, the head of the district of Vangaindrano in the southeast of Madagascar thus called for increased surveillance of the Antaisaka people who flouted statute labor through their nomadic lifestyle.[91]

In the final analysis, Vichy officials on the Red Island sought, with varying results, to associate the National Revolution with Malagasy custom. The projection of Vichy's National Revolution onto Malagasy cultures made for an often gawky and even unwieldy fit, but Vichy administrators persisted in seeing in it nothing short of a new form of colonialism. Their vision of Madagascar was very much in keeping with metropolitan Vichy nostalgia for regional folklore and tradition. As in Vichy France proper, the peasant and the artisan were at once glorified and kept firmly in their social place in the new Madagascar.[92] Armand Annet vaunted the virtues of the artisan, proclaiming in a March 8, 1942, circular:

> The restoration of the artisanal spirit is considered by the Government of the Marshal to be one of the essential reforms of our educational system. Furthermore, it is urgently needed in Madagascar to adapt the colony to its new living conditions.[93]

Ceaselessly invoking both the National Revolution and the British blockade, Annet established a blueprint for a new Madagascar—at once artisanal, rural, traditional, eminently hierarchical, and nonassimilated.

Of course such schemes predated Vichy in some respects. Scholars such as Gillian Feeley-Harnik and Gwendolyn Wright have documented the efforts of the French to exploit and indeed reinvent Malagasy customs for their own ends well before 1940.[94] My research suggests that the apogee of antiassimilationist, antirepublican (and hence explicitly antirevolutionary), nostalgic, and folkloric trends occurred in Madagascar under Vichy. From 1940 to 1942, Vichy colonial officials in Madagascar went about inventing folkloric ceremonies and rituals, as well as practices and legislation. In the minds of unrelenting reactionaries, the resulting construction became a blueprint not only for France's colonies but also in some cases even for metropolitan France. It is important to underline that Vichy's folkloric ultraconservative projects did not remain dead letters in Madagascar: they were accompanied by real and oppressive consequences, most notably the impoverishment of the island (through taxation, "voluntary" or otherwise) and the massive recrudescence of forced labor. In both cases, ideology and economic contingency were invoked simultaneously: the British blockade was employed to justify the exaltation of the artisan, the return to the soil, the ruralization of education, and the recrudescence of forced labor, all of which also held a central place in the pantheon of Vichy ideals. Moreover, the dramatic impoverishment of the island during the war would of course have political consequences of its own. As Lucile Rabearimanana has argued in a local study, the dramatic drop in the standard of living begun in 1941 certainly contributed to "make ... the ... rural population [all the more] ready to follow the rebels in 1947."[95]

Cooperation and Resistance

Vichy ideology, and its visions of a future Madagascar, stirred both resistance and enthusiasm among the Malagasy. It seems undeniable that at least some Malagasy were seduced by Vichy traditionalism. A Malagasy pharmacist headed an indoctrination organization known as "Young Malagasy Volunteers for the National Revolution."[96] During May Day 1942 — a festivity that Vichy appropriated for its own ends — a certain Laurent Ralaimanisa declared: "[T]he words of the Marshal have not slipped off our spirits and our hearts like water slips off of *saonjo* leaves." Ralaimanisa, claiming to speak in the name of all Malagasy workers, concluded: "Pétain ... will always be the Great *Ray-aman-dreny* of all the *Ray-aman-drenys*."[97] That the new regime's ideology appealed to some Malagasy is demonstrated by a police report, according to which a Malagasy entrepreneur stated on October 11, 1940, in Tananarive: "Mr. Ravelojaona, the delegate of Madagascar to the Conseil Supérieur des Colonies, is the accomplice of Mr. Mandel, former minister and of other *vazaha* (whites) who betrayed France during the 1939–1940 war."[98] The scapegoating of the Jewish former minister of the colonies, Georges Mandel — who would later be assassinated by Vichy's *milice* — and the designation of a camp of traitors for the military defeat of May–June 1940 both reflect a certain allegiance to Vichy ideology. Some Catholic and Protestant Malagasy also approved of Vichy, on the basis of Vichy's reintroduction of prayer and religious instruction in public schools and its repudiation of an official secularism that had been the rule since the governorship of Victor Augagneur (1905–10).[99] In one important respect, however, Vichy officials failed to tap the potential appeal of Pétain and his traditionalist propaganda. Despite interest from Malagasy "functionaries and notables" in joining the Légion Française des Combattants et Volontaires de la Révolution Nationale as volunteers, the Legion in Madagascar resolved to accept only Malagasy veterans and to reserve the ranks of the volunteers to whites.[100] Vichy's racism toward the Malagasy (admittedly far less pronounced than toward other groups), and related antiegalitarianism and antirepublicanism, dictated that Malagasy participation in the new regime would be restricted from the outset.

A few isolated cases of cooperation or enthusiasm notwithstanding, it seems apparent that an overwhelming majority of Malagasy were, in the words of a November 1942 Gaullist report on Madagascar, "staunchly anti-Vichy."[101] Resistance to the colonizers had never truly ceased in Madagascar, with revolts in 1896–98 making way in the twentieth century to underground resistance movements such as the VVS (1913–15).[102] Historians of Madagascar have suggested that under Vichy, Cayla and Annet succeeded in muting all dissent.[103] It will be argued below that, contrary to received wisdom, the Vichy period in Madagascar saw its share of resistance—although rarely expressed through spectacular shows of defiance—and played an important part in shaping Malagasy nationalism. Specifically, Vichy's uncompromising colonialism, as well as its antiassimilationism and traditionalism, contributed to the metamorphosis of Malagasy resistance, transforming a prewar assimilationist current into a postwar nationalist movement.

There can be little doubt that Vichy officials in Madagascar dealt firmly with all forms of dissent. In March 1942, Annet inquired to the public prosecutor of Tananarive whether "marauding brigands" could be legally dealt with through summary executions.[104] Meanwhile, scores of political dissidents were preventively incarcerated as of 1940.[105] In spite of this crackdown, many did dare to express their opposition to the new regime, be they Communists or non-Communists. Among the latter, a Malagasy priest, Father François Razakandrainy, emerged as an outspoken detractor of Vichy oppression. He bitterly complained to the local administrator in Faratsiho, near the capital, in January 1941:

> The head of our district no doubt wishes to starve us. ... Many of us have had to sell our rice even before harvesting it, in order to avoid being sent to work in the gold mines, which amounts to a hard labor camp. ... No doubt the people of France are suffering greatly, but is that a reason to starve us to death?[106]

Razakandrainy's resistance, which led him to come to blows with the head of the district, was inspired by humanitarian rather than strictly ideological considerations; indeed, the priest suggested revealingly that he would send his grievance for arbitration to Pétain himself, if the need arose.

For their part, the more politically charged underground activities of Malagasy Communists did not fail to capture the attention of the colonial police. In March 1941, in the port city of Tamatave, later to become one of the focal points of the 1947 insurrection, the police reported the distribution of pamphlets reading *Miraisa Hina* ("Unite!"), written by a person bearing the pseudonym of *Ratiatanindrazana* (the patriot), and another entitled "The Politics Necessary for the Malagasy."[107]

Forced labor, perhaps more than any other individual measure, galvanized resistance in Madagascar under Vichy.[108] One basic form of opposition to forced recruitment involved migration. This practice was not restricted to the nomadic south, however. In the Befandriana district of the Majunga region in the northwest of the island, inhabited by the traditionally sedentary Sakalava people, a functionary observed in a July 29, 1942, telegram to his superior: "I have already pointed out in a previous report that the natives do not appreciate in the slightest the recruitment of workers. To escape it, many flee their villages before the arrival of recruiting agents."[109] Resistance seems to have arisen throughout the Majunga region, as evidenced by the report of the head of the Soalala district on October 1, 1941: "I confirm the existence of a general resentment expressed by the native populations toward requisitioning workers for the Marseillais sugar factory in Namakia."[110] Similar observations were recorded well beyond the Majunga area, near Fianarantsoa: "[P]unishments are frequent because of the population's resistance to the execution of corvées."[111] Opposition to these corvées spilled over into the post-Vichy era; from 1942 to 1944 the Free French—invoking the ongoing war effort—continued to employ statute labor widely in Madagascar. The wide-scale return of forced labor had clearly elicited more Malagasy opposition than any other Vichy-era reform. In October 1943, the Mutual Aid Society for French Citizens of Malagasy Descent (l'Amicale des citoyens français d'origine malgache)—one of the few organization to represent Malagasy interests at the time—singled out "forced requisitions of labor … as the abuse about which the Malagasy complain the most bitterly."[112] The practice would be curtailed on an empirewide basis only in 1946, after much lobbying on the part of Aimé Césaire, Léopold Senghor, Félix Houphouët-Boigny, and Lamine Guèye, to name only a few.[113]

Detested though it was, forced labor was certainly not the only policy resented by Malagasy dissidents. Police reports from the Vichy period reveal glimpses of the rich but shackled political culture of Madagascar under Vichy, and of various grievances against the new regime. These reports offer a rare sampling of Malagasy reactions to Vichy. For example, a spy overhearing two merchants in Tananarive on December 26, 1941, transcribed the following: "Ralaimongo, Ravoahangy, and Randriabolollona whom the pro-Nazis have persecuted will one day be covered with glory. Do not despair for we will eventually be governed by the sound principles of Communism."[114] This equation of Vichy repression with "pro-Nazism" seems highly revealing: it shows that rank and file Malagasy Communists, far from siding with the Nazis against the Free French as some historians have suggested,[115] clearly regarded Vichy as a profascist enemy, at least after Hitler's breaking of the Nazi-Soviet pact. Another conversation, between two Malagasy women on February 11, 1941, was overheard by a "native spy." It points to fluctuations and changes in opinion: "Marshal Pétain can try all he wants to ensure the revival of France and its Empire.

From now on, I hate the French. We nationalists are also Communists, and the administration is starting to arrest us."[116] This example of disillusionment with France and Pétain might be fruitfully compared with another dialogue of January 2, 1942, between a shopkeeper and his customer: "Where is the Popular Front to repair the injustices currently being committed in Madagascar?"[117] This passage clearly contrasts Vichy's brand of colonialism with that of the Popular Front, and suggests a political repudiation of Vichy in favor of the left.

By 1942, police reports began to register mounting hostility to Vichy. A February 1942 exchange on the *Boulevard du Maréchal Pétain* in Tananarive between two Malagasy functionaries underscores this increasingly bitter mood: "The French are cruel. They turn to the Malagasy only to collect funds, to recruit soldiers for combat, or to do their dirty work. The word of Marshal Pétain is therefore not trusted."[118] Finally, a January 10, 1942, conversation in a Tananarive bar concluded with a message that the colonial police no doubt found more ominous than most: "The hour of revolution is upon us. Our Malagasy brothers must educate themselves and support one another in order to regain our independence."[119]

This increasingly nationalist resistance to Vichy was as multifaceted in its manifestations as complex in its origins — at once formulated as a reaction to Vichy repression, marked by the VVS legacy of anticolonialism, informed by Communist condemnations of "pro-Nazis," and influenced by Gaullism. On an institutional level, it is likely no coincidence that the PANAMA movement was founded in 1941. PANAMA, a Malagasy acronym for Parti National Socialiste Malgache, later paved the path to the insurrection of 1947.[120] Likewise, the anticolonial MDRM (Democratic Movement for Malagasy Renovation) also made use of the Vichy episode in subsequent years. Jacques Rabemananjara, a leader within the organization, utilized the precedent and memory of French resistance to Vichy and the Nazis so as further to legitimize the cause of Malagasy liberation. As in the case of the main avenue in Tananarive, baptized Avenue de la Libération after the war and renamed Avenue de l'Indépendance after 1960, Rabemananjara played with the term "Liberation" by linking the French resistance of the Second World War to Malagasy independence. He declared, in a 1946 speech that was reported verbatim by a French police infiltrator: "The people of Paris rose up against the Germans, sacrificed themselves for the love of their country. Is it a crime that the Malagasy should [likewise] love their country, and should demand their independence?"[121] Unfortunately, aside from such glimpses into the workings of Malagasy separatist parties, the institutional history of Malagasy resistance to Vichy is almost impossible to trace in its early phase, due in part to its clandestine nature. Paradoxically, everyday oppositional practices emerge much more clearly from the archival record.

Under Vichy, when all public assemblies were banned and arbitrary arrests became commonplace, opposition to the regime—and to the French in general—grew by definition less overt and more anonymous. Outbursts of Free French and anti-Vichy sentiments surfaced in cinemas, whose dark confines facilitated precisely such anonymous political expression and whose very socialness transformed them into popular political tribunes. During the projection of a newsreel in a Diego-Suarez theater on December 31, 1940, spectators "applauded frantically and uttered admiring exclamations when English military forces were shown,"[122] prompting the banning of the newsreel in question. In a similar incident in Majunga on August 9, 1941, "whistles were heard in the Rex cinema when the projectionist showed newsreels portraying the Marshal touring the Free Zone. These whistles emanated from the Malagasy section."[123] This display of heckling triggered the closure of the Rex, and the ensuing surveillance of all cinemas by police officers.

Perhaps the most striking example of oppositional practice under Madagascar under Vichy was anonymous, and could consequently have emanated from either a French or Malagasy dissident. The police chief of Diego-Suarez reported the following episode during the normally solemn occasion of the first anniversary of the Legion on September 1, 1941:

> The marks of respect were given, and *Au Drapeau* was trumpeted. But several people, even officials, could no longer keep a straight face after the loudspeakers began playing the national anthem, because, just as the officers and crowd prepared for the anthem, the *Marseillaise* faded and made way to profane music. A clandestine radio was scrambling the reception. [This] angered many against the guilty prankster or antinational.[124]

This remarkable act of resistance—reminiscent of the oppositional culture of the French Resistance—utilized a prank to deride and subvert the solemnity and hence the very legitimacy of this new ceremony invented under Vichy.[125] Perhaps even more than the *V*s for Victory, which were scrawled at night upon the walls of Tananarive, this anonymous show of defiance was directly aimed at ridiculing the trappings of the new regime. The substitution of "profane" music for the *Marseillaise* might further suggest that this represented a Malagasy act of anti-French resistance.

In the final analysis, Vichy's attempt to forge a new Madagascar in line with the National Revolution failed, due in part to the short period that Pétain's regime held the island and in part because of opposition to the new regime. The very authoritarian and repressive nature of Vichy in Madagascar undoubtedly contributed to its unpopularity. Indeed, after the fall of Vichy in Madagascar, when a measure of freedom of expression was reinstated, a delegation of Malagasy notables expressed their desiderata to France. One grievance in particular reveals the shadow cast by Vichy over the Red Island: "The Malagasy bitterly complain that the policy of the Vichy government was crystallized in the words 'discipline and authority.'"[126]

Seen in the larger context of French colonial history, the Vichy years in Madagascar marked critical turning points. The highly symbolic denaturalization of Jules Ranaivo in 1942, and the formation of a new nationalist resistance, signaled both a hiatus in pro forma republicanism and the genesis of wide-scale organized nationalist opposition. Vichy itself unwittingly contributed to stirring Malagasy nationalism, through its fostering of Malagasy traditionalism. Clearly, Vichy—or at least its local representatives—sought to find resonance in the hierarchical, premodern, and authoritarian world of eighteenth-century Madagascar. This, in conjunction with a hardening of colonial practices encapsulated by a drastic increase in forced labor, made the two years that Vichy ruled the Red Island decisive in antagonizing Malagasy opinion and in fomenting wide-scale opposition. If the Vichy years in Madagascar were decisive in the island's eventual emancipation from the French, such was not the case elsewhere. In colonies like nearby Réunion, or distant Guiana, Martinique, and Guadeloupe, which had been French some six times longer than Madagascar and had witnessed long cycles of reform and reaction, resistance to Pétainism would have an altogether different outcome.

"Marshal Pétain and Madagascar." Propaganda poster by the Malagasy artist Ranivolon, 1941. This poster was rejected by the Vichy authorities for being insufficiently flattering toward the marshal. Courtesy Centre des Archives d'outre-mer, Aix-en-Provence (Archives Nationales, France).

Malagasy youngsters performing *mouvements d'ensemble* during a Legion celebration on January 18, 1942, at Tananarive's Mahamasina Stadium. Courtesy Centre des Archives d'outre-mer, Aix-en-Provence (Archives Nationales, France).

A delegation of Malagasy farmers in Tananarive, carrying a portrait of Marshal Pétain. Courtesy Centre des Archives d'outre-mer, Aix-en-Provence (Archives Nationales, France).

Vichy youth camp, January 8, 1942. Note the prominence of Pétain's portrait.
Courtesy Centre des Archives d'outre-mer, Aix-en-Provence (Archives Nationales,
France).

Ponvienne, the secretary general and commissioner to youth in Madagascar under Vichy, handing a banner reading "Travail, Famille, Patrie" to the leader of a Vichy youth section. Courtesy Centre des Archives d'outre-mer, Aix-en-Provence (Archives Nationales, France). All rights reserved, 31 Fi 241.

May Day, 1942, in Tananarive, Madagascar. In the foreground are processions comprising various corporations, including the leather industry, soap makers, and book binders. A larger sign declares that work is to be honored. On the right, the portrait of the marshal towers above the entrance of the *Printemps* (today the Ibis Hotel, Place de l'Indépendance). In the background is the governor general's palace. Courtesy Centre des Archives d'outre-mer, Aix-en-Provence (Archives Nationales, France). All rights reserved, 31 Fi 247

CHAPTER 4

Suppressing the Republic
in Guadeloupe

The complete loss of political power under the present regime has
been a blow to the local Negro and its recovery constitutes his
greatest revendication vis-à-vis the colonizing power.

— Marcel Malige, U.S. consul to the
French West Indies, Apr. 7, 1943[1]

They were upset there b/c they had rights for a while

In this dispatch to Washington, the American consul to the French West
Indies captured the essence of the Vichy years in Guadeloupe. Whereas indigenous populations in Madagascar and most other French colonies had
little reason even to hope for consultation on political matters, in Guadeloupe election by universal male suffrage had been the norm since 1871. The
hijacking of Guadeloupe by pro-Vichy officials on July 1, 1940, and the
subsequent disenfranchisement of the island's male electorate, conspired to
strip Guadeloupeans of perhaps their greatest right of all—that of citizenship. The experience of the island under Vichy is therefore largely a dual
history of ideological reaction and subsequent indignation.

The French Caribbean island of Guadeloupe covers 1,633 square kilometers (including its dependencies) and counted 304,329 inhabitants in
1940. It lay nestled between the then British islands of Montserrat and
Dominica, the latter separating Guadeloupe from its sister island of Martinique to the south. As one of the *vieilles colonies*—so named because Guadeloupe had been French since 1674, long before the "new" colonies of the
nineteenth century—the island featured total male enfranchisement. The
island therefore presents a fascinating case study: unlike Madagascar, it

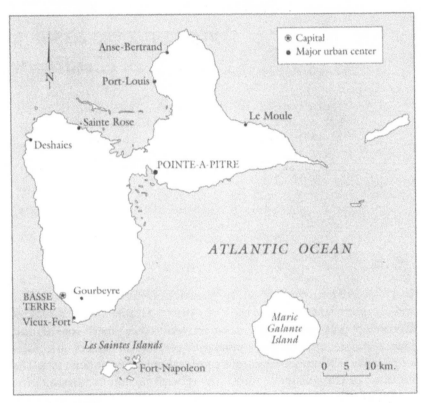

Map 2. Guadeloupe

boasted a public political culture that was trampled between 1940 and 1943. It provides, moreover, a rare instance of popular pressure having led directly to the overthrow of local Vichy colonial authorities. Finally, as in Metropolitan France, the Vichy years (known in local Creole as *"En Tan Sorin"*—or "In the Time of Sorin") left deep scars well into the postwar era. In few territories other than Guadeloupe and of course the metropole can one still today accurately diagnose the presence of a "Vichy syndrome," or malaise stemming from the Vichy experience.

Before the war, Guadeloupe had benefited from the special status unique to *anciennes colonies,* a rank shared only with Martinique, Réunion, French Guiana, and the *quatre communes* of Senegal. As such, it had enjoyed universal male suffrage and was represented in Paris by two senators and one deputy.[2] In the island's administrative capital, Basse-Terre, a Conseil Général made up of thirty-six members actually wielded greater powers than its institutional counterparts in the metropole. An independent judiciary dispensed metropolitan legislation, rather than either the iniquitous *indigénat* or customary law used by the French in other colonies. In sharp contrast with Madagascar, where the transition to Pétainism involved primarily a difference of degrees of authoritarianism and repression, in Guadeloupe the advent of the National Revolution ushered in wholesale changes in kind, both through institutional reform and political about-faces. The Vichy regime's colonial reforms essentially relegated Guadeloupe to the status of any other colony by obliterating limited democracy, the main political feature that had distinguished it from the likes of Madagascar.

To gain a fuller understanding of the situation of Guadeloupe in 1940, however, requires greater hindsight. The nineteenth century had seen both momentous transformations and certain continuities in Guadeloupean society, the echoes of which were still being played out under Vichy. Although slavery was abolished for the second and final time in 1848, the specter of a return to servitude continued to haunt the island under the authoritarian regime of Napoleon III, from 1849 to 1870. Even after the establishment of the Third Republic in 1870, the newly acquired right of universal male suffrage seemed in jeopardy, and it was only in 1876 that the island became represented at the Chamber of Deputies in Paris.[3] Under the Second Empire and the Third Republic, however, the French Antilles began to be recognized as more inherently French than the lands being colonized under the impulse of the New Imperialism in Africa, Asia, and the Pacific. The heterogeneity of Guadeloupe's population, its uprooting and generations of enslavement at the hands of the French, the absence of a single pre-existing, unifying national culture, and the emergence of a powerful and assimilated black elite in the nineteenth century, all contributed to the picture of Guadeloupe as an "evolved" territory in the colonial imagination. Martinique and Guadeloupe consequently became the sites of a full-fledged assimilationist experiment.[4] Yet, before 1946, Guadeloupe, Martinique, and Réunion were still in an administrative no man's land: at once thoroughly assimilated members of the French Republic but not quite *départements* (a duality reflected by the presence of both a republican Conseil Général and a colonial governor in Basse-Terre).

Assimilation was not only imposed from Paris but also came to be demanded locally, too. Already anticipating Albert Memmi's theory that assimilation could constitute the contrary of colonialism[5]—or at least a safeguard against its most arbitrary and brutal manifestations—prominent black politicians of the interwar years pressed for total integration. Guadeloupe's two black deputies on the eve of the war, Gratien Candace and Maurice Satineau, were at the forefront of this proassimilationist movement (ironically, both would vote to grant full powers to Marshal Pétain on July 10, 1940).[6] From 1918 to 1939, veterans of the First World War invoked the blood tax that the island had paid to France. The island's abundant war memorials represent, I have argued elsewhere, veritable monuments to Frenchness articulated by Guadeloupe's black elite and veterans.[7] A rumor first spread in 1919, according to which the French Antilles were to be ceded to the United States, further galvanized assimilationist forces on the island.[8] However, assimilation failed to break down tensions between a host of communities that resisted being subsumed into a single mold. This vast array of amorphous and self-delineated categories included new immigrants, most notably Indians and Syrians; a majority of blacks, mulattos, *créoles,* and *békés* (Guadeloupean whites of subtly different shades); and *blancs-France* (freshly arrived white French administrators). By the 1930s, assimilationism was also on the defensive on another front. Guadeloupe's non-white elite endeavored to counter the racist strains of associationist theories (such as those advanced by Louis Vignon) that were gaining sway in a metropolitan France increasingly hostile to its own assimilationist and revolutionary legacies.

The interwar years in Guadeloupe profoundly shaped the Vichy era in a multitude of other ways. The Great Depression ushered in economic hardship, a series of strikes, and the introduction of Communism to the island.

Marxist ideology, one expert on Guadeloupe has argued, was brought to the island almost single-handedly in 1928 by one Max Clainville-Bloncourt.[9] This Guadeloupean mulatto had previously acted in 1920 as secretary general for a Paris-based organization devoted to granting French citizenship to the Malagasy; then, between 1922 and 1925, he had served on a French Communist Party commission on the colonies alongside N'Guyen Ai Quoc, alias Ho Chi Minh. Clainville-Bloncourt's efforts at spreading Communism in Guadeloupe, themselves facilitated by the effects of the Great Depression, led to major strikes throughout February 1930. These occurred in the sugar sector, where wages were low and where industrial barons proved unyielding in salary negotiations. The strikes of February 1930 marked several important breaks with social movements of the past. They were crushed with particular brutality, as police forces fired upon and killed a number of strikers. They were also widespread, encompassing more than eight factories at their height and spanning the entire Grande-Terre (or eastern half of Guadeloupe). Most important, they cemented an alliance of Communists and Socialists, prefiguring the *Cartel des Gauches* and the Popular Front of 1936. Indeed, Clainville-Bloncourt was joined at the head of the strike movement by Paul Valentino, a young Socialist and mulatto who would later become the greatest Guadeloupean opponent to Vichy.[10] February 1930 was undoubtedly his baptism of fire in resistance.

Another cataclysm, of a quite different sort, had struck Guadeloupe two years earlier. A great hurricane devastated the Emerald Island in September 1928. The storm killed between one and two thousand Guadeloupeans and reduced to ruins much of the island's largest urban center, Pointe-à-Pitre. The island's infrastructures and public buildings would need to be entirely rebuilt over the next decade.[11]

Perhaps more seriously for the long term, from 1918 to 1939 the island's governors, elected officials, and entrepreneurs failed to diversify an economy that was still essentially mercantilist—depending on finished goods from the metropole—and producing almost exclusively bananas, sugar cane, and its by-products. This inability to diversify, combined with the effects of the Great Depression, only heightened social inequalities. By 1933, the Paris-based newspaper *Le Cri des Nègres* could write with little exaggeration of "the appalling misery of Guadeloupe's workers next to the scandalous profits of rum and sugar magnates."[12] Guadeloupe was consequently becoming politically radicalized; thanks to Clainville-Bloncourt, the Communist Party made significant inroads in Guadeloupe, while in *blancs-matignon,* or "poor white" circles, the attraction of the far right grew considerably. This constituency lambasted and exploited for its own ends the island's notoriety for electoral fraud. The reputation of the French Antilles for political scandal, their cases of influence peddling, and tales of long-deceased voters did indeed lead to a steady stream of political crises throughout the interwar period. To these problems one should add the enduring racism of the former slave-owning classes, whose descendants in the early twentieth century still pointed to Haiti as an example of black empowerment gone wrong.[13]

Finally, the Popular Front and its aftermath saw yet another settling of political scores, this time between the partisans of the newly appointed black Guianese governor Félix Eboué and the followers of the *député* Maurice Satineau. This wrangling was often more a matter of personal vendetta than one of political conviction, and it eventually played a part in Eboué's dismissal in 1938. Nevertheless, the Popular Front years would also be remembered for remarkable reforms; following the lead of the new Socialist prime minister Léon Blum, Eboué introduced a standard forty-hour work week to Guadeloupe. In a similar vein, Eboué instituted paid vacations and established the legitimacy of union bargaining rights.[14] Overall, then, a balance sheet on interwar Guadeloupe yields a brighter picture than might be expected.

For all of the fissures and strains in Guadeloupe's French republican system, the island's institutions had shown no signs of crumbling and the official ideals of "Liberty, Equality, Fraternity" few signs of wavering prior to 1940. In spite of its scandals and divisions, Guadeloupe represented something of a Third Republican success story: its black and mulatto political class stood as a model of multiracial entitlement and of racial, if not social, equality of opportunity.[15] In this sense, one should not fall into the trap of credulously accepting Vichy's claim that interwar Guadeloupe had been inherently decadent, or that its politics had been rotten to the core. If, prior to 1940, some newspapers could claim that election results were increasingly determined by financial influence or Parisian pressures,[16] this only serves to underscore the freedom of the press that reigned on the island during the Third Republic. In sharp contrast, after the advent of Vichy in 1940, censorship would become so severe that it was not uncommon for nine-tenths of an article to be cut. Certainly, as the American vice consul of the time remarked, no piece critical of the regime or of its officials was ever permitted.[17] This state of affairs stemmed from a series of reforms, implemented by Admiral Robert, giving the newly created and centralized "Information Services" on the island a monopoly over news, the ability "to control and, practically speaking to direct the local radio and press," as well as to mount propaganda campaigns.[18]

During the 1939–40 Phony War period in Guadeloupe, as throughout the empire, French propaganda had contrasted images of an exaggeratedly assimilationist France with more accurate depictions of Nazi racism. From 1938 to May 1940, Guadeloupeans had enlisted in the armed forces by droves, no doubt convinced that they could lend a hand in a titanic global struggle between racism and republican humanism. The slogan, already professed during the First World War, that France embodied civilization in the face of German barbarism now seemed more pertinent than ever to Guadeloupeans made all too aware of Hitler's perception of blacks. Interestingly, this late Third Republican campaign aimed at educating Guadeloupeans about the evils of Hitlerian racism would later haunt Vichy officials. Pétainists would be forced to argue before decidedly unconvinced Guadeloupeans that the Vichy regime's "partnership" with the Third Reich in no way signaled an adhesion to National Socialist theories of Aryan supremacy.

Guadeloupe's new governor, Constant Sorin, freshly arrived on April 30, 1940, had been appointed several years earlier by the Third Republican Radical minister Georges Mandel. Sorin was a former officer from St. Cyr military school and then a student at the Ecole coloniale who seemed ill inclined to become a staunch Pétainist. His wife was British and believed to be Jewish,[19] and his own prewar sympathies had been resolutely left of center. On June 18, 1940, a day after France requested an armistice and the very day of General de Gaulle's famous call to fight on, Sorin's determination appeared clear. Seemingly challenging Pétain's defeatism, Sorin cabled the following message to the new colonial minister, Henri Lémery: "I ask you to please transmit to Marshal Pétain the pledge of all Guadeloupeans to be victorious in this war, or to die."[20] Certainly, in early June, nobody could foretell Sorin's abrupt July 1, 1940, acceptance of Pétain's defeatism, nor his espousal of Vichy ideology. In order to elucidate this about-face, one must examine both the power dynamics of the French administration in the Antilles and the events that in the summer of 1940 precipitated Guadeloupe into Vichy's camp.

governor
in Guadaloupe
leu detractist
man de faih

(handwritten margin notes: "indigenous had no say in who either sided w/ Gaulle or Pétain")

A Quiet Naval Coup

The historian Marc Michel has argued that throughout France's empire, the decision in 1940 to rally to de Gaulle or to remain loyal to Pétain was made exclusively by high-ranking officials, with little or no consultation of indigenous populations.[21] Guadeloupe, in spite of its institutional safeguards, its elaborate system of balance of power, and its seemingly liberal governor, was no exception. In Guadeloupe's case, however, it would be misleading to attribute entirely to Sorin the decision to side with Vichy.

Before the war, a French military training ship, the *Jeanne d'Arc*, had traveled regularly to the French Antilles for military exercises and perhaps incidentally to defy the Monroe Doctrine. With the impending defeat of June 1940, the *Jeanne d'Arc*, along with the aircraft carrier *Béarn* (carrying more than one hundred airplanes) and several other formidable war vessels, sailed to the French Antilles. One ship, the *Emile Bertin*—among the fastest cruisers in the world at the time—had left France for Halifax, Canada, with the bulk of the gold from the Bank of France. Once it became clear that France was engaging not merely in a neutral armistice but in an actively anti-British one, the *Bertin* fled Halifax shortly after its arrival on June 18, 1940, threatening the use of force to leave dock, and soon reached Martinique.[22] Intrigues over the French West Indies were only just beginning to brew. After the American intervention in the war in December 1941, Congress and U.S. public opinion pressed for the overthrow of the Antilles' Vichy rulers. In February 1943, a major diplomatic incident was narrowly averted after an injured German U-boat sailor sought refuge and was treated for his wounds in Vichy-controlled Martinique.[23] For the purposes of this chapter's political analysis, however, what seems significant to stress is the importance of Vichy's armada. Once anchored off Guadeloupe's and Martinique's largest cities, Pointe-à-Pitre and Fort-de-France, it served not merely to protect France's bullion but also to ensure that the French Antilles would remain firmly in the camp of Pétain.

This fleet, reinforced by American-built fighters, troubled both British and American diplomacies, which resolved not to intervene in Guadeloupe but instead to tightly control imports and exports, while striking a deal known as the Robert-Greenslade accords. These established a modus vivendi with the island's authorities. The foremost of these authorities was not Sorin, but Admiral Georges Robert. An ultraconservative whose politics served to confirm that the French navy deserved its title of *la Royale*, Robert had been pulled from retirement shortly before the war to occupy the newly created backwater position of high commissioner representing the government in the French Antilles. Robert was not, as an American historian has suggested, merely a "realist" who ruled over complacent subjects, themselves "indifferent to colonial politics."[24] The admiral was in fact a staunch Pétainist who carried out the unpopular directives of National Revolution with unusual zeal. At the first sign of Sorin's wavering in his intentions, Robert dispatched his henchman Admiral Rouyer to bring Guadeloupe in line. At Robert's trial after the war, one Guadeloupean witness recounted: "In reality, it was Admiral Rouyer who ruled Guadeloupe, and Sorin only obeyed the directives of this high navy official."[25] Rouyer would leave a lasting mark on Guadeloupe: from 1940 to 1943 he single-handedly fired a number of blacks, whom he saw as unfit to serve as functionaries, as well as homosexuals and Jews whom he claimed "infested" the island's administration.[26] He hounded proponents of what he called "the democratic ideals which have cost France so dearly."[27] As the head of a police force that islanders soon dubbed the "Gestapo," Rouyer was also responsible for the arbitrary imprisonment and torture of numerous Guadeloupeans suspected of Gaullism.[28]

In retrospect, the decision to choose loyalty to Pétain in June–July 1940 seems more imputable to a low-key navy putsch engineered by Robert than a natural rallying to the "savior of Verdun." The island's main elected assembly, the Conseil Général, convened on July 1, 1940, to respond to Sorin's official declaration of fidelity to Vichy issued that very morning. The Socialist lawyer Paul Valentino dominated the meeting with an eloquent speech demanding that Sorin continue to abide by the laws of the republic. If Sorin and Robert became known as the local incarnations of Pétain, then one can say that Valentino emerged as a worthy Guadeloupean de Gaulle. Before the Conseil Général in Basse-Terre, he elaborated the bases of what would later become René Cassin's Gaullist legal rationale for viewing the armistice as null and void, and considering the Vichy regime itself illegal. Valentino invoked Article 1 of the law of February 15, 1872, which stipulated that the Conseils Généraux were to take over if pressure were brought to bear upon the National Assembly. Valentino then put to the lie Sorin's promise that Pétainism would not spell the advent of unabashed racism. Valentino argued that Lacrosse, Napoleon's representative, had made similar hollow promises prior to re-establishing slavery on the island in 1802. Before the "vigorous applause" of a frenzied audience, he expressed his wish to see maintained "French laws as they were before the Armistice," and ultimately "the liberation of France from the clutches of its invaders."[29] Orator upon orator, claiming to speak in the name of their constituents, demanded that the French republican tradition in Guadeloupe be safeguarded.

The administration's response was swift and unambiguous. When on the same day a delegation of five conseillers généraux led by Valentino confronted Sorin "with the pretension of governing the colony,"[30] the governor refused to meet with them. The Conseil Général, long considered the voice of the people of Guadeloupe, had been silenced by a governor serving the interests of the navy and the Vichy regime. Shortly thereafter, on July 21, 1940, Valentino was arrested and exiled to the infamous penitentiary of the Île du Salut off of Guiana. A wave of other arrests followed, with lesser figures incarcerated at the Fort Napoleon on the nearby archipelago of Les Saintes, located between Guadeloupe and Dominica. The witch-hunt of representatives of parliamentary democracy soon reached a climax. On October 27, 1940, at the suggestion of the zealous colonial minister René-Charles Platon, and in consultation with Constant Sorin, a law was passed at Vichy suspending indefinitely all Conseils Généraux and other elected assemblies in the colonies.[31] This law was itself in keeping with a metropolitan reform passed on October 12, 1940. The latter had suspended all Conseils Généraux in the *hexagone* (metropolitan France), while vastly increasing the authority of prefects. In Guadeloupe, as in all other *anciennes colonies,* the law of October 27 accordingly vested colonial governors with full powers.[32]

Sorin himself appeared metamorphosized. After having vowed that Guadeloupe would fight to the death to save the republic, by October 1940 he emerged as a convinced Pétainist. By November he sought to impress Vichy with his zeal, boasting that he had forbidden listening to Allied radio long before any orders had instructed him to do so.[33] A year later, Sorin once again exhibited the extent of his allegiance to Vichy after a letter was intercepted from a Guadeloupean student in the metropole who had written home that "a majority of French people are still Anglophiles and against Collaboration." Sorin immediately cut off the young man's funding and denounced him to Metropolitan officials.[34] A Vichy inspector's private assessment of Sorin seems to have hit the mark: "impulsive, authoritarian in words rather than deeds, Sorin is in reality quite undecided and feeble, wavering depending on the influences of the day."[35] In midcrisis, however, the Ministry of the Colonies was unable to follow upon this inspector's suggestion that Sorin be banished to a remote African outpost.

As early as 1940, Sorin, Rouyer, and Robert set out to define clear policy objectives. Their delicate goal involved the implementation of the National Revolution without alienating a black population that feared a recrudescence of racism and even an outright return to slavery. Such apprehensions had emerged during the Conseil Général's extraordinary assembly of July 1, 1940, when one representative revealed: "The population today thinks that their 1848 emancipation is directly threatened."[36] Responding to this concern, on February 18, 1941, René-Charles Platon ordered all Vichy officials in the Antilles to "show that in the metropole there is no more racial prejudice than before the war."[37] The other principal points of this policy directive involved curtailing inflation and instilling laborers with the sense of "the important role which the Marshal symbolically assigns to *Travail,* along with *Famille* and *Patrie.*"[38] Admiral Rouyer, as head of security on the island, set his own calendar for the propagation of the New Order. November 1940 to June 1941, he reported to Robert, had marked a phase of "repressive actions" aimed at crushing dissent and dismissing foreign propaganda.[39] Once this was accomplished, from August 1941 to January 1942, Rouyer conducted a thorough purge of the administration as part of a "National Redressment," in line both with the spirit and laws of the Vichy regime.[40]

In the end, however, neither coercive nor propaganda measures succeeded in winning over the vast majority of Guadeloupeans. Seeking to explain this failure, Vichy's inspector to the Antilles, Devouton, invoked first "the racial tensions in our *anciennes colonies*" and second "the occult workings of local functionaries under the influence of Freemasonry." Third, and most important, Devouton deplored "the difficulties of winning over to the new regime the insufficiently evolved black masses that fear a return to a disguised form of slavery and the introduction of Hitlerian racism."[41] In early 1944, well after the fall of Vichy on the island, Devouton further refined his arguments. The only reasons that Vichy had been able to reign on the island for three years, he suggested, were "the presence of important naval forces" and "the adhesion of a majority of white administrators to the National Revolution."[42] In other words, Vichy had failed to garner the support of the island's vast majority of blacks. All firsthand accounts of popular opinion seem to validate this last theory. Jean Cazenave de la Roche, a former ally and advisor of Félix Eboué's, observed in 1943: "In a country where freedom of … opinion has come to be considered sacred, [Vichy] has stiffened the population in its opposition. But one cannot fight with knives against rifles and machine guns. That is the only reason why there is a surface calm in the West Indies."[43]

Dismantling the Republic

Of the many charges registered against Admiral Robert at his postwar trial, one stands out for the number of times it was raised in court by witnesses: "Robert proscribed even the word *République*. The motto of *Liberté, Egalité, Fraternité* and *République Française* were replaced in the *Journal Officiel* by the words *Etat Français, Travail, Famille, Patrie*."[44] The insignia of the new order made their appearance in even more prominent locales. On the front of city halls, republican symbols par excellence, the triptych of the National Revolution replaced that of the republic. Streets honoring "representatives of the former regime or of nefarious doctrines" were re-baptized and given the names "of good Frenchmen."[45]

These were merely the external manifestations of far-reaching reforms intended to gut Guadeloupe of its rich republican legacy. In Guadeloupe, as in the metropole, Robert Paxton's words ring true: "Vichy was not a Band-Aid. It was deep surgery."[46] The law of October 27, 1940, dissolving once powerful colonial Conseils Généraux, was but the first stage of this operation.[47] A Guadeloupean who witnessed the Sorin era has summarized political life under Vichy in two sentences: "The Vichy Government ... revoked elected mayors and replaced them with designated replacements who shared its views. The Conseil Général was shut down altogether."[48] These momentous reforms were initiated in part following the lead of the metropole, of course, but also in accordance with the convictions of the island's new rulers. Admiral Robert's contempt for representative government in general, and toward the Third Republic in particular, leaves no doubt. He declared over the airwaves of Radio Martinique on April 22, 1942:

> We are lucky enough, for the first time in seventy years, to have a Leader who imposed himself by his actions rather than being the product of electoral intrigue, a Leader who is unanimously respected, and who is able to speak the language of statehood by declaring: "I alone am responsible before history; follow me."[49]

This cult of the "natural" leader, verging on the *Führerprinzip*, was projected down to the lowest administrative echelons, making local dictators not only of Robert and Sorin but also of their recently hand-picked mayors.

The wholesale revocation of mayors was rendered possible by yet another law, drafted on January 20, 1941. Article 2 held that "both mayors and their assistants are henceforth nominated by the governor."[50] Article 8 stipulated that municipal councils were also to be gubernatorially appointed, and that no former municipal councilors could serve on them.[51] In sum, Vichy elaborated a system of political clientage at the very antithesis of the democratic regime that had preceded it, and actually aimed at punishing the champions of republicanism on the island. This mirrored what was transpiring in the metropole, where, as Robert Paxton has suggested, the dissolution of municipal councils was intended as "a purge of the Third Republic's local cadres."[52] In Guadeloupe, almost by default, elections were suspended sine die, for all representative bodies had either been banned or rendered undemocratic.

The dismembering of the republic was felt on an almost daily basis. By late 1941, Sorin could proudly tell his superiors: "I have designated at the head of new municipalities individuals of unconditional national sentiment, independent both politically and materially, while avoiding stacking these positions with whites and industrialists."[53] Sorin's report itself constituted a contradiction: what he meant by the euphemistic "independent both politically and materially" was precisely wealthy industrial barons who had been left on the sidelines of republican politics. They now seized their chance to rule.

Political corruption was the most frequent pretext for revoking elected mayors. Convinced that "the democratic political regime ... had allowed a free-for-all and the massive waste of public moneys,"[54] Guadeloupe's Vichy officials saw corruption everywhere (admittedly interwar Guadeloupe had been plagued by bona fide influence scandals; however, under Vichy the gratuitous slandering of elected officials became systematic). To cite only a handful of examples, in January 1942, by virtue of the law of January 20, 1941, Sorin revoked Fernand Alidor, the mayor of Deshaies, on trumped up charges of embezzlement.[55] In January 1941, Sorin dismissed on similar grounds the entire municipal council of the island of Marie-Galante.[56] So thorough was this administrative purge that Sorin resorted to grouping revocations by tens and twenties in his telegrams to Vichy. Figures showing the number of mayors revoked are especially telling: by the end of 1941, twenty-one had been dismissed out of a total of thirty-four,[57] a figure similar to Martinique's, where by 1941 twenty-one had been revoked out of a total of thirty-two.[58] By the end of the Vichy era, the number of mayors revoked in Guadeloupe since the armistice reached twenty-three.

The composition of the new mayoral corps was not as balanced as Sorin's report to his superiors might suggest. Dominique Chathuant has estimated that of Vichy's new appointments, fourteen were white and only nine black. Furthermore, two more white than black mayors were confirmed in their positions. The net result came as a stark contrast to the racial ratio of mayors between 1935 and 1939, when twenty-seven of the island's mayors were black.[59] Equally denigrating to Guadeloupeans were the tasks now reserved to once powerful democratic institutions. Under Sorin, the municipal council of Pointe-à-Pitre was reduced to convening for the staged decision to rebaptize the city's main square, the Place de la Victoire, into the Place Maréchal Pétain.[60]

In another such charade, the pro forma Conseil Local, reinstated in the French Caribbean on September 25, 1942,[61] proved a pitiful and emasculated replacement of the once mighty Conseil Général. In October 1942, Marcel Malige, the American consul to the French West Indies, summarized the new role of this assembly in Guadeloupe:

> The Conseil Général … [is] revived … but all members and officers thereof chosen by Governor, sessions are not public, no resolutions of a political nature may be voted, only questions approved by the Governor may be considered, and its decisions subject to veto by the Governor when supported by the Minister of Colonies.[62]

As Malige noted, the very idea of reintroducing even this sham of consultative government emanated not from Robert or Sorin, but from institutional changes in the metropole "after whose government [Guadeloupe was] patterned."[63] The drive to apply such protoconsultative policies to the Antilles had been spearheaded by none other than Vichy's former colonial minister, the Martiniquais Henry Lémery. In a letter to Pierre Laval dated August 28, 1942, Lémery had actually proposed first that the Conseil Local be introduced to the Antilles, and second that Guadeloupe and Martinique be admitted as full-fledged *départements*.[64] This last act, he argued, would have convinced Antillais once and for all that Vichy was not attempting to relegate them from their status of *anciennes colonies*. Laval and the new minister of the colonies, Jules Brévié, acceded to the first clause but rejected the astonishing second facet of the proposal, leaving Guadeloupeans instead in an institutional void. Their new Conseil Local met only twice a year, and as Malige indicated, was entirely at the mercy of the island's governor.

Not content with shackling Guadeloupe's rich political culture, Vichy also overhauled a once independent judiciary. After arriving in Fort-de-France, Martinique, in early 1941, the anthropologist Claude Lévi-Strauss witnessed the new judicial system at work in the French Antilles. He recalled in *Tristes Tropiques*:

> One day I entered the *Cour d'assises* which was in session; this was to be my first and last ever visit to a tribunal. A peasant was on trial for having bitten off a piece of someone's ear during a fight. ... In only five minutes, the irascible black man was condemned to eight years in jail. In my mind, justice had always been associated with doubt, reasonable cause, and respect. The fact that a man's life could be disposed of in such a short time shocked me profoundly.[65]

In this sphere, what can be said of Martinique applies to Guadeloupe as well. For instance, the already imprisoned Paul Valentino was condemned in December 1940 to an additional six months in jail and a fifty-franc fine for the new crime of "publishing information that had unfortunate consequences on the population's morale."[66]

At the basis of Vichy's judicial and political reforms was the simple conviction that "the people" were incapable of exercising intelligent judgment. To Vichy officials this was clearly exacerbated when "the people" happened to be black. Accordingly, in late 1940, Guadeloupe's magistrates, in conjunction with Constant Sorin, drafted a proposal intended to abolish the jury system altogether. Their official motives included "the low morality of Guadeloupean jurors compared with those in France" and "widespread ignorance among the masses."[67] Guadeloupe's *procureur général* (district attorney), Viennet, used these racist stereotypes to explain a series of "scandalous acquittals," "a tendency to judge on purely emotional bases," and "an inability to comprehend certain abstract notions."[68] In another instance, Viennet went a step further, accusing juries not only of incompetence but also of deliberate collusion. He suggested: "[T]here seems to have been a strike mentality among people called upon for jury duty, in a direct attempt to defy justice and hence the Government, by deliberately fomenting disorder."[69] Persuaded that juries represented at best a waste of money,[70] and at worst a bastion of popular resistance, Guadeloupe's judicial establishment sent Vichy's colonial secretary Platon the draft of a bill intended to eradicate the jury system entirely.

This scheme called for the revision of the law of July 27, 1880, which had instituted trial by twelve-member jury in Guadeloupe, Martinique, and Réunion. An accompanying report by the head of Guadeloupe's judicial services under Vichy asked rhetorically: "Is the jury an institution that we must be resigned to maintain merely because it was born of the Revolution? We do not feel that this origin should render it untouchable."[71] This remark betrayed perhaps the most significant dimension of the projected abolition of juries, and of Vichy's institutional reforms in general. They were intended as a direct assault upon the legacy of both 1789 and the Third

Republic. Guadeloupe's Vichy officials seemed to be drawing a blueprint for a return to either the *Ancien Régime* or to the *Ordre Moral* of MacMahon, which had preceded 1789 and 1880, respectively.

By the time Platon examined the proposed revision of Guadeloupean justice in February 1941, new legislation was being elaborated in Vichy proper that "coincidentally, reached precisely the same objectives as those sought by the Governor of Guadeloupe."[72] Once again, colonial officials had beaten metropolitan Vichyites to the mark in matters of reaction. The resulting metropolitan law associated magistrates with juries in determining guilt or innocence, and halved the number of jurors from twelve to six. Platon wished to use the Guadeloupean case to extend metropolitan plans for judicial reform uniformly to all *anciennes colonies*.[73] This, he reasoned, would lay to rest any criticisms that *anciennes colonies* were somehow being treated differently from the metropole. Guadeloupe's Pétainist judges, however, were not satisfied by this measure, which they considered far too timid. Guadeloupe's civilians could be trusted even less than their already irresponsible metropolitan counterparts, they reasoned. They requested, through the colonial inspector Devouton, that juries consist of four members at most. These, in turn, were to be chosen from "notables of the colony," although to sidestep any potential uproar, the phrase "French citizens benefiting from high political consideration"[74] might be used instead. Platon acceded to this request that further eroded republican justice. The law of June 30, 1941, on the judicial system in *anciennes colonies* consequently went further yet than its metropolitan Vichy model. Juries were "associated with the opinion of the Court in determining guilt," and reduced from twelve to four members in Guadeloupe, Martinique, and Réunion.[75] As Lévi-Strauss attested, Vichy rule alone guaranteed that the judiciary would mold itself to the trappings of the new regime: at once arbitrary, authoritarian, and explicitly antidemocratic. What he could not have surmised, however, was that magistrates actually stood at the vanguard of the ideology of National Revolution in the French West Indies.

In the name of garnering elusive popular support, and in accordance with its traditionalist leanings, Vichy would break down an even more sacrosanct French republican mainstay in Guadeloupe—the division of church and state. In a transparent appeal to Guadeloupe's Catholic majority, on January 12, 1942, Sorin instructed that Guadeloupe follow the lead of Martinique in conducting a "referendum" on the introduction of religious images in public buildings.[76] This was a "popular consultation" *à la vichyssoise,* with only the island's mayors (nonelected, of course), priests, and local Legion officials invited to offer their opinion on the issue.[77] With little suspense, the measure passed unanimously in January 1942.[78] It was itself based on a metropolitan Vichy directive—a prefectoral circular of July 18, 1941—that allowed for the presence of religious emblems in public buildings when in keeping with local traditions and when receiving the full approval of the population.[79] In lavish ceremonies across Guadeloupe running from February to April 1942, the image of Christ crucified was introduced into city halls, schools, hospitals, and courts. The gesture could not have been any more anathema to republican secularism.

Scapegoats of the New Order

In addition to abrogating universal male suffrage, the republican judicial system, and the division of church and state, Vichy officials in Guadeloupe set about persecuting those perceived as the "unnatural elite" or "occult forces" behind the previous regime. These included elected officials, of course, but also Jews and Freemasons, the perennial scapegoats of the French far right. The impetus and origins of such discriminatory measures stemmed from Vichy directives. Their implementation would not have been possible, however, without the zealous cooperation of Guadeloupe's rulers, who evidently shared both Vichy ideals and scapegoats.

As in Madagascar, and throughout the "loyal" empire, the law of June 2, 1941, on the status of Jews was adopted in Guadeloupe. A census was accordingly conducted of all *Israélites* on the island.[80] On August 12, 1941, Constant Sorin further informed his administration that "any personnel conforming to article one's definition of a Jew … will cease to serve in any official function as of August 15."[81]

One example in particular serves to illustrate Sorin's punctiliousness in the application of Vichy's anti-Semitic laws. On October 11, 1941, a prominent Pointe-à-Pitre business personality requested to be admitted to the new veterans' organization, the Légion Française des Combattants et Volontaires de la Révolution Nationale. He explained that although both of his parents were Jewish, he had been baptized in 1912 in Pointe-à-Pitre, had since married in a Catholic church, had eleven Catholic children, and served with the highest distinction in the First World War (having fought for thirty-six consecutive months on the front, received the Croix de Guerre, and been wounded twice). This veteran provides an interesting test case, for other than his Jewish origins, he conformed almost perfectly to the Pétainist ideal: father of a Catholic *famille nombreuse*, he had fought gloriously in the Great War. Sorin's response was firm: "Mr. X must be considered Jewish in the eyes of the law of June 2, 1941 ... and as such all elected assemblies are off limits to him."[82] This example clearly demonstrates the extent to which Sorin was prepared to follow the letter of Vichy's discriminatory laws on an island where direct Nazi pressure was non-existent.

More incriminating yet for Sorin was his role in aborting a scheme to send to the Antilles French Jews and foreigners deemed "over-represented" in the metropole.[83] This plan, which has gone totally unnoticed by historians, took shape in late 1940. On November 29, 1940, Vichy's minister of the interior, Marcel Peyrouton, informed colonial minister René-Charles Platon that he was planning a "massive emigration policy for foreigners."[84] The scheme, couched alternately in racist and humanitarian terms (foreigners were "over-represented," and yet "the rules of humanity could not be ignored"), specifically mentioned the French West Indies as an appropriately distant destination. The project was ultimately scuttled, not in the hotel corridors of Vichy but in the Caribbean by Robert and Sorin. When consulted by Vichy, the former responded that the Antilles could in no case accommodate more than four hundred refugees.[85] By March 19, 1941, Sorin for his part declared unequivocally that Jews were to be denied passage to Guadeloupe.[86]

The initiative for abandoning this plan belies any notion that Vichy's West Indian authorities were somehow moderate or marginalized from the ideals of National Revolution. Indeed, in this instance, the new rulers of the French Antilles appear even more Pétainist than their Vichy counterparts, insofar as their anti-Semitism and xenophobia seem to have surpassed those of many high-ranking metropolitan officials. As Robert Paxton and Michael Marrus have observed, the first solution put forward to resolve the "Jewish question" in metropolitan France between 1940 and 1941 had been emigration, not extermination.[87] However, Paxton and Marrus place the responsibility for the failure of emigration plans entirely upon the weight of French bureaucracy, arguing that outside of this explanation "there seems to have been no special reason for this failure of Vichy to bring procedures into line with its stated policy on encouraging emigration."[88] The new archival evidence presented above suggests that it was specifically the anti-Semitism of Vichy colonial authorities that closed this final escape route for Jews desperately seeking to flee metropolitan France.

By virtue of the law of August 11, 1941 (adapted to the colonies on August 18, 1941), Freemasons in Vichy colonies were subjected to treatment similar to that of Jews. They were forbidden to hold public offices, to serve as civil servants of even the lowest rank, and their names were published in the *Journal Officiel*.[89] Sorin called upon all administrators to sign two separate declarations: one certifying that they were not Jewish, the other swearing that they had never been affiliated with a Masonic lodge.[90] The persecution of Freemasons in Guadeloupe, as in the metropole, was conceived as an act of retribution against an organization seen as embodying all of the ills of the former regime. These included most notably the belief in Enlightenment and republican ideals as well as secularism, and the alleged practice of sedition and corruption (anglophilia was an additional sin many Vichyites attributed to Freemasonry). In Basse-Terre under Vichy, the Disciples D'Hiram lodge was actually razed, its contents pilfered, and its operating budget confiscated. Over its ruins a church was to have been erected; however, republican rule was restored before the church could be constructed.[91] This projected substitution was of course highly symbolically charged. Like Catholic parishes built over the vestiges of Roman basilicas, themselves constructed over "pagan" temples, it conveyed the message that Catholicism had triumphed over its foes. Such a gubernatorial endorsement of a Catholic revenge over the *République laïque* appears all the more surprising in light of the strained personal relations between Constant Sorin and the island's bishop, Msgr. Genoud.[92] Yet even personal animosity could not overshadow the natural alliance that emerged between reactionary Vichy ideologists and a local Catholic establishment eager to erase seventy years of republican secularism.

Vichy officials in Guadeloupe seem to have achieved greater success in disbanding Freemasonry than their counterparts in other colonies. On October 10, 1941, Platon called to Robert's attention reports that Freemasons continued to convene in Martinique and French Guiana, in blatant defiance of the National Revolution.[93] That no mention was made of Guadeloupe is doubtless a testimony to the particular zeal with which the island's Masons had been hunted.

It appears probable that local Vichy officials saw the potential of appealing to Guadeloupean Catholic circles through the relentless victimizing of Freemasons. In a similar effort to curry the favor of social conservatives, in November 1940 Sorin adopted Vichy legislation limiting the number of women in the workforce. That Sorin had public opinion in mind when he introduced this sexist law (originally aimed at reintroducing male prisoners of war into the metropolitan workforce) is suggested by a postwar report. The interim postwar governor of Guadeloupe observed in

1945 that "Sorin had personally insisted that this measure be extended to ... teachers so as to satisfy public opinion. It was thus not only an administrative reform but also a political maneuver."[94] Irrespective of motives, the application of this law in Guadeloupe is sufficiently telling in its own right. The original legislation of October 11, 1940, intended only for mainland France, had stipulated first that all hiring of women in the administration would henceforth be frozen; second, that any woman under twenty-eight years of age who voluntarily resigned so as to marry was to be awarded a stipend. Third, the law held, in families earning above a certain income in which the husband worked and the wife had fewer than three children, that the wife could legally be placed on indefinite leave without pay. Lastly, any woman over fifty operating in the public sector could be immediately retired.[95]

These measures went into effect in Guadeloupe after their publication in the *Journal Officiel de la Guadeloupe* of November 21, 1940. Following earlier orders from Platon,[96] Guadeloupe's governor established lists of quotas on women, post by post for all administrative sectors. Sorin noted that in several departments all subaltern jobs were held by women, a figure he initially hoped to cut in half.[97] Sorin demonstrated uncommon zeal in applying this discriminatory law. He advised administrators that those who had received promotions placing their families in excess of the total earnings allowed under the law on *Travail féminin* should expect their wives to be laid off.[98] He further insisted before Vichy inspectors in the Antilles that the law be extended to teachers, arguing that to exclude them (as Platon and his inspectors had suggested) would make for an "unfortunate exception."[99] In all, sixty-four female schoolteachers were thus revoked in Guadeloupe under Vichy. In spite of the poor economic conditions on the island, only one—not included in this last figure—opted to leave voluntarily so as to marry and accept Vichy's stipend.[100]

The aims of this law were naturally in keeping with the role assigned to women by National Revolutionary ideology.[101] Women were urged, even bribed by the state, to marry. In an effort to curb what Vichy ideologues portrayed as the catastrophic depopulation of France, women were further encouraged to bear as many children as possible (the quintessential Vichy heroine, Mrs. Jacquier, was a mother of seven at age twenty-one).[102] In Guadeloupe, one teacher was rewarded for the birth of a third child by being reinstated in May 1943.[103] To Vichy officials, the legislation on *travail féminin* was thus perceived as doubly beneficial, serving to reward women with many children by exempting them from the measure, while allowing women who were too busy occupying "unnatural positions in society" to devote themselves fully to procreation. It is in this light that one should understand why Vichy officials in Guadeloupe especially targeted childless teachers.[104]

Sorin may well have been convinced that Vichy's view on the status of women concorded with that of conservative currents in Guadeloupean culture, by at once glorifying motherhood and seeking to return women "to their rightful sphere." However, the manner in which this law was implemented guaranteed its unpopularity. Jacques Grandjouan, the Guadeloupean head of youth affairs under Vichy, resisted the firings vigorously, "only consenting to apply the law on *travail féminin* after the formal insistence of Vichy inspectors [taking their orders directly from Vichy]."[105] Grandjouan had cited the blatantly racist inconsistencies involved in the law's implementation. He noted that two white female teachers in Pointe-à-Pitre who were, respectively, married without children and married with one child, were kept on.[106] Conversely, black teachers with better credentials, and mothers of two, had been swiftly dismissed.

The law on *travail féminin* was only formally abrogated in 1945, although many of the teachers expelled by Vichy were rehired in 1943. In his final assessment of the measure, Guadeloupe's postwar interim governor observed with a hint of irony: "[T]he regime which pretended to protect and value families has ruined no fewer than thirty-nine innocent families."[107] The law on *travail féminin* in Guadeloupe also betrays an interesting repercussion of duplicating Vichy legislation overseas. It reveals at once how ill adapted Vichy reforms could prove in a colonial context, and how they caused an important impact thousands of kilometers away from their intended targets. Indeed, while in the metropole the law on women's work was rationalized by pointing to the influx of returning prisoners of war into the workforce, in Guadeloupe no specific local conditions—save perhaps the regime's pandering to conservative circles—could even begin to justify this measure.

Elected officials, blacks, Jews, Freemasons, and gainfully employed women were not the only scapegoats of the new regime. Constant Sorin also played upon popular resentment toward the freshly arrived Syrian community. The Syrians had established themselves as successful merchants in the interwar period, especially by introducing door-to-door sales on an island where many a hamlet was devoid of even a *lolo*, or general store. On April 10, 1942, Guadeloupe's governor reported to Robert: "I have banned all traveling salesmen in the entire colony," adding: "[T]he activities of the Syrian and Lebanese communities in Guadeloupe are not dissimilar from those in West Africa, which led Governor Boisson to take extraordinary measures against them." Sorin concluded: "[S]uch a measure was needed in Guadeloupe, and the population has approved it."[108] Popular support was not the sole catalyst for this crackdown: after Syria fell in the camp of the Free French and British in April 1941, retributions against Syrians were orchestrated throughout France and the "loyal" empire. Falling short of confiscating Syrian properties and auctioning them, as Governor Boisson had done in Vichy West Africa,[109] Sorin nonetheless singled out this immigrant community and curtailed its professional activities.

The Foundations of the New Order

After an initial stage of repression, persecution, and revocations, Vichy officials set out to pave the way for a future Pétainist Guadeloupe. This brave new world would closely follow blueprints elaborated for the metropole: at once rural, corporatist, hierarchical, and in line with the values of *Travail, Famille, Patrie*. The transition between the repressive purge phase and the utopian future was perhaps best articulated in September 1941, by Amédée Cabre, the vice-président of Guadeloupe's Legion, when he declared:

> Should we be ashamed [of the defeat of 1940]? No. ... Were we ashamed of the hurricane of 1928? ... With every generation comes new sap which produces anarchical sprouts. [They, in turn] require the firm hand of a gardener to twist and tame them, in accordance with tradition, so as to perpetuate order and measure in a garden where one will enjoy living. For a long time, we lacked such a gardener. Today we have one who will be able to twist, trim, and if necessary, cut. You are his faithful workers. ... [Before the war] our beautiful *jardin à la française* had become a horrid fallow land.[110]

Here, both Le Notre's literal, and Voltaire's figurative, rationalized gardens of the Enlightenment are crudely transformed into metaphors for the cult of leader and the almost fascist catharsis from decadence and decay into order and youth. The tropics, both lusher and "wilder" than the metropole, were to be "tamed" and pruned by Vichy ideology.

To Cabre, the defeat of 1940 was clearly something of a "divine surprise," providing a tabula rasa for Vichyite social engineering. Constant Sorin shared this view of a future Pétainist utopia on the island, as reflected by a defining speech he delivered on Armistice Day 1940. Conscious that too coercive an emphasis on *Travail* might conjure up the memory of slavery, he cautiously glorified the first of Vichy's commandments as follows:

"It is through Work that man truly attains freedom."[111] Utilizing classic Vichy imagery, which Cabre would imitate a year later, Sorin proclaimed: "[R]emember Marshal Pétain's words: *a field that falls into fallow is a part of France that dies; a newly planted field is a part of France reborn.*"[112] Sorin was on much firmer ground when he evoked *Famille* and *Patrie*. He asserted: "[Y]ou will help me create a great Christian Guadeloupean family, whose primary cell will be the home, organized so that a child returning from school will find both his parents."[113] (in this interpretation, prior to 1940 the father would have been away from the home, inebriated at a *débit de boissons*). Like his counterparts in Madagascar, Sorin clearly sought to superimpose Vichy ideology upon a local culture he perceived—rightly or not—as favorably disposed to conservative, Catholic, and authoritarian discourse.

As in Madagascar as well, the principal ideological and administrative apparatus of the National Revolution were introduced to Guadeloupe. First and foremost, the ideological canon of the new regime was omnipresent. In January 1942, for instance, Sorin advised Robert that he had duly ordered copies of Charles Maurras's *La Seule France* for his administrators.[114] Secondly, the main agencies of the new regime quickly made their appearance on the island. After some initial friction with the Légion Française des Combattants et Volontaires de la Révolution Nationale, which he suspected of wanting to infringe upon his powers, Sorin came to endorse this organization as an enforcement arm of the new regime. He attributed this role to the Legion during swearing in ceremonies in 1941, when he announced: "[Y]our cries of 'Long live Pétain!' constitute a warning to those on this island who have not yet understood. You will help me to unmask these enemies of France. Either they will rally to our side or be crushed."[115] If Sorin perceived the Legion as a policing agent against detractors of the regime, Legionnaires themselves were convinced that they were waging a crusade of another sort. Amédée Cabre formulated the mission of Guadeloupe's Legion in terms of generational conflict, arguing:

> Tired by four years of war, betrayed by words and vain promises, we, veterans of the Great War, have not passed on the flame to the next generation. ... Morality and honor, the guides of our ancestors since the days of chivalry, fell by the wayside before the war. Some even mocked these values.[116]

Ironically, the failure of the Legion to propagate the new ideology stemmed in part from conflicts between rival institutions supporting Vichy, yet clearly at odds over how to remedy what Cabre stigmatized as prewar "decadence." Seeking to harmonize support among Pétainist stalwarts, in November 1942 Sorin called for increased cooperation between priests and Legionnaires.[117] In short, Sorin envisioned an updated form of the nineteenth-century conservative alliance known in French as the pact between *le sabre et le goupillon*—the sword and the clergy. However, despite obvious affinities in their moralistic discourse, in reality tensions between proponents of Vichy were so acute as to contribute to the regime's ultimate undoing. In practice, Legionnaires and clergymen, priests and administrators, and Legionnaires and administrators were often caught in triangular loggerheads.[118]

Nevertheless, when the local regime succeeded in muting such discord, it presented a formidable front. An August 3, 1941, swearing in ceremony for the Legion at Pointe-à-Pitre flaunted the multiple trappings of the new ideology. The procession began with a fanfare at the First World War monument, after which the *cérémonie des couleurs,* or the raising of the flag, was performed before two distinct rows of soldiers: one composed primarily of colonial troops, the other of white naval elements. This was followed by a Mass at Pointe-à-Pitre's Cathedral. In a practice intended to mark the subsuming of all veterans' organizations into one, groups of *anciens combattants* then offered their banners to the head of the Legion. After a speech by Constant Sorin, and the singing of the *Marseillaise,* came the ceremony's climax. The republican tricolor flag was blessed by the bishop of Guadeloupe—in an act typifying Vichy's collapsing of the boundaries of church and state. The sailors of the *Jeanne d'Arc* oversaw the entire proceedings, led by Admirals Robert and Rouyer.[119] This curious hybrid cortege then marched through Pointe-à-Pitre—to the military cadence of a naval parade, but presenting the exterior appearance of a Guadeloupean Saint's Day procession. By associating Catholicism with the cults of the flag and of the dead, this procession was intended to reflect the supposed unity of the regime's main constituents, composed of a bizarre and in reality fragile alliance of veterans, Catholics, young fanatics, and of course the French naval forces.

If the Legion was eventually to have constituted a single party in Guadeloupe, then corporatism was seen as representing the island's future social and economic structure. Sorin seems to have been especially seduced by the propaganda potential of corporatism. He declared shortly after the armistice:

> To the deadly slogan: "workers of the world, unite!" Marshal Pétain is opposing a vital formula: "Frenchmen of all classes and categories, unite!" ... This

true Revolution—yet peaceful and constructive—this National Renovation, requires a corporatist social system.[120]

Here Sorin captures the essence of Pétainist social propaganda, which utilized corporatism as a weapon against Communism and simultaneously pilfered Marxist discourse of its most appealing notions of "revolution" and "social justice," and then transferred them to a nationalist register. Like Mussolini, Pétain and his local minion, Sorin, set out to neutralize unions by overriding them. Hence, Sorin "invite[d] people of the same profession to form unions based on their craft, then to unite in corporations."[121] No doubt because he was not altogether conscious of the very limited scope of corporatist developments in the metropole, Sorin took corporatism seriously indeed. He called upon newly formed corporations to appoint "natural leaders." Accordingly, in November 1941, Guadeloupe's freshly composed banana, coffee, cocoa, and sugar corporations nominated their respective presidents.[122] Sorin sought to accommodate this local sugarcane corporatism to the ill-adapted typology of its metropolitan model, which featured the distinctly less Guadeloupean categories of "heavy industry" and "furs."[123]

Corporatism seems to have stirred considerable interest in Guadeloupe. In April 1942, the island's sugar magnates clamored for a corporation of their own, arguing that they were full-fledged industrialists, having in reality little to do with the agricultural corporation to which they had been assigned.[124] Constant Sorin, for his part, saw corporatism as a method for strengthening hierarchies while curtailing individual freedoms. He declared before the island's chamber of agriculture in September 1940 that the chamber itself would soon become corporatized. Corporatism, he contended, would prove of the utmost benefit for an island where "everyone thinks he is a one man show. … It … will introduce an organization based on discipline and hierarchy."[125] Clearly, then, corporatism was conceived by both the island's administrative and economic rulers as a method of social control that could both guarantee order and increase productivity.

By 1942, Sorin had elaborated a plan to integrate new Vichyite institutions on the island, by associating the Legion with artisan corporations.[126] A year later, a Sorin still seemingly captivated by the potential of corporatism cabled Admiral Robert to request the government's approval for a corporation of Guadeloupean fishermen.[127] After having dismantled republican institutions, Sorin thus demonstrated personal initiative in formulating a new political and institutional future for the island. His blueprint, in keeping with the ideals of the National Revolution, proposed nothing short of a society of notables, operating under a corporatist veneer. This vision of society was of course in perfect harmony with Vichy's ideals of inegalitarianism, hierarchy, and antidemocracy. In the span of only three years, Guadeloupe had undergone a thorough transformation. An island once governed by universal male suffrage, possessing a republican judiciary, and advocating integration through assimilation now found itself ruled by a regime that abrogated democracy, utilized the judiciary as a tool of political repression, and singled out for persecution supporters of the republic as well as imagined enemies of the new order.

In the final analysis, the main element differentiating Vichy rule in Guadeloupe from that in Madagascar and Indochina involved the presence and subsequent curtailing of a pre-existing and deeply entrenched republican legacy. While in most colonies the Vichy episode was marked primarily by a hardening of colonialism and by the reinvention of indigenous cultures in accordance with Pétainist ideology, in Guadeloupe the advent of Vichy spelled above all the suppression of republican institutions and their replacement by the hallmarks of Pétainism. Since 1880, republican government, law, and secularism had represented the backbone of a society born of the Second Republic and fiercely attached to its republican political culture. The impact of Vichy rule upon this society should therefore provide a logical sequel to the above political analysis.

unlike places already colonial here

vichy rly got rid of colonial infrastructure

CHAPTER 5

Guadeloupean Society
under Vichy

> Marshal Pétain holds you, farmers and peasants, in the highest es-
> teem, for he knows it is you who will rebuild a rich France, a rich
> Guadeloupe. He knows, as do we all, that although it is God who
> makes the plants grow, you, by farming, help God.
>   "God's Own Helpers." What more beautiful a name could you
> want?
>
> —Maryse Condé, *Tree of Life* [1]

Subsistence

This reference to Guadeloupe under Vichy, penned by the Guadeloupean
novelist Maryse Condé, sheds light on the ruralist dimension of Sorin's *Effort Guadeloupéen*. This campaign involved a call to produce crops and
goods that had heretofore been imported from the metropole. Such a move
toward autarky, in turn, cannot be understood independently from the effects of the Allied blockade. The naval surveillance of Guadeloupe and
Martinique began in earnest in August 1940 and was aimed at bringing
about the downfall of Vichy in the Antilles. It was organized primarily by
the British navy on the high seas, with the tacit cooperation of its American
counterpart. The wartime "siege" of the Antilles has become as legendary
in the French Caribbean as the "Guadeloupean Effort" it engendered. The
one resulted directly from the other, responding to an abrupt reduction in
metropolitan imports. Because Sorin and Robert were the architects of the
"Guadeloupean Effort," they are still today seen by some as having introduced "order and work" to Guadeloupe. [2] Sorin in particular has benefited

from a "posthumous nostalgia"[3] in some circles, not for his political repression, of course, but for his supposed ingenuity in the face of autarky. It is in this light that one should regard the fascination of some modern-day Guadeloupean secessionists with the Vichy era, perceiving it as a period of glorious self-sufficiency.[4]

In reality, the blockade around Guadeloupe was not as hermetic as some might suggest. Nor can it alone account for all economic crises on the island. It was still in its infancy when Guadeloupe suffered the most from hunger, in July 1940. Moreover, even at its height, American authorities allowed a significant amount of trade to continue (and this much to the annoyance of the British). The American consul to the French Caribbean kept the State Department abreast of the exact nature of all merchandise leaving Guadeloupe for the metropole. By way of example, on January 30, 1941, Howard Blocker, the U.S. vice consul, reported to Washington: "9 A.M. French vessel Paul Lemerle departed [from Guadeloupe] for Marseilles via Casablanca January 29 with ten thousand barrels of rum, twenty thousand cases of pineapple, and about sixty bags of coffee."[5] It appears, then, that the American allies of the British blockaders closed their eyes to certain food shipments to and from the Antilles. So loosely enforced was this blockade that the United States actually opened its markets to Guadeloupean goods, importing rum, bananas, and other products while claiming to bear economic pressure upon the island's Vichy rulers.

This in no way detracts from the genuine suffering experienced by most Guadeloupeans during the Vichy period. Shortly after the armistice, the economic plight of the island—whose supplying had been neglected by a defeated France—was so dire that in 1940 the American consul, Marcel Malige, reported to Washington: "The economic situation in Guadeloupe is very serious. To July 2, Guadeloupe had no communication with France. Revolution due to hunger is possible in thirty days if no help comes."[6] Three factors contributed to alleviate this imminent threat of famine: first of all, Guadeloupeans resorted to the famous *système D*, barely getting by on the island's natural food supplies. Second, Sorin and Robert successfully lobbied American authorities to permit minimum shipping service to and from the Antilles. Third, Sorin did indeed call for a "Guadeloupean Effort," combining the food drives, conservation, and austerity measures also undertaken in the metropole. In Guadeloupe, this included increasing agricultural yields, recycling (old tires were used for shoe soles, for instance),[7] and the production of a range of goods from soap to fuel, which Guadeloupe had traditionally imported from the metropole.

Although outright famine was averted in 1940, the island continued to endure harsh economic conditions that translated into a subsistence economy from 1940 to 1943. As in the metropole, where specialized cookbooks suggested tips for preparing salads without oil and a host of recipes for rutabaga,[8] so in the French West Indies did ersatz materials come into play. The official news bulletin of the French Antilles found a makeshift solution to a problem with which all inhabitants grappled: the sudden absence of wheat on islands that had come to adopt the metropole's taste for baguettes. The local *Bulletin de France* recommended:

> To make "local bread" [*pain pays*], cook a little bit of breadfruit [large, Tahitian tropical fruits found in the Antilles] with salt. Cook till tender, cut into slices, then grill. Or: make a batter out of manioc powder passed through a sieve. Add beef fat and sea water. ... [P]lace in hot oven till ready.[9]

The inhabitants of the town of Anse-Bertrand turned to perhaps more appealing but no less Spartan diets based primarily on roots and green bananas, occasionally confectioning salads out of sugar-cane leaves.[10] Privation and restrictions led to collective fantasies of Rabelaisian feasts. A reporter in 1943 Martinique, for instance, imagined that Guadeloupeans were gorging themselves on a delectable local specialty, *court-bouillon de daube*. The author confessed, however, that such rumors might well be the products of empty Martiniquais stomachs and fertile imaginations.[11]

The "Guadeloupean Effort," although undoubtedly part myth in its own right, also played an important role in stemming famine. A Guadeloupean reminiscing about this era explained that although Vichy was "a period of great misery," it was also one of "industrial and rural resurrection," and, as such, "many Guadeloupeans remember it with nostalgia."[12] Sorin had a hand in this revival, as is suggested in his February 1942 orders to all mayors to leave no fields fallow, given that "it is absolutely necessary for Guadeloupe to make a maximum effort to be self-sufficient."[13]

However, to take Sorin's assertions at face value and to portray the island as having lived in absolute autarky would be misleading. Many still prepared the classic Guadeloupean cod fritters, or *accras*—a remnant from the days of the triangular rum, slave, and cod trade. Even the legendary "Guadeloupean Effort" cannot account for cold-water cod suddenly appearing in Caribbean waters. Instead, the explanation stems from the fact that the United States did not follow Britain's hard line on blockading the Antilles, thereby allowing residual shipping to continue. This is clearly evidenced by a May 1943 U.S. naval dispatch addressing the cod question:

> The Islands are quiet and there is apparently no concentrated local effort to remove Robert. ... A solution of the situation may be had through an enforced blockade to eliminate smuggling between St. Thomas, St. Martin and St. Barts ... and by preventing the entrance of schooners under British flag which leave Newfoundland carrying codfish. In the period between November and March, about 800 tons of codfish, which is the food staple for the Negroes, has arrived on two trips of the schooner Izarra from St. John's. Further cargoes are expected. ... It is recommended that ... the schooner be captured en route.[14]

This 1943 suggestion to cut off imports so as to foment revolt illustrates the extent to which American naval forces had hitherto permitted the carefully filtered supplying of the Vichy French Antilles. It would seem then that a combination of factors contributed to staving off famine in Guadeloupe: foremost among these were the porousness of the blockade and the industrial and rural élan of the "Guadeloupean Effort."

The Return to the Soil

In Guadeloupe, the sudden paramountcy of crops under the *Effort Guadeloupéen* concorded perfectly with the new regime's call for a "return to the soil." On an official visit to Martinique in March 1941, Constant Sorin reminded sugar-cane producers that the metropole was entirely dependent upon the Antilles for its sugar (presumably, metropolitan beet-root sugar production was for its part being entirely absorbed by the Reich), for the British naval blockade around Vichy's other sugar-producing island, Réunion, was tighter than in the Caribbean.[15] Having established the material imperatives of sugar production, in July 1941 Sorin underscored the moral and ideological facets of ruralism, declaring to Guadeloupean youngsters: "You will understand even better than your fathers that on an agricultural island, the tilling of the earth should be held in a position of honor."[16] The sacrosanctity of the harvest was no vain expression for Sorin and Robert. In June 1941, Vichy passed a law rendering the destruction of crops in *anciennes colonies* punishable by death.[17]

The cult of the earth was also encoded into a set of freshly invented traditions. On the occasion of the island's first ever sugar-cane day, on February 1, 1941, Sorin explained:

> The Ancient Greeks teach us a great deal about the harvest; they had their protecting deities which were celebrated annually with great pomp and pageantry. In France, we inherited the ancient custom of blessing providence in order to spare crops from calamities. ... This benediction is accompanied or is followed by popular amusements such as local dance and songs. It is therefore to say the

least surprising that during the three centuries that Guadeloupe has been harvested, the fundamentally natural benediction of ... crops has not yet been adopted by local custom. [To reverse this situation] ... three ceremonies overseen by Msgr. Genoud and Governor Sorin will now open the sugar harvest.[18]

Sorin promised that a uniquely Vichyite coffee harvest festival would soon follow. Here Vichy introduced a series of hybrid celebrations to Guadeloupe—at once classical Greek, but also French medieval, and a harvest festival laden with both Catholic and pagan influences that have long constituted the semiotic bread and butter of the French far right.

The Ailing Motherland

In addition to transposing Vichy's brand of French folklore to the Caribbean, the new regime sought to instill Guadeloupeans with a sense of heightened loyalty for the suffering metropole. This phenomenon alternately took the form of generous self-abnegation for occupied and martyred France and of solidarity through a kind of guilt-induced penitent thanksgiving for being spared such miseries. Guadeloupe's tightly controlled press dwelled upon this last notion. The newspaper *La Raison* asked rhetorically, in October 1941: "Is your child cold? No, but children in France are. Give to the *Secours National*."[19] Similarly, Sorin declared in April 1941:

> Every Guadeloupean, even the most miserable, must understand that he is privileged next to his French brothers. On this magnificent island where fruits and vegetables abound ... you have never really experienced hunger. On your fields, basking in the sun, you have never known the bitter cold of winter.[20]

One can only imagine the popular reaction provoked by such propaganda, especially among Guadeloupeans suffering from protein deficiency and living in unprecedented squalor. Raphaël Confiant's *Le Nègre et l'Amiral*, which takes place in Vichy Martinique, addresses this very question. Upon hearing Vichy radio pronouncing: "The Marshal has faith in you. ... O inhabitants of the fortunate islands of Réunion and the Antilles,"[21] one of the novel's main characters responds to the title of "fortunate islands" by bursting into derisive laughter.

Such an emphasis on the suffering of the mother country must be situated in a larger context. Vichy was of course waging a battle for legitimacy against the Free French, and emotional appeals of this sort were common currency in what was in reality a vast imperial civil war. Hence, for Imperial

Week 1941, Sorin proclaimed on behalf of Guadeloupe:

> Today, although wounded and distressed, O Mother country you still find enough love in you to care for us. ... We hereby swear to you, Marshal, to be always by your side. We pronounce our faith in France's destiny and our will always to remain French.[22]

Other no less contrived appeals were politically charged along different lines, focusing on anti-Allied rather than pro-Pétain sentiments. On November 21, 1940, for example, Sorin personally opened a subscription in favor of the victims of Mers-el-Kébir and Dakar. Sorin also seized such opportunities to promote Vichy's brand of folklore. During Youth Day of Imperial Week 1941, each of Guadeloupe's communes adopted a metropolitan province, offering donations to it and showcasing its traditional dances and customs.[23] What more evocative a form of fidelity to the motherland, after all, than Guadeloupean villagers dancing *la bourrée*, or dressed in Provençal attire — practices steeped in both traditionalist and "regional" meanings.

Educational Reform

Youth day 1941 was no isolated festivity, but part and parcel of an ambitious campaign to indoctrinate and regiment Guadeloupean children. Youngsters were targeted as potential adepts of Pétainism, and of the new regime's cult of youth and vitality in particular. Sorin showed no qualms about introducing the National Revolution into the island's classrooms. On the first day of school in 1941, he told children: "Each of your actions can assist the National Revolution. Each of your actions as schoolchildren can contribute to the salvation of France, and to the future of Guadeloupe."[24] Behind such window-dressing, Guadeloupean schools were being radically transformed. The salute of the flag became obligatory every morning,[25] while the traditional emphasis on a balanced general curriculum made way for new concentrations on sports, hierarchy, religion, and patriotism. One witness attests that in Guadeloupean schools under Vichy,

> teachers actually taught very little. Students gardened in the courtyard, sang songs all day long glorifying Marshal Pétain, and prayed constantly. Each day they were required to salute the flag and to sing the hymn to Marshal Pétain (*Maréchal, nous voilà!*).[26]

Propaganda seems to have stolen top priority away from teaching: ten-year-olds were recruited for a letter contest to the marshal. The winning entry read:

> Marshal Pétain, you saved France in 1914–1918, thanks to a brilliant victory at Verdun. Once more you are saving France and you want to make her strong again. I, a little Guadeloupean schoolgirl, send you my gratitude and my respect.[27]

Sorin also appears to have been something of a pioneer in stressing physical over general education. He received high praise at Vichy proper for his ideas on the matter. The head of the Ministry of the Colonies' political bureau congratulated him in February 1941, writing: "I am entirely in agreement with you on the role that schools must play in teaching hygiene and physical education."[28] So similar were Sorin's reforms to metropolitan Vichy ones that the *Commissariat Général* to youth commented in 1940 that Sorin's proposals were: "remarkable and entirely in unison with our own reforms."[29] The glorification of physical education did not remain a dead letter: in March 1941, a team of Vichy pedagogical experts prepared Guadeloupean teachers for the new regime's curriculum. A newspaper chronicling this program observed: "[F]or a week these teachers became students, learning the joy of teamwork, singing and hiking—in a word they learned how to live simply, healthily and rationally like Scouts."[30] Male teachers were shown how to teach *Hébertisme,* but also gardening and manual labor, while their few remaining female colleagues were tutored in the finer points of household science and boot making.

Indoctrination and regimentation of youngsters were not confined to the classroom. At Sorin's initiative, a section of the main Vichy youth movement, the *Chantiers de la Jeunesse,* was established in Guadeloupe. That none were ever introduced to Martinique speaks to Sorin's insistence on the question of the *Chantiers.* Opened near the town of Vieux-Fort, this camp came to serve essentially as a screening center for naval recruits, a bitter disappointment for Sorin, who had hoped to endow it with "great significance."[31] The Vieux-Fort camp ultimately failed because of lack of Vichy support. Indeed, the law instituting the *Chantiers* as a substitute for military service was never extended to the Antilles, for fear that it might smack of forced labor or even slavery. In this instance, Vichy's colonial minister, Admiral Platon, personally scuttled what he perceived as too thorough and enthusiastic an exporting of the National Revolution to Guadeloupe.[32]

Other youth movements also made their appearance under Vichy, with mixed results. Admiral Robert bemoaned that Guadeloupe's boy scouts never flourished to the same degree as their Martiniquais counterparts because of tensions between Guadeloupe's civil and religious authorities.[33] Nonetheless, some organizations did achieve a measure of success. Such was the case of the town of Gourbeyre's youth group. Led by a committee of notables composed of the local mayor, teacher, priest, and doctor, it was intended for teenagers to practice physical education and "build character" by instilling "team values and the notion of duty."[34] Its avowed foundations were patriotism and Catholicism, and its goals: "to train men, namely French and Catholic men, capable of serving in a traditional setting at their work, in their family, and in their town—itself the new vital cell of the colony and the empire."[35] A second branch, reserved for girls, featured "activities which will always be directed in a feminine direction, be it for physical, professional or moral education, in view of raising a family."[36] This extracurricular organization fit the mold of metropolitan Vichy youth movements perfectly. It offered a religious and moral upbringing, stressed the primacy of the village as the cornerstone of the new order, and prepared boys for leadership, girls for child-rearing.

Decay and Regeneration

If targeting younger generations with Pétainist dogma was seen as guaranteeing the long-term success of the National Revolution, that measure alone failed to remedy the supposed decadence afflicting prewar Guadeloupe. The alcoholic, represented in the metropole under Vichy as a prime enemy of the family—alongside the prostitute, the abortionist, and the career woman[37]—came to embody degeneracy in Guadeloupe under Vichy as well.

Unlike the governor of Indochina, who could boast to inquiring Vichy authorities that "alcoholism is virtually unknown among the Indochinese,"[38] Sorin was faced with the task of transforming an island whose image—at least in the metropole—was closely associated with rum production. Vichy officials in Guadeloupe soon singled out alcohol as the island's social bane. In January 1941, Sorin accordingly established a commission to "examine all possible measures to be taken against alcoholism."[39] As usual, Sorin appointed representatives of the new regime's main constituencies to this purely consultative body. These included the bishop's assistant, the island's chief prosecutor, and a pedagogical expert. That temperance in Guadeloupe was perceived primarily as a moral cleansing can be of little doubt. A law dated January 18, 1941, instructed that any *débit de boisson* located fewer than two hundred meters from a church, cemetery, or school was to be closed immediately.[40]

Political considerations also contributed to Vichy's crackdown on bars and cafés. As during MacMahon's Moral Order, when in the metropole *débits de boissons* were singled out as hotbeds of popular political dissent,[41] so in Guadeloupe under Sorin were such establishments tightly controlled. A 1940 law prohibited the opening of any "new café, cabaret, or other *débit de boisson*" in Martinique and Guadeloupe.[42] During the 1941 Carnival, Sorin instructed that all bars were to close at 10:00 P.M., in view of "maintaining moral order given the serious and tragic hours which the metropole is enduring."[43] Lists of all *débits de boissons* were drawn up that same year, and taxes on all alcoholic beverages raised considerably.[44] This near prohibitionism seems all the more revealing given the pressing need to sell the island's rum stocks. And yet, moral and political considerations manifestly superseded economic imperatives. The war against alcohol was waged with such zeal that inspectors searched individual homes for liquor stashes. In one instance at least, local adepts of the island's famous *ti-punch* outwitted inspectors by concealing rum bottles in the cinders of their fireplaces.[45]

Modern and Traditional Aesthetics and the Eden of the New Order

Guadeloupe's Vichy officials were convinced that dismantled social structures needed to be replaced by a new, utopian National Revolutionary edifice. The "moral cleansing" inherent in both the repression of alcoholism and in the creation of a new generation of Pétainists was consequently accompanied by an even more pervasive urban renewal. This physical renovation, in turn, was viewed as the foundation of any future society. Vichy would accordingly strive to mark the very face of Guadeloupe with an indelible stamp of Pétainist aesthetics, reflecting both the regime's visual trappings and its penchant for social control.

To be sure, the architectural transformation of Guadeloupe had begun well before Vichy. In the wake of the devastating hurricane of 1928, and in a *grands travaux* response to the Great Depression, a vast urban facelift was undertaken on the island. In the early 1930s, the Tunisian architect Ali Tur was called upon to create palaces for the republic—from the governor's building in Basse-Terre to courthouses, city halls, and schools. These concrete structures, in a style similar to that of the Musée des Colonies in Paris, were part of a larger urban colonial experiment in social control, analyzed by both Gwendolyn Wright and Paul Rabinow.[46] That Ali Tur's disproportionately grand projects also constituted the first stage of a vaster vision for Guadeloupe is suggested by G. Robert, the engineer in charge of public works in Guadeloupe in the mid-1930s. He explained:

> It has been written of Guadeloupe that nature has blessed it but that man has done little to profit from it aesthetically. One must recognize that if the beautiful mountains provide pleasant sights, the *cases* [Guadeloupean homes] built along roads ... detract from the agreeable impression a visitor might otherwise feel. We must therefore embellish this island, but that is a long term project that has only just begun.[47]

Under Sorin, the emphasis would shift from monumental urbanizing projects to an almost fascist campaign of everyday small-town beautification, reminiscent of Nazi "strength through joy" programs. As in the metropole, where in the Provençal village of Oppède-le-Vieux, Vichy established a community of artisans and artists in hopes of fostering an elitist rural utopia,[48] so in Guadeloupe was aesthetic renovation closely associated with the idealization of the village as the cellular foundation of the new order.

This "beautification" project took shape in 1941. From the outset, it was highly ideologically charged. Sorin proclaimed in April 1941: "There can be no moral renovation without physical cleanliness and without elegance."[49] He added: "On this island where beautiful flowers flourish on their own and which is spared the rigors of winter, one need not spend much to achieve quaintness."[50] It was above all village quaintness (*coquet*) that Sorin desired. He instructed the mayor of Basse-Terre to render the capital "quaint" and "clean."[51] In October 1941, he explicitly associated salubrity and regeneration, informing all mayors:

> Everyone must understand the need to rid Guadeloupe—an island blessed by God—of hideous *cases* and from the ugliness engendered by man. A quaint and clean Guadeloupe where strong, unified and healthy families can prosper, such is the objective I ask of all Guadeloupeans.[52]

Sorin's antipathy for the Guadeloupean *case* seems to have been particularly intense. After touring a poor quarter of Pointe-à-Pitre in August 1941, he wrote to the city's mayor:

> The visit of this neighborhood left a painful impression [on me]. I demand that you immediately prevent the installation of any more hideous *cases* in regenerated areas, and that you combat slums in Pointe-à-Pitre by any means necessary.[53]

Especially repugnant to Sorin was the wide-scale use of sheet metal on and around these homes. This material had been utilized in Guadeloupe since the turn of the century, after it was found to resist downpours better than wooden roofs.[54] Sorin's solution was to order the replacement of sheet metal fences by hedges, and for all sheet metal roofs to be painted red.[55] Sorin thereby combined French traditionalist nostalgia for mythical flowered villages, and for all things recently extinct,[56] with a modernist distaste for what he characterized as "abominable huts with ignoble roofing unfit for human beings of the twentieth century."[57] That Vichy's governor offended islanders with this discourse seems probable, especially given the ancestral Guadeloupean customs associated with selecting, then constructing, the almost sacred *case* so as to protect it against malevolent spirits.[58] What Sorin abhorred as bricolage were in reality staples of black domestic Caribbean architecture.

Sorin's alternately modernist and traditionalist discourses and aesthetics might at first seem contradictory. However, as Paul Rabinow suggests, Vichy's rural and traditionalist dimensions, and its modernist and technocratic components, can actually be perceived as the flip sides of the same coin.[59] This dichotomy constitutes in reality a hallmark shared by both Vichy and bona fide fascist regimes. It should therefore come as no surprise that Sorin rested his urban transformation upon both the models of the modernist architect Le Corbusier and on those of the traditionalist pro-Vichy artist Henri Cortot. The government-controlled *L'Hebdomadaire de la Guadeloupe* printed the following excerpt from Le Corbusier, which seemed to validate both Sorin's aesthetics and National Revolutionary thought: "The problem of lodging is not a secondary one. It is the key to the rebirth of the family and to that of the spirit, the key to the rebirth of the Nation."[60] Le Corbusier had indeed been appointed to a committee on urban and architectural affairs by Vichy in 1940, before falling out of favor with the regime in July 1941.[61] The fact that Sorin should have invoked this quintessentially modernist architect, however, reveals more about the former's *Weltanschauung* than about the latter's ideological sympathies. Sorin manifestly believed that Vichy values and modernist architecture could coexist and even flourish together; this postulate seemed all the more valid in the colonies, where Le Corbusier's architecture had already been exported and tested in the past.

Sorin appropriated not only Le Corbusier's notions of creating housing for a "new universal man"[62] but also Vichy's ideal of beauty. According to Sorin: "The Beautiful can only be the result of Order"[63]—an expression that would no doubt have made surrealists shudder, but which certainly concorded with Nazi notions of beauty. Here, Guadeloupe's governor invoked the "great French artist Cortot,"[64] actually an obscure Pétainist sculptor and engraver who had written, "You can see that the culture of the superfluous cannot be separated from the indispensable. It is at once a moral value, an enriching of the spirit, and a character builder."[65] Sorin thus interwove Le Corbusier's notions of practical architecture with concepts of superfluous and ordered beauty. The end result was an imagined Guadeloupe with flowered hamlets, uniformly red roofs, and leveled shantytowns. In such an idealized world, Sorin hoped to propagate the National Revolution by fostering village pride and rural values.[66]

In September 1943, two months after Vichy finally fell in the French Antilles, a journalist called for Guadeloupeans not to renounce Sorin's urban accomplishments. After remarking that "the return of elected assemblies ... offers us the occasion to speak freely again,"[67] this anonymous author implored Guadeloupeans not to turn their backs on the ideal of "beautification" merely because it had been associated with Pétainism. The journalist argued: "It would be unfair to deny that in our two principal cities and in many towns, considerable urban efforts were made over the last few years. These have undeniably led to increased cleanliness and order."[68] The author concluded that it would be an unforgivable error to return to the "indolence and lack of taste[,] ... incompatible with the twentieth century,"[69] that had supposedly characterized the prewar period. This suggests that in Guadeloupe, as in the metropole, the end of Vichy spelled anything but a return to the status quo of the Third Republic. Instead, some Guadeloupeans came to share at the very least Vichy's technocratic and modernist utopian vision of a new society, as well as the Pétainist assertion that the Third Republic had embodied both moral and physical corruption and disorder. In short, this journalist clearly betrays residual postwar sympathy for Sorin and his regime.

Cooperation

Not all of the island's inhabitants resisted the new regime; some, like the aforementioned journalist, even regretted that it fell. Supporters of the National Revolution under Vichy included of course Legionnaires, naval commanders, and ultraconservative clergymen. Many of these Vichyites were white, either long established on the island or freshly arrived from the metropole. However, as Richard Burton has commented for Martinique, to pose the question of cooperation and resistance solely in terms of race is as misleading as it is problematic.[70] The archives reveal the presence of both black and white Pétainist sympathizers on the island. Foremost among such black Vichy supporters, ironically, were some heretofore steadfastly loyal representatives of the republic. Vichy's first minister of the colonies from July 12 to September 6, 1940, was Henri Lémery, a Martiniquais mulatto who had previously served as that island's senator. A close friend of Philippe Pétain, he carried considerable political sway in the Antilles. The American vice consul to the French West Indies illustrated this influence when he remarked in August 1940:

> The inhabitants of these colonies are divided on the question [of loyalty], many thinking that the colonies should have declared for General de Gaulle. ... However, it is noticeable that much of the local public talk against the Pétain government has ceased since the receipt of a telegram from Monsieur Henri Lémery, Senator from Martinique and now Minister of the Colonies, requesting that the people support the present regime in France.[71]

Guadeloupe possessed its own equivalent of Lémery, equally capable of steering public opinion. Gratien Candace, former deputy of Guadeloupe at the National Assembly, likewise paid homage to the new regime, providing it incalculable propaganda services. In February 1941, Pétain appointed him *Conseiller National*—an essentially honorific title.[72] Earlier that same month, he had declared to his fellow Guadeloupeans:

> I know the profound attachment of all of you to the Government and to the person of Marshal Pétain. I insist that you maintain the strictest cohesion around the Leader who is pursuing the work of National Resurrection. I am happy to personally salute Governor Sorin ... for his actions which are entirely in line with those of the Head of State.[73]

The precedent for cooperation was thus set at the highest echelons. Guadeloupeans would therefore have to decide whether to follow the ideological lead of Candace and Lémery, or that of the island's black former governor Félix Eboué, who on August 26, 1940, became the first governor of a sizable colony to rally a territory (Chad) to General de Gaulle's Free French.[74]

Guadeloupe's Vichy supporters were not all celebrities residing in the metropole, however. Like Bertrand Mauville, an "ordinary Martiniquais" won over by the National Revolution in Raphaël Confiant's *Le Nègre et l'Amiral*,[75] many were unassuming citizens who were seduced by Pétainism. Some might undoubtedly have borne grudges toward ousted republican dignitaries; Félix Eboué, for example, had no shortage of enemies on the island. Others might have been genuinely converted to the new ideology, or perhaps found profit in serving it. Thus, as in the metropole, denunciators thrived under Vichy. According to the resister Jean-Charles Timoléon, "a system of denunciations wreaked havoc even within the tightest knit families."[76]

Among ideological collaborators, one unlikely candidate figured prominently. Henry Thomasset was a native of Haiti, former director of Port-au-Prince's and then Pointe-à-Pitre's branches of the Royal Bank of Canada.[77] During the war, American intelligence reports characterized him as "pro-Vichy and pro-Nazi."[78] Thanks to his multilingualism, he was able to serve as the regime's anglophone radio propaganda agent. According to American sources, "his broadcasts were reported to be violently anti-British."[79] This curious personality seems to have amply deserved his popular title of "the Laval of Guadeloupe."[80] After the war, Thomasset sought to clear Constant Sorin's name, by contending that the governor had every intention of siding with the Allies but had been stopped in his tracks by Admiral Robert.[81]

Resistance

The factors that engendered Guadeloupean resistance against Vichy were equally complex. Manifestations of resistance themselves assumed a multitude of forms, from everyday oppositional practices to numerous defections to the Free French via the nearby British isle of Dominica. Admiral Robert himself offered perhaps the most surprising explanation for opposition when he wrote about Martinique:

> The idea was spread around the island that de Gaulle was a black general, wishing like [the Haitian revolutionary] Toussaint Louverture to free the people of color from the yoke of white land owners. ... To complete this fable, *La Dissidence* [as resistance in the Antilles was known] was imagined either as the wife of the General, or as an island under his control.[82]

This gendering, personalization, and racial construction of resistance seems highly significant, and should not be dismissed out of hand, as it is by the Guadeloupean historians Laurent Farrugia and Eliane Sempaire, as a mere "slandering of ... Antillais resistance and patriotism."[83] On the contrary, it would seem to indicate that resistance captivated the popular imagination. In the process, the idea of resistance was infused with distinctly Antillais meanings. The decision to leave for Dominica or to resist in some other capacity was thus not informed solely by ideological and international considerations, but was in reality also influenced by a set of cultural, political, and historical factors.

Guy Cornély, a former sailor aboard the *Jeanne d'Arc* who left Vichy-controlled Guadeloupe to join the Free French, confessed to me that he had been criticized in the past precisely for suggesting that not all of his fellow resisters had chosen the path of "dissidence" purely out of self-abnegation and patriotism.[84] His suggestion is borne out by primary sources, which reveal that a host of motives—not the least of which were misery and rumor—actually contributed to swelling the ranks of the resistance.

More than any other single cause, however, the loss of political freedom and the spread of racism played crucial parts in galvanizing dissent. Cornély recalls one oppositional practice that was specifically devised as a reaction to Vichy's suppression of the republic. According to this witness, resisters often displayed a ten centime coin when approaching Vichy officials. The hidden meaning encoded in this practice was that Vichy had "dissolved" the republic.[85] Here, the French expression for "ten centimes"—*dix sous*—was employed as a rebus for the verb *dissous,* or "dissolved." This encoded practice is reminiscent of one devised by metropolitan "passive resisters," who displayed two fishing rods, or *gaules,* as a symbol of their support for de Gaulle *(deux gaules* being of course a rebus for the general's name).[86] In this instance, Guadeloupean opponents likewise exercised their now proscribed democratic voice by inventing forms of expression that speak at once to the resourcefulness of popular culture and to the determination of popular resistance.

Not all manifestations of opposition were so cryptic, nor were they solely fueled by sympathy for the republic. Other considerations also contributed to fanning the flames of resistance. The Martiniquais thinker and politician Aimé Césaire declared at Admiral Robert's 1947 trial: "Governor Robert created for us, men of color, a situation which pitted blacks against whites."[87] Vichy's assurances that France had not become negrophobic overnight in 1940 had done little to alter this perception, especially since everyday racism was manifestly on the rise in the Antilles under Vichy. One Martiniquais witness reveals that under Robert, "racism constituted a form of widespread moral torture."[88]

Thus, although the official government line had been expressly to claim that Vichy was no more hostile toward blacks than the republic,[89] Vichy rule nevertheless spelled an augmentation in expressions of racism from

[handwritten margin note: Creative small act) of resistance]

(margin handwriting: "many outright racists held power")

those whites who believed that the new regime should openly champion racial supremacism. The fact that some such vocal racists held positions of power in Guadeloupe under Vichy only serves to underscore the gap between official discourse and government practices. Admiral Rouyer, for instance, had no qualms in asking Robert to fire the head of the island's agriculture department on the grounds that he was "a local colored man."[90] Furthermore, in spite of Sorin's assurances that he wished to maintain blacks as mayors, statistics demonstrate that under Vichy the proportion of white to black mayors was practically reversed.

The closely related specter of a return to slavery also played a defining role in the formation of Guadeloupean resistance. Jean-Charles Timoléon attributed his rallying to the Free French in Dominica almost entirely to this *primum mobile*, when he wrote:

> Here are the reasons for my departure: rumors were spreading that … Senegalese troops were being brought in. … It was also rumored that industrialists were planting karata with which to whip the blacks. At the end of the war, slavery would be re-established. Friends and I often discussed this possibility. Some … found it unlikely … but others said that in the event of a victory by Hitler … a return to slavery was entirely possible. One day, returning from our agricultural work … we saw two policemen talking to the proprietor. A few minutes later, the boss assembled all of us, men and women. The officers wrote down our names, ages and addresses. They asked us to sign a register and gave each of us a work pass. … The officers … told me that we would henceforth be allowed to leave the plantation only after having informed the police. This event confirmed our fears, and … I declared to my companions that things had been exactly the same under slavery; slaves too were not allowed to leave their quarters.[91]

This testimony sheds light on the extent to which some Guadeloupeans associated Vichy with the period of prerepublican authoritarianism, when slavery still existed. The pre-1848 era of bondage was then less than a century behind, after all, and still deeply embedded in Guadeloupe's collective memory. Although archival sources reveal that Vichy was on the contrary wary of any measure that might even evoke the memory of servitude, it seems clear that Vichy officials failed to understand the repercussions of their actions. In particular, they were unable to see that Pétainist political reforms could quite reasonably be interpreted by the population as markers of a more generalized return to a pre-1848 society. Timoléon's testimony further serves to confirm Richard Burton's theory that passage to *la Dissidence* was understood as a continuation of the legacy of marooning—when slaves had once fled Guadeloupe for freedom in nearby British islands.[92]

No less significant a catalyst for resistance were international developments. Unlike Madagascar, which was invaded by British forces before the
tide of the war began to turn, Guadeloupe remained in the camp of Pétain
well after the first signs that the Axis was faltering. The events of November 1942 received special attention in Guadeloupe, and certainly helped
spur defections to Dominica. On November 20, 1942, Sorin briefed all of
the island's mayors on Pétain's radio address a day earlier, in which the
marshal had announced his loss of control over North African colonies
now faced with a full-fledged American invasion. The marshal had declared, in a speech foreshadowing one that de Gaulle would deliver decades later: "Frenchmen, Generals in the service of a foreign power are refusing to obey my orders. Officers and soldiers of the African army, do not
obey these unworthy leaders."[93] In Guadeloupe, as in the metropole, the
prestige and credibility of Pétain were greatly tarnished by this admission
of powerlessness. Just over a week later, word also reached Guadeloupe of
the scuttling of the French fleet at Toulon, following the German invasion
of the "Free zone" (itself a reaction to the American landings in North Africa).[94] In spite of calls "not to spread rumors,"[95] news of both of these
events undoubtedly made its way across Guadeloupe by way of mouth,
bringing potential resisters much-needed hope.

The first and most vocal expressions of opposition to Vichy in Guadeloupe had of course come during the July 1, 1940, extraordinary session of
the Conseil Général. On this occasion, Valentino had called for the respect
of pre-armistice institutions and laws, and for Guadeloupe's continued engagement in the war among the ranks of the Free French. After Sorin's refusal even to negotiate with Valentino, and the latter's subsequent deporta-
tion to the Ile du Salut later that month, opposition to Sorin seemed tem-
porarily quelled.

However, barely a month later, another quite different plot was
hatched to rid Guadeloupe of its Vichy rulers. This scheme, which has
gone entirely unnoticed by historians, was elaborated by an anonymous
"committee of [Gaudeloupean] notables."[96] In late August 1940, their
leader traveled to Martinique to meet the American consul to the French
West Indies. This delegate hoped to "make known to President Roosevelt
the decisions of the inhabitants of Guadeloupe relative to their desire to be
freed from France and placed under American protection."[97] The anonymous representative proceeded to declare solemnly:

> The indignation, contempt and disgust of a government itself accused of
> treachery, and hunger have made the inhabitants of Guadeloupe turn toward

their sole hope for protection against the Nazis and for their immediate commodities: the United States of America. Of the population a committee of notables was formed and, after being approved, took the following decisions.

1) Proclaim the independence of Guadeloupe.

2) Place the Free State of Guadeloupe under American protection. ...

As soon as the American Government will send three warships and a boat with commodities to Guadeloupe, the Initiative Committee of which I am President will proclaim the independence of the island under the American protectorate. ... Signed at Fort de France, Martinique, August 20, 1940.[98]

This remarkable proclamation emanated from a current of resistance that was clearly at odds with Valentino's, insofar as he seemingly did question French sovereignty over Guadeloupe at this stage. The above statement also underscores both the political and material distress of Guadeloupe in the early days of Vichy rule, as it calls for American military protection but also for much-needed food supplies. It also points to the genesis of the first consequential secessionist resistance on the island—which would gain greater amplitude in the postwar era. In any event, American officials took this August 1940 declaration seriously indeed, deeming that "the plot is significant due to the fact that it apparently represents the feelings of a large part of the population of both Guadeloupe and Martinique."[99] And yet, American noninterventionism, as well as the complexity and fragility of U.S. relations with both Vichy and the Free French, conspired to doom this project. American authorities never dispatched the three warships the Guadeloupean committee confidently claimed would suffice to bring down the local Vichy authorities.

Although popular opinion under an authoritarian regime is always difficult to gauge, it seems safe to suggest that this secessionist group was in reality a fringe movement, on the margins of the general thrust of Guadeloupean resistance. The August 1940 plot should therefore not undermine Eliane Sempaire's assertion that, generally speaking, "participation in the resistance was seen as a revendication of the right to be French, and was actually perceived as a proof of Frenchness."[100] Certainly, Guy Cornély professes to have left Guadeloupe for Dominica so as to fight a war for France, as his father and uncles had done before him.[101]

The trickle of resisters who made their way across the channel to reach Dominica from 1940 to 1942 soon grew into a steady flow from 1942 to 1943. Colonel Jean Massip, the Free French official in charge of receiving Guadeloupeans in Dominica, recalled that by May 1943 even sailors and officers aboard Vichy vessels were leaving Guadeloupe in droves.[102] In all, roughly two thousand Guadeloupeans joined "La Dissidence" in Domin-

[handwritten marginalia: anonymous / some nice proposal / Americans support of they resist]

ica, approximately as many as left Martinique for St. Lucia for the same ends.[103] So considerable and sudden was this exodus, and so specific was the age and gender bracket involved, that its repercussions were soon felt on the island. On April 30, 1943, the head of a sugar factory in Sainte Rose telegraphed Sorin: "Despite the use of prisoners in our fields, the numerous daily departures of dissidents has created a labor shortage which is such that the crops cannot be harvested."[104]

A year earlier, when the situation did not yet seem irreversible, Constant Sorin had confronted the question of departures for Dominica directly. He had announced to the island's mayors on May 18, 1942:

> I am well aware that a certain number of young Guadeloupeans have left Guadeloupe for a neighboring British island. The reasons which lead them to flee are not always honorable and few are those who have acted out of patriotism. ... There is therefore no cause for excessive alarm. But it would be wise for the population to be informed, and that it know from the outset that those who leave will never return. Their case is closed. They have emigrated permanently. People will understand ... for [they will be reluctant to leave] their native village, the cemetery where cherished ones lie, their parents, friends, etc.[105]

Here Sorin utilized scare tactics, while also relying upon both Guadeloupean and Vichyite senses of regional and village pride. Oblivious to these appeals, Guadeloupeans were ever more numerous in braving the channel between their island and Dominica, often aboard rowboats that were at the mercy of storms, currents, and Vichy patrols.

Opposition was by no means the preserve of young men who left to join the Free French forces. Guadeloupeans of all ages and of both sexes expressed their antipathy to the new regime by any means possible. However, the stifling of political freedoms under Vichy dictated that shows of opposition be deftly and discretely conceived. With assemblies of more than five people banned under Sorin, and with an impressive ratio of police and naval forces to the population at large, overt armed resistance was no easy task. Accordingly, Guadeloupeans devised oppositional practices such as one chronicled by Guy Cornély: at an auction at Pointe-à-Pitre under Vichy, a number of objects were presented for sale, among which were both a puffer fish and a portrait of Marshal Pétain. Bidders haggled frantically over the fish, raising its price disproportionately, while the marshal's picture fetched a pittance.[106] With traditional avenues of expression curtailed, Guadeloupeans displayed remarkable ingenuity in inventing such forms of and stages for everyday popular resistance. No greater an offense could have been achieved than this deliberate denigration of the icon of a regime that attributed such importance to the cult of its leader. Similarly, when on January 24, 1941, Pointe-à-Pitre's Place de la Victoire was officially rebaptized the Place du Maréchal Pétain, dissidents sullied the square's new name sign with a black paste, in a visceral and almost excremental expression of their contempt for the new regime.[107]

Guadeloupeans remained a step ahead of Vichy administrators in coining new forms of opposition before officials could unmask and interdict them. Thus Sorin was forced to ban drivers from honking out the letter *V* for "Victory" in Morse code.[108] One potential arena for opposition proved particularly difficult to shut down entirely, for paradoxically, it also held a privileged place in the ideology of National Revolution. Indeed, Robert and Sorin had resolved to propagate *hébertisme* and other sports in Guadeloupe by any means possible. And yet local officials were all too conscious that stadiums could serve as more than the regulating mechanisms of social control Vichy intended. They could also constitute forums for popular protest on an island where all conventional political assemblies had been systematically dissolved. Accordingly, in February 1941, Sorin had ordered an increased police presence at all sporting events on the island.[109] It should come as no surprise, then, that a soccer match would be used as the pretext and indeed the starting point for one of the greatest acts of resistance on the island, which would occur on May 2, 1943.

The social unrest of April–May 1943 had been brewing for months. American officials had already observed that something was amiss in March 1943. The U.S. consular shipping advisor in Guadeloupe reported on March 21 that:

> possibly a local revolt and race revolution similar to that which took place in Guiana was being organized. There is also involved a group of about one hundred enlisted men, whose leader, a junior officer of the *Jeanne d'Arc*, now fears that about fifty men may not be controllable and is afraid of a mutiny. ... The French navy are preparing for trouble. It is reported that Martinique is calm.[110]

That this source should have termed the peaceful rallying of Guiana to the Free French on March 16, 1943, a "race revolution" speaks more to the state of mind of 1940s white America than anything else.[111] Nevertheless, this account does serve to show that the overt resistance of 1943 originated in Guadeloupe, rather than Martinique, and that an atmosphere of extreme tension prevailed on the Emerald Island that year.

Armed resistance broke out for the first time on the evening of April 30, 1943, in the town of Port-Louis, on the northern extremity of the island.

There, the local police station was stormed by sixty to eighty individuals wielding machetes, sticks, axes, and any other rudimentary weapons they could get their hands on. Constant Sorin conceded that the plot "was not hatched by an imbecile,"[112] for it had involved a multipronged attack. Telephone lines had been severed beforehand, and an attempt had been made to cut off the bridge before the assault on the *Gendarmerie*. This charge was itself aimed at securing firearms with which to invest the Beauport sugar plant. Sorin believed that the insurrection had been triggered by the policies of the Beauport factory, which Sorin recognized, monopolized all of the lands in the region while its workers suffered from hunger.[113]

Whatever the immediate and local causes for this rebellion, it seems also to have reflected a broader malaise that spanned the entire island. Indeed, only a few days later, on May 2, 1943, a second more peaceful protest sprang up at the opposite end of the island in Basse-Terre. There, a group of protesters assembled the day after the regime's nonobservance of the May Day holiday. They were joined by a second column, returning from a soccer game in which the Cygne Noir team had defeated its Racing Club rival, thanks to the splendid performance of the goalie, Micaux.[114] Members of the march interspersed cries of *Vive le goal*—"Long live the goalie!"—with the phonetically close but infinitely more politically hazardous *Vive de Gaulle!* In front of Basse-Terre's main square, the Champ d'Arbaud, the cortege was met by police forces, blocking the way to the governor's palace. Without warning, the police opened fire on the unarmed crowd, wounding many and killing Serge Balguy, a seventeen-year-old fan of the Cygne Noir. Balguy had none of the makings of a subversive: he was the son of a metropolitan white police officer and a black Guadeloupean mother, and by all accounts simply happened to find himself at the wrong place at the wrong time.[115] The crowd quickly dispersed, only to congregate once again in front of the home of a doctor suspected of sympathizing with Vichy. Balguy's death brought resistance to a head. Even the appointed municipal council of Basse-Terre and the mayor, Gaston Feuillard, dared to resign collectively in protest on May 3.[116] Two days later, a "pious commemorative manifestation" was held at the Cygne Noir's stadium.[117]

These demonstrations failed to topple the regime directly but certainly lit the spark of "Dissidence" that would soon consume the French Antilles. On June 3 to 4, yet another attempt to overthrow Sorin was foiled. Paul Valentino, who had been liberated when the Free French gained control of Guiana in March 1943, had disembarked clandestinely on the island to mastermind this aborted plot. After failing to capture a radio station in

Pointe-à-Pitre, from which he had hoped to announce Guadeloupe's rallying to de Gaulle, Valentino barely escaped a second arrest by fleeing to Dominica.[118] According to Jean Massip, the events of May–June 1943 in Guadeloupe were the determinant catalysts for the subsequent overthrow of Vichy in Martinique in June 1943.[119] Antillais resisters had become convinced that actions directed at Sorin were futile as long as Robert himself (residing in Fort-de-France) was not overthrown. Consequently, and on orders from the Algiers Free French Liberation Committee, a rally was mounted in Martinique on June 18, 1943, to commemorate the third anniversary of de Gaulle's call to fight on.[120] When Martinique's police and naval forces refused to disband this protest, Robert's fate was sealed. The next few weeks saw the United States broker a deal whereby Sorin and Robert gained *saufs conduits* to North Africa.[121] Upon his arrival in the Antilles in July 1943, Henri Hoppenot, the Gaullist delegate assigned the task of restoring republican rule in the French West Indies, declared: "It is to your … honor that you liberated yourselves from this tyrannical regime which never succeeded in breaking your spirits."[122] Guadeloupeans had led the way in this revolt and were frustrated in their attempts only by military and police forces that proved more loyal to Vichy than their Martiniquais counterparts.

What precisely did it mean to be a Guadeloupean resister? In parallel with the metropole, there had been both active and passive opposition in the Antilles. Much like their metropolitan counterparts, Guadeloupean resisters had also risked their lives to join the Free French (actually in much greater numbers, proportionately, than in the metropole). From Dominica, Guadeloupean dissidents were initially sent to the United States, Canada, or Great Britain to receive military training. Some, like Guy Cornély, later participated in D-Day; others distinguished themselves in the campaign to liberate France and in North Africa. In short, many Guadeloupeans had resisted Vichy on their own island, and many more had volunteered to combat the Germans in the North African and European theaters of war.

And yet, archival sources demonstrate that, after the war, political considerations conspired to exclude Guadeloupeans from mainstream resistance organizations. On July 21, 1945, the postwar colonial minister Paul Giacobbi issued the following advice to the Conseil National de la Résistance (CNR):

> At a time when in various colonies, certain groups are constituting themselves under various resistance titles, and when the CNR might be solicited, it is my

duty to attract your attention to the character that such associations are taking, especially in the Antilles, and in our Indian territories. One must underline such associations' political afterthoughts, which are often outright anti-French, although sometimes hiding under the mask of a prestigious umbrella organization. … The titles of their members are hardly comparable to those of our heroes of the *maquis,* and bear in reality only a distant similarity to groups composed of authentic "Resisters," having proven themselves in the face of the enemy occupation, or during the Liberation. I therefore advise you to avoid granting membership to any such groups, so as to avoid serious inconveniences.[123]

Giacobbi's message was unambiguous. On the pretext that Guadeloupeans did not conform to the emerging *Bataille du rail* conception of Resistance, and for fear that they might use the CNR as a platform for independence, Guadeloupeans and other colonials were not to be considered full-fledged resisters. An association of former political internees led by Paul Valentino was therefore expressly denied membership to the CNR.[124]

It is undoubtedly one of Vichy's great outrages that it exported its policies to colonies outside of German influence, while simultaneously preventing these territories from joining the Allies. All the greater irony then, that the absence of Germans should be held against Guadeloupean resisters. In Guadeloupean culture, however, resistance to an unfettered and unwarranted form of Vichy rule came to be perceived as analogous to metropolitan resistance. The epitaph on Basse-Terre's memorial to Serge Balguy was consequently no different from those of partisans in the metropole. It read simply: "Here fell … Serge Balguy, who died for Liberty."

Re-establishing the Republic

In Guadeloupe, the transition from Vichy to the Free French was as remarkably smooth as it was unrewarding for resisters. Vichy laws were abrogated without fanfare, and male suffrage reinstated; in 1946, full universal suffrage was introduced to the island, a year after it was at last adopted in the metropole. Beginning in July 1943, political captives were released from prisons, in which no Pétainist sympathizers came to replace them, however. Sorin himself was never tried as a Vichy official. Ever the ideological chameleon, he later joined the Free French and participated in the campaign to liberate Alsace.[125] In Guadeloupe, some isolated voices did call in vain for a metropolitan-style *épuration*. A September 1944 article in the newspaper *l'Homme enchaîné* observed that in the *hexagone* collaborationist intellectuals were being punished; why not, the author asked, pursue Jean Rocailleux, the principal of a Basse-Terre school who had supposedly "tarnished the Republic through his writings and speeches"?[126]

The memory and consequences of the Vichy years would play a crucial role for the Antilles in the postwar era. General de Gaulle set the tone for events to come when he declared on July 24, 1943: "The National Liberation Committee is pleased to welcome the patriotic people of Martinique and Guadeloupe into a French empire unified for the Resistance and for the Liberation of the metropole. I know how long you have yearned to join us."[127] Like Pétain, de Gaulle stressed Guadeloupe's loyalty to France — but couched it in assimilationist terms.

Less than three years later, on March 19, 1946, Guadeloupe, Martinique, Réunion, and Guiana became full-fledged French departments, upon approval by the island's Conseil Général. This major change of status was presented in part as a "reward" for the wartime efforts of these regions first in rallying to, and then within, the ranks of the Free French. Departmentalization was further hailed as "a rejection of the racist theories which had recently cost humanity so dearly."[128] In the words of Guadeloupe's governor Ernest de Nattes: "Guadeloupeans are now French to the same degree as Basques, Bretons or Lorrains. They have the same rights, but also the same duties."[129]

The legacy of the Vichy period had come full circle. Between increasingly secessionist elements and an assimilated elite (the categories sometimes overlapped, and members of both had resisted Vichy), the republic pandered quite logically to the assimilationists. In 1949, the bodies of the nineteenth-century abolitionist Victor Schoelcher and of the black Guianese Free French leader Félix Eboué were inducted together in the Pantheon, in a glorification of the very Antillais republicanism that Vichy had sought to bury between 1940 and 1943. The literal entombment of the two figureheads of Antillais assimilation into the republic's foremost *lieu de mémoire* constituted — through both its theme and its visual narrative — a dual homage to assimilation.

Sorin's memory was not entombed quite so easily. Today, some look back with wistfulness at a time when "Guadeloupe could produce more than it consumed," and when "people were given jobs." Others continue to harbor more acrimonious sentiments. Already in 1943, a popular song castigated Sorin as a "brigand" who "laughed while we starved." Rifts in opinion were apparent at his death in 1970. He was the subject of a rather indulgent obituary in the largest local newspaper, *France-Antilles*. To this, a rival Guadeloupean journalist remarked irreverently, "[N]ow that he has croaked, we respond simply to the Vichyite flatterers of *France Antilles*: 'Exit Soso.'"[130] The myth of Sorin would stir the same emotions as his rule: derisively reproved by some, while admired by others.[131]

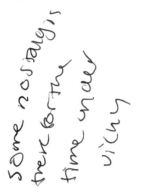

some nostalgis there for the time under vichy

CHAPTER 6

Adapting the National Revolution to Indochina

In Indochina, the Marshal enjoyed great prestige, and was the object of boundless veneration. This is a historical fact, which no one can dispute. For nearly all the French in Indochina, the Marshal incarnated the distant fatherland. He was the savior and the preserver of France, and embodied its flag. For the Indochinese, this feeling ran deeper still, and I would have acted criminally had I attempted to stem it. By virtue of his age, his peasant origins, his experience, his victory at Verdun, and also his new slogan "Travail, Famille, Patrie"—which corresponded admirably with the profound and traditionalist aspirations of the masses, and fit unexpectedly well into Confucian philosophy—Pétain, one must admit, received from the outset the respect and admiration of Indochinese peoples.

—Vichy's governor in Indochina, Admiral Jean Decoux[1]

This effort at vindication by Vichy's governor of Indochina elucidates many aspects of Vichy rule in the region. At one level, it illustrates the dissemination of National Revolutionary ideology—which was intimately associated with the image and "person" of the marshal—in French Indochina. It also likens Pétainism to Confucianism, a central and rich theme of the Vichy years in Indochina. It further betrays a reliance upon Pétain's prestige, one of many nonmaterial forms of power retained and wielded by the French in Indochina. At a more basic level, though, Jean Decoux's words attest to the permeation of Vichy in Indochina. They reveal, in other words, the seemingly evident, yet historiographically neglected, fact that a crucial Vichy moment occurred in French Southeast Asia.

Second World War Indochina

Even though it has long been known that between 1940 and 1945 "Indochina became an outpost of the Pétainist National Revolution, in many ways more fervent than France itself,"[2] scholars have nevertheless almost altogether failed to examine this remarkable phenomenon. Instead, historians have focused upon either the Japanese presence in Indochina during this period, or upon strictly diplomatic or external developments. Stein Tønnesson perhaps best summarized the continuing historiographical silence surrounding the Vichy period in Indochina when he wrote in 1991:

> So far, the Vichyst *Révolution nationale* in Indochina, and its repercussions on the relationship between French and natives, has attracted little attention from professional historians. Indeed, the only historian to have exploited some of the voluminous files of the Decoux regime in the French colonial archives is Pierre Lamant of the *Institut national des Langues et Civilisations orientales* in Paris.[3]

For a host of diplomatic specialists, the Vichy era was significant only insofar as it could be seen as leading up to armed conflict in 1945–46—itself the first step of escalation to the Vietnam War.[4] For a number of experts on the Vietnamese resistance, meanwhile, the Second World War is seen in much the same light—except that, in this teleology, the August 1945 Revolution is substituted for the Vietnam War.[5]

The Vichy episode in Indochina has no doubt been obscured precisely because it has not been defined as such. To many experts of the region, the years between 1940 and 1945 are identified as "the Japanese period."[6] Diplomatic historians have scrutinized the Washington, Tokyo, London, and Algiers perceptions of Vichy-controlled Indochina, leaving the most voluminous archival documentation—that of the Vichy-Hanoi channel—virtually ignored.[7] In fact, the designation of the Second World War as the "Japanese period" has sometimes led historians quite simply to overlook the basic fact that Vichy ran Indochina. Archival records demonstrate irrefutably that Vichy officials controlled the everyday administration of the region from the armistice of 1940 to March 1945—well after the metropolitan Vichy regime had fallen. Most official activities, from the police force

Map 3. French colonial Indochina

to education, tax levying, banking, and governmental decision-making, remained in Vichy hands, in spite of a Japanese military presence after 1940. As late as January 1945, American Intelligence sources confessed to being "surpris[ed] ... by the extent of power retained by [Vichy governor] Decoux."[8] To reduce the years from 1940 to 1945 to the "Japanese period," then, can be compared to dismissing Vichy in the metropole as the "German era." In attempting to rectify this historiographical imbalance, these chapters deliberately afford maximum attention to Vichy's role in Indochina. Readers interested in the intricacies of the Japanese presence can be directed to a host of existing sources.[9]

L'Indochine française

Unlike Madagascar, where the French inherited a highly centralized Merina administrative structure, French Indochina was largely a colonial invention, a patchwork of regions and ethnicities, comprising Laos, Cambodia, Tonkin, Annam, and Cochin China—the last three composing modern-day Vietnam. This vast, diverse realm was governed through a host of different and often conflicting mechanisms. It included colonies—such as Cochin China—as well as protectorates, such as Tonkin, and of course kingdoms, like Annam or Cambodia (to further complicate the picture, Tonkin was also technically part of the Empire of Annam; and Annam, Cambodia, and Laos were at once kingdoms and protectorates). As one scholar has recently indicated, the very term *Indochine*—which for the purposes of these chapters will be used interchangeably with "Indochina"—was laden with meanings. *L'Indochine* came to embody a set of fantasies in the colonial imagination that ranged from "military, erotic, textual ... [to] visual adventures."[10] Such mythical Indochinas were themselves superimposed upon a diverse political and administrative pastiche that was the *Union indochinoise*.

In running Indochina, French officials had shown little pretense of introducing representative government, of tolerating political dissent, and even less of fostering republicanism or assimilationism. Indochina, significantly, had originally been a colonial project not of the Third Republic but rather of the Second Empire (the first French efforts at conquest date from 1859). Even under French republican regimes, its administrators had maintained an unwaveringly authoritarian character. Military rule by naval admirals, upon which Vichy's own admiral-governor would inspire much of his heavy-handed leadership, had made way for a civil administration only in 1879. Indeed, Vichy's governor general associated himself on more than one occasion with the autocratic pre-1879 era; in his inaugural speech of July 21, 1940, he pronounced his desire to "carry on ... some fifty years later, the tradition of the Admiral Governors."[11] An editorial two years later remarked that "by practicing a policy of encouraging the artisan classes, Admiral Decoux has been following the path first outlined by the great Admiral Governors—a path from which we had strayed for too long."[12] By 1940, civilian leadership in Indochina was thus equated with metropolitan democracy as a weak regime, in need of toppling by paternalistic military leaders.

Owing perhaps in part to the absence of gubernatorial continuity in Hanoi, several distinct and conflicting indigenous policies had clearly emerged in pre-1940 Indochina. Gallieni's *Politique des races,* utilized during the conquest and so-called pacification phase, gave way after the turn of the century to the associationist doctrines of Governors Doumer and Sarraut.[13] This loosely defined program called for a revalorization of indigenous cultures and hierarchies—especially insofar as they could benefit the colonizers. In 1930, Governor Pasquier explained the principal objectives of association in the following terms: "France once more will follow through on the nobility of its intentions and the largesse of its ideas. It will restore, instead of dissolving; and it will restore in the direction of Annamite national tradition."[14] In stark opposition to Pasquier's vision, which was based in part on his fascination with ancient Vietnam, the policies of Alexandre Varenne and other liberal republicans sought indigenous cooperation, not from mandarins versed in Vietnamese history or from conservative notables but rather from "the Vietnamese who had a French-style education and had gained 'up-to-date' qualifications."[15] Vichy would later build upon Pasquier's seminal 1930 declaration, adopting a carrot-and-stick policy intended to bolster Indochina's conservative notables—most especially the mandarin class in Annam and Tonkin—on the one hand, while striking fiercely at revolutionary militants on the other.

A number of great upheavals in the 1930s rattled the colonial edifice in Indochina, setting the stage for a series of complex retributions under Vichy. The Great Depression severely damaged what had been the most sizable French colonial economy alongside Algeria's.[16] Uprisings at Yen Bay, and the Nghe Tinh soviets of 1930, were met with brutal repression by a colonial administration increasingly reduced to a policing role.[17] According to Patrice Morlat, a specialist of French colonial repression in Vietnam, the Nghe Tinh soviets of 1930 marked a great "militarization" in the French response to Indochinese communism.[18] Ironically, the coercion meted out by the Sûreté, the Légion étrangère, and other instruments of repression virtually guaranteed that more moderate and less secretive forms of resistance would be crushed: Ho Chi Minh once predicted that Gandhi would not have gotten far in Indochina. On another level, the combined effect of the Yen Bay and Nghe Tinh uprisings in 1930 was to disabuse the French from their "relative complacence"[19] toward Indochinese demands.

By 1931, it had become apparent to many Europeans that unyielding repression was losing potential indigenous allies. Historians of this period generally depict French rule in Indochina as more coercive even than Dutch rule in Indonesia or British domination in India.[20] This turn toward greater repression can be ascribed in part to a conservative and repressive brand of colonialism that alienated nearly every stratum of society. The head of Indochina's police admitted as much in 1931:

> We no longer have anyone on our side. The mandarins, to whom we never offered sufficient moral or material benefits, serve us only prudently, and cannot do much anyway. The bourgeoisie probably does not desire communism, but it considers that it might well be, as in China, an excellent recipe for external use. ... Youth is entirely opposed to us: much like the immense masses of miserable peasants and workers. Truthfully, what is needed here is much more than repression.[21]

Broadly speaking, one can consider that between 1936 and 1938, the Popular Front would seek to appeal to some of these disgruntled groups, while from 1940 to 1945, Vichy would attempt to satisfy quite different communities—especially the conservative notables previously courted by Pasquier.

In contrast to the repression and conservatism that had characterized the first half of the 1930s, the Popular Front years, from 1936 to 1938, saw a reversal of some hard-line policies. Concretely, an August 27, 1936, amnesty guaranteed the release of some 1,500 political prisoners from Indochinese jails and from the dreaded penitentiaries of Poulo-Condor and Guiana (it seems worth noting that Indochina accounted for 1,532 of the 2,028 total colonial amnesties pronounced by the Popular Front).[22] Among these were many prominent Communist leaders. Under the Popular Front's governor Jules Brévié, political dialogue became relatively open for the first time since the French conquest, with even Communist leagues openly voicing their opinions. Some of the Popular Front's reforms were admittedly superficial—unions remained officially illegal, as they were anathema to many intransigent *colons*.[23] Though they doubtless failed in the end, the colonial minister, Marius Moutet, and Governor Jules Brévié had also attempted to carry out their reforms in a peaceful social environment, reaching out to workers, peasants, and intellectuals in particular.[24] Between the release of Communist dissidents and the courting of certain constituencies—workers and intellectuals—the Popular Front did not gain many friends in either Indochinese or French conservative circles. In a striking parallel with the political course of the metropole, in Indochina under Vichy such circles would later caricature the Popular Front as an era dominated by Communism and Freemasonry. What rendered the Indochinese case so curious, however, was that the former Popular Front governor, Jules Brévié, would return to power in April 1942 as Vichy's colonial minister. He would then be responsible for governing a French bureaucracy that had largely come to detest what he represented in 1936. Brévié, like his other colleagues in Hanoi, had been part of a complex cycle of reaction and republicanism, association and assimilation, that had characterized Indochina under the Third Republic. Versed as he was in the local context, he no doubt understood full well that the nomination of Admiral Jean Decoux[25] to head Indochina in 1940 had signaled a step back toward the iron-fisted rule of the late nineteenth-century admiral-governors.

Throughout the colonial period, the tiny European community in Indochina, estimated at between twenty-five thousand and thirty-nine thousand in 1940—roughly 0.2 percent of the overall population[26]—enjoyed for the most part a luxurious life in the opulent French quarters of cities like Hanoi and Saigon, or at the hill stations at Tam-Dao, Sa-Pa, Ba-Vi, Dalat, and Bokor, chosen for their gentle "metropolitan climate." Indochina became reputed to the French as a land in which the most humble European—not to speak of high-ranking officials—could live in opulence and afford a coterie of servants.[27] Hanoi's disproportionately vast and lavish opera house, for its part, stands as a lasting testimony to the delusions of grandeur of Indochina's supercilious *colonat*. Built shortly after the turn of the century, the structure was described by some as "a pretentious caricature" of the Paris Opera, with enough seating to accommodate the entire European population of Hanoi in 1886, the year it was planned.[28] Economically, until the Great Depression, the colonizers thrived off the so-called *mise en valeur* of Indochina, especially from sectors such as the booming rubber industry.[29]

It is difficult of course to speak of a single French colonial Indochina. There was the idyllic, phantasmatic Indochina often dreamt of in the metropole, considered a land of adventure, opportunity, and exoticism.

(handwritten margin note: *dreamy Indochine sep from the reality?*)

For Europeans, one's perspective on Indochina varied according to occupation. Indeed, the military, *petits blancs,* business community, missionaries, and administration, to cite only five sectors, rarely saw eye to eye. Among the richer settlers, some did indeed live the "Indochinese dream"; consider the Guillaume brothers, who arrived in Indochina in 1888 with twenty thousand francs, and ten years later owned a plantation containing two hundred thousand coffee trees, a milk farm, a construction firm, and a marble quarry. However, this Indochina of (European) opportunity was more often than not the stuff of fiction, and in any event it ground to a halt after the Great Depression reached the colony in 1931. For the most part, Indochina was a colony marked by hierarchies: the French administration itself was more stratified than at home. The domestic economy of the colonial home comprised a vast pyramid of specializations, predicated on racial stereotypes, and typically featuring a Chinese cook, Annamite servant, and Cambodian gardener, to mention only a few. Vestimental difference accentuated the chasm between colonizer and colonized. And petty rivalries constantly divided *colon* and administrative circles, often pitting the one against the other. The *colon*'s universe was of course a world removed from his or her previous life in the metropole. A metropolitan visitor described the average *colon*'s situation rather unflatteringly: "[They obtain] land from free concessions, employees through forced labor, and remuneration through bonuses."[30]

Politically, the sympathies of Indochina's European population lay overwhelmingly to the right, if not to the antirepublican far right. The historian Vu Ngu Chieu has quite logically remarked that "very few radicals or communists had wanted to settle down in a colony where the way of life was predicated by the law of survival, and the cardinal principal was militant racism."[31] Vichy's National Revolution would find many an adept in such a favorable political climate. Precious little has been written about local precursors to Vichy in Indochina (or in any other French colony for that matter). And yet, the archives do provide evidence of significant antirepublican extremist activity in the 1930s. For example, a branch of the *Croix de Feu,* whose fascism is sometimes disputed by historians but whose antidemocratic and far-rightist penchants can leave no doubt, was founded in Hanoi in April 1935.[32] It was soon abolished under the Popular Front in August 1936.[33] Its members would no doubt be all too eager to exact revenge upon *Frontistes* after 1940.

The War Reaches Indochina

In a matter of months, from June to September 1940, Indochina's French rulers were abruptly threatened in their position of power. The war, which the ill-prepared and poorly equipped French forces stationed in Indochina had so dearly hoped to avoid, was suddenly at Indochina's doorsteps in June 1940. As France crumbled in early June, Japanese authorities began to mount pressure upon the governor of Indochina, Georges Catroux, to break the chain of supplies that ran from Haiphong in Indochina to Japan's enemy, China. Faced with an ultimatum and conscious of Japan's overwhelming military superiority, Catroux ceded to this demand. The new Vichy regime, which saw in Catroux a potential threat, dismissed him on June 30, on trumped up charges that he had not sufficiently consulted his superiors before entering into diplomatic negotiations.[34] As a replacement for Catroux—who soon became a prominent figure in the ranks of the Free French—Fleet Admiral François Darlan nominated a career naval officer, Rear-Admiral Jean Decoux, the "loyal" head of the French navy in Indochina. This hard-nose disciplinarian's devotion to Pétain can leave little doubt; long after the end of the Second World War he would become vice president of the league to defend and preserve the memory of Marshal Pétain.[35] Decoux, if infinitely more obedient to Vichy, proved no more successful than his predecessor at heeding off Japanese threats. July and August 1940 were marked by almost weekly Japanese menaces.

The ensuing struggle for influence in Indochina involved a number of conflicting agents on both sides.[36] At Vichy, the prime question involved whether Pétain would accept another armistice, or perhaps a third occupier. No sooner had the ink dried on the June 22, 1940, armistice with Germany, than the French government was faced with a seemingly identical situation more than eight thousand miles away. The foreign minister, Paul Baudoin, counseled conciliation, compromise, and ultimately collaboration, contending, as had Pétain before him for the metropole, "that in the present circumstances our duty was to save everything which could be saved in French Indochina."[37] In a meeting with the marshal himself, Baudoin's view prevailed over the firmer line advocated by the colonial minister, Henry Lémery.[38] The Vichy regime, which would, throughout the war, oppose Allied attacks with force, while acquiescing to Axis demands, had demonstrated in Southeast Asia that this policy would be global and not merely metropolitan.

In this instance, Baudoin and Decoux had, in all fairness, negotiated with a far mightier foe.[39] The resulting treaty was actually twofold, the first economic and the second military. It was accordingly signed at two ceremonies, on August 29 and September 22, 1940. The first phase paved the way for the isolated Indochinese economy to be integrated into Japan's economic sphere. The second guaranteed French sovereignty over Indochina, while allowing for the stationing and passage of Japanese troops. All-out conflict was only narrowly avoided. Baudoin's theory that "the Japanese want the right for their troops to enter Indochina, and enter it they will with or without our consent,"[40] seemed confirmed when, on the very day of the second accord, the maverick Japanese general Nishihara launched a devastating unauthorized attack on French positions at the Tonkin Border post of Lang Son. In the wake of this battle, Japanese authorities formally apologized to the French and forced Nishihara into retirement.[41] Japanese forces then re-entered the Tonkin in a more orderly fashion, by virtue of an agreement that had come none too soon for a French community shell-shocked by the show of military force at Lang Son.

The defeat of Lang Son, which cost 150 lives on the French side, taught Vichy officials in Indochina several lessons, not the least of which was their utter inability to repel a Japanese invasion.[42] More humiliating yet, confidential reports suggest that Vietnamese auxiliary troops deserted at Lang Son, and that a local minority people, the Thô, actively joined the Japanese side during the battle (note that the ethnonym Thô now designates a different group; the minority people that the French called Thô are now known as "Tay").[43] This raised the specter of an Indochinese-Japanese alliance against the French, a fear that would soon become a perennial obsession of French authorities in the area. The Vichy foreign minister, Paul Baudoin, who had served as head of the Bank of Indochina before the war, was among the first to articulate the closely related concern that weakness before the Japanese might signal the end of "white superiority" in the eyes of the Indochinese. Indeed, the French population, which had based its subjugation of *indigènes* on notions of racial dominance, was dealt a severe blow by the sight of Japanese occupying forces. Before the accord with Japan, Baudoin had pleaded for both German and American assistance on precisely this score. He had used just such a racist rationale, arguing before German officials that "it was not in the interest of the white race to hand Indochina over to Japanese, Chinese, and Siamese troops."[44] To the Americans, Baudoin employed precisely the same language as with the Nazis, asking: "[C]an one let Japan settle itself in the center of a region so vital to the interest of whites? ... Do we have the right—vis-à-vis other white nations which have colonized the Orient—to let a small European army be crushed by the Japanese, thereby making Indochina the first and only country in Asia lost by the white race[?]"[45] These arguments—so telling about the sudden collapse of the entire racist underpinnings of French rule in Southeast Asia—fell on deaf ears in both Berlin and Washington. Remarkably, however, far from being the only European colony to fall to the Japanese, as Baudoin predicted, after the fall of the Dutch East Indies, the Philippines, British Burma, Shanghai, Singapore, and Hong Kong, by 1943 French Indochina would in fact become the last remaining functioning European colony on the continent east of India. The French administration had been left in place by a Japanese government that, like its German ally, saw in the maintenance of French rule a way of sparing valuable military and administrative resources for other more pressing missions.[46]

Throughout these many crises, officials at Vichy and Hanoi bemoaned that "Indochina was absolutely alone,"[47] abandoned by allies of yesterday and today. But in spite of its obvious isolation, and of major concessions to the Japanese, French Indochina remained remarkably autonomous from September 1940 to March 1945. A French witness of this period recalls: "If the Japanese presence in Indochina might in appearance have seemed to limit our sovereignty, in reality, it respected its fundamental principles."[48] To be sure, Japanese generals did eventually pressure Vichy officials into further concessions. In July 1941, the Japanese requested and received permission for their troops to enter all of Indochina, not merely the Tonkin and Annam.[49] Then too, the economic "partnership" between Japan and Indochina proved one-sided. French officials in Indochina complained of the absence of metropolitan goods—including fuel, but also wine and bread (as in the metropole, food cards were distributed to Europeans in Tonkin)—which unilateral, exclusive trade with Japan entailed.[50] Ersatz elements were swiftly elaborated, to maintain the colonial way of life. Thus, a 1941 report on Tonkin noted that after much experimentation in baking with local wheat, "very acceptable results" had at last been achieved.[51]

More than in any other French colony, the consequences of the plans elaborated in response to wartime economic circumstances would have devastating effects in Indochina. While Europeans complained of having to consume ersatz products, it was the indigenous populations that suffered most from rampant inflation and dire privations. Between 1940 and 1943, the price of rice in Tonkin rose eightfold.[52] Poor distribution of food and the appropriation of rice stocks by the Japanese army combined for the greatest disaster of all: approximately one million Vietnamese would perish of famine in 1945 alone.[53]

Prior to these cataclysms, however, a modus vivendi was reached between local Vichy authorities and the Japanese—this in spite of an evident imbalance of power between the two. So harmonious seemed their relations at times that Communist sources have spoken of "a collusion between the French colonialists and the Japanese fascists, aimed at checking the Vietnamese National movement."[54] Ho Chi Minh himself saw the Japanese presence not as a prelude to liberation but as a "double yoke of oppression."[55] Within this complex relationship, the French were afforded virtually free reign in running Indochina. To be sure, as a satellite of the Axis, Vichy represented a more acceptable form of government to the Japanese than the prospect of Gaullist rule, which would no doubt have been tantamount to a declaration of war. However, beyond this point—a moot one since other than Catroux and a minority of administrators, the French in Indochina were overwhelmingly Pétainist from the outset—French officials possessed great latitude in all civilian matters.

As a result of this modus vivendi, planners at the colonial ministry in Vichy began to consider Indochina as relatively secure. On a list of colonies at risk, drawn up in May 1942, Indochina did not even figure among the top five "territories in danger."[56] In Indochina itself, some contemplated turning foreign policy attention away from what had become a routine and courteous entente with Japan. Incredibly, in February 1941 a high-ranking French naval official in Saigon put forward a plan to organize an expedition from Indochina to reconquer New Caledonia from the Free French[57] (the plan was only definitively abandoned at the highest level in January 1942).[58] Although the Ministry of the Colonies objected to the brash proposal, it betrays at once the enthusiasm for Vichy in some French circles in Indochina, and the remarkable stability of an Indochina considered firmly in Vichy French hands. To the French of Indochina, no signs seemed to augur the fateful Japanese *coup de force* of March 9, 1945, when, without warning, the Japanese would eradicate the entire French administration—decapitating resisters and arresting entire government branches—before setting up a temporary Vietnamese puppet government.

Foot Soldiers and Enemies of the National Revolution

For most of the war, however, the French population of Indochina, in blissful ignorance of Japan's inclination eventually to annihilate it, marched to the tune of the famous ode to Pétain, *Maréchal, nous voilà.*[59] In the shadow of the Empire of the Rising Sun—as indeed Vichy proper had operated in the shadow of the swastika—the National Revolution thrived in European circles in Indochina. According to the French General Sabattier, who would later lead a small group of surviving French troops across the border into China in March 1945, "Generally speaking ... the vast majority of French people had adhered to the internal politics of National Revolution."[60] This confirms the impression given by an admittedly partial Decoux, when he telegraphed Vichy in April 1942:

> For many long months now Indochina has been cut off ... from the metropole. Yet she has never been closer to France than she is now. We are closer to France intellectually, having adopted as our guiding principle the National Revolution. We are closer morally, through our total adhesion ... to the ideals of the new national and imperial order. [Finally], Indochina is at one with the French community through their shared cult ... of the person of the Marshal, Head of State, Leader of the Empire.[61]

Pétain's maxims were published in a 1941 Hanoi volume entitled the *Words of the Marshal,* and his paternal portrait became omnipresent throughout Indochina between 1940 and 1945.[62] The marshal's bust adorned local city halls, and his image dominated landmarks as varied as Hanoi's opera house, Saigon's cathedral, and the waterfall of Kam-Ly in the outskirts of the French colonial hill station of Dalat.[63] In April 1941, Decoux reported back to Vichy that no fewer than seventy thousand portraits of Marshal Pétain had already been sold or ordered in Indochina. They had been printed locally, from a handful of models dispatched from the metropole to Hanoi.[64] Pétain's every trip in the metropolitan unoccupied zone was projected in cinemas throughout Indochina, provoking "emotion and intense enthusiasm."[65] A Haiphong newspaper took the cult of Pétain to new heights when in March 1941 it reproduced the marshal's birth certificate, so as to demonstrate his hearty peasant stock.[66]

To many colonizers the National Revolution signaled wholesale social and moral regeneration. In 1942, for instance, novelist and member of the Académie Française Thierry Maulnier published a tome in Hanoi, entitled *Révolution Nationale, the Future of France,* in which he argued: "[We] must create new mores, new values, and new ways of thinking."[67] For his part, a local figure, Pastor Lehnebach, head of a Vichy youth league in Cochin China, presented the National Revolution as nothing short of a religion, writing in 1943: "The National Revolution is at once carnal and spiritual. France's flesh is wounded, but we are not blinded. Under the National Revolution, nothing will ever be the same, and, above all, the spiritual will triumph."[68] Lehnebach also elaborated a Vichy teleology, describing to his compatriots in Indochina the "moral disintegration that France underwent before 1940."[69] To Georges Taboulet, a high school history teacher in Indochina, the National Revolution represented a "return to common sense, to the wholesome traditions of our race."[70] Taboulet's 1941 pamphlet and series of speeches given throughout Indochina, entitled *Le retour à la tradition, ou la cité reconstruite,* served as an introduction to the main tenets of Pétainism, from its ideological influences (including Charles Maurras and Charles Péguy) to its cherished themes of hierarchy, obedience, the family, and the return to the soil.[71] Nothing seemed to escape the Pétainist "spirit"; a 1941 censorship report gave as its first criterion the "verification that any film must conform to the principles of the National Revolution."[72] Meanwhile, a Vietnamese theater troop in Hanoi prefaced each of its performances by a "living tableau" of *Travail, Famille,* and *Patrie.*[73] So pervasive was the phenomenon in Indochina that the Vietnamese writer Nguyen-Tien-Lang prefaced one of his 1943 re-editions with the mention "Year III of the National Revolution."[74] Like the great Revolution of 1789, Vichy's National Revolution had succeeded in rewriting the calendar.

As in all other colonies loyal to Vichy, the new regime set out to destroy or erase its predecessors and enemies—in a purge presented as a cathartic amputation. Taboulet, in distant Indochina, justified metropolitan Vichy Jewish laws by arguing that "Jews are being treated as elements belonging to a foreign body, whose gradual inroads had compromised the health of the social body as a whole."[75] In Vichy Indochina, such rationalizations of anti-Semitism as an act of "civic sanitation" were accompanied by deeds. The colony's administration was thoroughly purged of all Vichy scapegoats, from Jews to Freemasons and Gaullists.

The latter, presented as the scourge of Indochina, were subject to intense persecution. So serious was the witch-hunt that separate detention camps were set up throughout Indochina for Gaullist political prisoners.[76] The largest camps in Cochin China were those of Nui-Bara, near Saigon, Baria, and Long-Xuyên. These terrible detention centers were well frequented. A certain Rouan was condemned in 1941 to five years of forced labor for having privately pronounced his sympathy for the Free French.[77]

same as madagascar

Another Gaullist, an engineer in Laos by the name of Auvray, was detained at Long-Xuyên in November 1942 for having "expressed in writing sentiments hostile to the National Revolution."[78] This in fact constituted one of Decoux's sharpest breaks with the past. Never before had Europeans—the very group that had previously benefited from sacrosanct colonial privileges—been so prone to random persecution and imprisonment in Indochina. As Philippe Devillers has observed, "Thanks to the Légion ... Vichyite zeal in Indochina reached greater heights than in the metropole. Gaullist activities were mercilessly hunted, and some [dissident] administrators ended up serving hard labor terms."[79] While harsh police practices toward the Vietnamese were certainly nothing new, the stiff sentences and hard labor meted out to Europeans reflect a form of persecution entirely new to Indochina.

Along with Gaullists, Jews and Freemasons constituted the principal European victims of Vichy rule in Indochina. Of the 187 revocations among European cadres in the Indochinese civil service between 1940 and 1942, thirty were dismissed for having been members of secret societies, and fifteen in accordance with anti-Semitic legislation (others yet fell victim to Vichy's new retirement laws aimed at older officials).[80] Governor Decoux requested that all functionaries answer a questionnaire that bore only two possible answers, "#1) I have never been a member of a secret society; or #2) I declare my definitive renunciation from any secret society to which I might have previously belonged."[81] Initially, confusion arose over whether Vichy's laws interdicting secret societies were to be directed at Europeans only, or whether they were to be extended to the Indochinese as well[82]—thereby opening the Pandora's box of what precisely constituted a secret society in a different culture from that for which the law was intended.[83] By 1942–43, Vietnamese functionaries began to fill out these declarations on a regular basis. Every conceivable colonial service was involved in this witch-hunt. Forms were received from organizations as varied as the port authority of Haiphong, to the prestigious Metropole Hotel in Hanoi, to the garbage collectors in that same city.[84]

Similar zeal was displayed in applying Vichy's notorious Jewish statutes. The metropolitan law of June 2, 1941, calling for a census of Jews and banning *Israélites* from exercising a number of professions, was adopted in extenso in Indochina. Accordingly, in early 1942, Jews were fired from a wide range of professions, from banking to the insurance, advertising, administration, and business sectors.[85] A hand-scrawled note emanating from the Résident Supérieur of Tonkin's office demonstrates that great efforts were made just to understand Vichy's Jewish statute:

Scenario #1)   4 Jewish grandparents = a Jew
  #2)   3 Jewish grandparents = a Jew
  #3)   2 Jewish grandparents—2 possibilities:
  a) married to a Jewish spouse: then = Jew no matter what religion they may be
  b) married to a non Jewish spouse: then [2 options]: Jew if one cannot prove one's religion as being other than Jewish; or non-Jew if one can prove that one is Catholic and not Jewish.[86]

This witch-hunt was greeted with some perplexity by several high-ranking French officials in Hanoi. The mayor of Hanoi noted in March 1943 that not a single Jew could be legally fired in his city; the only "high-ranking" Jews he had been able to find, Lipschutz and Belliscia, escaped the letter of the law on professions as they were, respectively, a subaltern bank employee and a self-employed landlord.[87] The Résident Supérieur of Tonkin was initially even more baffled by Decoux's original memorandum, dated October 7, 1941, specifying the number of grandparents required for one to be considered Jewish: the memorandum is replete with marginalia reflecting the reader's annoyance, confusion, and disbelief. One annotation reads: "None of this gets us very far."[88]

Still, Vichy's Jewish statutes were widely implemented in Indochina. A special commission was appointed within the Indochinese University in Hanoi to enforce quotas on the number of Jewish students.[89] Decoux went out of his way to fire Léo Lippmann, the former director of Hanoi's tram company, who had sought to circumvent the Jewish statutes by remaining in his company, but in a secondary capacity.[90] The zeal with which Decoux hounded his perceived adversaries was of course illogical even by his own standards. After all, he constantly bemoaned a lack of qualified European personnel. And Indochina's handful of Jews occupied some positions crucial for maintaining his power: out of the eighty Jews in Tonkin, forty-nine were in the military, and twenty-seven of those were Foreign Legionnaires.[91] Surrounded as he was by military threats, Decoux could hardly have spared a single man.

Interestingly, the extension of such anti-Semitic measures to French Indochina made for a situation wherein Jews in Indochina were subjected to injustices similar to those faced by the Jewish refugees in Japanese-controlled Shanghai.[92] This was but one consequence of Vichy's insistence at hounding its scapegoats as far as Indochina. Another more unexpected consequence were cases of Vichy's discriminatory laws coming back to haunt the French administration in Indochina. Governor Jean Decoux reported from Hanoi to Vichy in August 1942 that "the application of laws on Jewish companies and goods has brought considerable difficulties to Indochina."[93] Decoux evoked one case in particular to his superiors at Vichy, which, sui generis, seemed to backfire on French interests:

> I call to your attention the case of the *Société des Ciné-Théâtres de l'Indochine*. This cinema company was, until March 1941, considered Jewish, for it was managed by Mrs. [Ruby] Schwoerer, a person belonging to the Jewish race, who held a majority of the company's stock. Since March 1941, Mrs. Schwoerer ceded the entirety of her stock to non-Jews, and the company therefore now escapes our control. ... I am now advised that the cinema chain is on the point of being sold to a Japanese firm. As a result, I am unarmed against a sale which would threaten the Indochinese Federation ... by seeing a prime propaganda vector fall into foreign hands.[94]

Indeed, Decoux argued, the owner of the cinemas would not have resorted to their sale to the Japanese, had she not been imminently threatened with dispossession under Vichy's Jewish laws. In spite of Decoux's conclusion that extending Vichy's anti-Semitic laws to Indochina had brought only "difficulties to the colony,"[95] their application continued unabated, at the request of Vichy's Ministry of the Colonies.

A similar incident occurred in relation to Pétainist anti-Masonic laws. In October 1942, Decoux reported with regret that he had been forced to sack a loyal and patriotic officer by the name of Colonel Bertaux, because the latter had confessed to having once been a Freemason. Decoux complained bitterly that the removal of this exemplary "pro-Pétain" officer could have deleterious consequences on both the security and morale of Indochina. Though Decoux seemed to challenge the wisdom of such discrimination overseas, he nonetheless once again adhered to the letter of the law.[96]

Decoux's political troubles were not limited to his dialogue with Vichy over how thoroughly to implement Pétainist discrimination. Locally, his vision of the National Revolution was also contested by some colonizers who found even Pétain's politics not rightist enough. In Indochina, more than in any other distant colony, Vichy's governor was openly challenged by fascists comparable to Parisian ultracollaborators. One such individual, a low-ranking official with the forestry division in Cambodia by the name of Pierre Rothé, wrote Marshal Pétain personally in February 1941, decrying the alleged moderation of Governor Decoux. Rothé reproved: "I do not sense that spirits have changed much since before the war. Freemasons and unions continue to meet secretly in small groups, and, when the situation is ripe, they will resume their nefarious Masonic influence." Rothé concluded with an unwittingly ironic plea to the octogenarian marshal: "[We] ask you to please purge the Indochinese administration. Send us young personnel."[97] This official in remote Cambodia had crafted his own ideological trajectory to the far right. General Sabattier suggested in his memoirs that Rothé was no isolated case: "There was ... especially in Cochin China, a minority of ultras, more Pétainist than Pétain, who found Admiral Decoux timorous, and argued that insufficient measures had been taken against Jews and Freemasons."[98] In July 1944, Admiral Decoux himself addressed the dissent of the far right when he declared to an inquiring journalist:

> Certain quixotic fanatics would have liked me to ... go further than the Marshal himself. They asked for blood, and for me to give in, in the name of orthodoxy, to the petty struggles and the personal interpretations of the National Revolution by ultras. The Marshal never asked us to make of the National Revolution in Indochina an unintelligent or exaggerated version of that in the metropole. He expects us to build, with our available resources of men of goodwill, a structure adapted to our climate and to our unique situation.[99]

To construct this adapted version of the National Revolution, and to channel fanatics away from dissident ultras, Decoux would count on the support of two agencies in particular, the navy and the Légion Française des Combattants et Volontaires de la Révolution Nationale—the spearhead of National Revolutionary ideology in the metropole.

Even more than in Guadeloupe, where its importance was reflected by the powers wielded by Admirals Robert and Rouyer, the navy played a dominant role in first introducing, then reshaping, the National Revolution in Indochina. As Vichy's commissioner to youth in Indochina, the naval captain Maurice Ducoroy remarked, "Admiral Decoux seemed to have surrounded himself with a large number of naval comrades—which my presence only increased."[100] General Sabattier went a step further, suggesting that the navy represented in fact the vanguard of the National Revolution in Indochina. He observed:

> Both official and unofficial propaganda tended to present the navy as a model of discipline and cohesion. From that to making it the guardian of the principles of the National Revolution, and by extension a political instrument of Vichy, was but a small step. This step was indeed taken.[101]

Of course, the navy had long stood as a bastion of reactionary politics—well before Pétain came to power in 1940. Thereafter, it had found its way into Pétain's small circle of trusted agencies. It had, after all, stood firm under British fire at Mers-el-Kébir, and, until 1942, its leader, Admiral Darlan, appeared the loyal Pétainist par excellence. In Indochina, *la Royale,* as the navy was fittingly known, had been responsible, to borrow Decoux's hyperbole, for the greatest French naval triumph of the war, the victory over the Siamese at Koh-Changh.[102] Armed with a Pétainist blessing and with the prestige of Koh-Changh, naval officials like Robbe, charged with information, or Ducoroy, commissioner to youth, soon became the stewards of the National Revolution in Indochina. That this naval stranglehold on power irritated some can leave little doubt. The novelist Morgan Sportès's depiction of General Mouche—in reality General Martin—complaining bitterly of "naval officers who honeycombed the entire administration, and who captured all of the most prized positions,"[103] is quite true to life.

For those excluded from the naval clique of command, Decoux reserved another National Revolutionary agency, the Légion Française des Combattants et Volontaires de la Révolution Nationale. The Legion's role in Indochina was also more extensive than in any other colony.[104] Its goals were outlined early on. According to the head of the Legion in Cochin China: "[Legionnaires] must become Leaders. They must be the cadres of the National Revolution who will orchestrate the French resurrection. Legionnaires, you, at the head of this Revolution, are entrusted with building this new France."[105] To Decoux, the Legion further constituted a direct link with Pétain, for "it answers directly to the Marshal."[106] In a sense, it therefore represented a bridge with the distant metropole. It was also, along these same lines, a vector for disseminating the cult of the marshal. At a swearing in ceremony for Legionnaires in Hanoi in May 1942, the Résident Supérieur of Tonkin, M. P. Delsalle, described Pétain as follows:

> His figure dominates us. It is the very image of the nation. As a vast rock imposes its mass over the seas, the solid and firm Marshal opposes his mastery and calm to adversity. His clear eyes guide us. His tenderness of voice moves us. His sure-handed judgment leads us and helps us to avoid the pitfalls of sinuous paths. To serve him is to serve France. To love him, is to love our beautiful homeland and its past.[107]

In this way the Legion became a site of worship of Pétain, with his portrait dominating all public buildings at Legion ceremonies. As the vanguard of National Revolutionary ideology, the Legion also organized a series of events designed to popularize Pétainist precepts. Thus, in April 1942, Legionnaires were invited to attend a conference in Saigon on "the miracle of the new race: France and the New France."[108] To which "race" this referred, and for whom reinvigoration was intended, became important topics of debate within Decoux's inner entourage.

The question of who could join the Legion served further to define not only National Revolutionary institutions but also Decoux's political agenda as a whole. While Decoux is considered by some to have acted magnanimously in his effort to hire native Indochinese functionaries, the same cannot be said of his stance on Indochinese legionnaires. In October 1942, he had cabled Vichy to inquire whether in Algeria and West Africa "natives" had been admitted to the ranks of the Legion—either as veterans or volunteers.[109] In November 1942, the colonial secretary, Charles Platon, replied that the Legion of North and West Africa had indeed admitted "natives," but that he was given full discretionary powers in this matter for Indochina.[110] Instead of admitting Indochinese elites, Decoux proposed, then later abandoned, a scheme whereby "Asians" would be accepted as "Friends of the Legion."[111] So true was Decoux to the French policy of segregation in Southeast Asia that he failed to seize a golden opportunity to curry the favor of Indochinese collaborators. The motives for having eschewed this propaganda bonanza are outlined in Decoux's memoirs. There, he reveals: "I saw [in the Legion] a powerful tool to assert the solidarity and cohesion of the French population in the face of 25 million native onlookers, and in front of the Japanese army."[112] Convinced that the National Revolution must serve as a spectacle of French power as well as a bastion of National Revolutionary ideology, Decoux would mount grandiose Legionary rallies—worthy of miniature Nurembergs—which will be examined in a coming chapter.

If the Indochinese were cast out of the Legion, Europeans, conversely, were assigned to it by force. Decoux issued strong warnings to magistrates in Saigon who had failed to join the Legion.[113] Little wonder, then, that the Legion's ranks swelled from 2,637 members in January 1942 to 6,576 later that same year, and finally to more than 7,000 by June 1943—out of an estimated European population of 34,000.[114] Still, coercion alone cannot explain the phenomenal success of the Legion among the French in Indochina. The occupations of its five principal leaders lend us an impression of how pervasive a movement it became. Its heads included Lafferanderie, director of education at Hué; Truc, a labor inspector in Phnom Penh; Paris, a lawyer in Saigon; Allemand, the head of civil servants in Vientiane; and Barth, the manager of a major department store in Hanoi.[115]

Preaching to the Converted?
Vichy Propaganda in Indochina

If the French in Indochina could have been considered favorably disposed to Pétainist ideology from the outset, one might assume that the same could not be said of the Indochinese. But Vichyites would argue the contrary: "No other people of the Empire are as prepared for the National Revolution as are the Annamites, for it concords surprisingly well with their traditions."[116]

Even before concocting a dual strategy of superimposing the National Revolution onto local cultures and simultaneously appealing to indigenous conservatives—be they Buddhist or Catholic—Vichy officials set about limiting the tremendous diminution in prestige caused by the armistice and treaties with Japan in 1940. In addition to grappling with the loss of stature brought about by defeat, Decoux also sought to counter Japanese propaganda, which played admirably upon pan-Asian and anti-French themes. Indeed, between 1940 and 1945, the French were caught in a "triangular game," to borrow Pierre Brocheux's expression, between themselves, the Indochinese, and the Japanese occupiers.[117] For Decoux, a major step toward damage control came when he personally bade the marshal to pronounce a radio speech containing the following reassurance: "Annamites, Cambodians, Laotians, France remains. Do not doubt its destiny which is tied to yours."[118] Similarly, Vichy officials directed the once relatively autonomous Indochinese press to exalt the virtues of the new regime. Thus *Nagaravatta*, a Cambodian-language newspaper, explained to its readers in July 1940: "The republican regime, which once had worked well for France, is now overhauled. Democracy no longer exists since President Lebrun was succeeded by Marshal Pétain."[119] Meanwhile, *Tuan-Le*, a Vietnamese-language weekly based in Hué, asserted in November 1940:

> France, our metropole, has already begun a thorough purge. Under the enlightened guidance of Marshal Pétain, it has not hesitated to sweep away old prejudices and erroneous beliefs. The motto "Liberty, Equality, Fraternity" is now replaced by "Work, Family, Homeland," which speaks volumes on the rational nature of the reforms undertaken by Marshal Pétain. ... We hope that Indochina will likewise promptly repent for past errors, and engage on the path of necessary reforms.[120]

In addition to accounting for a change of regime, *Tuan-Le* unmistakably sought to endear its Vietnamese readers to the father figure Pétain, by stressing his "enlightened" and "rational" approaches to government. The parallel between Pétainism and Confucianism was all but drawn. In a 1941 article, a French journalist would sketch the outlines of Vichy's theory of congeneric Vichyite/Annamite development, when he wrote:

> Traditional Annamite morality is based [first] on the accomplishment of social duties [*Tam cuong*] ... toward one's elders, toward one's parents, toward the state, and [second] on the practice of social virtues [*Ngu thuong*]: humanity, fidelity, politeness, and wisdom. The Annamite learned as of a tender age of the five social relationships: of prince to subject, of father to son, of husband to wife, of brother to brother, and of friend to friend, and teaching had as a sole objective the training of men instructed in their duties toward themselves, their peers, their region, and their state. Here, we find the main concerns of our own "Leader" who considers "the social in its spirit and its traditions" to be an essential trait of his regime. How could Annamites not adhere with all their hearts to this program that makes the family the central nucleus of ... society?[121]

This almost Machiavellian conflating of Vietnamese traditionalism and Vichy *völkism* would become a cornerstone of National Revolutionary propaganda in Indochina. It would also soon be utilized for different ends altogether by Vietnamese nationalists.

Pétain as Confucius Reincarnated: Indochinese Cultures and the National Revolution

In a volume published in Hanoi in 1941, prefaced by the emperor of Annam, Bao Dai, an Indochinese journalist bearing the royal name of Ton That Binh outlined the fundamental affinities between Confucianism and Pétainism. With syllogistic reasoning, he first established that "the Annamite instinctively loves his *Patrie*," then argued that "the Annamite is profoundly attached to his *Famille*." Finally, he maintained, the industrious Annamite is devoted to *Travail*. He then concluded:

> All of these virtues of our people are well established. Therefore, when ... the great voice of the Marshal spoke of *Travail, Famille, Patrie*, we naturally adopted this slogan, which the glorious warrior intends to use as the basis for national resurrection. ... The new French maxim strongly resembles a Confucian one. It is akin to the four essential duties taught by Confucius ... *Tu, Tê, Tri, Binh*, in other words individual improvement, the family nucleus, the government, and the pacification of the universe. From now on, the maxim of the new France is our own.[122]

my n draw parallels between them

Echoing this theory, another journalist, named Nam Dong, contended in 1942 that "there are many analogies between [Indochina's] traditions of order, discipline, authority, work and sacrifice ... and those of ancient France ... [which the marshal is seeking to resurrect]."[123] As if copying the same press release, another Indochinese writer, under the revealingly nationalist nom de plume of Nguyen Viet-Nam,[124] had noted in 1940 the remarkable congruence of National Revolutionary and Indochinese values. He commented: "For us Annamites, [the motto *Travail, Famille, Patrie*] cannot leave us indifferent. I will go further. It has actually been ours for years, so close is it to the four duties enumerated by Confucius, *Tu, Tê, Tri, Binh*."[125] In 1943, a European writer for the local pedagogical bulletin further refined this argument. A certain Agard posited that the National Revolution stemmed from a fusion of Eastern and Western cultures—a reformulating of the nineteenth-century idea of a "Europe regenerated by Asia."[126] Agard advanced circumstantial evidence to this effect; Confucius's supposed influence on Pétain was reflected in his cults of authority, work, hierarchy, and the soil. Agard foretold that Pétain would become to the West what Confucius was to the East. Agard determined that Pétain was fusing the best of Western and Eastern canons.[127]

The finest example of Confucian-Pétainist parallelism, however, can be found in a 1942 text that presented side-by-side aphorisms and maxims from both philosophies. The book, *Sentences parallèles franco-annamites*, bore on its cover the nationalist pseudonyms of Jean François (read Français) and Nguyen Viet-Nam (no translation necessary), and contained nearly one hundred pages of cultural similarities designed to startle, but that in reality sometimes amounted to universal truisms rather than truths. Pétain's statement that "the individual exists by definition within a family, a society and a nation, from which he receives, along with life, all the means of existence" was juxtaposed with the Vietnamese verse "it is from the Heavens, the Earth, the Nation and the Family that we receive all of our means of existence."[128] On some scores, such as self-improvement, one does indeed find genuine common ground. Thus Pétain's pseudo-religious phrase "in the new France, none will be saved who haven't already tried to reform themselves" was likened to Confucius's principle that "[f]rom the emperor to the people, [all] must first perfect themselves."[129] Then too, shared notions of hierarchy were fruitfully exploited, with Pétain's famous expression "the new regime will be a social hierarchy" compared to the Sino-Vietnamese dictum "the State is a social hierarchy."[130] But even where Vichy ideologues were on shakier ground, they ventured full speed ahead.

Oblivious to the possibility that they might offend what was very much a "bookish" Vietnamese intellectual elite, bent on studying ancient canons, Vichy's propaganda team quoted the marshal at his most anti-intellectual: "We will try to destroy the morbid prestige of a pseudo-culture that is purely bookish, generating only sloth and uselessness." As a Vietnamese equivalent, the authors could dig up only a popular saying: "[T]he reading of philosophers is not as fruitful as the realistic meditation of the human condition"[131]—hardly a literal translation.

To be sure, at one level these thoughts fit perfectly with Decoux's scheme to "adopt the National Revolution to new climes." The recurrence, in virtually identical form in Indochina's press from 1940 to 1943, of the theme of Pétainist and Confucian congeneracy, can doubtless be attributed more to orders issued from Decoux's own political offices than to some sudden collective consciousness. French newspapers, following similar instructions from Decoux, had mentioned even the most superficial and tenuous parallels between the new France and Indochina—noting for example that the marshal's eighty-fifth birthday coincided with the death of Monivong, King of Cambodia (a coincidence that would—ironically—probably have been seen as inauspicious from an Asian perspective).[132]

Equally important, however, is the fact that Vichy's traditionalist and antiassimilationist penchants seem genuinely to have stirred considerable interest among Indochinese monarchists, conservatives, and nationalists alike. In a speech delivered at Hué, Saigon, Vientiane, and Phnom Penh in 1942 and 1943, the ultraconservative Nguyen Tien Lang underscored how Vichy's essentialism, folklorism, and rejection of assimilation could be seen as both a blessing and a vindication. According to this observer:

> The Third Republic, every time it had sought to assimilate, managed only to accentuate the differences it was seeking to erase. ... The National Revolution [conversely] asks for natives to be themselves, and far from breaking with the past, to conjure it up, and be complete Annamites, complete Cambodians, and complete Laotians, rather than caricatures of the French.[133]

Vichy officials had fostered this formation of new reductionist identities, of "total Cambodians" and "total Annamites," countervailing the identity of a "True France." Indigenous conservative nationalists proved all too willing to turn this new colonial discourse on its head by employing it for different ends. From 1940 to 1945, long stymied local patriotisms were suddenly encouraged as part of a generalized "return to the past."[134] Decoux himself played an important part in this new spirit, visiting for example the temple of Kiêp Bac, dedicated to none other than Tran Quôc Tuân, conqueror of the Mongols and Annamite hero.[135] Decoux also called for the simultaneous celebration of Joan of Arc and the Trung sisters, who had expelled the Chinese from the Red River Delta much as Joan had ousted the English from France.[136] This was all the more daring because the Trung sisters had previously been upheld as symbols of anticolonialism by some Vietnamese writers.[137]

On this same symbolic register, in December 1941 the colonial government press in Hanoi produced a remarkable book entitled *Hymnes et pavillons d'Indochine*. The work featured the insignia, heraldry, anthems, and flags of the colonizing nation, of course, but also of the so-called *petites patries* of Laos, Cambodia, and Annam. Some anthems were more recent inventions than others. Thus, Laos's reads as a transparent ode to Pétainist folklore:

> Our Lao race once benefited from great renown in Asia.
> Back then, the Lao were united.
> Today once again they love their race and their country, and are uniting around their leaders.
> They have maintained their fathers' religion, and the soil of their ancestors.
> …
> All together we will be able to restore the antique glory of Lao blood, and help each other in times of trouble.[138]

Sovereigns also featured prominently in this book. In fact, kings Bao Dai of Annam, Norodom Sihanouk of Cambodia, and Sisavang Vong of Laos were assigned the same status as Pétain. The marshal, for his part, prefaced the colorful album with the words: "I know how devoted you are to France. Love her … but also love your own, small country because this will help you understand and love France all the more."[139] Like the *Sentences parallèles franco-annamites*, this book literally invited the appropriation of symbols and discourse for nationalist ends. Whereas the British in India had resisted the propagation of nationalist flags that could undermine colonial domination,[140] under Decoux in Indochina the French themselves sought to impose "folkloric" heraldries, flags, and anthems upon the colonized, in a bid to rekindle an imagined and idealized "authentic" past.

Everywhere, colonial officials now promoted notions of organic difference and diversity under the mantle of the National Revolution, as well as the idea of a mythical synergy between Pétainism, Buddhism, and local Indochinese identities. Thus Decoux stressed in a speech at an Indochinese school: "You are all the more prepared for [the National Revolution] because the Annamite race possesses in it the two great notions of family and labor which the Marshal ... has chosen for the new motto ... of the French State."[141] Decoux, then, through a set of praxes and through the elaboration of a new discourse of racial reductionism blended with nostalgic folklorism, actively promoted a "return" to a wide range of Indochinese customs—in reality the invention of a set of traditions—be they in the form of folk songs, anthems, or rituals of government.

Such a concerted effort to rekindle a distant Indochinese past, and to construct an integralist Annamite identity, served to sharpen a new nationalist rhetoric in many Indochinese circles. This language played upon not only the National Revolution's reactionary regionalism but also upon its systematic denigration of the republic. Along precisely such lines, in 1941 Nguyen Manh Tuong, a Vietnamese high school teacher in Hanoi, launched a scathing attack on pre-1940 France, while calling for a revival of wholesome Vietnamese values, which the new French regime now championed. He reasoned:

> Our old Annamite civilization recognized long ago the primacy of the family over the individual. Our legislation, our literature, our morals revealed the existence of a hierarchical society, acting under the paternal authority of responsible leaders, informed only by sentiments of duty and sacrifice. The contact with republican ideas wreaked havoc upon this harmonious ensemble.[142]

Here, Nguyen Manh Tuong employed a set of complex literary maneuvers to subvert French dominance by borrowing the very language of Pétainism. By implying that the Vietnamese had themselves long ago invented a form of National Revolution, which had subsequently been steered off course by the deleterious effects of French republicanism, this author effectively subverted the intended National Revolutionary message, reinscribing it with truly national and revolutionary meanings. Nguyen Manh Tuong deftly utilized two arsenals, and ably shifted between two registers, in creating a dialogical and opportunistic nationalist discourse. Nguyen Manh Tuong's rhetoric is of course subject to interpretation. This passage could show him as either a nostalgic Vietnamese monarchist, or as a nationalist using the language of tradition. In either case, the central point is that the condemnation of "French republican ideals" could easily slip into explicitly anti-French, and hence anticolonial, sentiments.

In some cases, then, the very implications of Vichy propaganda clearly placed the Decoux administration on the defensive. Indeed, the simple hypothesis that "natives" might have coined the principles of the National

Revolution long before the French seemed itself tantamount to undermining the French ingenuity and superiority that supposedly underlay colonialism. Thus, even the authors of the *Sentences parallèles franco-annamites* acknowledged that

> some might interpret the extraordinary similitude between new French and ancient Annamite ideals ... to mean that the sages of China and Annam had long ago arrived at the principles of [the National Revolution], and that consequently the Marshal is teaching [the Vietnamese] nothing new.[143]

The authors added hastily that such a conclusion would be erroneous, and that the clear parallels between Confucianism and the National Revolution could be simply imputed to the fact that they constituted absolute, eternal, and universal truths.[144] But to arrive at this set of logical contortions, which denied any influence of Confucius on Pétain, one had essentially to post the dubious disclaimer that any similarity between the two philosophies was purely coincidental. Such a statement seemed all the more at odds with the intended objective of underscoring the affinities between Pétainism and Confucianism. The entire malaise resulted quite simply from the indisputable fact that Confucius had preceded Pétain.

Vietnamese undermining and appropriating of the National Revolution did not always hinge on such colonial inconsistencies; often, it simply seized an opportunity presented by the new prevailing reductionist rhetoric. In 1942, Vietnamese students at the new *Cité Universitaire* of the Indochinese University in Hanoi composed a school song that clearly appealed to Decoux's nostalgism, while simultaneously brandishing a set of Indochinese nationalist images. The first two couplets read:

> From the coast of Annam to the Ruins of Angkor,
> Across the mountains of the South to the North.
> A voice rises:
> Serve the beloved homeland,
> Always without reproach and without fear,
> To make the future brighter.
> Joy, fervor and youth
> Are full of firm promises.
> To serve you, Dear Indochina!
> With heart and discipline!
> Such is our goal, such is our law,
> And nothing will make our faith waver.
> Students! Our glorious past
> Remains present in our memories,
> Of these great heroes who fought long ago

For this beautiful land, we are the sons.
Let us be proud of our ancestors.[145]

Here, the beloved homeland is certainly Indochina, rather than France. The ancient heroes of bygone wars of liberation, whose cult Decoux had fostered in tandem with a new sense of discipline and fervor, are intended to show the way for a newfound resurgence and unity. One is tempted to ask, though, against whom this fervor, resurgence, and unity are to be directed.

Even when Indochinese sources fell short of employing National Revolutionary discourse directly to undermine French rule, they still suggested novel nationalist readings of Pétainist texts. The newspaper *L'Annam nouveau* published a series of articles in 1940 and 1941, encouraging "parallel revolutions" in the metropole and Indochina. The journalist Tao Trang penned a first article in December 1940, holding that "*Travail, Famille, Patrie* translates into a concise motto for the once confused aspirations of the children of Viet-Nam. Indeed this triple motto summarizes for us too, all of our own program of reconstruction."[146] *L'Annam nouveau* further pursued this theme of Vietnamese ownership of the National Revolution. An anonymous editorial in September 1941 asserted that "[Pétain's] program of restoration of moral values, of reinvigorating youth, is indeed applicable to the Annamite people."[147] A month later, Pham Quynh, education minister to Emperor Bao Dai (and soon to become minister of the Interior), was described by this same newspaper as seeking to demonstrate "the parallels which exist between the policy of renovation undertaken in France by the Marshal, and the restoration of ancient ideals and moral principles which is needed in Annam."[148] Pham Quynh went on to summarize recent decades in Indochina as "[a period when] we thought that we should shed our own souls." The emperor's right-hand man, described by historian David Marr as an "arch-conservative,"[149] concluded: "This Annamite soul must be rediscovered. We too have an important work of restoration ahead of us."[150] The National Revolution, resting at the crossroads of restoration and revolution, became, in Indochina, a concept laden with notions of national rediscovery.

"Pure" Viet, Lao, and Cambodian identities were constantly affirmed, emphasized, and ultimately reified in the French-language Indochinese press under Vichy—a press aimed at French and indigenous elite consumption. In November 1940, one Vu Ngoc Lien condemned the culture of métissage and the métissage of culture, rejecting the very idea of hybridity. He chose the field of popular music, arguing against the importing and Vietnamization of French songs. Taking aim at this "musical renewal, or cái-luong," the author concluded: "[We] find this hasty métissage and forced marriage a shocking outrage to art—not all reforms are desirable."[151] Here, the marriage of French scores and Vietnamese lyrics, itself a cultural by-product of the colonial contact zone, was rejected as inauthentic by the colonized, with the full blessing of the colonizer.

Decoux's officials had intentionally initiated this ideological throwback to an invented bygone era of Indochinese "authenticity." Far from merely jumping on a bandwagon or "getting into the spirit of things" and acting "benignly" toward "local patriotisms,"[152] as one historian has suggested, in reality Decoux took the first step by vigorously endorsing cultural activities that renounced assimilation, while redefining Indochinese identities along regionalist lines dear to the National Revolution. He did so pragmatically, and in concert with Vichy. On April 11, 1941, he had reported to Platon: "[We] are witnessing in some bourgeois circles an attempt to regroup once-divided political tendencies into a common nationalist program, that we will watch, and steer into a favorable direction."[153]

In precisely such a spirit of "channeling Indochinese nationalisms," from 1940 to 1945, a plethora of writings set about investing Indochinese cultures with National Revolutionary meanings. In a book entitled *Popular Wisdom in France and Annam*, the Vietnamese thinker Chi Qua Ho Phu suggested that the local peasant embodied the noblest virtues of the An-namite people, at once simple and frank in manners. A reviewer commented that such a vision of rural Annam concurred perfectly with the newfound importance of the peasant in the National Revolutionary ethos.[154] Another journalist went a step further, applying a Pétainist maxim to Annam. Indeed, this source maintained, "Annamites, like the French, are laborious, agricultural people, faithful to *the earth, which never lies*."[155] Similarly, in an article on "indigenous theater," a French observer outlined the qualities of an art form that "stresses events of the national past," thereby enabling its public to "assimilate the classical bases of its race and culture."[156] Indochina's minority peoples, once romanticized by some Europeans, while considered uncivilized and backward by others, were now upheld as models of "natives acting like natives." This tension reflects what Frances Gouda describes as a dual discourse of "domination and con-trol [and a concomitant] ... rhetoric of desire" toward the "primitive."[157] Better yet, a certain D. Antomarchi implied, simple, hierarchical minority peoples could provide a valuable lesson in National Revolutionary values. Among the Rhadé people of the Darlac province, he argued, "the family is the essential nucleus of society. ... Sterile wives go so far as to give their young husbands a concubine ... so that she might have children."[158] The Rhadé thus seemed to espouse in their own way both the National Revolutionary glorification of the family and the Pétainist obsession with denatality. Another Indochinese columnist interpreted the National Revolution as signaling "the return to Chinese characters for Annamite people."[159] In sum, to such thinkers, Pétainist cultural policy seemed to mark an about face, ushering in true associationism, which recognized difference, hierarchy, and tradition, while rejecting a language of assimilation equated with cultural alienation.

Such theories received widespread attention, even reaching the heart of the metropole. Near the capital of Vichy, the Vietnamese scholar Hoang Van Co delivered a keynote address at the University of Clermont-Ferrand in February 1942. The lecture, entitled "The Renovation of Native Economies: The Overseas Peasantry and Artisans," once again associated traditional Vietnam with the National Revolutionary *Weltanschauung*. Hoang Van Co affirmed:

> Like ancient France, most of our colonies are the preserve of small enterprises and artisans. ... The taste for small companies and for family operated artisan work was so crucial to our colonies that artisans in an urban center like Hanoi once constituted its backbone: Hanoi was popularly known as the "town of the thirty-six crafts."[160]

Nor did Hoang Van Co stop at drawing parallels between ancient Hanoi and future Pétainist retro-urbanism. Like Nguyen Manh Tuong before him in Indochina, and thanks in no small part to the Vichy French eagerness to condemn the legacy of the Third Republic, he dared to suggest that France had in fact long ago ruined a premodern National Revolutionary experiment in Indochina. He concluded: "Then France came, and the prestige of traditional crafts was soon eclipsed by modernization."[161] Sharing Vichy's professed distaste for both modernism and modernization, this text also seems emblematic of an important current of Indochinese thought, at once cautiously nationalistic and intensely reactionary. Indochinese conservative notables, who were at the forefront of this movement, represented at once Vichy's staunchest supporters and—setting aside Communist and other nontolerated forms of resistance—France's sharpest critics.

As the historian David Marr has indicated, the period from 1940 to 1945 saw Vietnamese intellectuals engage in a profound "reassessment of

Vietnam's heritage."[162] To the disgust of some radicals and Communists, conservative nationalists were undoubtedly seduced by Vichy's retrogressive cultural discourse. In this sense, one might posit that the Decoux administration, far from being duped by traditionalist praxes encoded with nationalist meanings, had instead intentionally endeavored to hijack Indochinese nationalisms by cultivating conservative notables, while articulating a new reductionist vision of what it meant to be "Indochinese."

In such a light, Ho Chi Minh's wartime decisions to cancel the Agrarian Revolution, to veer from internationalism to nationalism, and explicitly to associate the seemingly contradictory tenets of Communism and nationalism,[163] can be seen as informed in part by the threat of Vichy's appeal to Indochinese traditionalists (though one could of course question just how exposed Ho Chi Minh and the early Viet-Minh were to Vichy propaganda: this is obviously a matter of speculation). It was coincidentally in June 1941 that Ho Chi Minh drew up a legitimizing and eminently nationalist historical lineage to his revolutionary movement, referring to the Vietnamese as "the twenty-odd million descendants of the Lac and the Hong," and eulogizing "our predecessors, such as Phan Dinh Phung, Hoang Hoa Tham and Luong Ngoc Quyen."[164] As for the very programs of the Viet Minh, some French observers themselves noted a curious affinity with Decoux's agenda. French intelligence reports remarked that the Viet Minh's cultural plan included "developing a new Culture—the Culture of Vietnam" and "[e]ncouraging and stimulating a national program of physical education so as to fortify the (Vietnamese) race."[165] These two points clearly intersected with Decoux's stated objectives of rekindling and rewriting the Vietnamese past by adulating its heroes, and of reinvigorating the Vietnamese through a strict and disciplined regimen of physical education. Whether Ho Chi Minh had simply plundered selectively from Decoux's programs, had on the contrary attempted to counter them strategically, or had perhaps managed to maintain the strategic initiative remains unclear. Regardless of the precise modes and parameters of intellectual interaction and cross-fertilization, one can certainly conclude that the Vichy era left an important mark on Vietnamese politics and culture.

Whether as an intentional ploy to steer Indochinese nationalisms in their direction or as a genuine belief in the congruence of transcultural traditionalism, one thing seems certain: Vichy actively promoted a vision of an idyllic and regionalized ancient Indochina, in step with a backward-looking Vichy France. The linchpin of this conception involved the grafting of the cult of Pétain onto local pantheons. If one is to believe Vichy's secretary general in Indochina, Georges Gautier, Marshal Pétain was revered as the incarnation of a new Franco-Indochinese congruence from 1940 to 1945. According to this source:

> For the peoples of the Orient, Marshal Pétain was the very embodiment of a superior man. Advanced in years, and hence in wisdom, covered in the triple glory of the scholar, the diplomat and the military mandarin, expressing himself in straightforward yet profound prose, translatable into all the languages of Indochina, and transposable to all traditional philosophies, never had a French head of state garnered such respect and admiration in Indochina.[166]

Gautier, like Decoux, was no doubt prone to exaggeration on this point. Nonetheless, there can be little doubt that Vichy's sensibilities were shared by significant numbers of Indochinese conservative notables. According to Gautier, however, Decoux had not necessarily set the first stone of the policy of appealing to Indochinese elites and superimposing the colonial edifice onto local customs. Indeed, Gautier argued, the foundations for such an approach had been established at the turn of the century by Marshal Lyautey, who had first seen the wisdom of protectorates,[167] which ensured that native societies would not become "uprooted" or "mongrelized."

In a sense, then, Decoux was not the first to showcase "cultural authenticity" and to contrast it to "mongrelization." As Herman Lebovics, Gail Paradise Kelly, and others have shown, assimilationism had been rejected by French officials in Indochina long before 1940. Still, as Lebovics himself concedes, the vestiges of "republican egalitarianism"[168] provided a veneer of assimilationism prior to 1940. This veneer was definitively shed under Vichy. The Vichy regime, then, marked the high-water mark of a reductionist, traditionalist, hierarchical, regional, and rural vision of Indochina. Bereft for the first time since 1871 of a modicum of republicanism, Indochina's French rulers would implement far-reaching and profoundly reversionary reforms, in tune with both National Revolutionary and Lyauteytian doctrines. Whether, as the colonial expert Charles Robert Ageron has suggested, "the Indochinese ... were the ones to profit from the National Revolution"[169] or, as Ho Chi Minh asserted, "[under Vichy] the French rulers ... bec[ame] even more ruthless in carrying out their policy of exploitation, repression, and massacre"[170] will be discussed in the following chapter.

CHAPTER 7

Toward a New Indochina

I can still remember the primary school where every morning little Vietnamese children, lined in formation, sang at the top of their lungs: "Maréchal, nous voilà."

— Kim Lefevre, Franco-Vietnamese author
born in Hanoi, later exiled in France[1]

Admiral Toudebout ... asked Mr. Phan Ky to share his "charming little anecdote," which proved how much France was profoundly anchored into the hearts of even Indochinese children. ... [Phan Ky recounted: We] entered into an elementary class of Tien Yen, where we found thirty or so adorable little Tonkinois schoolgirls. Choosing the prettiest of these ... I asked her, pointing at the wall to the portrait of the Victor of Verdun: "Who is this Gentleman?" The little girl, anything but shy, answered "He is the Marshal!" I continued: "[A]nd what is the Marshal's name?" She responded: "Nous voilà!"

— Morgan Sportès, Tonkinoise[2]

Here Morgan Sportès's historical novel set in Indochina under Decoux exposes at once the gulf between colonial and metropolitan realities, and the ironies inherent in the ill-adapted and unfettered Pétainist indoctrination that Vichy dispensed in Indochina. Indeed, the ideological lesson sought by "Toudebout" and "Phan Ky" (who are in reality none other than Decoux and the right-hand man of Pham Quynh) completely misses its mark. This schoolgirl's constant exposure to the hymn Maréchal, nous voilà ("Marshal, Here We Are") has brought her no closer to understanding the marshal on Vichy's terms.

Such critical approaches have remained largely the preserve of the novelist. Historians have tended to accept at face value—with varying degrees of acceptance—Decoux's professed desire to "renovate French policies in an occupied Indochina, [to] achieve an association with [indigenous] elites, and to put in place a genuine protectorate."[3] It is true that on the surface Decoux introduced a series of seemingly progressive reforms to Indochina. In December 1941 he banned the derogatory term *indigène* from administrative parlance, recommending *Indochinois* in its place.[4] Then too, Decoux is generally recognized as having hired many Indochinese into administrative posts hitherto reserved to Europeans. And yet, overall it is amply evident that Decoux's designs in Indochina were actually as complex as they were deeply ideologically motivated by the regime he served. Behind a veneer of reform, Decoux introduced Pétainist regimentation, ideology, and new degrees of repression to Indochina.

Repression

Most obviously, those who persist in believing Decoux's claim that his rule was somehow magnanimous toward the Indochinese, or perhaps a "lesser evil," have chosen not to grapple with the ferocious repression that occurred in Indochina under Vichy. To be sure, between 1940 and 1945, Decoux succeeded in currying the favor of many of Indochina's traditional elites. Nevertheless, at the same time he also proved implacable toward mounting Vietnamese Communist resistance. When in November 1940, Communist guerrillas rebelled in Cochin China, Vichy officials orchestrated amazingly brutal reprisals. After the initial *mise au pas* of the revolt— during which French troops are said to have pierced the hands and feet of Communist captives with wires, in lieu of handcuffs[5]—colonial justice took over where the Foreign Legion had left off, meting out one death sentence after another. As a measure of this ruthlessness, one can turn to correspondence from Vichy's minister of the colonies, Admiral Platon, to the governor of Indochina, Jean Decoux.

Although no pacifist himself, Platon nonetheless urged Decoux in July 1941 to cease persecuting Cochin Chinese insurgents after the fact. By comparison with Decoux, Platon seemed uncharacteristically lenient, observing that "nine months after the rebellion, native populations will no doubt fail to understand the ongoing punishment."[6] Some two months earlier, another loyal Vichyite at the Colonial Ministry, political bureau chief Gaston Joseph, had similarly remarked on "the high number of death sentences pronounced recently in Indochina." Noting that "repression seems extremely stiff [even by comparison with the crushing of Yen Bay and the 1930 soviets]," Joseph implored Decoux to consider the political consequences of his actions. Joseph reasoned: "It is not through ruthless and blind repression that we will endear ourselves to [the Indochinese]. ... Stiff sentences will appear to them to be racially motivated."[7]

Decoux, in a position of absolute power in distant Indochina, seems to have disregarded these persistent pleas for moderation. Nor were such voices from Vichy the only factors which might logically have dictated that Decoux show a measure of restraint in dealing with internal opposition. At a time when the Soviet Union was still considered a partner of Germany's (by virtue of the Molotov-Ribbentrop Pact), and well before Vichy's July 7, 1941, orders on the repression of Communism—which would follow Hitler's invasion of the USSR—Decoux was already mercilessly persecuting Southern Vietnamese Communists.[8] Indeed, between the armistice and June 1941, 108 death sentences were carried out in Indochina—a figure accounting only for judicially endorsed executions. The vast majority of these were of Communists involved in either the Cochin China rebellion of November 1940 or the unrest at Vinh in January 1941. Far from heeding Platon and Joseph's appeals for restraint, Decoux instead "deplored the lengthy procedures necessary for pardon procedures to be presented to [the head of state, Pétain]" (pardons that were mere formalities prior to executions, that Decoux thus wished to hasten).[9] Decoux recommended only two pardons during his four years in power. He furthermore firmly rebuffed Platon's broader orders on clemency, defiantly responding to his superior in Vichy on August 19, 1941: "[T]he masses would not understand any leniency; they would see in it only weakness. To change our stance, as the Japanese are preparing to occupy the South, might let the natives think the Japanese [are behind this proposed indulgence]."[10] Employing the Japanese presence as a pretext for intransigence, Decoux continued on this unwaveringly stern course toward those he considered France's—and indeed colonialism's—inveterate enemies.

The Carrot and the Stick

Why then, given such ruthless repression, have some observers sung the praises of Decoux's "native policy," from remarks that "Admiral Decoux's indigenous policies were not without their merits,"[11] to bolder claims that "Decoux implemented an indigenous policy whose liberalism was without precedent in French colonial history"?[12] The answer resides precisely in the plurality of Decoux's indigenous doctrines. While vigorously suppressing Communist uprisings on the one hand, Decoux on the other formulated a quite lenient project for Indochinese conservatives and for the crowns of Annam, Cambodia, and Laos, which has been variously termed one of "patriotisms" or *politique des égards,* insofar as it both rested upon, and sought to appeal to, traditional elites and national sentiments. Contemporaries understood how the seemingly lenient *politique des égards* was at loggerheads with Decoux's other goal of crushing dissent. In the words of a liberal French colonial dissident: "The multiplication of stadiums, the promotion of indigenous elites, the permission to use the term Viet-Nam and to wave the Vietnamese flag, the official recognition of a Vietnamese culture and nation ... might indeed have seduced some nationalists away from the Japanese, had Decoux not, at the same time, so mercilessly and indiscriminately crushed all those who dared [challenge him] by arms, pen or word."[13]

But for Decoux, far from constituting a contradiction, firm resolve against Communism and the courting of traditionalists away from both Communism and the threat of Japanese pan-Asianism seemed to constitute a coherent course of action—one eerily prefiguring later, equally unsuccessful American attempts to woo and indeed shore up resolutely anti-Communist elements of Vietnamese society. In fact, the very act of crushing Communist resistance no doubt served to endear traditional elites to Vichy. For all of its Machiavellic reactionism, however, the *politique des égards* was anything but straightforward, desperate, or ill-conceived. It was at once successfully interwoven with Vichyite themes, and profoundly rooted in a local Indochinese context.

This complex agenda, ranging from the advancement of Indochinese cadres and mandarins, to the promotion of regional identities, and the final rejection of assimilation, was perhaps first put forward by a Vietnamese notable. In October 1940, a provincial mandarin by the name of Nguyen Trong Tan submitted a proposal to Vichy's colonial minister, René-Charles Platon. In it, Nguyen Trong Tan drew the outline for a new Franco-Indochinese relationship, wherein French and Indochinese elites would be treated equally. This document detailed a seemingly eclectic program, including "the re-establishment of traditional schools, the return to former [read precolonial] educational programs," and the "safeguarding of ancient principles in keeping with morality, while adapting them to modern life."[14] Building upon two Vichyite themes—the idea of 1940 as a clean slate on which to draw up models for a new society, and the notion of returning to an idealized past—Nguyen Trong Tan presented a timely project, intended at once to appeal to Vichyites and promote an "authentic" and restored Vietnam.

It would seem too great a coincidence if Decoux's outlook had not been at least indirectly shaped by such proposals. To some degree, Vichy's colonial ministry actively endorsed the ideas contained in Nguyen Trong Tan's manifest. On August 8, 1941, for instance, Gaston Joseph advised Decoux's personnel bureau that "greater and greater room must be afforded to the Indochinese in the administration."[15] Clearly, however, Decoux made this particular theater of courting elites his own cause célèbre, taking it to ends Platon and Joseph could not have imagined. Might other factors also have motivated Decoux's reforms in this arena? Already in October 1941, Platon had asked Decoux to consider solutions "to avoid that Indochina lose, little by little … its French [officials]" to repatriation.[16] A February 1942 telegram to the Ministry of the Colonies confirms that Decoux was confronted with a dearth of European administrators. He noted that no replacements had arrived from the metropole since maritime links had been practically severed in 1940; hence, retirements, deaths, and leaves, not to mention the creation of new positions, had left voids that could be filled only by hiring "indigenous" replacements.[17]

In addition to this underlying factor, one must recognize that Decoux soon became a staunch advocate of measures intended to appeal to traditional Indochinese elites. His determination actually pitted him against Vichy officials—this time not as a zealot of repression, but of reform. On October 20, 1941, Admiral Platon firmly reproved Decoux's first bid to open some of the highest-ranking administrative posts to the Indochinese—a suggestion that took to unforeseen ends the reform advocated by Joseph. Platon stated unequivocally: "[A]dmitting non-French citizens to management positions poses delicate questions, and simply cannot be undertaken."[18] Undaunted, Decoux prepared to stand firm, claiming to "want to give to indigenous elites the satisfaction which they are due."[19] Decoux justified his position by pointing to the need to counter Japanese propaganda, and by implying that the reform concurred with Pétain's desire for decentralization. Finally, however, a stern October 29, 1941, rebuke from Platon, accusing Decoux of insubordination, forced Vichy's governor of Indochina to postpone the implementation of the reform until May 1942.[20] By then, Jules Brévié, a former governor of Indochina himself, had been appointed secretary of state to the colonies. Thanks to this change in leadership, in May 1942, Decoux at last issued a decree opening the access of

Indochinese functionaries to even the highest administrative positions.[21] An Indochinese journalist, drawing a balance-sheet on the reform two years later, concluded that it "has been universally well received. ... The numbers are eloquent. They indicate the willingness of the government widely to utilize the intellectual elites of this country."[22]

It seems fair to question what factors might conceivably have driven Decoux to direct confrontation with Vichy in his bid to garner the sympathies of Indochinese elites. The answer lies in the fact that the law on Indochinese cadres was but one dimension of a much vaster program undertaken by Vichy officials in Indochina. A government publication, chronicling the successes of the National Revolution in Indochina, affords us perhaps the best sense of Decoux's overall political objectives. These included, first, "the creation of a stable social state ... through a fusion of ancient traditions, and taking into account the needs of an evolving Indochinese society." The second doctrine involved "the respect of local nationalisms," and the objective of "harmoniously guiding the evolution of elites and the masses in the direction of traditions, and national facts." Lastly, Vichy officials wished to undertake "the development and [achieve] federal solidarity of the different countries which compose the [Indochinese] union."[23] The keystone of Vichy's first goal in Indochina—achieving a new social order—involved wooing the landed and established elites, ranging from high-ranking functionaries to mandarins and monarchs.

The New Social Order and the Return to Traditions

In seeking to bolster the status of elites, and mandarins in particular, Vichy was entering a delicate arena, which had long constituted a source of tension in Annam and Tonkin especially. As recently as 1938, the leftist Saigon-based newspaper *La Lutte* had depicted local mandarins as "ignorant country squires ... who mismanage their villages."[24] On the opposite end of the spectrum, Governor Pasquier, a proponent of association between the wars, had clamored in 1930 for "a revival of mandarin power."[25] Traditionalists like Pasquier contended that mandarins were underpaid and underutilized, while Communist and even moderate reform voices countered that this corrupt feudal class already wielded far too much arbitrary power.

As in the case of Indochinese functionaries, much more was at stake here than the issue of mandarin status alone. In reality, two contesting visions of Indochina had vied for supremacy between the wars. Broadly speaking, the first, championed by Pham Quynh and other social conserva-

uncharted modern state or traditional hierarchical monarchy

tives, involved the resurgence of precolonial monarchies and hierarchies within a rigid "traditional" framework. The second, championed by revolutionaries, consisted in brushing aside such traditional trappings in favor of a new, still largely uncharted modern state.

Vichy officials took sides early on in this Vietnamese socio-ideological schism. So desirous was Decoux to pander to Indochinese sovereigns and mandarins that he bade Vichy to consider an Indochinese exception to its laws on insignia. In an effort to ban all symbols of Gaullist resistance—most notably the Croix de Lorraine and the *V* for Victory—Vichy had extended to the colonies December 24, 1940, legislation prohibiting insignia other than those of the new regime (such as the Francisque, for example). In January 1941, Decoux entreated the Ministry of the Colonies to "exempt from the law ... decorations relating to the crowns of Annam, Cambodia and Luang Prabang [Laos] ... so as not to offend sensibilities."[26] This was achieved on March 14, 1941, when this exemption was codified as a law, allowing the sovereigns of Annam, Cambodia, and Laos to wear or endorse whatever decorations they so wished.[27] In Laos, meanwhile, Decoux's bolstering of the monarchy was accompanied by a fostering of Lao nationalism. By encouraging Lao literature and theater, and the rediscovery of Lao history, Decoux had hoped at once to counter Siamese territorial designs and to adapt National Revolutionary ideology to the remotest Indochinese "province."[28]

In Annam, Tonkin, and Cochin China, meanwhile, mandarins were transformed from the scapegoats of Third Republican colonialism into the prominent local embodiment and conveyors of Vichy's traditionalism. They accordingly represented the sine qua non of the new regime's social agenda. Addressing a class of graduating mandarins in December 1941, Jean Decoux declared that, henceforth, "you must be the principal architects ... of the restoration of Indochinese traditions."[29] Decoux, and Bao Dai's prime minister, Pham Quynh, went on to associate the recrudescence of mandarin power with the fostering of local nationalisms—encouraged by Vichy as part of a generalized return to an imagined past. During this same speech, Decoux became the first French governor to utilize a term that was gaining in popularity to denote Annam, Tonkin, and Cochin China, when he asserted: "Every mandarin must consider himself responsible for the destiny of Vietnam."[30]

That mandarins were in fact conceived as agents for Vichy's nostalgic traditionalism is amply evidenced by both Decoux's and Pham Quynh's speeches. In December 1941, the latter had announced to a class of graduating mandarins:

> Experience has shown ... that it is by turning to traditional institutions, and by reinvigorating and consolidating them, that we can best ensure the progress ... of this people. You know these fundamental institutions well: they are the patriarchal family, the oligarchic community, and the monarchic state. They rest on the same traditions of order and discipline, of hierarchy and authority which are the bases of Annamite society.[31]

Here, Vichy's Indochinese ally clearly elaborated a vision of a Vietnam that went well beyond an abstract precolonial status quo ante. He infused this invented Vietnam with Pétainist concepts of natural, reactionary, and autocratic order. Notions of oligarchy, patriarchy, monarchy, discipline, and hierarchy were, after all, some of the very ideological bedrocks that underlay the National Revolution as a whole. In a 1943 telegram to Vichy, Decoux made a more explicit parallel between the new orders in France and Indochina, when he observed: "[Thanks to our new mandarin policy,] the principles of authority are being rehabilitated in Indochina, just as they have been in France."[32]

As indicated in a previous chapter, this language served as more than a marker of Vichy essentialism and inegalitarianism; it was intended to win over a segment of Indochinese society to Pétain, by underscoring the affinities between French and Indochinese traditionalism. Concretely, Decoux also endeavored to inveigle the Indochinese "establishment" with material benefits. Mandarins, for example, were awarded considerable pay increases from 1941 to 1943.[33] In Cochin China, meanwhile, the status of *grand notable* was carefully delineated under Vichy, so as to include traditional elites, without however in any way democratizing the institution.[34] This revivification of the power of traditional elites was carefully coupled with National Revolutionary tenets. In precisely this vein, Decoux introduced courses in physical education at the new Vichy youth camp at Phan Thiet, as part of a new mandarin training curriculum.[35]

There can be little doubt that at least some Indochinese found advantage in, and publicly gave thanks for, this oligarchic renaissance put forward by Vichy. In 1943, Hanoi's government press produced a fascinating "who's who" of Indochinese high society. In it, many a notable publicly acknowledged the munificence of the new regime toward established elites. One dignitary in particular, the elder Buddhist priest Pham-Van-Tien, listed under his own credentials a religious ceremony he had performed in July 1941 in honor of Marshal Pétain.[36]

In short, then, Vichy appealed to a Vietnamese constituency that might be characterized as neotraditionalist, or as Philippe Devillers has labeled it: "the anti-communist Vietnamese right."[37] That such a group existed, and in fact thrived between 1940 and 1945, has been somewhat obfuscated by the subsequent meteoric ascendancy of Vietnamese Communism. It should not come as a surprise, however. According to Hue-Tam Ho Tai's analysis of Indochina in the 1920s, Social Darwinism had provided a radically new lens through which Vietnamese intellectuals came to view themselves and their rapport with others. Hue-Tam Ho Tai contends that a crisis of Vietnamese culture, a veritable "spiritual malaise," ensued. To this author, both Cao Daïsm and Marxism offered comforting solutions to this crisis.[38] Reductionist neotraditionalism may also have followed such a trajectory by building upon Social Darwinian theories while appealing to a bygone ethos. In this sense, the dynamics underlying Vichy's integralist ideology in Indochina were not those of colonial diffusion, but rather of encounter and even symbiosis—between ultraconservatives with admittedly differing agendas, but a shared vision of authenticity, and an equally shared aversion to métissage and "mimicry."

In this way the image of the unspoiled paddy field became closely intertwined with Pétain's cult of the earth—"the soil that never lies." At the forefront of Vietnamese Vichy sympathizers was Pham Quynh, the avid reader of Maurice Barrès and Charles Maurras, and dogged opponent of Marxism. Pham Quynh and Decoux found common ultraconservative ground on most issues: like Decoux, Pham Quynh was persuaded that traditional authority, family values, and elitism needed to be restored. Pham Quynh and his entourage, in the words of one observer, "constitute an important current of thought: a nationalist current, resolutely hostile to communism, which was conferred power by Admiral Decoux."[39] Thus Pham Quynh's assassination by the Viet-Minh in September 1945 is reminiscent of Admiral Platon's at the hands of the French Resistance a few months earlier: the pragmatic ultraconservative alliance they embodied had been almost instantly swept away by the course of the war, and by two Liberations.[40]

The Return to the Soil and the "Restoring of Authority"

As in the metropole, where Vichy's cult of the chief was rivaled only by its fixation with the return to the soil and the glorification of the peasantry, so in Indochina did the question of the Indochinese village preoccupy the

French administration as much as the related issue of "natural leadership." This particular leitmotiv of the National Revolution was easily transposed to Indochina. A Saigon newspaper explained to its readers in 1941: "[We] believe it necessary to inform our men of the soil of the misery caused throughout the world by ... urbamania, and the abandonment of the countryside."[41] In a bid to stem the supposed desertion of the countryside, Vichy officials drafted sweeping rural reforms for Indochina. These shared one important trait. Once again, all advocated increased powers for country notables, previously lambasted as corrupt and self-interested, not only by Indochinese Communists but even by French officials.

In 1939, several experts on Cochin China had advanced the theory that the local *commune*, or smallest administrative unit of the colony, was in dire need of revamping. To summarize, these critics postulated that the powers of notables had been gradually eroded since the early days of colonialism, to the detriment of the Cochin Chinese way of life.[42] Arguing that it had been an error to strip notables of their judicial functions, these sources recommended "restoring to notables the authority and the prestige which they once enjoyed."[43] Under Vichy, the need for rural reform in Cochin China came to be considered all the more pressing, because the November 1940 uprisings were imputed in part to the diminishing prestige of conservative, pro-French village patriarchs. In consultation with conservative Cochin Chinese dignitaries such as Tran Van Kha, Jean Decoux accordingly set out to curb the supposed "desertion of the countryside,"[44] now presented as endemic in Cochin China. In order to ensure that "the peasant love his village," Decoux, in keeping with earlier proposals, set about "revalorizing the status of notables."[45] In substance, Decoux's administration reduced the number of administrators in Cochin Chinese villages, thereby vastly increasing the powers of individual town magnates. In a note on this almost seigniorial reform, a French administrator concluded: "[T]hus rejuvenated and reinforced, local government—a daughter of tradition—will continue to run to the satisfaction of Cochin Chinese peasants."[46]

Much more was at work here than a simple administrative overhaul, or infusion of quaint folklore into local government. In its report on communal institutions, the Conseil Fédéral Indochinois noted in July 1942:

> In Cochin China the status of the heads of *cantons* has been profoundly modified. The basic principle behind the reform is the replacement of elections with appointments. The French administration is thereby returning to the regime once in place under the mandarins, under whom village notables met in groups of two or three per village to examine the titles of candidates and to propose to

the competent authority the nomination of a single person. This very simple system is in keeping with tradition, and offers the advantage of reinvesting the local leaders and the Governor General with their [respective] rights; it is therefore inspired by the same principles that underlay the *Etat Français* [that is, the Vichy regime].[47]

This passage seems especially telling, for it plainly advocates authoritarianism over even rubber-stamp elections, and further invokes a distant past, reinvented so that Governor Decoux could sit in the throne of Viet emperors. In this manner Vichy nostalgism served both to introduce unabashed authoritarianism and to invest the colonizer with former imperial powers.

Vichy officials undertook very similar steps in Tonkin. There, by virtue of reforms dating from the 1920s, communal councils had been popularly elected, albeit by a very restricted all-male electorate. Although this system could in no way be termed democratic—even by colonial standards—Vichy would first revile, then eliminate it altogether. A certain Le Dinh Chan justified this 1941 abrogation by affirming that "elections—the basis of power in Western democracies—are not an article which can be imported [to Indochina]."[48] A French journalist echoed these sentiments, asserting that "[Vichy's abrogation of elections] answers the desires of an essentially conformist people, accustomed to a patriarchal regime, which has lasted thousands of years, and has proven most efficient."[49] Nowhere was the allegation clearer that the republic had erred in even its most timid efforts at liberalization. Nowhere was the essentialist argument as strongly advanced that Indochina should be run as it had been before it was "tainted" by Westernization.

Tonkin reforms were further presented as directly in step with National Revolutionary ideology. By "replacing a regime of elections for a system of official nominations" and "concentrating all government functions in the hands of a few"[50]—as was also done in Cochin China—Vichy officials manifestly intended to emulate Pétain's curtailing of representative government in the metropole. Although in Indochina there was plainly much less of a democracy to trample in the first place, Vichyites nonetheless vented their bile upon any institutions that even hinted at republicanism. They condemned the "gossipy chimera of democracy,"[51] which one would be hard pressed to discern in pre-1940 Indochina. It was in this spirit that the journalist Le Dinh Chan quoted Pétain ad nauseam, in particular the marshal's assertion that the future social hierarchy "will no longer rest on the false idea of natural equality." Le Dinh Chan further expressed the hope that in both the metropole and Indochina, "true elites will be reborn."[52]

[margin note: similar al in i out place even though never had direct democracy]

A Modern or Traditionalist Indochina?

While the main thrust of Vichy rule in Indochina went in the direction of authoritarian elitism and traditionalism, some Vichy officials nonetheless conceded the potential significance of modernization and of nonelites in a future Indochina. In reality, ambivalence toward modernization constituted nothing new for Vichy: as Robert Paxton and Richard Kuisel have shown, Pétainist discourse and praxes were very much double edged, insofar as they were at once profoundly nostalgic and forward looking.[53] Nor were "utopian" schemes for workers and farmers of the future entirely foreign to Vichy.

It is in this sense that one should understand a 1944 Vichy Indochinese blueprint drafted by Decoux's political bureau, outlining the social and cultural programs needed to accompany a foreseen rapid growth of industrialization. The authors of this report manifestly turned their backs on earlier conceptions of an artisanal and rural National Revolutionary Indochina. Acknowledging that Indochina was in dire need of an industrial as well as a "National" Revolution (especially now that commercial ties had been practically severed with France), they endeavored to ensure that such a momentous transformation would not uproot Indochinese cultures. Specifically, one major concern emerged from this source, namely that "[t]he common spectacle in other colonies, of workers surrendering to alcohol, living in shacks, and reduced to a deplorable physical state must be avoided at all costs in Indochinese factories."[54] Vichy's social engineers consequently advocated the creation of "pleasant worker cities ... responding to normal conditions of salubrity, where each family will have its own home."[55] The prime regulator of these industrial paradises of the future would be Indochinese elites, who were to exert a positive "cultural action" upon displaced laborers. If this "great social project"[56] did not correspond to most of Vichy's traditionalist themes, it did conform to the Pétainist topoi of the cult of the family and of physical, social, and cultural "hygiene." In many ways, it mirrored at once late-nineteenth-century Benthamian models of social control, and new Italian fascist and Nazi plans for "worker cities."

Federal Indochina

Hand in hand with modernist, reactionary, and oligarchic utopianism, Vichy officials promoted a new federalist mapping of Indochina itself. Federalism, it should be stressed, was very much a misnomer for Decoux's Indochina. What to us might evoke notions of an alliance among equal partners signified something quite different to authoritarian colonial officials, borrowing their language from Vichy. In his memoirs, the Vichy minister of the interior, Marcel Peyrouton, provides a useful definition of Vichy's brand of "federalism":

> [T]he fathers of the National Revolution ... were federalists. They thought of retooling France by creating representative assemblies, elected and representing newly revived old French provinces, sorts of local *parlements*. ... It was not so much a matter of reviving dead [democratic] institutions, but rather of retaining their essence and transforming them. ... By dividing France into provinces [rather than the *départements* of 1789], the federalist doctrines of the National Revolution sought only to obey geographical and moral realities, and to consolidate them, by allowing these natural units—provinces—a means of being heard.[57]

In other words, in mainland France, federalism involved replacing republican *départements* by royalist provinces, and rekindling a regionalism reminiscent of the *parlements* of *ancien régime* France.

In Indochina, Vichy officials would transpose the notion of "province" to the five *pays* of the federation, namely Tonkin, Annam, Cochin China, Laos, and Cambodia. Decoux instated a policy of fostering carefully channeled local nationalisms, becoming in fact the first governor to employ the word "Vietnam." At the same time as championing local patriotisms, however, Decoux also "tried to create a 'real' and 'living' Indochinese identity," to quote an expert on spatial definitions of Indochina.[58]

Locally, federalism became the catchword for Vichy's new "idyllic" Indochina. Pétainists utilized this term, evocative of an ordered relationship among many equal or at least representative parties, to designate something quite different. Decoux's federalism would indeed be ordered, but also hierarchical, explicitly antidemocratic, and inegalitarian. It would, above all, designate an abstract union of various Indochinese identities under the protective and fundamentally antiassimilationist umbrella of Vichy France. Finally, as Philippe Devillers has remarked, the new "federalism" was part and parcel of a "mythical Indochina" invented by the French largely to counter the themes of Japanese pan-Asian propaganda.[59]

The concomitant endorsement of "federal" pan-Indochinese, and local allegiances, be they Laotian, Cambodian, or Vietnamese, fell in line perfectly with the plurality of National Revolutionary identity construction. The review *Indochine, hebdomadaire illustré* was quick to point out, for instance, that "ever since taking power, the Marshal specified that families, *communes,* crafts and provinces were to be the pillars of the new Constitution."[60] Along these same lines Decoux exhorted the Indochinese to demonstrate a visceral attachment to their villages, *communes,* and *pays*—much as Pétain was doing in the metropole—but also toward a new diverse and "authentic" pan-Indochinese union. In short, Decoux transposed Vichyite typologies to the Far East. Local identification with the soil, village, *commune,* and province was retained, while the marshal's plea for a united empire was simply transferred to an Indochinese register, under the umbrella term of "federalism." The official press defined Vichy's brand of federalism as follows:

> We needed a doctrine: the Admiral has elaborated one in keeping with National Revolutionary principles and has summarized it in one word: federalism. … Federalism does not signify a precarious association … of intolerant, suspicious and petty nationalisms; nor does it cover a nefarious desire for uniformity and assimilation. It signifies at once unity and diversity: unity of all the countries of Indochina under the mantle of the federator, France—at once the generous and indispensable common denominator—respecting local cultural diversity.[61]

In this way, federalism was articulated as an offshoot of the National Revolution, in direct opposition to assimilation. However, it did manifestly stand, in many ways, as a traditionalist precept akin to Lyauteyian associationism. In this way, Vichy officials in Indochina found in the respect, and indeed the promotion of difference under a federalist umbrella, a highly original application of Pétainist ideology in Southeast Asia.

Concretely, a number of ventures contributed to making federalism a reality. Some, like the *Tour d'Indochine* bicycle race, or the new Indochinese councils, warrant separate treatment. Suffice it to emphasize here that federalism was conceived as a system somewhat similar to the more recent EEC, insofar as it was intended to act upon and to bolster the region, as its primary cell.

Government agencies actively propagated the image of an Indochinese Federation composed of many strong and unique parts. At the exhibit *L'Indochine dans le passé,* on display in Hanoi in 1941, the new regime showcased its dual glorification of Annam and Tonkin as regions, and Indochina as federation. The very objectives of this "state of the art exhibit" are revealing of Vichy's cultural project in Indochina. According to its organizer, Paul Boudet:

> The merit of this exposition goes to Admiral Jean Decoux who intends for the past to have its place beside the present. … Two ideas emerge from this un-

precedented exhibit. First, the power of expansion of the Annamite people. Second, the fruitful collaboration of France and Indochinese Annam, Cambodia and Laos in maintaining the equilibrium between disparate peoples, both internally, and before outsiders.[62]

Here, Decoux's cultural team—which as one observer has remarked, carried greater weight and disposed of more resources than Ho Chi Minh's at this time[63]—articulated a vision of the Indochinese past in accordance with the doctrine of ethnic pluralism and with Vichy's folkloric nostalgia, while at the same time shoring up notions of Indochinese uniqueness in the face of Japanese "outsiders" (this as an "antidote" to Japanese pan-Asianism). So important was this exhibit in expressing a vision of Annam's and Tonkin's past that one Vietnamese observer suggested it be employed as a model for future national history textbooks, which would "purge us from the virus of denigration which poisons and blinds us."[64] To the colonizers, meanwhile, ancient Vietnam was fascinating insofar as it represented a distant "great civilization." As Edward Said has argued, in the colonial imagination the glorious "indigenous past" was constantly contrasted with alleged "modern-day decadence."[65]

While the Hanoi exhibit quite logically constructed a narrative of Annamite/Tonkinois history, actually depicting the birth of Vietnam, other sources drew up a Vichy teleology of Cambodian and Laotian history. A 1944 textbook, intended for French children in Indochina, recounted how the "Khmer kingdom once shone brightly," while stipulating, however, that before the French invasion "the Indochinese peoples quarreled endlessly."[66] This last point constituted in effect the key to Vichy's federalism: France, it was now argued, stood not as conqueror, assimilator, or even protector (a difficult claim, given the Japanese presence), but as arbiter, providing a supposedly indispensable cement for the Indochinese edifice.

Federalism amounted to far more than a redefining of France's role in Indochina, however. As already observed, the review *Indochine, hebdomadaire illustré* presented the new doctrine as nothing short of a new colonial philosophy, destined to replace assimilation and association as a framework for imperialism. To be sure, in reality neither undiluted assimilationism nor associationism had ever been practiced extensively in Indochina. Nevertheless, 1940 spelled an important turning point, insofar as it marked a clear break with colonial doctrines of the past. During France's debacle in early June 1940, René Caty, a French headmaster in Indochina, already sketched the outlines of what would become Vichy's colonial ethos. He observed in his private journal:

The French believe themselves entrusted with a so-called civilizing mission. They want to make the natives in their own image. ... They are satisfied only when the natives become caricatures of the French. They forget one important thing: the essence, the genius of the race, is not the same. ... [Our] civilization does not necessarily—if ever—suit other races which possess their own bases, needs and aspirations. ... Our supreme error has been to believe that these people who mimic us awkwardly ... are exactly the same as us. We must simply remember that they are different, and will remain so no matter what.[67]

This pre-Vichy text shows a propensity for French elites in Vietnam eventually to sanction Decoux's repudiation of assimilation. Caty defined what would become Decoux's overriding principle: under the guise of respecting "otherness," Indochinese peoples were to be rerooted in their cultures and "races," and in fact increasingly segregated, under the aegis of a traditionalist regime capable of conjuring up a folkloric past. In this light, federalism became synonymous with fanciful re-creations of Indochinese cultures.

Rejecting Assimilation

As in most colonies that remained loyal to Vichy, assimilation was openly rejected by colonial administrators in Indochina from 1940 to 1944. This repudiation is perhaps best illustrated by judicial decisions over both name changes and naturalizations. Whereas prior to 1940 it had been possible, albeit rare, for Vietnamese to adopt European names, and difficult for the contrary to occur, Vichy eliminated the former of these two options. While "natives" could no longer "impersonate" whites, however, Eurasians were permitted to modify their names, and hence their identities—but in the direction of "Vietnamization" only.[68] Thus under Vichy, a certain Félix Paul Hauser was at last granted his wish, first expressed in 1934, to change his name to Hoang Huu Phuong.[69]

On a more general basis, Decoux's administration set about determining the precise status of Asians before the law. Successive pieces of legislation passed in February 1942, and March and July 1943, defined an Asian nearly as restrictively as Pétain and Laval had defined a Jew: "any functionary who cannot trace his ancestry to two European grandparents is to be considered Asian."[70] No doubt inspired by models of affidavits arriving from Vichy, asking all administrators to pledge their non-Jewishness and their disassociation from "secret societies," in September 1943, Decoux conceived a form to be filled out by all new functionaries in Indochina, asking them for racial identification. The form, dated September 14, 1943, ran as follows:

> I the undersigned, X, candidate for the position of X, having read the decrees of March 16 and July 22, 1943, declare under my oath of sermon [to the marshal]:
>   1) being of French nationality, but of Asian origin
>   2) being an Indochinese subject …
>   3) being of French citizenship and European origin, having at least two grandparents of European origin.
>   My grandparents are, on the paternal side, Mr. X, of European, Eurasian or Asian background (circle the appropriate category), Mrs. X of European, Eurasian or Asian background. … [same for the maternal side][71]

This declaration broke with traditional understandings of citizenship as theoretically colorblind, rendering race the sole measure of status. Though this had of course been an integral part—if not the cornerstone—of the colonial modus operandi long before Vichy, the ideal of citizenship had nonetheless been hitherto formally disassociated from race in official correspondence. In Decoux's new typology, race superseded citizenship.

Officially at least, the rationale behind this campaign involved harmonizing European and Asian salaries. But even the most credulous observer must have conceded that this purpose was at odds with a vast survey on racial origins. To be fair, Decoux did attempt to bridge the tremendous gap between Asian and European salaries. However, Asians were still prevented from collecting the "colonial stipend" and a number of sizable bonuses.[72] As for Eurasians, whose identity had heretofore been hazy, they were clearly assigned a new status: Asian if descending from fewer than two European grandparents, and European if such a white lineage could be verified "with tangible evidence."[73]

These two examples reflect a fundamental shift away from pre-Vichy French approaches to Eurasians, who had long served as the litmus test for perceptions of "Frenchness" and "otherness." Indeed, the métis question had, in the words of the anthropologist Ann Stoler, "produced a discourse in which facile theories of racial hierarchy were rejected."[74] Nonetheless, Stoler argues, "the fear that métis might revert to their natural inclinations persisted … [in the 1930s]."[75] From 1940 to 1944, Eurasians were thus assigned the status of "Indochinese" or "European," under a regime that championed, rather than questioned, "facile theories of racial hierarchy."

Finally, under Vichy the number of French naturalizations of Indochinese "subjects" dropped significantly. Between 1940 and 1942, Decoux's administration conformed to instructions sent from Vichy that stipulated that "all requests for naturalizations should now be suspended,"[76] with only a handful of exceptions. These exceptions, moreover, involved mostly members of the French Foreign Legion and French women who had previously lost their citizenship by marrying foreigners. The Indochinese, in other words, did not enter into the equation at this juncture, for their naturalization would have run contrary to Vichy ideology on several scores. Only around 1943 were naturalization requests from Indochinese again considered. In all, during the entire Vichy era (1940–44), only twenty-nine naturalizations of Indochinese people took place.[77] While naturalizations tapered off, a new tendency emerged—that of stripping French citizenship from "natives." In fact, the file labeled "naturalizations" in the archives of Hanoi's governor general's office (still on location) contains only *denaturalizations* for the Vichy era.[78] This dossier follows in some detail the fate of two Vietnamese notables, Duong Van Giao and Phan Van Thiet, who saw their French citizenship removed in 1942–43 in accordance with the same law of April 17, 1942, used to denaturalize the Malagasy nationalist leader Jules Ranaivo.[79]

Duong Van Giao's professional trajectory before 1940 had been typical of that of many other French-educated indigenous elites, once considered valuable allies by the French. He had served in the First World War, had obtained a doctorate in law in Paris, and had taught at the Parisian school of Oriental languages. It was in the 1930s that his relationship with the French began to sour, at least according to Vichy jurists. Under the Popular Front, he had written for the leftist newspaper *La Lutte*, so despised by Decoux's regime. He also apparently had dealings with the Caodaïst religion, which Vichy soon suspected of Japanese sympathies. Finally, he was said to have participated in the creation of the Unified Revolutionary Party of the Annamite People, an allegation that almost single-handedly contributed to his denaturalization on the grounds of "anti-French activities."[80] The lesson to be drawn from Duong Van Giao's case, though, involves not so much his disillusionment with the French—assuredly not uncommon—but rather the fact that a member of the learned elite, a fellow lawyer in fact, had seen his citizenship removed by a French colonial court and had been unceremoniously relegated to the rank of "native." To add injury to insult, in spite of unspecified "attenuating circumstances," Duong van Giao, at age fifty-three, was sentenced to eight years of forced labor without parole.[81] Clearly, Vichy had repudiated the republican effort to woo the "Westernized" intelligentsia, turning instead to Vietnamese mandarins and conservatives as allies.

Nevertheless, it would be a grave error to suggest that assimilationist discourse disappeared altogether with the advent of Vichy. It seems important to point out, for example, that Vichy attempted in vain to "romanize" Cambodian (though this decision might be attributed also to a desire to distance Khmer script from Thai alphabetically, thereby reaffirming Indochinese "oneness" and fending off Thai designs). Jean Decoux clearly labored over this decision, acutely conscious that it ran contrary to antiassimilationist currents which underlay his regime. In justifying his December 1, 1943, decree making romanized Cambodian obligatory in "all administrative branches of the Kingdom," Decoux reasoned:

> If traditional Cambodian script is indeed part of the national heritage, and must remain a medium of sacred and ancient literature, if it must obviously continue to be taught in schools, it did seem necessary in the name of progress to institute a simpler, clearer and faster alphabet, which is more easily adapted to typing.[82]

Despite clear reservations, in this instance Decoux followed the main thrust of the French assimilating impulse. Where the Jesuit missionary Alexandre de Rhodes had long ago introduced the Western alphabet to what is now modern-day Vietnam, it was Decoux who sought to extend it to Cambodia. He did so at tremendous cost, for the romanization affair sparked a serious opposition movement. Buddhist priests steadfastly refused to utilize Western script, and by July 1942 Decoux's representative was confronted by thousands of protesters in Phnom-Penh.[83] As usual, Decoux's short-term solution was repression. But the lesson he no doubt drew was to embrace and steer individual nationalism rather than obstruct it.

In spite of this retention of some facets of assimilationist doctrines, Decoux evidently sought to steer a new course, described as a third path between assimilation and association (much as the National Revolution itself was presented as a third way between Communism and fascism). From 1940 to 1944, it was federalism that was depicted as the culmination of French colonialism. It promised deeper reforms than even its associationist precursor. According to the Vichy-endorsed newspaper *l'Echo annamite*:

> Association marked a real progress compared with assimilation, but it unfortunately had a tendency to stress the economic side of colonialism. A moral and intellectual element was lacking—that element has made our colonial action today a true collaboration between colonizers and colonized. France's true indigenous policy, that which we claim as characterizing the French colonial genius, is collaboration. ... The recent creation of the Federal Council of Indochina marks the triumph of this philosophy.[84]

Here, the colonizers, all too aware that they had themselves become colonized in Europe, employed the protean word "collaboration" to denote what they considered a radically new colonial paradigm. Collaboration and federalism became catchwords for a doctrine that sought to infuse association with essentialism, rather than content itself with employing it for economic *mise en valeur*—as had allegedly been the case in the 1930s. This new brand of imperialism would seek to erase the innumerable errors now imputed to republican colonialism. At the forefront of these were the handful of meager, yet highly publicized and controversial, reforms taken in the direction of liberalization immediately before Vichy.

Federalism and Indochinese Assemblies

In keeping with both National Revolutionary and federalist precepts, Indochina's mostly rubber-stamp representative bodies were abolished in 1940, only to be replaced in 1943–44 by a federalist and corporatist assembly of notables. In this arena, the admittedly parochial observations of a Communist scholar seem to have hit the mark:

> Admiral Decoux, appointed Governor-general of Indochina by the Vichy Government, carried out a double-faced policy of dictatorship and demagogy. At the end of 1940, the few councils which had been set up to give the colonial regime a semblance of democracy were dismissed and all powers fell into the hands of the Governor-general.[85]

Abolishing pre-existing representative bodies—regardless of their actual representativeness—became paramount to a regime bent on destroying what came before it and convinced moreover of the global ascendancy of "enlightened" authoritarianism over democracy. Thus, when discussing the creation of new councils, Vichy ideologues reasoned:

> It seemed that the principles on which older assemblies were created were no longer in keeping with the evolution of metropolitan politics, and though it was necessary to consult the more enlightened portion of the Indochinese population, it was clearly impossible to return to an antiquated [political] system. Such was the idea underlying the project ... of endowing the Indochinese federation with new councils at once more in keeping with the spirit of the National Revolution, and adapted to an increasingly federal Indochina.[86]

This mission statement for Indochina's Vichy assemblies betrays an inherently elitist attempt to govern in cooperation with a tiny Indochinese constituency—that of the conservative elites, deemed "enlightened" for their anti-Communist and traditional leanings.

When placed in context, the November 8, 1940, Pétain-endorsed dissolution of all Indochinese assemblies, including the important Grand conseil des intérêts économiques et financiers de l'Indochine and the Conseil Colonial de Cochinchine, appears all the more significant in light of recent pre-Vichy bids to democratize and bolster Indochinese assemblies.[87] As recently as April 1940, Governor Catroux had taken an albeit largely symbolic step in the direction of representative government in Cambodia. American consular authorities, at least, seemed convinced of the magnitude of this reform, when they reported to the State Department:

> [A new law,] dated April 19, 1940, … transforms the Native Consultative Assembly in Cambodia into a Chamber of People's Representatives. This change increases the participation of the natives in their government, and in some quarters is attributed to the generally progressive policy of the former Minister for the Colonies in Paris, Georges Mandel.[88]

This was by no means an isolated case of pre-Vichy wartime liberalization. Catroux had issued another decree on May 10, 1940, increasing the number of "indigenous councilors" in the municipal assemblies of Saigon, Hanoi, and Haiphong.[89] In an act indicative of his own Vichyite sensibilities, but also in keeping with Pétain's November 8 law, Decoux rescinded both of these reforms. In fact, a decree dated April 27, 1941, further stipulated that "the municipal councils of Saigon, Hanoi and Haiphong will no longer be elected, but instead will be appointed by the Governor general."[90] The repealing of even the most modest pre-Vichy liberalizing measures was emblematic of Pétainist authoritarianism, both in the metropole and overseas.

Equally revealing of Decoux's political outlook were the substitute assemblies he conceived. Decoux established two new bodies in "accordance with National Revolutionary principles."[91] The first, the Conseil fédéral indochinois, founded in June 1941, was intended to promote pan-Indochinese federalism. It was by design hierarchical, corporatist, and explicitly undemocratic, reserved exclusively to "Indochinese notables, designated by the Governor-general."[92] Its numbers read like a roll-call of potentially pro-Vichy traditional elites. Their ranks included the Southern Vietnamese Truong Vinh Tong, hailed by Vichy's press as "one of the last representatives of a phalanx of lettered men who maintain the cult of traditional writing in its most polished form."[93] Truong Vinh Tong was, moreover, in the words of this same source, "the son of the famous scholar, and great friend of France, Pétrus Truong Vinh Ky."[94] Nguyen Van Huyen, a federal councilor representing Tonkin, also seemed the very prototype of the elite courted by Decoux. A scholar specializing in such anthropological and folkloric questions as "traditional songs for boys and girls in Annam," "marriage in the populations of High-Tonkin," "the Pha-dong celebrations," and "popular imagery in Indochina," Nguyen Van Huyen appeared a proponent of the cultural revival championed by Decoux.[95] Overall, though, this assembly seemed most geared toward gratifying its honorary members. It wielded in reality only ceremonial power, as its consultation in all matters was by definition "never mandatory."[96]

Reliable Vietnamese reactions to institutional and federal reforms are difficult to recover from archival or press records—as Decoux authorized only laudatory press articles on this topic, as on any other. However, an intercepted message from a Communist guerrilla to the Japanese authorities in November 1943 provides a rare, though uncorroborated, glimpse at public responses to the Conseil Fédéral Indochinois. According to this source, "the Conseil Fédéral Indochinois formally endorsed by the Vichy government is but another delusion for the Indochinese people ... giving them the impression of ... [political] participation." Most interestingly, this source perceived the Conseil as part of a new system of "small autonomous states" promoted by Vichy so as to subvert Vietnamese nationalism.[97] In this sense, the impotence of new federal institutions, and their purpose of dividing and conquering, clearly did not escape the attention of Vietnamese contemporaries.

While Decoux's first creation was reserved for the Indochinese, his second—which, either as a way of stressing the "federal" or in a staggering lack of imagination, was given exactly the same title—was, conversely, composed of both European and Indochinese elements. Established in 1943, the Conseil fédéral indochinois II was designed to replace the Grand conseil des intérêts économiques et financiers de l'Indochine, itself abolished in November 1940. It presented two important distinctions from its predecessor. Members of the new body were to be designated rather than elected by limited suffrage, and its majority would be Indochinese, rather than French. This reflected Decoux's will to appeal to Indochinese notables, while simultaneously eradicating all markers of representiveness or republicanism. Interestingly, Henri Bléhaut, secretary of state to the colonies since late March 1943, had expressed initial concern that Decoux's Conseil fédéral indochinois II would do more harm than good, by underscoring Vichy's distrust of popular suffrage. On April 29, 1943, Bléhaut had asked Decoux:

> I would, however, like to have your assurance that this reform will be well received by local opinion. Specifically, I am concerned that the French and Indochinese will see in the suppression of an elected body ... a distinct regression of their rights, insofar as the new assembly is to be ... purely consultative and appointed.[98]

On May 9, 1943, the governor of Indochina responded to this reproving remark:

> No doubt on the French side, some beneficiaries of the old regime will regret seeing their opportunities for democratic machinations disappear. But the wholesome element ... will accept with satisfaction a reform marking the government's desire to apply to Indochina the principles used to restore our *Patrie*. ... None of those who recognize the dangers of elections ... can interpret this reform as a regression. [On the Indochinese side,] the evolved Indochinese element, in other words the key to indigenous opinion, has embraced wholeheartedly the principles of the National Revolution, and never had any delusions about the powers of former assemblies in the first place. However, they do lend considerable importance to the numerical proportion of representation. ... The new system will allow them to gain satisfactions that the previous regime denied them through quotas, which guaranteed a French majority.[99]

Decoux's direct challenge to his superior is revealing indeed. At one level, it betrays the governor of Indochina's hard line on issues such as antirepublicanism. Here Decoux took it upon himself to remind Bléhaut that Vichy was antidemocratic. In this instance, as in so many others, a metropolitan Vichy minister like Bléhaut appeared more prepared to compromise on Pétainist orthodoxy—in the name of placating public opinion in colonies at risk—than did intransigent colonial governors. At another level, the governor of Indochina seemed paradoxically to express his objectives entirely in terms of the responses of Indochinese elites. One can only conclude that while Decoux was intractably opposed to elections and fiercely loyal to Maurassian philosophy and to the ideals of the National Revolution, he was, ironically, prepared to satisfy Indochinese elite desires for a greater slice of this undemocratic pie.

Steering Public Opinion

Decoux's assertion that Indochinese elites represented the key to public opinion raises a number of separate issues. Perceptions of public opinion shaped much more than Decoux's visions of Vichyite assemblies; they seem to have constituted a general and perennial obsession of his authoritarian regime. Most important, Decoux was preoccupied by a host of foreign and internal propaganda threats, ranging from Japanese to Allied, Communist, Caodaïst, and Siamese sources. As a result of this constant apprehension, Vichy administrators journeyed to some of the remotest corners of Indochina to spread the gospel of Pétainism. In rural Cambodia in the spring of 1942, for instance, a touring *chef de province,* or low-ranking French official, proclaimed before local notables and Indochinese functionaries:

> [C]ompare what we have gained by listening to and following the Marshal, with what we would have lost by listening to dissidents. To each his own task, questions will be better handled thus. A wood worker would never consider criticizing a surgeon, but ordinary people still tend to think that they have the right to second guess diplomats and policy-makers.[100]

In a Cambodia that was exposed to the triple influence of Thai, Japanese, and Gaullist propaganda (the latter through the airwaves of Radio New Delhi), Vichy authorities resorted to an elitist and paternalist discourse with which to steer popular opinion. This discourse was novel only insofar as it called for total and unquestioning allegiance to a specific French regime, rather than to a colonizer per se.

The effectiveness of such ventures is naturally difficult to determine with any precision. Nevertheless, if one is to believe a June 1941 Gaullist secret report on propaganda, it would seem that Allied anti-Vichy propaganda was very much on the defensive in wartime Indochina. This source commented:

> Liberty, Equality, Fraternity, Democracy, Parliament, Elections, Unions and all that can be considered "international" have become dirty words, and no longer interest anyone in Indochina. Even if we were right a thousand times over on such issues, it would be totally inopportune to raise these matters now.[101]

Throughout much of the war, Vichy consequently succeeded in curtailing any potential Free French pledges—however empty—of future liberalization. Decoux was in effect left to win the battle of indoctrination over "indigenous policies."

This is in no way to suggest, however, that Decoux was without detractors. His industrious postal censorship bureau—merely one branch of an elaborate and efficient intelligence apparatus—kept him abreast of even the slightest murmurs of discontent with Pétainism. By way of example, an intercepted April 1941 letter from Bui Lang Chien in Saigon to a certain Mi Van To revealed concerns that Pétain had come to consider Indochina as a secondary colony. The author of this missive noted: "The Marshal declared over the radio that North Africa will have a place in the future National Council. Indochina was never even mentioned. I intend to write a grievance to the Governor-general about this matter."[102] Nor was this the only reproach that would unwittingly reach Decoux before it was intended. This same Bui Lang Chien remarked:

> Some are claiming that Vichy is contemplating ... abandoning Asia so as to retain Africa. ... As proof, they point to the [Vichy] decision to [resurrect] plans for the Tran-Saharan railroad, while Indochina is to benefit from no significant grand project, either for the present or the future.[103]

Vichy's governor of Indochina, benefiting from the knowledge of such desiderata even before they were publicly voiced, responded swiftly to allegations that the marshal—whom he had elevated to the status of chief sovereign of a federal Indochina—might be neglecting his subjects. Decoux therefore lent satisfaction to specific grievances of this nature, a task rendered all the easier as it essentially involved purely symbolic recognition of the vested interests of Indochinese notables. In November 1941, Decoux consequently recommended to his superiors at Vichy that Indochina be represented by no fewer than five members at the projected empirewide Conseil Colonial. The Tonkinois and Annamite appointees to this purely consultative organism were Nguyen De, a "pioneer in the development of Franco-Annamite collaboration," and Pham Duy Khiem, a twenty-two-year-old veteran and an "emerging notable." Tran Van Don, another veteran of the 1939–40 campaign, and Var Kam, an "indigenous leader," were to be "deputies" for Cochin China and Cambodia, respectively.[104] It seems noteworthy that in this case Decoux turned not to elder leaders and established mandarins, but to younger "emerging notables."

Of course, one can question the representativeness and validity of various records emanating from what are essentially espionage files. At times it would seem that Decoux's information specialists read good omens into plainly bad news. Scanning over a series of intercepted personal letters from 1943, complaining about the inadequacy of civil servant salaries, and the high cost of living, Vichy officials underlined the surprising desirability of the resulting message. The lesson drawn by one corespondent, a certain Mrs. Ai, living in Hué, was: "[if you wish to earn a living], then return to the soil, or turn to commerce."[105] Another corespondent, Ho Van Tieng, living in Cantho, Cochin China, reported home to his wife: "I now intend to leave the administration in order to take up a trade or to cultivate the land, or to do anything else that might earn money. How can one make money by being an administrator?"[106] To officials at Vichy's postal censorship offices in Hanoi, these signals seemed to confirm the effectiveness of Pétainist ideology; the return to the soil, and the return to traditional crafts, were, after all, what Decoux preached on a daily basis. The more ominous message, that of despair and mounting hostility to the French, seems to have been somehow lost in the euphoria of a chimerical National Revolutionary success.

Still, there can be little doubt that Vichy officials saw themselves waging a battle for the "loyalty" of the Indochinese. One case in particular illustrates the struggle for influence between the Vichy French and the Japanese occupiers. By all accounts in his dossier, Tran Trong Dai had been a model young employee, serving from 1938 to 1942 as a typist for the French Military Cabinet in Indochina. On two occasions, in fact, his superiors had recommended, and obtained, salary increases for the twenty-year-old, noting in his file that he was a stellar employee.[107] Nothing seemed to augur the fact that in the summer of 1942, Tran Trong Dai would abruptly defect to the Japanese side, taking up employment with the Japanese police.[108] This defection was received as a slap in the face by the French Military Cabinet, not just because its security had been compromised by a typist who had gained valuable information but also because of the accompanying realization that even model and seemingly loyal indigenous employees could be potentially "anti-French." This last lesson was clearly expressed in a note from July 23, 1942, requesting a "female European typist to replace Tran Trong Dai, fired from his position." Such an appointment was deemed "indispensable in order to maintain secrecy in matters of national defense."[109] Incidents such as this one, so common under any occupation, clearly took their toll on French morale. If Europeans need be hired even for menial administrative tasks—once "reserved" to the Indochinese—then perhaps the war for influence against Japan was being lost. In this sense, Decoux may have realized, the best hopes for maintaining Vichy French power over Indochina lay in battling Japan for the loyalty of Indochinese youth.

A Regenerated Indochina: Vichy Youth and Sports Movements

To Decoux, Vichy's traditionalist and utopian projects for a future Indochina—be they federalist, essentialist, or hierarchical—all hinged precisely upon the condition of winning over Indochinese youth, perceived as the key to any future National Revolutionary enterprise in Indochina. The very elite courted by Decoux was consequently young. He declared before a graduating class of boys at the Lycée Pétrus Ky in Saigon in July 1941:

> Tomorrow's Indochina will require much work, and to accomplish it we will call upon all of the elites of this country. ... These elites will have the fascinating mission of constructing the future. You must, my dear children, through your work, your will and your discipline, show yourselves worthy of figuring among this phalanx of young men of good will.[110]

Vichy's governor of Indochina, then, elaborated a vision of a Pétainist Indochina in which Vichy-trained young leaders would play a fundamental role.

Nowhere are the pervasiveness and intended longevity of Vichy's reforms, or Vichy's ideal of a regimented and authoritarian future Indochina, as clearly illustrated as in Decoux's sports and youth directives.[111] Assisted by Vichy's high commander to youth and sports in Indochina, naval captain Maurice Ducoroy, Decoux drew up blueprints for a new Indochina, in line with Pétainist notions of physical education and social control. In fact, archival sources reveal, Decoux became convinced that Vichy's actions in the field of youth and sports could actually contribute to the construction of an Indochinese *Übermensch*. He observed in 1943:

> It is an important consequence of the rebirth of sports [under Vichy], that ... physical education has not only improved the race, but actually transfigured it. As a result, a new type of man is being born, or should I say, the true type of Indochinese man is being reborn, after centuries of indifference to physical development. [This new type] is at once fine and highly muscular, endowed with a straight and direct gaze, and contrasts strongly with the sickly young man of the past, who cared only for intellectual speculations, despising all other activities.[112]

This transposal to Indochina of Vichy's ideal of a "regenerated Frenchman"—at once male, a leader, young, vigorous, and "racially pure"—captures the main tenets of the National Revolution under Decoux. In adapting Pétainism to Southeast Asia, Vichy officials claimed to resurrect (and in reality, strove to create) an essentialist and long-lost Indochinese identity and "race." Thanks to a Pétainist regimen, this new authentic Indochinese superman would supposedly shed his unnatural, Europeanized, and intellectualized shell, to re-emerge as a model of physical strength, vigor, and untainted "authenticity."

To present such projects as having been entirely Vichy-generated, or as merely passively accepted by the thousands of Indochinese who underwent Vichy physical education and leadership training, would be to strip the colonized of any agency in this matter. In reality, Decoux may not have been far off the mark when he spoke of a Vietnamese fascination with his program of physical and moral regeneration. Not only did an estimated six hundred thousand Indochinese[113] participate in Vichy's training, or elite camps, sporting leagues, or youth movements, but some elements of Vietnamese and Cambodian societies in particular seem to have shared Vichy's desire to "vivify and resurrect Indochina" through methodical regimentation. While Vietnamese social conservatives had no qualms in upholding Confucianism as a precursor to Pétainism, they clearly rejected what one historian has termed "the Neo-Confucian model of pallid, frail students cloistered for years over classical texts."[114] In 1943, a cartoonist captured the irony of notables who had previously shared such Neo-Confucian ideals suddenly espousing Vichy's model of reinvigoration through sports. Some Vietnamese pedagogical experts proved to be enthusiastic crusaders for a regimented Vietnam. Pham Xuan Do, a local notable (Kiêm-Hoc, or educational inspector) from Sontay province, was one such specialist. He had proven invaluable to the French administration in his home province by indoctrinating local schoolteachers and students. In 1941 he had regaled them with Vichyite propaganda of his own creation, including a speech "on the life and work of Marshal Pétain" (a remarkable talk for someone who had never been to France, noted the local French official with typical condescension).[115] Convinced that this Vietnamese convert could spread the gospel of Pétain, Decoux's administration enrolled him on a tour of Indochina to deliver a series of addresses to schoolteachers and principals. In a public speech delivered at Hanoi's municipal theater in late 1942, this same Pham Xuan Do is reported to have

> cited the example of Italian and German youth leagues, which by their remarkable spirit of patriotism and their moral virtues, deserve to be imitated by young Annamites. These will be able to appreciate in future the virtues of leading a simple and rugged existence.[116]

Here Pham Xuan Do went well beyond Vichy's youth policies. Choosing to imitate instead the more successful models of those who had themselves conquered the French, he conceived of nothing short of a Vietnamese version of fascist and Nazi youth leagues.

Pham Xuan Do was not alone in seeing the potential of Vichy's cult of physical fitness. Young king Norodom Sihanouk of Cambodia, who came to the throne in part as a choice of Decoux's (the latter had bypassed Monireth, the elder son of the former king, whom most expected to take over the throne),[117] launched a youth movement called Yuvan in 1941. This youth league, closely modeled upon Vichy's *Compagnons,* organized vast rallies, while mobilizing and regimenting the youth of Indochina and decrying an idleness associated in the metropole with the *zazou* and in Cambodia with intellectuals. Like Ducoroy's vaster program, Yuvan sought to stir Cambodians from their supposedly engrained "indolence" and to "form in the people [of Cambodia] a martial soul."[118] It further exalted a "Cambodian national ideal,"[119] and was in fact designed to disseminate Khmer royal sentiments to the farthest reaches of a kingdom already partially occupied by Siam. Yuvan was thus intended to foster "a new ideal of Khmerity which would penetrate into the heart of the country, reaching remote regions where dense rain forest still imposed harsh manners."[120] Yuvan therefore acted on one level as a national unifying agent, and as a catalyst for a new "Khmerity." At another level, the spirit of Yuvan was one of "simplicity" and "ritual,"[121] and its avowed goal was to regiment Cambodian youngsters. As in the Annamite and Tonkinois youth leagues, Yuvan employed the fascist or "Olympic" salute—an outstretched right arm—and featured a new uniform, "more sober than that of scout movements."[122] King Sihanouk himself, as supreme leader of the Yuvan, donned this uniform on special occasions, such as his birthday on November 6, 1943. At another "magnificent and spectacular parade," intended as an homage to Pétain, throngs of Cambodian boys sang first the *Nokoreach,* or ode to the Cambodian king, immediately followed by the Pétainist anthem, *Maréchal, nous voilà.* Whereas under the Third Republic the French Revolutionary *Marseillaise* had always been the musical mainstay at official occasions, under Vichy a new personal eulogy to an authoritarian supreme French leader was superimposed upon the cults of local sovereigns. According to one observer, "the two songs ended up by merging into a *Sire, nous voilà,* expressing simultaneously a profound love of the new legitimate sovereign, and a desire to return to the race ... the confidence which it once lost."[123]

While some Indochinese doubtless possessed separate or even hidden agendas in their support of Ducoroy's campaigns, the French made no secret of anchoring this not so benign cult of physical and moral fitness into a Vichy framework. Decoux argued, for example, that

> the spirit which moves Indochinese youth is one which the Marshal would approve: more virility, more elevation of hearts, more rectitude of conscience, ... patriotism and a sense of belonging to a moral and political elite like the Indochinese Federation or the French Empire.[124]

The Vichyite all-male schools at Phan Thiet, east of Saigon, constituted the principal embodiments of this new spirit in Indochina. Like their distant cousin in the metropole, Vichy's École des Cadres d'Uriage, Phan Thiet schools upheld a set of "austere, almost monk-like" ideals, while preparing youngsters to be "loyal workers of the New Indochina."[125] Phan Thiet, chosen for its rural setting, so as to "steer its cadets away from temptation,"[126] featured in reality two separate schools. The first, dubbed Indochina's Physical Education School, was called ESEPIC (Ecole Supérieure d'Education Physique d'Indochine). Its three-month program conditioned youngsters to become physical education instructors themselves. It utilized the French navy's disciplining method of "natural physical education" known as *hébertisme*.[127] At ESEPIC, *hébertisme* promised nothing short of "forming men in a same mold."[128] In fact, conformity pervaded most practices at these new centers. Thanks to sketches drawn by Ducoroy in the review *Indochine, hebdomadaire illustré* in 1941,[129] *hébertiste* exercises and facilities had become commonplace throughout Indochina, thereby providing a common, and indeed identical, register of physical training. At ESEPIC, students awoke at 5:30 A.M.; they then followed physical education classes, received instructions in "sports pedagogy," anatomy, and morality.[130] The homoerotic cult of the male body represented another important theme at ESEPIC. Decoux recalls in his memoirs that students were "tanned, like gods of the stadium, and displayed large chests revealing sculpted pectorals."[131] The ESEPIC further served as something of a eugenics center. Thanks to extensive pseudo-scientific eugenic data obtained there, Ducoroy reached the astounding conclusion that Indochinese "races" were predisposed for basketball, ping-pong, and the European regional sport of pelote Basque.[132]

The seemingly fantastic idea that the Vietnamese were predisposed for a sport practiced very locally at the other end of the globe was taken quite seriously by Ducoroy's services.[133] In a bid to apply the "findings" of Phan Thiet, and to establish pelote Basque in Southeast Asia, several of its expert

European practitioners toured Indochina in 1942.[134] This was followed by the construction of fifteen pelote Basque courts, discernible by their large walls, or *frontons*. Alongside this far-fetched experiment, Ducoroy supervised the construction of hundreds of self-contained hébertiste stadiums across the federation (600 were erected across Indochina between 1940 and 1943).[135] In addition to these smaller facilities, between 1940 and 1942 some 271 new multipurpose stadiums were erected, 80 in Tonkin, 89 in Annam, 61 in Cochin China, 26 in Cambodia, and 15 in Laos. By the end of the Vichy era, the total number of new full-scale stadiums throughout Indochina reached 991 (only 120 had existed before), new swimming pools 188 (22 predated Vichy), and new obstacle courses 286 (a mere 4 dated from before 1940).[136] One can conclude without exaggeration that the sports infrastructure of postwar Vietnam had been almost entirely built under Vichy, owing to an obsessive desire to reinvigorate and discipline a people considered bookish and frail in the colonial imagination.

While the ESEPIC camp disciplined "mostly the body"[137]—to borrow Decoux's expression—the *cadre* school at Phan Thiet proper was designed to build character and to train future leaders. Dubbed ESCJIC (an acronym for *Enseigner à Servir dans la Confiance et la Joie d'un Idéal Commun*—or Teaching to Serve in the Confidence and Joy of a Common Ideal), this center offered month-long crash courses aimed at "creating leaders."[138] Instructions to provincial youth leaders specified, however, that "natural selections" need be made even before Phan Thiet. Indeed, the camp, they were told, could not operate miracles, and therefore could not "transform a lost youth with none of the requisite baggage into a great leader."[139] Those graduating from this rigorous *cadre* school would become youth leaders themselves, and were in turn to have hand-picked future generations of Phan Thiet students. In this way, Decoux and Ducoroy created a closed-circuit system of leadership and physical conditioning, at once eminently elitist and rigidly hierarchical.

The most interesting feature of the ESCJIC center at Phan Thiet involved the common ideal contained in its acronym. Surprisingly, this lofty goal was neither French patriotism, nor the cult of youth, nor even Pétainism, but rather "the love of our respective *patries*."[140] Here the combination of federalism and the fostering of local patriotisms made for fascinating results. Students at this self-described "new tower of Babel" were encouraged to sing both the *Marseillaise* and their respective national anthems, and to "exalt the love of their small nations." The knowledge they gained was to be transmitted to their compatriots "in their respective languages."[141] In short, ESCJIC training involved a re-education in "authenticity." Youngsters were explicitly reimmersed into the history and identity of their respective *pays*, before being assigned the task of sharing these teachings with their compatriots. Decoux's promotion of the *petites patries* thus played a much overlooked role in the problem studied by Benedict Anderson in *Imagined Communities*: it helps to explain in part why former French Indochina splintered into three independent countries, while nearby colonial states such as former Dutch Indonesia remained united, during their respective national liberation struggles.[142]

Thus, if one scratches beneath their boy-scoutish veneer, Ducoroy's programs were manifestly intended to promote not only Pétainism per se but also Vichy-style federalism. The very administrative structure of new youth leagues was inherently federal, with each of Indochina's five *pays* operating a separate youth program.[143] Federalism and the cult of the five *pays* were to be found throughout Ducoroy's programs. In a pamphlet distributed to provincial youth leaders, Ducoroy outlined the chief objectives of regional youth priming. His principal recommendations involved "making frequent references to the rich folklore of your *pays*," "rediscovering beautiful and original traditions," "reviving the memory of the great moments which abound in your rich pasts," and "making known the great figures of the French empire."[144] These instructions prompt two related observations. First, Ducoroy did seem to achieve an ex post facto understanding that he might have inadvertently transformed Vietnamese national sentiments through such naïve and literal applications of metropolitan Pétainist youth directives.[145] Second, one cannot help but remark upon the very universality of National Revolutionary traditionalism, whose hallmarks were dispensed perhaps as widely, and arguably with greater results, in Indochina than in many parts of Vichy France proper.

Decoux's federalism and its maxim "Unity through diversity"[146] also found their expression in Pan-Indochinese sporting events pitting the various *pays* against each other. A December 1942 soccer match at Hanoi's stade Mangin, for example, showcased Annam's brightest soccer stars against those of Tonkin.[147] More spectacularly, Ducoroy orchestrated a number of grandiose pan-Indochinese sport extravaganzas from 1941 to 1944. These included a November 1941 trans-Indochinese torch race, a January 1942 circuit of Indochinese capitals, a March 1942 athletic day in Laos and Annam, in January 1943 a first—and then subsequently annual— bicycle *Tour d'Indochine,* and finally an Olympic relay foot race from Phnom Penh to Hanoi in December of that same year.[148] Of these many events, the torch race and *Tour d'Indochine* receive the greatest attention in Maurice Ducoroy's memoirs. The former event departed from the Temple of Angkor, as a token of Vichy and Khmer traditionalism, then crossed Cambodia, Cochin China, and Annam, before arriving in Tonkin. By superimposing this freshly invented tradition upon Cambodian royal rituals, Ducoroy achieved a hybrid celebration. According to his own account, opening celebrations presided over by the young King Sihanouk took on the aura of a "religious ceremony." Throughout Cambodia, onlookers "knelt before the flame," which symbolized to them their young sovereign.[149] Ducoroy, conversely, interpreted the flame as representative of a "nascent sporting spirit."[150] This torch race, like the *Tour d'Indochine* bicycle race that would soon follow, was clearly encoded with federalist meanings. The *Tour d'Indochine* closely followed the lead of its metropolitan prototype, the *Tour de France*—down to the yellow jersey used to designate its leader. Like its hexagonal model, the *Tour*'s itinerary was crafted as a delineation of national—or in this case, "federal"—space. The *Tour* began in Saigon; its grueling itinerary of more than two thousand kilometers then took it through Cochin China, Cambodia, Laos, Tonkin, and Annam, stopping in such sites of Indochinese Pétainism as the elite Vichy *cadre* training center at Phan Thiet.[151] The *Tour* also stopped at major sites of Vietnamese history, including the imperial city of Hué, where Emperor Bao Dai greeted the hundred racers; once again, Decoux had sought to superimpose a new ethos onto sites and memories of ancient Southeast Asia.[152]

It would be difficult to overstate the pervasiveness of Decoux and Ducoroy's programs. Centers inspired by the Phan Thiet model soon sprang up throughout Indochina. In Cambodia, an institution at Tonlé-Bati, modeled upon Vichy's metropolitan *Compagnons* youth league, served as a center to produce candidates for Phan Thiet.[153] At Sam Son, a seaside resort halfway between Hanoi and Vinh, Father Vacquier, the Catholic priest of Nam Dinh, founded a camp that groomed its one hundred hand-picked students into "future leaders."[154] The Sam Son camp's very maxim, "A leader is formed through discipline, obedience and suffering,"[155] was informed by both Catholic and Pétainist teachings. The camp's format, for its part, bore the stamp of Vichy-style corporatism, as it featured a panoply of different crafts, accepting among its ranks electricians, astronomers, barbers, carpenters, and artists, to name only a few.

A similar camp, perched atop an eight-hundred-meter hill at Ba-Vi, northwest of Hanoi, and reserved for ten- to twenty-year-old male young-

sters (both Indochinese and French), stood as a model of Pétainist inculca-
tion. Notre-Dame du Bavi, as the camp was known, interwove the cults of
Pétain, of youth and vigor, and Catholicism.[156] Readings for youngsters attending the camp included Alexis Carrel's seminal work on human inequalities, *L'Homme, cet inconnu*.[157] Most interestingly, Notre Dame du
Bavi was modeled upon a curious amalgam of colonial hill stations and
medieval monasteries.[158] One journalist claimed that it exuded a "monastic
aura." He elaborated:

> Life at the camp gives rise to a totally different spirit than that below—a com-
> mon phenomenon in communities of men living in isolation. This particular-
> ity, made possible ... by altitude and remoteness, renders the pedagogical
> training of leaders all the easier. ... The great tradition of the tree-cutting
> monks of Gaul seems renewed [at Ba-Vi]. Our ancestors tilled the earth, felling
> trees to elevate their souls, at a time when all needed to be constructed. Today,
> over the ruins of a glorious past, we must build a new France.[159]

A careful reading of this passage reveals monastic and Dalat-inspired hill
station ideals converging with invented ancient French images, and
Pétainist notions of 1940 as a year zero, to elevate Ba-Vi's youth to the vanguard of a future Pétainist crusade.

Such camps constituted in reality a network parallel to the pyramid of
cadre training culminating in Phan Thiet. These summer camps set out to
expose both French and Indochinese youngsters to National Revolutionary doctrines. The camps thus took over where in-school physical training
left off, by indoctrinating children around campfires. As early as December
1941, four thousand youngsters had already attended Vichy summer
camps. Roughly 70 percent of these were Indochinese, and approximately
22 percent of the total were female.[160] Camps shared several traits, be they
located at an archeological site in Cambodia designed to rekindle Khmer
culture, or in mountainous terrain conducive to reinvigorating hikes. Everywhere, children duly observed the ritualistic pageantry of the *cérémonie
des couleurs*—morning and evening; everywhere the values of team work,
responsibility, and patriotism were stressed.[161] Also ubiquitous were the
Olympic rings, Olympic slogan, and Olympic salute—not coincidentally
identical to the fascist salute. In his memoirs, Ducoroy reveals his lifelong
fascination with the Olympic spirit, and for Pierre de Coubertin, the man
responsible for its modern rebirth.[162]

Indochinese children attending summer camps followed a special curriculum—in addition to the standard physical, patriotic, and Olympic
training—outlined in 1941 by the Conseil Fédéral Indochinois:

In the intellectual and moral realms, the young Annamite, Laotian or Cambodian needs to be directed to all that can make him proud of his homeland, of his
traditions, and of his culture. [This can be achieved] by reintroducing ancient
games, dances and tales transmitted through an especially rich folklore, as well
as the performing of traditional theater, and diffusing national literatures by
translating into *quoc-ngu* (romanized Vietnamese script) the Chinese classics,
and into Khmer the Sanskrit classics.[163]

In the realm of youth indoctrination, as in so many other theaters, Vichy
planners plotted the "rebirth" of Khmer, Viet, and Lao cultures, closely
tied in their eyes with Indian and Chinese traditions respectively.

Besides government-endorsed youth associations and camps, the Vichy
era saw five competing scout movements introduced to Indochina.[164] A
special center at Bach-Ma near Hué served to train Scout leaders. Scout
values were prized by Vichy ideologues and their conservative Vietnamese
allies, who lauded the movement's attempt to "follow a model in which
youngsters educate one another, and employing methods ... that make a
man ... morally, physically and socially complete."[165]

Although the new regime's efforts at regimentation targeted mostly
youngsters, they also sought to discipline Indochinese adults as well, by introducing work breaks, early starts or early dismissals from the public sector so as to encourage physical education on the job.[166] Vichy thereby unwittingly bequeathed to Indochina what would become a postwar Vietnamese taste for physical exercise before and at work—admittedly inherited in part from Chinese culture, and of course later refined and altered by
the Viet-Minh. Still, it was under Vichy that physical exercise became
codified as an integral part of the Vietnamese workday.

Although like adults, Indochinese girls may have constituted something of an afterthought to Vichy pedagogues, a handful of special camps
were nonetheless established for them beginning in late 1941. In December
1941, a conservative Vietnamese observer remarked in the newspaper
l'Annam Nouveau: "[O]ur [Vietnamese] conception of the role of women
fits well with the renovation of mores being undertaken in France and the
Empire at this time: the place of women is in the home."[167] As in the
metropole, then, where maternity was exalted, while women working outside the home were chastised, so in Indochina did Vichy promote a set of
ultratraditional gender roles. Interestingly, this had not always been the
case—at least for white women in Indochina. One of the few contemporary examples of public—and indeed published—discontent from Euro-

peans in Vichy-controlled Indochina emanates from a *femme moderne* who complained bitterly to S. Lehnebach, a pastor friend of Decoux's,[168] of Vichy's intention to relegate women to the kitchen.[169] The colonial context, ironically, had previously liberated many French women from such tasks, displacing the burden onto indigenous servants.[170]

Perhaps to "rectify" this exception, the new female training camp in the Europeanized hill-station of Dalat stressed "household science," hygiene, and physical education, inasmuch as the latter could serve to encourage fertility. According to a report drafted by the Conseil Fédéral Indochinois, the school was intended to "develop amongst female youths the taste for appropriate physical exercises, and for their application in a methodical and rational manner."[171] The school, managed by the order of the Daughters of Charity in Indochina, was "blessed" in June 1942 by Mrs. Decoux, after whom its first graduating class was named. A journalist attending the ceremony remarked:

> The Mrs. Decoux class left the quaint school perched upon a hill at Dalat, which dominated the countryside. It will, through its training, teach Indochinese youth the principles of educating the soul and the body, as the Marshal has required of youth in all the communities of the Empire, in order for a new, stronger and more beautiful imperial France to emerge.[172]

The "quaint" buildings of Dalat's girl camps included a shelter for Indochinese and Eurasian girls, a maternity school, where girls were taught the finer points of child-rearing, and a model farm. Regimentation was a mainstay at Dalat. A journalist recounted in 1943: "[Among the younger girls], a five year old 'leader' heads a marching battalion, complete with Olympic [fascist] salute and songs. Everything here is charming, pink and white."[173]

Dalat's female indoctrination center was open to all three categories identified by Vichy in its youth directives: Asians, Europeans, and Eurasians.[174] Ducoroy worried at first about the scarcity of interested candidates, imputing this initial hesitancy to Asian conservatism on gender issues. But, he added, no sooner did elements of Indochina's high society—including several members of the royal families—apply to the center, than it became intensely popular.[175] In reality, this sudden appeal of physical invigoration for women had stemmed at least in part from an intensive press campaign. The Vietnamese-language newspaper *Bao-Moi* declared in January 1942: "[We] hope that the Vietnamese woman will liberate herself from old prejudices, and think about her training to become a healthy wife, a good mother, for more than ever our country needs brave and vigorous women."[176] Whatever the actual reasons for its sudden rise in popularity, the fact remains that by 1942, some two hundred candidates applied for the twenty-five openings at the Dalat center.[177]

The Legacy of Vichy Rule

Like Phan Thiet, Ba-Vi, or the hundreds of sports leagues founded under Vichy, Dalat's hilltop indoctrination center was intended to discipline, regiment, and condition a new generation of Vietnamese youngsters. This would prove to be one of Vichy's most important legacies in Southeast Asia. After the Japanese coup of March 9, 1945, which on the surface erased most markers of Vichy's presence in only forty-eight hours, various new entities sought to utilize, and indeed recruit, from Ducoroy's networks. Thus, Phan Anh, youth minister of Tran Trong Kim's short-lived government under the Japanese occupation, transformed many of Ducoroy's youth leagues into paramilitary organizations.[178]

So pervasive was the Pétainist indoctrination and regimentation of youth from 1940 to 1945, that South Vietnam later borrowed for its national anthem the musical score of the Vichyite patriotic hymn "Call to Youth."[179] Then too, as early as July 1945, Vichy's *Chantiers de la Jeunesse* were readily converted into a Viet-Minh movement known as "Sports and Youth." The so-called avant-garde youth movement that later composed the elite corps of the Vietnamese military was itself a carryover from the Phan Thiet system.[180] Although it might be an exaggeration to suggest that Ducoroy essentially outperformed clandestine Communist camps in breeding future Viet-Minh followers,[181] it nonetheless seems clear that Vichy's youth officials contributed to fashioning a regimented, martial, and disciplined generation of Vietnamese youngsters. Not all of these became Viet-Minh, of course. Many appear to have subsequently followed a course more in keeping with their Vichy training and become members of the anti-Communist, ultranationalist South Vietnamese militias.

Jean Decoux during a religious procession in Phat-Diêm, Tonkin, April 26, 1942. Note the fascist salute used by the assembled onlookers. Courtesy Archives Municipales de Bordeaux (France), Fonds Decoux.

Ceremony during which mandarins and other high administrators received medals from Admiral Decoux. Hanoi, courtyard of the governor general's palace, December 8, 1943. Courtesy Archives Municipales de Bordeaux (France), Fonds Decoux.

La remise en honneur du Confucianisme

Lý-Toët. — « Confucius l'a toujours dit, Maître Xã-xệ : « les rites d'abord, l'étude ensuite » (Tiên học lễ, hậu học văn).

A political cartoonist lampoons the sudden *engouement* for sports among the conservative Indochinese establishment, embodied here by the comedic figures of Xa-Xe and Ly-Toet. Title: "The Revalorizing of Confucianism." Translation: Ly-Toet: "Confucius always said, master Xa-Xe, 'Rites first, studies later.'" *Indochine, hebdomadaire illustré*, Nov. 11, 1943.

Lý Toët et Xã Xệ, qui pratiquent maintenant tous les sports, disputent la finale du championnat de tennis de Đình-Đù. Bang Banh a consenti à arbitrer, en raison de l'élévation de la chaise d'arbitre. — Le conseil des notables a été convoqué pour la circonstance.

Translation: "Ly-Toet and Xa-Xe, who now practice all sports, are playing the final of the Dinh-Du tennis tournament. Bang Banh has agreed to referee, due to the elevation of the referee chair. The council of notables has been convened for the occasion." Note the stereotypical depiction of Indochinese notables as particularly ceremonious and pompous. *Indochine, hebdomadaire illustré*, Dec. 2, 1943.

HUMOUR ANNAMITE

« Le mouvement sportif ne cesse de gagner en profondeur. — Dans tous les villages grands et petits font de la culture physique ». (Les journaux).

Au village de Đinh-Đủ, Lý-Toét et Xã-Xệ, entourés de leurs enfants, donnent l'exemple.

Translation: "Sports and athletics are constantly gaining in popularity. In all villages small and large, physical fitness is now being practiced (say the newspapers). In the village of Dinh-Du, Ly-Toet and Xa-Xe lead by example, surrounded by their children." *Indochine, hebdomadaire illustré*, Nov. 18, 1943.

Vichy-era mural depicting the flame used in the November 1941 pan-Indochinese torch race. Dalat, Vietnam. Author's photograph.

Vichy-era Indochinese stamp, showing a Vietnamese athlete extending the "Olympic" salute. Author's collection.

A highland minority man, upheld by Vichyites as models of "authenticity," watching the *Tour d'Indochine*. Maurice Ducoroy, *Ma trahison en Indochine* Paris: Les Éditions internationales, 1949).

Maurice Ducoroy (first from right) and Jean Decoux (second from right) overseeing a "loyalty oath," during which a highland minority girl hands the governor a bracelet, Darlac Province, January 1943. Courtesy Archives Municipales de Bordeaux, Fonds Decoux, Photo box.

Scouts from Northern Vietnam parade before Governor Decoux, 1943. Courtesy Archives Municipales de Bordeaux (France), Fonds Decoux.

CHAPTER 6

The Pétainist Festival: Staging Travail, Famille, Patrie in the Tropics

That day, the scouts, the Eclaireurs de France, the Ames vaillantes, and of course the Légionnaires volontaires de la Révolution nationale began to parade across the town as of eight o'clock in the morning. ... On a podium surrounded by tricolor flags and francisques atop bamboo shafts, a dozen mostly white officers awaited the arrival of the gerontocrat. ... A choral of young girls from the Jeanne d'Arc boarding school, in light blue and white uniforms, struck up a song to the glory of "the Marshal, father of the nation, and savior of our army." A tiny contingent of black infantrymen seemed to form a khaki splash among the white splendor of the sailors from the "Emile-Bertin" and the "Jeanne d'Arc" [naval vessels].

— Raphaël Confiant, *Le Nègre et l'Amiral*[1]

One of the most puzzling aspects of Vichy's presence in the tropics involved its insistence at introducing such potentially dangerous trappings as the Pétainist parade described here by Raphaël Confiant. To be sure, celebrations in French colonies were nothing new; but they had never been so ideologically laden as under Vichy.

Long before 1940, quite different festivals had played a significant symbolic role in legitimizing French colonial rule. In 1930 and 1935, for instance, the centennial and tercentennial of French annexation were commemorated with re-enactments in Algeria and the French Antilles respectively.[2] Bastille Day, which was widely observed throughout the empire, represented a staple of the colonial calendar under the Third Republic.[3] Yet such local commemorations have received scant historiographical attention because they were dwarfed by colossal and phantasmatic colonial displays in the metropole. The grandiose *Expositions coloniales* of Vincennes (1931) and Marseilles (1922) fulfilled precisely the opposite function of humbler celebrations in the colonies themselves.[4] Whereas the former served to showcase France's diverse and exotic empire to metropolitan audiences, the latter provided a less grand spectacle of no less carefully crafted representations of the motherland to indigenous populations. As such, they constituted a visual cornerstone of the perpetuation of French colonialism—one whose importance would increase exponentially in times of crisis. Vichy would first revamp, then invest heretofore unprecedented efforts into such celebrations in the colonies themselves. Meanwhile, between 1940 and 1944, metropolitan colonial exhibits would be reduced to mere shadows of colonial apotheoses of years past.

Shortly after the fall of France, Vichy officials began to ponder possible strategies in their quest for imperial legitimacy—itself part and parcel of their struggle for "True France" and their imperial war against the Free French.[5] An August 31, 1940, memorandum on propaganda, emanating from Vichy's Secrétariat d'Etat aux Colonies, noted the resulting shift that would need to be, and indeed was, undertaken:

> The current situation, as paradoxical as it may seem, forces the Ministry of the colonies to modify radically its propaganda and information services. Whereas they were until recently almost exclusively directed from the colonies to France, in other words targeting metropolitans, current circumstances dictate that today France inform its colonies and shift its propaganda to the colonies themselves.[6]

In other words, the vector of colonial propaganda, which traditionally had run (and increasingly as the war approached) from the colonies to the metropole, was reversed after the defeat of 1940. Propaganda agencies that had heretofore been devoted to telling colonial tales in metropolitan France now performed an about-face and began to narrate Pétainism to the empire. The site of colonial celebration had shifted.

The predictions of the August 1940 memorandum were indeed borne out. A 1941 report on the *Service intercolonial d'information et de documentation*—the principal propaganda authority for all things imperial—confirmed the newfound preeminence of imperial propaganda in the colonies themselves over that in the metropole:

The activities of our service in the metropole are much less interesting. The limits imposed by the occupying forces on all national propaganda in the occupied zone, the impossibility of exalting the empire without arousing colonial vocations ... leave our services preaching only historical and geographical generalities. ... It is instead to our overseas territories ... threatened ... by dissidence that our Service is directing its action ... in view of reinforcing the moral unity of the empire and spreading word of the accomplishments of the National Revolution to colonial public opinion, both French and indigenous.[7]

In keeping with this logic, the colonial exhibit planned for Marseilles in 1941 was canceled outright (admittedly, the empire did figure prominently in the metropolitan press under Vichy, with Imperial Week enhancing "awareness" of the colonies).[8] In the place of the aborted Marseilles exhibit, a *wagon colonial* toured France in what seems retrospectively a pitiful, makeshift school project incommensurable with the lavish colonial exhibits of years past.[9] In the colonies under Vichy, conversely, no means were spared to produce grandiose celebrations of unity.

Events in metropolitan France, coupled with the exigencies of the new ideology of National Revolution, dictated that Vichy would not stop at reversing the traditional flow of propaganda. It would also create—sometimes ex nihilo—new celebrations of unity, thereby laying to rest the republic's *jours de mémoire* and establishing its own celebratory pantheon. Here Lynn Hunt's observations on French revolutionary celebrations find resonance in the twentieth century. She asserts, in a preface to Mona Ozouf's *La fête révolutionnaire:* "Whenever the regime changed, the festival calendar had to be rearranged. New festivals were created to celebrate each major alteration, and objectional reminders from the preceding regime were eliminated."[10] Similarly, Vichy's first steps in the realm of commemoration would involve the effacing of "objectional reminders" of the republic.

In the aftermath of the defeat of June 1940, Marshal Pétain had proclaimed July 14 a day of national mourning. November 11, meanwhile, was intolerable not only to the Germans in the occupied zone; it had also been claimed as a referent by opponents of the 1940 armistice—by students protesting at the Arc de Triomphe, on Armistice Day 1940, in one of the earliest acts of open resistance.[11] Ideological considerations also conspired to eclipse both July 14 and November 11. The former symbolized republican traditions anathema to Vichy, while the latter supposedly marked a victory from which no lessons had been drawn, shared with allies who had since shown their true colors.

It should come as no surprise, then, that Admiral Platon, acting on orders from Admiral Darlan, telegraphed all colonial governors the following message prior to Bastille Day 1941: "Due to the Nation's mourning, July 14 is not to be celebrated."[12] Similarly, Platon instructed in a November 7, 1941, cable to all colonial governors: "Due to [current] circumstances work will continue on November 11; public buildings will not be decorated. The Day should nonetheless be marked by profound reflection and contemplation."[13] Reflecting a veritable culture of defeat and of mourning, Governor Sorin inquired from Guadeloupe as to whether the French flag should be flown at half-mast on Bastille Day.[14]

Vichy's repudiation of official republican memories seems in retrospect a risky venture indeed, especially in colonies such as Madagascar or Guadeloupe, where July 14 had once been fervently celebrated. It did, however, present the advantage of affording the regime an iconographic clean slate. Out of the ensuing plethora of new Vichy celebrations, which included Mother's Day, Sully's anniversary, and Legion Day, the latter appears to have been most widely celebrated throughout the empire, and will therefore constitute a principal focus of this chapter. It will also consider two celebrations that had played secondary roles prior to 1940, only to be reinvented under Vichy: namely, May Day and Joan of Arc Day. Although each of these three occasions reflected individual themes dear to the National Revolution, they were all intended—even through their very uniformity of celebration—to rally support for imperial unity behind Pétain and to diffuse representations of the new regime.

Finally, Vichy's ceremonial slate was not completely blank in 1940. Pétainists did find models on which to inspire their new colonial rituals overseas. They pilfered indigenous cultures for their own benefit, but also turned to pre-1870 French commemorations. In many ways, Vichy's colonial celebrations were reminiscent of Louis-Napoleon's metropolitan *fêtes*—whose stock themes had included the cult of the leader, "the use of a romanticized past[,] ... [and] the images of suffering and sacrifice for the national community."[15] With the republic disgraced, Vichyites turned to paternalist and sometimes kitsch Second Empire rituals as blueprints for their colonial spectacles.

Travail

It may at first seem paradoxical that whereas July 14 and November 11 were practically erased from Vichy's calendar, May 1, the international day of labor so dear to Socialists and Marxists, was not. Instead, in both France and the empire, Vichy reinvented May Day, thereby running the risk—as Avner Ben Amos has pointed out—of changing the meaning of the celebration without altering the referent itself.[16] Flouting such a risk, Vichy did attempt to stage a new *Fête du Travail*, one that would supposedly elevate labor to the rank it deserved, alongside *Famille* and *Patrie*. In so doing, the new regime sought to defuse a popular celebration laden with leftist—or at least militant—connotations, by infusing it with Vichy values. Taking their cue from Mussolini's appropriation of Labor Day, Vichy officials promoted the new May 1 as not only a paternalist exaltation of manual labor but also a symbol of reconciliation of workers and management under the mantle of corporatism. As in Italy, where Mussolini hijacked May Day by associating it with a new festivity more in tune with the new order (April 21, commemorating the birth of Rome),[17] so too did May Day under Vichy conveniently coincide with the Saint Philippe, Marshal Pétain's name day. The latter had itself long been celebrated for other Philippes—Louis Philippe and Philip Augustus—by the royalist Action Française.[18] Vichy ideologues also endeavored to divest May 1 of its recent syndicalist past, preferring instead, through a *völkisch* pseudo-historical reconstruction, to re-enact a simulacrum of pagan festivals of spring.[19] As with every other imaginable colonial festivity under Vichy, May Day in the colonies also became a celebration of the supposedly indissoluble unity of metropole and empire. May 1, which in most French colonies had only recently begun to be either officially or clandestinely celebrated in the 1930s, would, under Vichy, become a staged show of loyalty not merely to Pétain himself but also to an ideology that ascribed mythical meaning to *Travail*.

May 1 in Indochina in the 1930s had witnessed sporadic outbursts of opposition and violence. In 1930 "relatively serious incidents" were reported in both Annam and Tonkin, one of which cost the lives of sixteen protesters.[20] In 1937, after the advent of the Popular Front, May Day was widely observed in Hanoi and Saigon.[21] Still, confrontations on May Day seemed the exception rather than the rule. May 1 actually represented a relatively insignificant date in the Indochinese revolutionary almanac. Communists lent greater importance to November 7, the anniversary of the Russian Revolution, and to the simultaneous celebration every January of the three *L*'s: Lenin, Luxemburg, and Liebknecht (the last two had been murdered on January 15, 1919, while Lenin perished on January 21, 1924).[22] In a sense, then, the celebrations staged by Admiral Decoux, intended to co-opt a festivity by displacing it from the anarchical streets to an orderly stadium,[23] actually missed the point. They spoke more to metropolitan concerns than to local considerations. Such was the result of a concerted effort by Vichy to export uniform celebrations as part of a larger desire to display imperial unity.

In precisely this spirit of uniformity, on April 25, 1941, Admiral Platon sent specific and identical instructions to all colonial governors regarding the celebration of the first May Day of the new order. Their main stipulation read:

> Take all measures to ensure that this day does not take on political overtones. Do not accept *cahiers de revendications*. Corporatist delegations will, however, be permitted to present a corporatist wish list elaborated in cooperation with workers, employers and specialists.[24]

Thereupon, Decoux responded by cable from Hanoi: "[U]nless you absolutely insist, I cannot allow the presentation of corporatist desiderata which would trigger inopportune social movements."[25] Interestingly, Admiral Decoux found threatening even Vichy's transparent transformation of a syndicalist tradition into a corporatist charade. This suggests that in some respects Vichy Indochina was less concealing of its authoritarianism than its metropolitan counterpart. In keeping with Platon's orders, May Day 1941 in Indochina was stripped of all recrimination and militantism and was instead marked primarily by religious ceremonies. The death of Monivong, king of Cambodia, on April 23, 1941, ensured that May Day would be mourned rather than celebrated throughout Indochina. Masses were attended by the royal family in Cambodia, while in Vientiane, the capital of Laos, "Buddhist priests implored Buddha to protect the Marshal so as to allow him to renovate France."[26] In Cochin China, the mise en scène was quite different. A group of French and Vietnamese "representatives of the nation," including farmers, industrialists, workers, administrators, and artisans assembled at Saigon's Chamber of Agriculture, not to submit a corporatist wish list but to formulate a corporatist vow "to serve Labor through peace in unity and concord."[27]

If May Day 1941 had involved sober prayers and vows, May 1, 1942, took on the character of a painstakingly choreographed mass rally more than a celebration. The day's program in Hanoi, staged to the minute by Decoux and the Legion, featured a speech by the Bishop Msgr. Chaize on the "religious and patriotic meaning of May 1"—in other words on all but its previous meaning—and an early 7:30 Mass. This was followed by a parade into Hanoi's stadium (Stade Mangin), where the Legion broke ranks:

the Volunteers of the National Revolution, surrounded by veterans, took their place in front of the female Legion, flanked to the right by youngsters. Some twelve hundred Legionaries attended what was essentially a swearing in ceremony for new members. At 9:55, the president of the Legion raised his right arm in the fascist salute and yelled: "Long live the Marshal." Once his arm lowered, the Legion replied with the same cry in unison. The entire ritual finished with the unavoidable commemoration at Hanoi's First World War monument.[28] This rally assumed some of the characteristics of what Emilio Gentile and George Mosse have seen as the "political religion" inherent in fascism.[29] The mass of Legionaries were intended to have participated, as one, in a literal communion with the metropole and in a prayer for the resurrection of France. Hence, Decoux reported to Vichy on May 5, 1942: "[The day's celebrations] demonstrate the population's profound attachment to the person and the accomplishments of the Marshal and its total solidarity with the martyred metropole."[30] Here, Pétain came to incarnate a distant collective subject—not dissimilar from what Claudio Fogu has termed Mussolini's "literal embodiment of the fascist mass subject."[31]

By 1943, May Day in Indochina became known officially as "the day of labor and of the Marshal" and was celebrated once again by religious services and "imposing rallies" organized by the Légion.[32] According to the weekly review *Indochine, hebdomadaire illustré*, May Day 1943 had been observed in "contemplation and confidence. ... Speakers at the Legion ceremony ... called upon everyone's sentiments of union and discipline."[33] By the next year, Vichy's May Day seemed, like the regime itself, to be waning, and was celebrated with "solemnity" according to Decoux.[34]

Prior to 1940, May Day had been observed even less widely in Madagascar than in Indochina. In 1934 and 1935, it was not celebrated on the Great Island. Not surprisingly, the local press did not report on May Day in the metropole either. The advent of the Popular Front seems to have changed little, save for the fact that newspapers now reported May 1 festivities in Paris.[35] Only in 1939 was May 1 finally seized as a politically significant moment. On this occasion, the leftist dissident Paul Ranaivo delivered a speech conflating Labor Day with an important date in the history of Malagasy nationalism—the protest of May 19, 1929, which gathered three thousand Malagasy demanding equal rights.[36]

The first May Day in Vichy Madagascar came only fifteen days after the arrival of Governor Armand Annet on the island. Conforming to the orders of Admiral Platon, he presented May Day as a celebration of "social peace"[37] and ordered his subordinates to ensure that "no demonstrations contrary to the new order take place."[38] On April 30, 1941, teachers in Malagasy schools delivered lectures glorifying manual labor. The next day was devoted to sporting events as well as public speeches on "the restoration of national unity."[39]

If Annet had been given insufficient time to prepare May 1, 1941, he would redeem himself the following year by staging lavish parades. This final mass celebration of the National Revolution in Madagascar, only days before the British surprise attack on Diego-Suarez, represented the symbolic apotheosis of Vichy on the island. In most respects, Annet faithfully followed the guidelines on the metropolitan 1942 May Day, forwarded to the colonies by the new colonial secretary, Jules Brévié. These read:

> Marshal Pétain has placed the morning of May 1 under the motto: *Le Travail est à l'honneur* ["manual labor is honored"]. This celebration will consecrate the new esteem in which manual labor is held. ... The afternoon ... will be under the sign: *Le Travail est en fête* ["labor is celebrated"]. Two banners will be displayed [one for each theme].[40]

That Annet duly reproduced not merely the spirit but the letter of the metropolitan *Fête du Travail* is evidenced in banners displayed across the streets of Tananarive bearing the words *Le Travail est à l'honneur*. However, on his own initiative, Annet also introduced two themes absent from Brévié's directives: forced labor and corporatism. He declared in a speech on May Day over Tananarive radio, on May 1, 1942:

> I am pleased to observe ... that the notion of obligatory work is becoming more and more engrained each day. ... Too often and for too long, in a curious and ... nefarious deformation of the principles of individual freedom, political authorities refused to force individuals to work who were openly recognized as being incapable of spontaneous effort, and who, lacking energy, remained in a state of physical resistance insufficient to safeguard the race.[41]

Annet, through his celebration of forced labor during *la Fête du Travail*, claimed to be impelling nothing short of the invigoration and rescue of the Malagasy "race," while also justifying the increasing recourse to forced labor.

The concurrent corporatist undercurrent of May 1, 1942, in Madagascar appears especially noteworthy in light of the relative insignificance of corporatist themes in the metropolitan *Fête du Travail* that year. Indeed, in mainland France the previous year had seen the apogee of corporatist rhetoric—not only during May Day, but also with the presentation of the

Labor Charter of October 1941. Thereafter, as Robert Paxton has observed, corporatism faded in metropolitan France, ceding way to more dirigiste economic schemes.[42] Conversely, by May 1, 1942, Armand Annet seemed prepared to enact the local Legion's corporatist projects in Madagascar. The very form of May Day 1942 was determined by corporatist considerations. The *Bulletin d'information et de documentation* issued by the French authorities in Madagascar described the day's main events in the capital Tananarive as follows:

> The representatives of the various corporations gathered in front of City Hall, in spots designated beforehand by separate signs for each profession. More than 1200 delegates were present, as well as schoolchildren from technical and agricultural ... schools, and youth movements. On the balcony of the *Printemps* building an immense portrait of the Marshal ... dominated by its majesty the popular assembly, reminding all that this was a day of reconciliation ... of all classes ... in closer cooperation between workers and management.[43]

This visual narrative presented corporatism as a new structural basis not merely for May Day but also for a future Madagascar under the paternal guidance of the marshal. The resulting hybrid May Day provided a telling self-representation of the new regime. Clearly, Annet considered Vichy's prime accomplishments in Madagascar to involve the recrudescence of forced labor and the introduction of corporatism as part of a new ideology. Annet felt satisfied to conclude that May Day 1942 had been "celebrated in the new spirit of the National Revolution."[44]

In spite of its active trade-unionism, Guadeloupe had likewise not experienced sizable May Day parades before 1940. Admittedly, even before the First World War, May Day had seen the distribution of medals to workers.[45] In the interwar years, the agency of celebration had shifted to unions; May Day had become an occasion, in 1934 and 1936 in particular, for workers to sing the "Internationale" in the streets of Pointe-à-Pitre.[46] Still, before 1940, May 1 had occupied a truly marginal rank among the profusion of Guadeloupean celebrations, political or otherwise, which included a host of Patron Saint days, Carnival, Bastille, and Armistice days, Abolition Day, and Victor Schoelcher Day.

The first May Day in Guadeloupe under Vichy presented a number of changes with years past. It was appropriated not only by the government but by the Church as well, for May 1, 1941, began with 9 o'clock Masses throughout the island.[47] The greatest pageantry on May 1 was reserved to Pétain's name day, as illustrated by Governor Constant Sorin's cable to Vichy on May 2, 1941: "Marshal Pétain was celebrated in an unforgettable manner in all towns ... where each house was decorated with thousands of pictures of him which had been sold for the benefit of the *Secours National*."[48] In 1941, *la Fête du Travail*, now rebaptised "the Celebration of Social Peace and of Labor," involved the rewarding not of workers, as in the prewar era, but of the favorites of the new regime, farmers and artisans.[49] Lastly, Sorin promoted a corporatist May 1, arguing that "all members of a sector are like members of a single family, whose interests, far from clashing, are complementary."[50]

By May 1, 1942, Governor Sorin, doubtless preoccupied by both the productivity of an island faced with autarky and the demands of a now all-powerful cast of industrialist pillars of the regime, declared that May Day would be celebrated through labor. Because early May coincided with the sugar cane harvest, Sorin decided that May Day could not be a holiday in 1942.[51] Instead, on the following Sunday, a Mass was held in Basse-Terre, followed by the awarding of prizes to 186 workers and farmers. During a lunch offered to these workers and their employers, allegiance was sworn to Pétain, "Father of the workers and savior of France."[52]

Nothing seemed to augur that May Day 1943 would differ from previous years. On April 30, 1943, the vice president of Guadeloupe's Legion gave Sorin his assurances that "on the occasion of May 1 and the Saint Philippe we are communing with you in the sacred love of our martyred homeland and swearing our attachment to our leader Philippe Pétain."[53] And yet, the dénouement of May 1, 1943, in Guadeloupe was to be radically different from that of years past, for it marked the first open rebellion against Vichy authorities in Guadeloupe. The fact that May 1 was no longer a holiday, combined with what Sorin himself recognized as the increasingly exploitative practices of sugar cane industrialists, contributed to galvanizing the resistance of workers who interpreted the new May 1 as nothing short of an exaltation of slavery. Workers at the Beauport sugar factory in Port-Louis revolted from the evening of April 30 to the early hours of May 1, 1943, attacking the town's police headquarters. By May 2, the movement had spread to the polar opposite end of Guadeloupe, to the capital, Basse-Terre, where Vichy troops opened fire on a crowd of political protesters.[54] Vichy's day of social consensus, of allegiance to the marshal and of exaltation of corporatism and manual labor had been openly contested in Guadeloupe. Demonstrators changed the site of commemoration—taking to the streets of Port-Louis and Basse-Terre, instead of joining the *Fête du Travail et du Maréchal* planned for the stadiums and squares of both towns.

Vichy's multifaceted self-representations across three continents on May 1 prompt several final observations. In attempting to establish a new commemorative culture in the colonies themselves, and in the name of imperial unity, Vichy exported a reinvented May Day, encoded with corporatist, traditionalist, and antirevolutionary motifs. This potentially explosive festival was introduced to colonies where May 1 had scarcely been celebrated before, on account of either colonial repression or the idiosyncrasies of the local revolutionary calendar. Throughout Vichy's empire the emphasis was placed upon the "political and religious" implications of May 1, which was intended to replace a sectarian and self-interested class struggle with a reconciliation under the ideals of Vichy, most notably the marshal, religion, and corporatism. In spite of this uniformity of celebration, some revealing differences do emerge from the spectacle of May 1 under Vichy. In Indochina, May Day was at times solemn and mournful, and at others martial and regimented, more reminiscent in 1942 of the choreography of the Nuremberg rallies than of the popular May 1 it sought to usurp. In Madagascar, May Day provided quite another reflection of the regime that staged it—at once corporatist and bent upon forced labor. In Guadeloupe, as well, May Day betrayed the essence of the local regime—its cult of the leader, proclericalism, and eagerness to satisfy the island's oligarchy to the point of imposing work on May Day. By superimposing these three lenses, one is also offered a telling *vue d'ensemble* of Vichy's commemorative culture—which assumed forms and utilized modes of representation eerily akin to those of fascist regimes. Under fascist governments, commemoration played an equally central role in the liturgy of a new political religion, which itself appropriated disparate elements from a variety of pre-existing cults.

Famille (coloniale)

Unlike May Day, appropriated by Vichy in an effort to subvert its original meaning, Legion Day constituted an original invention of the new regime. It commemorated the founding of the vanguard of the National Revolution, the Légion Française des Combattants et Volontaires de la Révolution Nationale, on August 29, 1940. Even more than May Day, Legion Day was conceived as a celebration of imperial unity—due in part to pressures from the secretary of state to the colonies. These themselves clearly resulted from the successive rallying of territories to de Gaulle's Free French. The schedule for the metropolitan 1941 Legion Day ran as follows:

> Vichy, August 28 at 7 P.M.: Marshal Pétain accepts the flame of the unknown
> soldier and with it lights three torches which are carried by runners throughout
> the free zone. A plane transports a flame to North and West Africa. On August
> 31, the runners arrive in one hundred and fifty towns of France and the empire
> at 9:45.[55]

This program, reminiscent of the carefully charted itinerary of the Olympic
flame, begs several observations. At one level, its form and ritual performances are clearly intended to emphasize the symbolic oneness of empire
and metropole. The very tools employed—the use of an airplane to deliver
a flame to Africa in a time of global war, served as a concrete token of
Pétain's imperial legitimacy and colonial solicitude. Legion Day actually
fulfilled multiple functions, exalting not only imperial unity and the tenets
of the new ideology but also the cult of the dead, crucial to the *Légion
Française des Combattants et Volontaires de la Révolution Nationale,* which
was first and foremost a veterans' organization. Indeed, with November 11
already erased from the calendar, August 29 became the principal day of
commemorating the losses of the First World War. This was orchestrated
not with static commemorations at First World War monuments but with a
torch race more in tune with the aesthetic ideals of the new regime, which,
like its fascist contemporaries, claimed to "make" rather than "write" history.[56]

August 29, 1942, presents perhaps the most fascinating and historiographically overlooked commemoration under Vichy.[57] Building upon Legion Day 1941, it stands as the apogee of a tangible, material symbolism intended to root the regime in a mythical *völkisch* past. Vichy's colonial secretariat issued its customary recommendations to all governors on July 22,
1942:

> On the occasion of the second anniversary of the Legion … a national com-
> memoration will take place on the Gergovie plateau. To crystallize the intimate
> union of French provinces, both metropolitan and colonial, each legionary sec-
> tion will collect a piece of French soil in a location chosen for military or relig-
> ious glory, or in ruins laden with centuries, failing this in cemeteries or in front
> of World War I monuments. These parcels of earth … will be mixed … [and
> sent to Vichy]. Thus assembled, they are to be planted in the Gergovie Plateau.
> A flag will be erected above them.[58]

No elaborate decoding or semiotic analysis is needed to comprehend that
this filiation rooted in the soil was intended to mark the ultimate proof of
national and imperial unity. As such, it provides a remarkable illustration of

Eric Hobsbawm's definition of an "invented tradition," seeking to "establish continuity with a suitable historic past."[59] In fact, Legion Day in the colonies from 1940 to 1943 seems to match all three types of invented traditions outlined by Hobsbawm:

> a) those establishing or symbolizing social cohesion or the membership of groups, real or artificial communities, b) those establishing or legitimizing institutions, status or relations of authority, c) those whose main purpose was socialization [and] the inculcation of beliefs.[60]

Each of the many topoi specific to this invented ritual—its choice of *lieu de mémoire,* its imagined historical continuity, its cults of the soil, of tradition, and of the dead, played a part in both the liturgy of the ideology of National Revolution and in perpetuating the myth of an indivisible France and French empire.

The choice of Gergovie, site of the short-lived Gaullish victory over Caesar, reflects an explicitly pagan dimension of Vichy's cult of, and return to, the soil (might it also betray a latent anti-German sentiment, with ancient Rome intended to evoke the Third Reich?).[61] Indeed, the unity of the empire's "provinces" was to be achieved by blending soils, in a sort of imagined druidic consanguination, before literally entombing and rooting them into a *lieu de mémoire* proper to the new regime.[62]

Such an entombing might be perceived as an exaltation of assimilation. But this was clearly the assimilation of soils, not blood. Such a baroque soil communion is all the more striking, then, because of its possible symbolic repercussions. The new regime, after all, disenfranchised and created difference by heightening racial barriers and countenancing theories of inequality. Yet at the same time as creating difference, Vichy dared to lay a symbolic claim to "assimilation." Such were the inconsistencies of the cults of "difference" and "multiculturalism" on Vichy's terms.

Richard Burton, the only historian to have touched on Legion Day overseas, takes this ceremony at face value and concludes that it exalted bona fide assimilationism.[63] A fundamental distinction should be drawn, then, between, on the one hand, territorial assimilation—which Vichy purported to embody—and on the other hand the classic Roman assimilation of peoples so frequently evoked to describe republican colonialism (sometimes erroneously), and which Vichy clearly did not incarnate. Even in its referent, Vichy had chosen a Gaullish, rather than Roman, moment for Legion Day. Where Vichy did innovate, however, was in the elaboration of a discourse of imperial unity heretofore without parallel in French colonial history. This it achieved through the invention of rituals, such as those of Legion Day, as part of a radically new commemorative culture.

In Madagascar, the head of the Legion of Tamatave rendered his own interpretation of Legion Day 1942. He declared on August 30, 1942:

> Gergovie was chosen for the assembly of these parcels. ... Thanks to the airplane of Commandant Gardillère, Madagascar, former Ile Dauphine, will be materially represented there, as will the Heart of Réunion, former Ile Bourbon, much like the Bourbonnais and the Languedoc. Periods, sites, and memories of history will be blended and mixed to form a single finality: France and its empire, the France of the Marshal, the France of 1942.[64]

This fictional genealogy, promoting once again the redemptive myth of imperial unity, seems at the very least determinist, selective, and anachronistic. It dwells, moreover, upon the term "provinces" already stressed in Vichy's directives to the governors. As Christian Faure has shown, Vichy sought to revive prerevolutionary French provinces, to the detriment of post-1789 departments.[65] In invoking a nonrepublican colonial tradition, the head of Tamatave's Legion drew a tenuous parallel between the Isle of Bourbon—as Réunion had been called prior to 1848—and the Bourbonnais in the metropole, in a concurrent glorification of imperial unity and nostalgic royalism. The juxtaposition of royalist names of provinces betrays more than the author's political convictions. It reveals a certain understanding of the past revolving around a carefully constructed historical lineage that disavowed the republican periods of the last 150 years of French history.

As for the remarkable image of the heart of the island of Réunion, and the mixing of soils as a blending of "periods, sites and memories of history," both point to a vision of the soil as nothing short of a holy relic. This was a veritable canonization of French colonial space. That colonial soils became artifacts, in a rite honoring the supposedly organic basis of France and its empire, falls in line with Vichy's vaster cult of the earth and the region *(terre and terroir*—the link is more explicit in French) as the wholesome, simple, and sturdy bases of a future society. If in 1931 the colonies had produced lavish, individualized, and exotic exhibits for Vincennes, a little over a decade later they were now asked for parcels of their soil to be entombed at Gergovie—in a reductionist tribute to unity and to the motherland, where they were thereby "represented."

In this last sense, August 30, 1942, in the colonies also constituted a pseudo-referendum intended to create a consensus on loyalty to Vichy—a "referendum" not only *à la vichyssoise* but also *à la coloniale,* in other words in consultation with only the governors of colonies.[66] This "consultation," orchestrated through a quasi-religious and freshly invented ritual performance, aimed at fostering an identification with a new France and hence at establishing nothing short of a new imperial identity through what George Mosse has termed "a shared worship that was so crucial to ... the sense of belonging [of the participants]."[67] The cult of the leader was paramount to this "shared worship." Pétain's estival *villeggiatura* at Villeneuve-Loubet, on the Riviera, was endowed with the status of an entire territory in its own right. In an article entitled "The Humus of Our French and Overseas Soils in the Crypt at Gergovie," a reporter in French Indochina declared: "At Villeneuve-Loubet, soil was gathered by local authorities at the Marshal's actual residence."[68]

If Legion Day 1942 in Madagascar and Indochina had extolled a nostalgic vision of *ancien régime* provinces and imperial unity based on an organic cult of the soil and the cult of the leader, so did the image of Pétain as thaumaturgical king become the curious leitmotiv of August 30, 1942, in Guadeloupe. On August 11, 1942, the head of Guadeloupe's Legion issued the following proposal to Governor Sorin:

> All samples of soil ... collected will be mixed and then divided into two parts. The first ... will be sent to Vichy. ... The second will serve for a ceremony we intend to organize here on August 30 which will re-enact that of the Gergovie Plateau. ... This mixture of soils will be buried at the cemetery of the Richepanse Fort.[69] ... In order better to mark the intimate union of Guadeloupe with the fatherland, we ask that a parcel of earth collected at Gergovie, and touched by the Marshal, be mixed with the samples from Guadeloupe.[70]

Sorin, accepting this project verbatim, telegraphed the colonial secretary, Jules Brévié, who himself informed the head of France's Legion on August 18, 1942: "All would be infinitely happy if this soil could be touched by Marshal Pétain."[71]

The request of Guadeloupe's Legion, duly transmitted by Sorin, prompts two observations. First, taken in conjunction with the fascination with the soil at the marshal's villa, it would seem to belie the 1923 assertion of the famous historian Marc Bloch that the French as a rule "no longer believe that political power or even royal lineage can confer supernatural grace."[72] Indeed, in this case, Marshal Pétain was clearly attributed the miraculous qualities, as well as the embodiment of power once considered proper to French monarchs. Thus, although Pétain was not presented as thaumaturgic per se, for he was not strictly speaking thought of as a healer, he was nonetheless explicitly conferred an element of an "ancient monarchical religion,"[73] namely the belief in a sacred "royal touch." In this respect, Marshal Pétain once again commanded a similar form of worship as Mussolini, who, as Claudio Fogu has shown, was imagined to have "transfigured" a war veteran with his caress.[74]

Secondly, the scheme hatched by the head of Guadeloupe's Legion to orchestrate a ceremony in Basse-Terre identical to that of Gergovie evokes quite another consideration. By proposing an exchange of soils, rather than the unilateral entombing of colonial soils at Gergovie, this Vichy official seemed intent on reminding his metropolitan counterparts of their pledge to promote Vichy throughout the empire, rather than vice versa.

These considerations relating to the cult of the soil, the personalization of power, and the site of commemoration should not obfuscate the fact that the overarching image of August 30, 1942, involved the unity of an indivisible colonial family fending off vultures allegedly prepared to prey on the empire of a weakened France. Hence, Vichy officials in some colonies, such as Madagascar and Djibouti, sent a parcel of soil to the metropole by airplane as an act of defiance against British "aggression." By expediting "a parcel of soil from a distant land," Djibouti's besieged and stubbornly pro-Vichy authorities intended to demonstrate the colony's "desire to remain French."[75] Similarly, in Indochina, Legion Day 1942 provided a tool by which to assert French pan-imperialism over Japanese pan-Asianism. In Indochina, moreover, the parcels of soil were not alone in being painstakingly selected. So too was the container in which they were embalmed. Thus Decoux reported to Brévié:

> In all the symbolic locations of Indochina parcels of earth were collected and mixed in an ancient urn from the Tan Hoa province. They will be sent to the metropole to take their place at Gergovie in the location I asked you to reserve for the great Asian colony.[76]

The choice of an ancient Vietnamese urn in which to encase the "holy soil" destined to Gergovie was itself encoded, for it identified Indochinese antiquity with the Gauls, in an allegorical fusion of civilizations. More obviously, such a stress on the ancient also betrays an attempt to legitimize both Pétain and his regime. By appropriating a dual antiquity, Vichy officials sought to convey an aura of authenticity, itself intended to endow Vichy festivals with a measure of respectability and even of sacrosanctity.

One cannot help but observe, moreover, a certain funereal morbidness to Decoux's reserving a plot for Indochina in what thereby becomes the cenotaph of Gergovie. The cult of the dead pervaded this ceremony from start to finish; parcels of earth were collected from First World War monuments (in a curious sacralization of a soil containing no remains), only to be reburied at Gergovie. To be sure, the exaltation of the dead was in no way unique to Vichy. During the interwar years, various veterans' organizations that later merged into the Legion had elaborated a series of intricate ritual commemorations revering the victims of the First World War. On Legion Day 1942, however, the cult of the dead was directly correlated to the myth of imperial unity, in a radically new visual and tactile commemoration.

By August 30, 1943, Vichy, left with only one loyal colony, avoided the embarrassment of staging shows of imperial unity. Nevertheless, in Indochina Governor Decoux dwelled upon "French unity," while also "reminding all of the principles of the National Revolution." In Saigon, Legionnaires and youth organizations paraded, bearing banners and singing *Maréchal, nous voilà.*[77] The following year, on August 30, 1944, Decoux encouraged Legionnaires "to remain faithful to [their] vow."[78] This display of fidelity was all the more remarkable because the Vichy regime proper had ceased to exist ten days before, when the Nazis in their retreat abducted Philippe Pétain and Pierre Laval to Germany. It certainly seems striking that while Vichy was reduced to tatters in the metropole, it was still celebrated in Indochina.

In sum, Legion Day, a ritual invented under Pétain, and the festivity most closely tied to the ideology of National Revolution, provides a rich self-representation of the Vichy regime. Beyond its cults of the soil, of Pétain as the embodiment of power, of traditions—be they Gaullish, royal, or ancient Vietnamese—Legion Day was above all an exaltation of French and imperial unity, whose oneness was cast in the very soil of the colonies. This pervasive topos was reflected in the very form of the August 30, 1942, ceremony, conceived as a shared worship, and in the semiotics of a festivity that rooted colonial soils into a new metropolitan *lieu de mémoire,* at once geographically and ideologically close to Vichy.

Patrie

If May and Legion days had revolved around imperial unity, no festivity came to consecrate the cult of the *Patrie* as much as Joan of Arc Day (May 10–11) under Vichy. Indeed, under Pétain, Joan of Arc was presented as nothing short of the *Sainte de la Patrie.* As with May Day, the *Fête de Jeanne d'Arc* had been much more widely observed in the metropole than overseas prior to 1940. In Madagascar, for instance, the paltry Joan Day festivities of 1934 were ridiculed by a newspaper which lamented that "the celebrations did not impress the crowd. ... [In fact,] the *Pucelle* did not have much success at all."[79] In Guadeloupe, meanwhile, Joan of Arc Day was celebrated for the first time "with fervor" in May 1939—in the face of the German menace.[80]

Vichy, however, annexed both the image of Joan of Arc and her commemoration for its own ends after 1940. It not only aggrandized both but also transformed the germanophobic Joan of the First World War and 1939 into an anglophobic guardian of French unity. Gerd Krumeich, the foremost expert on the representation of Joan of Arc, has argued that Joan was thus "conferred ... a ferociously anti-English character" under Vichy.[81] But contrary to what Krumeich has suggested, the mutation of Joan's image under Vichy did not end there. She was also associated with the cult of Pétain and transformed into a model for a regenerated, Catholic France. Furthermore, Jeanne d'Arc was tied explicitly to the cult of youth and vigor, while simultaneously becoming a protean model for Vichy's ultratraditionalist gender roles. Joan's image was, in addition, associated to an unprecedented degree to anti-Semitism and xenophobia.[82] In the colonies under Vichy, meanwhile, Joan of Arc Day celebrated an equally impressive range of cults, most notably those of the motherland, youth, and tradition. In this last respect, May 10 at times associated the veneration of Joan with reinvented local indigenous rituals, thereby subsuming the *petites patries,* as the colonies were sometimes called, into the greater *patrie,* while at the same time fostering a folkloric traditionalism so dear to Vichy.

Vichy's Secrétaire d'Etat aux Colonies issued precise and identical instructions to all colonial governors regarding the mise en scène of Joan Day. In a May 7, 1941, telegram, Platon asked governors to draw inspiration from the following metropolitan guidelines:

> The celebration of Joan of Arc Day will take place under the following conditions. ... The army will participate ... in the religious ceremonies with a guard of honor, but will not parade. ... Flowers will be laid before statues of Joan of Arc. Civil and Military authorities, members of the Legion ... and students are to attend the ceremonies.[83]

These general recommendations were accompanied by a more detailed circular from Georges Lamirand, Vichy's secretary general to youth.

The circular in question, addressed to youngsters of France and overseas, outlined the role of youngsters in the celebration of the *Sainte de la Patrie*. It began by calling for an almost Wagnerian decor:

> As much to mark the effort [of the participants] as to give the festivities a symbolism which will strike the imagination, we will have to extract youngsters from their usual milieu and find settings as evocative as possible for this event.[84]

Lamirand then outlined the form and principal themes of the festivity:

> The forms of celebration will depend largely upon available resources ... but one of the common goals of all celebrations will be to place the participants in communion with the French soil, and with the tradition of the purest heroes.[85]

Having defined the identity of the *patrie* as a function of its soil, heroes, and traditions, Lamirand proceeded to list the chief objectives of the celebrations:

> 1) Evoke and invoke Joan of Arc, the incarnation of the will to live French, of total devotion, of faith and heroism ...
> 2) Evoke ... the glories and history of the region, its great men and its great women.
> 3) Evoke legends, traditions, regional qualities and folklore—songs, dances, etc. ...
> 4) Draw a lesson by providing contemporary examples. Close the ceremonies by calling upon a collective act symbolizing the solemn pledge of youths to the French community.[86]

Clearly, Vichy sought to anchor France's "overseas youths" into the collective national imagination and memory, while paradoxically conjuring up in the same breath local history, tradition, and folklore.

Children, perceived as the first generation of a "new colonial order," constituted a primary target of Vichy ideologues. Interestingly, however, not all youngsters were assigned the same roles for these festivities. In an effort to ensure that Joan of Arc's image did not blur traditional gender boundaries, Lamirand concluded his circular with the following stipulation: "All programs are to be conceived in such as way ... as to clearly differentiate the input and roles of boys and girls, and to underline their respective natural vocations."[87]

Platon's and Lamirand's orders, although followed throughout the empire, found greater resonance in some colonies than others. Indeed, Joan of Arc Day 1941 was celebrated more widely and with greater pageantry in Indochina than in any other French colony—arguably even more than in much of Vichy France proper. In Hanoi, Admiral Decoux reported: "Sixteen thousand boys and girls took part in the largest celebration of the sort ever organized in Indochina and expressed their unanimous confidence in the destinies of the French empire."[88] Moreover, hundreds of French and Vietnamese youths staged a medieval mystery play, invoking Joan, God, saints, angels, and demons, while two thousand others paraded before twenty thousand onlookers in front of Hanoi's Joan of Arc statue, decorated for the occasion with a portrait of Pétain.[89]

In keeping with Lamirand's suggestions to associate the cult of the *Sainte de la patrie* with that of local heroes and heroines, Jeanne d'Arc was also identified for the first time with the three Trung sisters, who had expelled the Chinese from Vietnam in the first century after Christ, much as Joan of Arc had repelled the English from most of France in the fifteenth century. A historical reconstruction, staged by children from throughout Tonkin, celebrated all four figures simultaneously. It thereby allegorically bound Vietnamese and French cultures and subsumed Vietnamese nationalist figures into a new pan-imperial French liturgy.[90]

Nor was the pageantry of May 11 reserved to Hanoi. In Saigon, Vientiane, and Phnom Penh, vast "historical corteges" paraded down the main boulevards. In Hué, thousands of children participated in religious rites before Emperor Bao Dai. In the town of Thai Nguyên, an "immaculately white" statue of Joan of Arc, described by one account as "a statue whose white silhouette contrasts against the blue chain of the Tam Dao [mountains] on the horizon," was constructed on Joan Day.[91] Finally, as if to ensure that imperial unity and the cult of the *patrie* outshone all other themes, twenty thousand children from Tonkin bestowed their "veneration" upon Pétain, assuring him in a collective message of their "devotion and patriotic faith."[92]

Similarly, in Guadeloupe, Constant Sorin reported that Joan of Arc Day 1941 had been "celebrated under the triple sign of youth, national unity and fidelity to local traditions,"[93] in total accordance, in short, with both Platon's and Lamirand's instructions. On the morning of May 11 in Guadeloupe, a series of Masses were performed for youngsters, complete with special sermons on Joan of Arc. That same evening, the island's "young elite" assembled outdoors for songs, games, and campfires, all "evoking the memory of the National Saint and the rebirth of France."[94] Not content with associating Pétain's national redressment with Joan's fifteenth-century exploits, Sorin took the opportunity to express the youth of Guadeloupe's supposed "faith in the future and unity of the Empire," adding: "It knows that it will play its part in the National Revolution."[95]

By performing a ritual tribute to the *Sainte de la Patrie*, Guadeloupe's children were reminded of Joan of Arc's unquestioning devotion to France. In this sense, Joan Day fulfilled a function similar to that of Guadeloupe's abundant First World War memorials.[96] However, if First World War monuments in villages told of a supreme Guadeloupean devotion, Joan of Arc Day provided a more distant and abstract cult of a purely metropolitan sacrifice. Perhaps the veil of mystery enshrouding Joan of Arc compensated for this shortcoming. The novelist Raphaël Confiant suggests that in Martinique, at least, Joan was reinvented by *quimboiseurs* (sorcerers and witches), and other alike. Some anthropomorphized a warship named after her, and metamorphosed the *Pucelle* herself into a contemporary, supernatural ten-foot giant.[97]

While in Guadeloupe and Indochina Vichy authorities drew their inspiration primarily from Lamirand's directives, in Madagascar Armand Annet rigorously followed Platon's May 7, 1941, instructions. Annet's right-hand man, the secrétaire général, Ponvienne, advised all public officials in Tananarive: "In keeping with instructions from our ministry, there will be no parades ... on May 11, 1941 ... but rather religious ceremonies to which are asked to attend civil and military authorities, members of the Legion and schoolchildren."[98] Accordingly, on the morning of May 11, 1941, two separate religious ceremonies were held, one at the Andohalo Cathedral, the other at the Andohalo Protestant Temple (both in Tananarive), reflecting the regime's desire to propagate the National Revolution among both of Madagascar's powerful Christian communities. At the closing of each service, a guard of honor, comprising both metropolitan and Malagasy soldiers, saluted the *Sainte de la Patrie* with a fanfare.[99]

Joan of Arc Day maintained its character as a celebration of youth and unity in 1942. The new colonial secretary, Jules Brévié, cabled all governors on May 8, 1942:

> In the metropole, Joan of Arc Day ceremonies on May 10 will be held in cities and towns under the triple banner of Youth, Faith and Will. I leave it up to you to organize the actual festivities. The head of the Legion asks the overseas Legion to collaborate closely with local authorities to plan this solemn celebration symbolizing the unity of the patrie.[100]

The relative leeway accorded by Brévié to individual governors on this occasion, as well as the rapidly evolving international conjuncture, both translated into an even greater diversity of commemorative forms for Joan of Arc Day 1942.

In Indochina, Joan Day was marked once again by massive celebrations throughout the federation. A document held at the Vietnamese National Library in Hanoi, chronicling May 10, 1942, festivities in the town of Thai-Nguyên, offers a rare detailed account of a village celebration in a Vichy colony. In Thai-Nguyên, a town in Tonkin due north of Hanoi, Joan Day began with a Mass, during which the priest likened Joan of Arc to "a living church candle burning for France's salvation."[101] After this lesson in self-sacrifice evoking Joan's martyrdom in Rouen, another priest led "an imposing procession" to the town's statue of *la Pucelle*, constructed the previous year. The senior French official of the province, the *résident* Michelot, then delivered a speech comparing Joan of Arc with Philippe Pétain, before laying fleurs-de-lis—the symbols of the French crown—before Joan's statue. Thus, the image of the *Pucelle* was subject to interpretations similar to those in the metropole under Vichy: it was openly worshipped as a symbol of a royal, Catholic, and hence antirepublican France, while being concurrently associated to the veneration of Pétain. Moreover, in Thai Nguyên, as in the metropole, Joan Day 1942 was marked by sporting events intended to underscore the youth and vitality associated with the *Sainte de la Patrie*. Vietnamese youngsters participated in *mouvements d'ensemble*, while the athletes of the Indochinese Guard performed a human pyramid. Finally, as in 1941, Joan Day once again associated the image of the *Pucelle* with that of the Trung sisters. In Thai Nguyên, historical reconstitutions featured three young Vietnamese women, dressed in fanciful ancient garb, haranguing their troops. The significance of these performances was explained over a loudspeaker by two Vietnamese commentators.[102] However, the *pièce maîtresse* of this ceremony, which so far had extolled French royalism and Catholicism as well as Vietnamese traditionalism, involved the singing of the *Marseillaise* by a large chorus. This constituted a reminder that the cult of the *patrie* at once superseded and encompassed that of the *petite patrie*.

May 10, 1942, in Madagascar took on quite different connotations yet, in the wake of the English attack on Diego-Suarez only days before. Jules Brévié did not fail to exploit Joan's full anglophobic potential on this occasion, cabling Annet in Tananarive on May 9:

> At the moment when the metropole and the faithful empire are celebrating with fervor the National Saint, our thoughts go out to the battered colony and its heroic defenders. Against the same invaders this French island is demonstrating the same courage. It is the greatest honor which can be offered to Joan of Arc: the sacrifice to the *Patrie* and confidence in its destiny.[103]

As a result of the British attack, Joan of Arc Day festivities were postponed until August, when they were staged in conjunction with Legion Day. Once again, the head of Tamatave's Legion seized the opportunity to compare Annet's quest to repel the English from Madagascar to Joan's mission. However, he concluded his diatribe with a more ambivalent appeal to Jeanne d'Arc:

> To those who are believers, I ask you to invoke in your prayers the *Sainte de la Patrie,* Saint Joan, you who saved France and are as a result the second patron of France. Saint Joan of Arc, you who were a prisoner and whom we revere as the patron of prisoners, take pity on our prisoners.[104]

This last reference may point to a protean image of a Joan who was at once rabidly anglophobic and latently germanophobic. Such a Joan seemed concerned, at the very least, with the plight of French captives in German stalags, and perhaps with the soon to be captive Vichy loyalists in Madagascar.

The impact of the British attack on Madagascar was felt as far away as Guadeloupe, where it shaped the local *Fête de Jeanne d'Arc.* Indeed, Sorin informed the island's mayors that "because of the British attack on Madagascar, no balls are to be held in Guadeloupe for Joan of Arc's national celebration."[105] According to Sorin, in spite of this interdict, May 10, 1942, in Guadeloupe "was marked by manifestations of ardent patriotism and fervent piety and profound attachment to the Head of State."[106]

In Indochina, Joan of Arc Day's success grew exponentially, reaching mammoth proportions by 1944. In Saigon, for Joan Day 1944, a rally took place before an immense freshly constructed statue of the saint tending to her sheep. There Ducoroy, Vichy's commissioner to youth and sports in Indochina, harangued some twenty thousand youngsters. He stressed the "patriotic hope of the Maiden Warrior,"[107] whose lesson was to "keep intact one's faith in the destinies of the Nation—all the way to the stake." Here Ducoroy ascribed a certain fanaticism to Joan's mission, making it one with the objectives of a now desperate and futile Vichy regime. The "order, discipline and beautiful uniforms" of the assembled youngsters left a lasting impression on Ducoroy, who recalled vividly in his memoirs, published five years later, "the proud grandeur of this celebration."[108]

In the final analysis, the celebration of Joan of Arc Day overseas manifestly served to extol three main themes dear to the Vichy regime: tradition, youth, and the *patrie.* Constant Sorin's description of a 1941 Joan Day devoted to "youth, national unity and fidelity to local traditions" illustrates the principal leitmotivs of this celebration which Vichy had introduced to the empire. Moreover, the *Pucelle* provided a model of single-minded devotion, abnegation, and sacrifice, which Vichy attempted to redirect toward the cults of the leader and of imperial unity. Finally, by interlacing the cult of Jeanne d'Arc with that of the Trung sisters, Vichy officials asserted not only the primacy of the *patrie* over the *petite patrie,* but may in fact have begun to mold a single hybrid and pan-imperial female iconology, befitting the hagiography of integral nationalists who rejected the republican image of Marianne.

It seems germane to add that the republican calendar of festivals was eventually reintroduced to French colonies after the fall of Vichy, albeit with a few modifications. In Madagascar, for instance, November 11, 1943, combined Armistice Day with "a gala to benefit the Resistance."[109] In the French Antilles, meanwhile, November 11, 1943, was celebrated with unusual fervor, as a token of Antillais rejection of Vichy's defeatism.[110] In the Antilles, in 1944 demonstrators redefined May Day as a popular left-wing festivity. In so doing, they expressed their hostility to May 1 as "a day of idolatry to the cult of Pétain."[111] One Pétainist celebration was retained, however. It was associated with a new holiday so as to anchor it in a non-Vichy tradition. Hence, in postwar Tananarive, as throughout both metropolitan and "overseas France," World War II Victory Day and Joan of Arc Day were conflated on May 11, 1946.[112]

Using festivals as a prism through which to examine Vichy's self-representations, self-legitimation, and ideology, one is able to ascertain that Vichy disseminated a multifarious image and a multitude of themes overseas. These included notions of *travail, famille, patrie*, in addition to the cults of tradition, the soil, and of Pétain himself. The very forms of these celebrations raise several general considerations. First, they constituted, as in the case of Legion Day 1942, invented or at least reinvented traditions. By reinventing and staging commemorations, the Vichy regime not only diffused self-representations across three continents but also actually began constructing a new imperial identity.[113]

Secondly, the forms of Vichy's overseas ceremonies reflect major ideological precepts. They were elaborated in accordance with the National Revolution, in reaction to republican commemorations, perceived as descendants of the Revolutionary festival,[114] while also designed to reflect the myth of imperial unity. This overriding concern dictated that Vichy's commemorations would be staged with a high degree of uniformity (naturally, local cultures did shape these celebrations, with Joan of Arc Day in Viet-

nam involving historical reenactments featuring the Trung Sisters and processions of elephants, for instance). This unity of empire, and resulting
uniformity of celebration share an important point in common with the
genesis of a new imperial discourse, and with the exporting of the National
Revolution to the colonies. Indeed, Vichy's orders on reversing the flow of
imperial propaganda, its efforts, documented by William Cohen, to go so
far as to contemplate a sort of imperial constitution,[115] its fostering of a
pan-imperial iconology,[116] and its desire to stage imperial jubilees to unity
all reflect the following underlying precept under Vichy. Vichy officials at
the Secretariat d'Etat aux colonies were convinced that the best way to
maintain imperial unity in the face of Gaullism involved exporting the National Revolution and its liturgy to the colonies.

Still, this alone cannot explain the almost counterintuitive exporting of
"National" and "Revolutionary" festivals to distant colonies. Could Vichyites have completely ignored the possibility that statues to nationalist
figures like Joan of Arc, that the celebration of the Trung sisters, or more
generally the "Invoking of local heroes and heroines" might constitute potential time bombs to French colonial domination? Maurice Ducoroy, one
of the architects in adapting the National Revolution to local pantheons,
insisted that the festivals he oversaw had "made [Indochinese] youngsters
love France." He then elaborated that "they loved their own homeland all
the more because of it."[117] It would seem, then, that Vichy's unwitting fostering of nationalist sentiments can be attributed more to a particular vision of empire than simply to brash arrogance or incompetence. Vichy's
empire was to have been one of hedged or overlapping identities, in which
"natives" would owe tribute to a French marshal, while undertaking the
restoration, or reinvention, of local traditions.

Conclusion: The Sun
Sets on Vichy's Empire

This comparative analysis of three markedly different colonies over four years reveals both the remarkable diversity and constancy of Vichy ideology in a colonial context. Its diversity is evidenced most plainly by the ease with which colonial officials adapted Pétainist themes to radically different cultures and contexts. To take this argument further, Pétainism spelled a new, malleable instrument of authoritarianism—one that could be variously interpreted to legitimize the feudalization of Madagascar, to enable the subjugation of Guadeloupeans, or to buttress Vietnamese conservatism. Armed with new Pétainist legislation, colonial administrators were able to strip indigenous dissidents of their citizenship, to relegate them to a subservient status, and to rescind any previous liberalizing reforms. This in a sense constitutes an element of similarity and difference in itself: similarity in its unrelenting reaction, and diversity of forms of coercion. The constancy of National Revolutionary themes across four continents is thus illustrated by a pronounced uniformity and orthodoxy in such domains as celebrations, the systematic exporting of anti-Semitic and anti-Masonic measures, and the exact duplication of Pétainist institutions overseas. Only a comparative approach, in fact, can shed light on the many layers of interaction between Vichy's reductionist and authoritarian turn, and a host of local constituencies. Only through a broad comparison, then, can one achieve a picture of the multifaceted and novel colonial vision that was Vichy's.

Pétain's was a colonialism in three keys. It involved the wholesale invention and production of "authentic folklore," the introduction of hard-line colonial practices, and an overriding rhetoric of imperial unity. The language of unity was a fundamental motor behind the very introduction of the National Revolution to the tropics. Colonial officials under Pétain were convinced that only a uniform extension of the National Revolution overseas could guarantee colonial oneness. In this respect, Vichy, and not the Free French, coined the idea of the empire as a "French community." Indeed, in 1942, René Maunier could claim legitimately that "a new wind is blowing in the direction of integration and aggregation ... of the colonies to the nation; a situation which ... tends to transform the colonial empire into a narrow community."[1] He neglected to add that this community rested upon National Revolutionary doctrines. Blinded to the possibility that the National Revolution could backfire in a colonial context, Vichy colonial officials pursued their goals in the name of Pétainist unity. Like Vichy's vision of "Europe," its conception of "empire" would prove an alternate path never taken to its ultimate end.

Vichy's ultraorthodox colonial practices guaranteed the regime's unpopularity overseas. Vichy was of course bent upon satisfying *colon* demands; it was also genuinely convinced of the merits of transposing its ideology to the tropics. Hence, forced labor in Madagascar and the abrogation of universal male suffrage in Guadeloupe were as appealing to the Pétainist ethos as they were to colonial zealots.

Vichy's reinvention of indigenous customs, like so many other characteristics of the regime, involved at once a continuation and exacerbation of earlier currents. Traditional African elites had admittedly been courted by the French throughout the 1930s; but never had such policies been taken to the ends that Vichy would. The cult of the Trung sisters in Indochina, and of Andrianampoinimerina in Madagascar, had been carefully checked under the Third Republic. Only under Vichy's policy of rekindling indigenous pasts would they become encouraged by the colonizers. In retrospect, Vichy's colonial folklorism seems a precipitous forced marriage of imperial myths and viable ancient indigenous customs. This ideologically unwieldy amalgam unwittingly played into the hands of a host of resistance movements overseas. Politically, then, the National Revolution overseas represented something of a fanciful bricolage, a marriage of different ideological strains to the benefit of colonial rule. In practice, it often amounted to a dismal and contradictory eclecticism.

In this sense, Pétainism in the colonies stands in many ways as a history of opportunism. Colonial officials and *petits colons* alike delighted in the unchecked power they now wielded over natives whom they could suddenly denaturalize and disenfranchise. However, much more was at work than material opportunism. Politically, the colonizers zealously seized Vichyite ultraconservatism, applying it to suit their own ends, by erasing admittedly meager Popular Front reforms. Vichy colonial officials energetically applied Pétainist directives, staging Vichyite May Days, and commissioning gigantic statues to Joan of Arc, for example. Surely, such foot soldiers of the National Revolution were responding to motivations beyond imperial unity. The popularity of the Legion in Indochina, the zeal with which blueprints were formulated for a "utopian" Madagascar, and the energy with which Sorin and Robert hunted Guadeloupean republicans all suggest that Vichy provided a collective answer to long-standing colonial desiderata.

This history of opportunism is far from one-dimensional. If the National Revolution answered the every dream of some colonizers, it was seen in much the same vein by some of the colonized. Steeped as it was in the language of national rebirth, hagiography, regimentation, and reinvigoration, the National Revolution proved a catalyst in stirring what Benedict Anderson has termed the "imaginative power of nationalism."[2] It did so on many registers. In Madagascar, for instance, the rekindling of the cult of Andrianampoinimerina signaled more than a colonial resurrection of an ancient past. It betrayed a newfound endorsement of Merina power—the very power that Madagascar's conquerors had tried to stamp out at the turn of the century, through a *politique des races*. How did the Malagasy respond to Vichy's appropriation of Merina rituals? On a literal level, displays of Merina power certainly elicited nationalist sentiments. They did so at another level as well; revolted by the harshness of Vichy colonialism, some Malagasy appropriated National Revolutionary tools as weapons against French colonial rule. Hence, in Madagascar, some nationalists turned to the very symbolic practices that Vichy was so bent on staging.

This phenomenon is all the more apparent in Indochina from 1940 to 1944. There too, the French had long sought to check the power of certain groups—most notably the mandarins. These had been considered in some sense feudal, and hence antithetical to the French revolutionary tradition. In other words, before 1940 the mandarins had been resented not only as the former power-brokers in the region but also for their imagined conflation with anti-1789 reaction. This changed radically under Vichy. Mandarins, and other established elites, were upheld by Vichyites as the protectors and conveyors of tradition, and as the embodiment of discipline, hierarchy, and "authenticity." To be sure, the match was far from perfect. The irony involved in instilling regimentation and physical education in mandarins did not fail to capture the attention of contemporaries.

With the advent of Vichy, some Vietnamese nationalists saw the opportunity to propagate their theories under the cover of the National Revolution. The nature of Vichy ideology rendered this all the easier. At one level, the National Revolution reviled the preceding regime as decadent—a claim that Vietnamese nationalists could seize for different ends. At another level, Vichy ideology promoted national rebirth and authenticity—two linchpins of national liberation struggles. Utilizing these weapons—and many others—Vietnamese nationalists challenged French rule through the very avenues unwittingly availed to them by Vichy.

In Guadeloupe, resistance took quite another turn. Oppositional practices were employed to undermine the new regime and to reinforce the legitimacy of republicanism. On the Emerald Island, too, resisters opportunistically pinpointed Vichy's weaknesses. The new regime's cult of physical fitness proved to be part of its undoing in the French Caribbean, by providing forums for popular protest.

Vichy in the tropics also affords us a glance at perhaps the only unfettered form of Vichy rule. Devoid of German influence, between 1940 and 1942 the colonial realm underwent something akin to "pure Vichysm." In other words, in the colonies, a Vichy moment was achieved independently from the defeat of 1940, and certainly from the Occupation. Chronologically, the height of Vichy reforms across the empire coincides with the tenure of the extremist colonial minister René-Charles Platon. It was between his appointment in September 1940 and his revocation in April 1942 that the vast majority of Vichy legislation was extended overseas. It was then too that Vichy fought the most fiercely against Free French encroachments on the empire.

The Vichy colonial episode would have a lasting impact upon both the colonies and the metropole. Through its rejection of republican discourse, Vichy indirectly shaped the ultraassimilation of the postwar, which brought about the departmentalization of Guadeloupe, Martinique, Réunion, and Guyane. With its essentialist doctrines, it undoubtedly engaged and interacted with such ideas as *négritude*, providing an infinitely more pragmatic and cynical model of "difference"—but one that nonetheless shared certain notions of organic "authenticity." Vichy's transposal of nostalgic reactionism overseas, as well as its hard-line colonialism, helped stir multiple forms of indigenous nationalism. Finally, Vichy rule in the colonies provided a legacy for future integralist *colon* movements hostile to the French republic. The flame of integralist colonialism would be passed on to the last fanatical defenders of empire.

Notes

The following abbreviations are used in the Notes and Bibliography:

ADG   Archives Départementales de la Guadeloupe, Guadeloupe, French West Indies.

AMB   Archives Municipales de Bordeaux, France.

AN   Archives Nationales, Paris, France.

ARDM   National Archives of the Democratic Republic of Madagascar Antananarivo, Madagascar.

BDIC   Bibliothèque de Documentation Internationale Contemporaine, Nanterre, France.

CAOM   Archives Nationales, Centre des Archives d'Outre-mer, Aix-en-Provence, France.

GGI   Gouvernement Général Indochine.

PRO   Public Record Office, Kew Gardens, London, United Kingdom.

RSTNF   Résidence supérieure du Tonkin, Nouveau Fonds.

SHAT   Service Historique de l'Armée de Terre, Vincennes, France.

USNA   U.S. National Archives II, College Park, Maryland.

VNNA   National Archives of the Socialist Republic of Vietnam. Archives #1 (Colonial era), Hanoi, Vietnam.

BOOK EPIGRAPH: Alain Ruscio, ed. *Ho Chi Minh: Textes, 1914–1969* (Paris: L'Harmattan, 1990), p. 104. *All translations from the French are the author's.*

Introduction

1. To make matters worse, the handful of scholars who have examined Vichy in the tropics have concentrated almost exclusively on economics. These historians have suggested that Vichy policies were actually enlightened and forward-looking

in the colonies. Daniel Lefeuvre, "Vichy et la modernisation de l'Algérie: intention ou réalité?" *Vingtième siècle, revue d'histoire* 42 (Apr.–June 1994): 7–16. Jacques Marseille, *Empire colonial et capitalisme français* (Paris: Albin Michel, 1984), pp. 338–42. Marseille remarks upon Vichy's supposed dedication to the notion of tutelage, its alleged aversion to forced labor, and its "visionary" economic outlook.

2. Charles-Robert Ageron et al., *Histoire de la France coloniale, 1914–1990* (Paris: Armand Colin, 1990), p. 324.

3. In this respect, the Vichy expert Robert Paxton's 1982 observation still holds true; the colonies do indeed constitute "a neglected Vichy subject." Robert Paxton, *Vichy France: Old Guard and New Order, 1940–1944* (New York: Columbia University Press, 1982), p. 398. To be sure, a number of local studies have told the story of Vichy's presence in such places as Guiana or Martinique, but this literature has failed to receive a wide historical audience. See Rodolphe Alexandre, *La Guyane sous Vichy* (Paris: Editions Caribéennes, 1988); F. A. Baptiste, "Le Régime de Vichy à la Martinique," *Revue d'histoire de la deuxième guerre mondiale* 111 (1978): 1–24; Richard Burton, "Vichysme et Vichyistes à la Martinique, 1940–1943," *Cahiers du CERAG* 34 (Feb. 1978): 1–101; Camille Chauvet, "La Martinique pendant la deuxième guerre mondiale," Ph.D. dissertation, Université de Toulouse le Mirail, 1983.

4. See, for instance, Charles-Robert Ageron, *La Décolonisation française* (Paris: Armand Colin, 1991), pp. 45–78.

5. See, for example, Henri Grimal, *La Décolonisation de 1919 à nos jours* (Bruxelles: Editions Complexe, 1996), pp. 96–97.

6. On how the British dealt with Vichy's hostile imperial "neutrality," see Martin Thomas, "After Mers-el-Kébir: The Armed Neutrality of the French Navy, 1940–1943," *English Historical Review* 112 (1997): 643–70; and Desmond Dinan, *The Politics of Persuasion: British Policy and French African Neutrality, 1940–1942* (New York: University Press of America, 1988).

7. The original quotation from June 19, 1940, reads: "[It] would not be tolerable for the panic of Bordeaux to cross the sea." Because the French government had fled to Bordeaux before settling in Vichy, the city denoted something akin to "panic" or "defeatism." Charles de Gaulle, *Discours et messages pendant la guerre, 1940–1946* (Paris: Plon, 1970), p. 5.

8. Henri Du Moulin de Labarthète, *Le Temps des illusions: souvenirs, juillet 1940– avril 1942* (Geneva: Editions du cheval ailé, 1948), pp. 198–99.

9. On this single ministry under Vichy, see Bernard Bléhaut, *Pas de clairon pour l'amiral: Henri Bléhaut, 1889–1962* (Paris: Jean Picollec, 1991), pp. 62–67.

10. A plethora of reports were drawn up after each imperial loss. CAOM, Affaires Politiques 2555, dossier 9, "Note sur l'orientation à donner à notre politique coloniale." CAOM, Affaires Politiques 928, dossier 4, "Note … après l'agression britannique contre Madagascar."

11. As one scholar has remarked, it would be a grave error to reduce all the root causes of decolonization to the Second World War. Ageron, *La Décolonisation française*, p. 5.

12. Colonial policy under the Third Republic between 1924 and 1938 had been especially coercive, delivering on few of the promises of republicanism. Alice

Conklin, *A Mission to Civilize: The Republican Idea of Empire in France and West Africa, 1895–1930* (Stanford, Calif.: Stanford University Press, 1997), p. 247.

13. It is interesting to note that Vichy's colonial rivals, the Free French under Charles de Gaulle and Félix Eboué, elaborated an antiassimiliationist indigenous policy of their own in Equatorial Africa, in some respects as reactionary as Pétain's. For this argument, see Frederick Cooper, *Decolonization and African Society: The Labor Question in French and British Africa* (Cambridge: Cambridge University Press, 1996), pp. 157–58.

14. I borrow this expression from Pascal Blanchard and Nicolas Bancel, *De l'indigène à l'immigré* (Paris: Gallimard, 1998).

15. Martin Thomas, *The French Empire at War, 1940–1945* (Manchester: Manchester University Press, 1998); Kim Munholland, "Empire," in Bertram Gordon, ed., *Historical Dictionary of World War II France* (Westport, Conn.: Greenwood Press, 1998), pp. 120–22; Paul-Marie de la Gorce, *L'Empire écartelé, 1936–1962* (Paris: Denoël, 1988); Dinan, *The Politics of Persuasion*.

16. In addition to Ageron's contribution in Jean-Pierre Azéma et al., *Vichy et les Français*, see his section entitled "Le Mythe de l'empire dans la France occupée," in Charles-Robert Ageron, *France coloniale ou parti colonial?* (Paris: PUF, 1978), pp. 269–75. Also see the final section on Vichy in Pascal Blanchard, "Nationalisme et colonialisme: idéologie coloniale, discours sur l'Afrique et les Africains de la droite nationaliste française des années 30 à la Révolution Nationale," Ph.D. dissertation, University of Paris I, 1994.

17. A host of such individual studies exist, examining Vichy rule in such colonies as St. Pierre and Miquelon, Guiana, Martinique, Réunion, and West Africa. Unfortunately, none provides a sense of Vichy's pan-imperial designs, nor of the extent or pervasiveness of Vichy reforms in the colonies. In addition to the works already cited in note 3 on Guiana and Martinique, see Catherine Akpo-Vaché, *L'Afrique occidentale française et la seconde guerre mondiale* (Paris: Karthala, 1996); Michael Crowder, "Vichy and the Free French in West Africa during the Second World War," in M. Crowder, ed., *Colonial West Africa, Collected Essays* (London: Frank Cass, 1978), pp. 268–82; J. J. Foll, "Le Togo pendant la deuxième guerre mondiale," *Revue d'histoire de la deuxième guerre mondiale* 115 (July 1979): 69–77; James Giblin, "A Colonial State in Crisis: Vichy Administration in French West Africa," *Africana Journal* 16 (1994): 326–40; Martin Espérance, "L'île de la Réunion de 1939 à 1945," DEA (master's thesis), joint: Faculté de Droit d'Aix-en-Provence and l'Université française de l'Océan Indien. On St. Pierre and Miquelon, see William Christian, *Divided Island: Faction and Unity on St. Pierre* (Cambridge: Harvard University Press, 1969).

18. Gwendolyn Wright, *The Politics of Design in French Colonial Urbanism* (Chicago: University of Chicago Press, 1991).

19. This has recently begun to change. Historian Jacques Cantier has been one of the first to view long-restricted dossiers in France on the matter, and has presented some of his findings in his excellent article, "1939–1945: une métropole coloniale en guerre," in "Alger, 1940–1962," *Autrement* 56 (Mar. 1999): 16–61. Unfortunately, materials in Algeria themselves still remain largely inaccessible to Western researchers today.

20. Bao Dai, *Le Dragon d'Annam* (Paris: Plon, 1980), p. 97.

21. Hubert Deschamps, a former colonial administrator in Madagascar, places the origins of this change somewhat earlier, around the Popular Front period (1936–38). Hubert Deschamps, *Roi de la brousse; mémoires d'autres mondes* (Paris: Berger-Levrault, 1975), p. 178.

22. Huyn Kim Khánh, *Vietnamese Communism, 1925–1945* (Ithaca: Cornell University Press, 1982), pp. 259–63.

23. Paxton, *Vichy France,* p. 69.

Chapter 1: Vichy's Empire in 1940

1. De Gaulle, *Discours et messages*, pp. 18, 32.

2. Robert Paxton has noted that after the fall of France in 1940, "the colonies had become simultaneously even more precious and even more vulnerable." Paxton, *Vichy France*, p. 48. Paxton has also argued, regarding Vichy's use of the colonies as a leverage for achieving true collaboration with Germany: "The Archimedian Point from which Vichy finally interested Berlin in collaboration was the issue of how to defend the French Empire against British-Gaullist encroachment." Ibid., p. 68.

3. Thomas, *The French Empire at War*, p. 1.

4. On Pétain's vision of the colonies as "free territories," see Du Moulin de Labarthète, *Le Temps des illusions*, p. 197.

5. Marc Michel, "Les Ralliements à la France Libre en 1940," paper delivered at the journée d'études: "La Seconde guerre mondiale et son impact en Afrique," Université d'Aix-en-Provence, Feb. 10, 1996. I wish to thank Marc Michel for making available to me the following unpublished manuscript, which builds this same argument: "The *Ralliements* of the French Colonies to Free France."

6. "In spite of the false promises, of pressures and threats, only one-sixteenth of our colonial territories have given in to the call of dissidence." Vichy's colonial secretary, Charles René Platon, quoted in "Une Allocution radiodiffusée du Contre-Amiral Platon aux populations de l'empire," *Les Nouveaux temps,* Aug. 19, 1941, p. 1.

7. Raymond Betts has aptly described this phenomenon as "bureaucratic submission." Raymond Betts, *France and Decolonization, 1900–1960* (New York: St. Martin's Press, 1991), p. 51.

8. William B. Cohen, *Rulers of Empire: The French Colonial Service in Africa* (Stanford, Calif.: Hoover University Press, 1971), p. 42.

9. A pro-Vichy journalist summarized this theory of colonial vendetta as follows: "England would have liked to complete its dismemberment of French territories, begun in the eighteenth century with the conquest of the Indies and Canada." Jean Luchaire, "Incertitude vichyssoise: la collaboration et l'empire," *Les Nouveaux temps*, Jan. 12, 1941, p. 1.

10. Cohen, *Rulers of Empire*, p. 52.

11. The historian of the Second World War, Gerhard Weinberg, has argued that "the authorities in the French colonial territories were not only traditionally anti-British in their orientation, but they had acquired the *idée fixe* that the British

only hoped to seize parts of the French colonial empire for themselves." Gerhard Weinberg, *A World at Arms* (Cambridge: Cambridge University Press, 1994), p. 160.

12. Maurice Ricord has outlined the contradiction between Vichy's colonial apotheosis and its denial of Third Republican contributions to the empire (most notably those of Jules Ferry and Georges Mandel). Maurice Ricord, *Au service de l'empire, 1939–1945* (Paris: Société des editions coloniales et métropolitaines, 1946), pp. 6–7.

13. As Eugen Weber and Robert Paxton have noted, Maurras's surprise was actually directed at Pétain's political savvy. Eugen Weber, *Action Française* (Stanford, Calif.: Stanford University Press, 1962), p. 447. Paxton, *Vichy France*, p. 139.

14. François Zuccarelli, *La Vie politique sénégalaise, 1940–1988* (Paris: Cheam, 1988), p. 15.

15. Comité d'action anti-Bolchevique, "Le Parti Communiste et les colonies," July 1940.

16. Marius Leblond, "L'Empire et la France de Pétain," in *France 1941: la Révolution Nationale constructive, un bilan et un programme* (Paris: Editions Alsatia, 1941), p. 150. On Marius Leblond and his unrelated "white brother" Ary Leblond, see Françoise Vergès, *Monsters and Revolutionaries: Colonial Family Romance and Métissage* (Durham: Duke University Press, 1999), pp. 109–12.

17. "A travers l'empire," *La Dépêche de Toulouse*, Sept. 10, 1942, p. 1.

18. Jean Peyrade, "La France est un empire," *La Croix*, Jan. 19, 1942, p. 1.

19. *L'Africain: hebdomadaire de la France extérieure* 393 (Feb. 26, 1941): 4.

20. *Les Nouveaux temps*, Jan. 1, 1941, p. 4.

21. Charles Maurras, *La Seule France* (Lyon: Lardanchet, 1941), pp. 130, 305.

22. "La Réunion exprime sa fidelité et sa reconnaissance envers la France," *La Dépêche de Toulouse*, Nov. 5, 1942; "Le Loyalisme des Guyannais," *La Croix*, Oct. 8, 1941.

23. CAOM, Affaires Politiques 355, Sept. 3, 1940.

24. "Une Allocution radiodiffusée du contre-amiral Platon aux populations de l'empire," *Les Nouveaux temps*, Aug. 19, 1941, p. 1.

25. I borrow this expression from Yael Simpson-Fletcher, "Capital of the Colonies: Real and Imagined Boundaries between Metropole and Empire in 1920's Marseilles," in Felix Driver and David Gilbert, eds., *Imperial Cities: Landscape, Display and Identity* (Manchester: Manchester University Press, 1999), pp. 135–54.

26. "La Maison du missionnaire," *L'Illustration*, Jan. 25, 1941, p. 100.

27. Michèle Cointet, *Vichy capitale, 1940–1944* (Paris: Perrin, 1993), pp. 146–47.

28. E. Vivier de Streel, "Notre future politique coloniale," *Revue des deux mondes*, Nov. 15, 1940, p. 209.

29. CAOM, Affaires Economiques 68, dossier 3, "Wiesbaden, Oct. 21, 1940."

30. Ibid., "Délégation économique, compte rendu de la séance du 19 novembre 1940."

31. Paxton, *Vichy France*, p. xii.

32. CAOM, Affaires Economiques 68, dossier 3, "Compte rendu de la séance du 19 novembre 1940."

33. Ibid.

34. CAOM, Affaires Politiques 355, Contre-Amiral Marzin, 20 novembre 1941.

35. CAOM, Affaires Politiques 2659, dossier "opinions allemandes sur la colonisation française."

36. Vichy replaced the Ministère des Colonies with a Secrétariat d'Etat aux Colonies. The terms "secretary" and "minister" can therefore be seen as synonymous.

37. CAOM, Affaires Politiques 2555, dossier 9, Brévié to Laval, Nov. 12, 1940.

38. Early in his career, Brévié had been one of the few West African administrators to show much concern for the plight of slaves. See Martin Klein, *Slavery and Colonial Rule in French West Africa* (Cambridge: Cambridge University Press, 1998), pp. 134, 170, 211.

39. Cohen, *Rulers of Empire*, pp. 115–16; 130–31; Conklin, *A Mission to Civilize*, pp. 208–9, 313.

40. See Panivong Norindr, "The Popular Front's Colonial Policies in Indochina: Reassessing the Popular Front's 'Colonisation Altruiste,'" in Tony Chafer and Amanda Sackur, eds., *French Colonial Empire and the Popular Front, Hope and Disillusion* (London: St. Martin's Press, 1999), p. 210.

41. Ibid., pp. 240–41.

42. See Cyril Buffet, *La Collaboration ... à gauche aussi* (Paris: Perrin, 1989).

43. Pierre Lyautey, *Pour l'empire français: action et doctrine* (Vichy: Comité de la France d'outre-mer, 1940), pp. 16–17.

44. Paxton, *Vichy France*, p. 21.

45. Robert Poulain, "La Révolution Nationale et les colonies," *Le Temps*, June 6, 1941, p. 1.

46. Ibid.

47. Cohen, *Rulers of Empire*, p. 163.

48. CAOM, Affaires Politiques 1297, Platon to Darlan, Vichy, Mar. 7, 1941 (binder, p. 320).

49. Henry Lémery, *D'une république à l'autre: souvenirs de la mêlée politique, 1894–1944* (Paris: Table ronde, 1964), p. 260.

50. CAOM, Télégrammes 679, #234R, Aug. 16, 1940.

51. CAOM, Affaires Politiques 2520, dossier 9, report #2, Aug. 9–30, 1940.

52. Lémery, *D'une république à l'autre*, p. 262. A report from the Canadian representative at Vichy corroborates this version of a racially motivated dismissal: National Archives of Canada, Ottawa, King papers, Correspondence, 1940 (Dennis to F) MG26, J1, vol. 287, p. 242462; Dupuy to Mackenzie King, Oct. 5, 1940.

53. Du Moulin de Labarthète, p. 38.

54. Ibid., pp. 38, 198. Robert Aron offers an instructive description of Platon: "This ex-Professor from the École Supérieure de la Marine, an austere Protestant, believed that the salvation of France lay in total collaboration with the Reich." Robert Aron, *The Vichy Regime, 1940–44* (New York: Macmillan, 1958), p. 129.

55. Jean Paillard, *1940–1944: la révolution corporative spontanée* (Paris: Editions du Vivarais, 1979), p. 236.

56. CAOM, Affaires Politiques 768, Platon radio broadcast heard in Guadeloupe on Nov. 22, 1940.

57. AN 3W 316, 6. In his memoirs, Marcel Peyrouton specifies that Platon was

tortured by resisters, who dragged him behind a truck until he died. Marcel Peyrouton, *Du service public à la prison commune: souvenirs* (Paris: Plon, 1950), p. 140.

58. CAOM, Affaires Politiques 885, dossier 1. Note dated Jan. 27, 1942, chronicling the difficulties in arranging for the Legion to be extended to the colonies.

59. René Maunier, *Les Lois de l'empire, 1940–1942* (Paris: Domat-Montchrestien,
1942), p. 9.

60. CAOM, Indochine Nouveau Fonds, carton 133, dossier 1201. Platon to
Brenier.

61. Ibid.

62. Cohen, *Rulers of Empire,* pp. 161–62.

63. The historian Jacques Marseille asserts: "[Vichy] functionaries had the
merit of formulating a project next to which Brazzaville's reformism palled by
comparison." Marseille, *Empire colonial et capitalisme français,* p. 342.

64. Joseph Lehr, "Le Gouffre colonial," *La Dépêche coloniale,* Feb. 3, 1901, p. 1.

65. Raymond Betts, *Assimilation and Association in French Colonial Theory, 1890–
1914* (New York: Columbia University Press, 1961), p. 131.

66. Conklin, *A Mission to Civilize,* p. 210.

67. Betts, *Assimilation and Association,* p. 106.

68. Conklin, *A Mission to Civilize,* p. 175.

69. Alice Conklin, "'Democracy' Rediscovered: Civilization through Association in French West Africa, 1914–1930," *Cahiers d'études africaines* 145 (1997): 66.

70. Michael Adas, *Machines as the Measure of Men: Science, Technology, and Ideologies of Western Dominance* (Ithaca: Cornell University Press, 1989), p. 321.

71. Léopold de Saussure, *Psychologie de la colonisation française dans ses rapports
avec les sociétés indigènes* (Paris: Ancienne Librairie Germer Baillière, 1899); Louis
Vignon, *Un Programme de politique coloniale* (Paris: Plon, 1919); Arthur Girault,
Principes de la colonisation et de législation coloniale (Paris: Recueil Sirey, 1929) (there
were many re-editions of this work).

72. Deschamps, *Roi de la brousse,* p. 98.

73. Paillard, *1940–1944,* pp. 233–35; and Pascal Blanchard and Gilles Boëtsch,
"Races et propagande coloniale sous le régime de Vichy, 1940–1944," *Africa, Rivista trimestrale di studi e documentazione del'Instituto Italo-Africano* 49 (Dec. 1994):
542.

74. Jean Paillard, *La Fin des Français en Afrique noire* (Paris: Les Oeuvres françaises, 1935), p. 169.

75. Blanchard, "Nationalisme et colonialisme," vol. 1, p. 462.

76. See Jean Paillard, *L'Empire français de demain* (Paris: Institut d'études corporatives et sociales, 1943); and René Maunier, *L'Empire français: propos et projets*
(Paris: Librairies du Recueil Sirey, 1943).

77. René Maunier, *Sociologie coloniale,* vol. 3 (Paris: Editions Dumat-Montchrestien, 1942), p. 265.

78. Maunier, *Les Lois de l'empire,* pp. 10–11.

79. Betts, *Assimilation and Association,* p. 116.

80. Steven Zdatny, "Collaboration or Resistance? French Hairdressers and Vichy's Labor Charter," *French Historical Studies* 20, no. 4 (fall 1997): 741; and Paillard, *1940–1944.*

81. Paillard, *L'Empire français de demain*, p. 21.
82. Ibid., pp. 22–23.
83. Ibid., p. 41.
84. Ibid., pp. 28–29.
85. There is an ongoing historiographical debate over just how fascist the Vichy regime was. While Stanley Payne has argued that "[s]erious students have long appreciated that the Pétainist regime itself cannot be considered intrinsically fascist, but rather one of a large number of syncratic, conservative authoritarian regimes," and has been supported in this argument by a host of historians including Alain-Gérard Slama, a handful of scholars have seen Vichy as more fascist than is commonly allowed (most notably Michèle Cointet-Labrousse and Roger Bourderon). Taking a compromise position, historians like Cointet and Paxton have suggested that while Vichy was never strictly speaking fascist, it nonetheless starting leaning toward fascism in its later years. Robert Paxton offers perhaps the most balanced judgment by stating that "in [a] broader sense, Vichy was fascist," and then conceding: "[However,] no undiluted fascist regime has wielded power." See Paxton, *Vichy France*, pp. 228–30, 232, 233; Stanley Payne, "Fascism in Western Europe," in Nathaniel Greene, ed., *Fascism an Anthology* (New York: Thomas Crowell, 1968), p. 298; Michèle Cointet-Labrousse, *Vichy et le fascisme* (Bruxelles: Editions Complexe, 1987); Roger Bourderon, "Le Régime de Vichy était-il fasciste?" *Revue d'histoire de la deuxième guerre mondiale* 91 (July 1973); and Alain-Gérard Slama "Vichy était-il fasciste?" *Vingtième siècle, revue d'histoire* 11 (July 1986): 41–53.
86. Colonel Priou, colonial administrators Desbordes, Lawless, and Rouvin, "Mémoire sur la condition des indigènes détribalisés" (May 1944), p. 93. Located in CAOM, Agence FOM 393, dossier 4 bis/1a.
87. On these incidents, and on the French policing of foreigners, see Neil MacMaster, *Colonial Migrants and Racism: Algerians in France, 1900–1962* (London: Macmillan, 1997); Clifford Rosenberg, "Republican Surveillance: Immigration, Citizenship and the Police in Interwar Paris," Ph.D. dissertation, Princeton University, 2000; Gérard Noiriel, *The French Melting Pot* (Minneapolis: University of Minnesota Press, 1996); José-Ramon Cubero, *Nationalistes et étrangers: le massacre d'Aigues-Mortes* (Paris: Imago, 1996); Tyler Stovall, "The Color Line behind the Lines: Racial Violence in France during the Great War," *American Historical Review* 103, no. 3 (1998): 737–69; and Philippe Videlier, "Il y a soixante-dix ans la France expulse ses étudiants chinois," *Le Monde*, Oct. 14, 1991, p. 2.
88. Priou et al. CAOM, Agence FOM, dossier 4 bis/1a, p. 84.
89. Ibid., pp. 121–22.
90. The dread among such theorists of the "debaucherous native" is reminiscent of turn-of-the-century fears of the crowd. The crowd was presented alternately as a woman or an alcoholic—both of which were seen as "threaten[ing] to undermine French civilization." Susanna Barrows, *Distorting Mirrors: Visions of the Crowd in Late Nineteenth-Century France* (New Haven: Yale University Press, 1981), p. 46.

Chapter 2: The French in Madagascar

1. K. C. Gandar Dower, *Into Madagascar* (Harmondsworth: Penguin Books, 1943), pp. 88–89.

2. Yvan-Georges Paillard, *Les Incertitudes du colonialisme: Jean Carol à Madagascar* (Paris: L'Harmattan, 1990), pp. 13–14.

3. Pier Larson, "Desperately Seeking 'the Merina' (Central Madagascar): Reading Ethnonyms and Their Semantic Fields in African Identity Histories," *Journal of Southern African Studies* 22, no. 4 (Dec. 1996): 552.

4. Stephen Ellis, *The Rising of the Red Shawls: A Revolt in Madagascar, 1895–1899* (Cambridge: Cambridge University Press, 1985).

5. Maurice Bloch, *From Blessing to Violence: History and Ideology in the Circumcision Ritual of the Merina of Madagascar* (Cambridge: Cambridge University Press, 1986), p. 29.

6. Paillard, *Les Incertitudes,* p. 16.

7. Gillian Feeley-Harnik, *A Green Estate: Restoring Independence in Madagascar* (Washington, D.C.: Smithsonian Institution Press, 1991), p. 124.

8. Paillard, *Les Incertitudes,* p. 16.

9. "La Francisation des noms de lieux aux colonies," *La Quinzaine coloniale,* Feb. 25, 1902, p. 128.

10. Feely-Harnick, *A Green Estate,* p. 123.

11. Victor Augagneur, *Erreurs et brutalités coloniales* (Paris: Librairie Montaigne, 1927).

12. Deschamps, *Roi de la brousse,* p. 244.

13. Paul Pollacchi, *Atlas colonial français* (Paris: L'Illustration, 1929), p. 175.

14. PRO, FO 371/24336, p. 156.

15. Madagascar's first governor under Vichy addresses this issue in Philip Whitcomb, trans., *France during the German Occupation, 1940–1944: A Collection of 292 Statements on the Government of Maréchal Pétain and Pierre Laval,* vol. II (Stanford, Calif.: Hoover Institution, 1957), p. 727.

16. See Francis Koerner, *Madagascar: colonisation française et nationalisme malgache* (Paris: l'Harmattan, 1994), p. 316. A number of truly fascist movements were established in Madagascar in the 1930s, although none posed a significant threat until 1940.

17. On the plans for Jewish emigration to Madagascar, see Vicki Caron, *Uneasy Asylum: France and the Jewish Refugee Crisis, 1933–1942* (Stanford, Calif.: Stanford University Press, 1999), 146–57; Magnus Brechtken, *"Madagaskar für die Juden": Antisemitische Idee und politische Praxi, 1885–1945* (München: Oldenbourg Verlag, 1997); Michael Marrus, *The Unwanted: European Refugees in the Twentieth Century* (Oxford: Oxford University Press, 1985), pp. 186–87; and Michael Marrus and Robert Paxton, *Vichy France and the Jews* (New York: Schocken Books, 1981), pp. 60–62.

18. Pollacchi, *Atlas colonial français,* p. 175.

19. Two theses have dealt with Madagascar during the war, although with no special emphasis on either Vichy or the National Revolution. The first, moreover, is essentially devoted to Madagascar's economic plight under the British blockade:

See Dox F. Ratrematsialonina, "Madagascar pendant la deuxième guerre mondiale: un essai d'autarcie, 1939–1943," Ph.D. dissertation, Université d'Aix-en-Provence, 1986; and Christian Guérin du Marteray, "Une Colonie pendant la guerre ou les origines d'une révolte: Madagascar, 1939–1947," Ph.D. dissertation, Université de Nice, 1977.

20. CAOM, Madagascar PM 126. Concerning the experience of Malagasy soldiers fighting for France in the Second World War, and their subsequent fate in prison camps in Germany, then in detention camps in France, see Monique Lupo-Raveloarimanana, "Soldats et travailleurs malgaches en France pendant la seconde guerre mondiale," *Omaly sy Anio (Hier et Aujourd'hui)*, Université de Madagascar 28 (July–Dec. 1988): 23–42; and Chantal Valensky, "Soldats malgaches et culture française," *Revue française d'histoire d'outre-mer* 315 (1997): 78–83.

21. Monique Rakotoanosy Ratrimoarivony, "Histoire et nature de l'enseignement à Madagascar de 1896 à 1960," Ph.D. dissertation, University of Paris IV, 1986, p. 103.

22. CAOM, Madagascar PM 126 and CAOM, Madagascar 3A25 (Circulaires 1940), Apr. 22, 1940.

23. CAOM, Madagascar 2D 198.

24. Throughout this book, I will employ the former names of since-rebaptized cities, in an effort to avoid anachronisms. I will thus refer to Saigon instead of Ho Chi Minh City, and Tananarive in place of Antananarivo.

25. CAOM, Cabinet 54, dossier 344.

26. It is interesting to note that certain other European communities in Madagascar, most notably the Greeks, appear to have vehemently opposed Vichy. See AN 3W48, Gaullist secret report, Nov. 24, 1942: "I will not hesitate in saying that the Greeks were the most Gaullist of all in Madagascar."

27. OSS State Department Intelligence and Research reports, part XIII (Africa), reel 8, p. 556.

28. PRO, FO 371/24336, p. 155.

29. See Deschamps, *Roi de la brousse*, p. 172.

30. AN 3W128, procès Cayla, dossier 4, 14.

31. The expression was used by Jean Guéhenno to describe metropolitan France. Jean Guéhenno, *Journal des années noires* (Paris: Gallimard, 1947), p. 16.

32. CAOM, Affaires Politiques 2520, dossier 9, rapport #3, 1er au 15 septembre 1940; and rapport #6, novembre 1940.

33. AN 3W128, procès Cayla, dossier 3, 43.

34. PRO, FO 371/28238, Madagascar 1941, "Information on General Conditions in Madagascar."

35. Ibid.

36. CAOM, Affaires Politiques 2520, dossier 9, rapport #3, 1er au 15 septembre 1940; and rapport #6, novembre 1940.

37. See Ratrematsialonina, "Madagascar pendant la deuxième guerre mondiale," vol. 1.

38. Lucile Rabearimanana, "Le District de Manjakanandiana (Province d'Antananarivo) pendant la deuxième guerre mondiale: désorganisation économique et restructuration sociale," *Omaly sy Anio* 29–32 (1989–90): 450.

39. Henri J. M. Grapin, *Madagascar, 1942* (Paris: La Pensée universelle, 1993), p. 28. Catholic missionaries confronted autarky by redoubling production in their private "farms." See Michel Carle, ed., *Au pays des lambas blancs: documents pour servir à l'histoire du missionnariat québecois dans la première moitié du XXème siècle* (Ottawa: University of Ottawa Press, 1995), p. 58.

40. Madagascar et dépendances: direction des douanes. *Rapport annuel, 1941*, pp. 20–21. Martin Thomas has suggested that the British blockade was regularly breached by none other than the Americans. See Martin Thomas, "Imperial Backwater or Strategic Outpost? The British Takeover of Vichy Madagascar, 1942," *Historical Journal* 39, no. 4 (Dec. 1996): 1052. Conventional wisdom on this matter is perhaps best summarized by Pierre Vérin's assertion that "the island managed to export only a little vanilla and graphite to the United States." Pierre Vérin, *Madagascar* (Paris: Karthala, 1990), p. 169.

41. Armand Annet, *Aux heures troublées de l'Afrique française* (Paris: Éditions du conquistador, 1952), p. 98.

42. The Armand Annet trial record reveals that Vichy had ordered him not to consider the Japanese enemies, even if they violated French sovereignty in Madagascar. Henri Grapin, meanwhile, suggests that the British might have barely beaten the Japanese to Madagascar. See Procès Armand Annet, Bibliothèque de Documentation Internationale Contemporaine (hereafter BDIC), p. 72; Grapin, *Madagascar, 1942*, pp. 78, 110, 145. For the opinion that only scarce evidence pointed to a Japanese strike on Madagascar, see Thomas, "Imperial Backwater or Strategic Outpost?" 1056. On the sabotaging of bridges, see Dinan, *The Politics of Persuasion*, p. 229.

43. Martin Gilbert, *Winston Churchill*, vol. VII, "Road to Victory" (London: Heinemann, 1986), p. 105.

44. Ibid.

45. Grapin, *Madagascar, 1942*, pp. 110, 135–45, 226. For the British casualty figures, see Dinan, *The Politics of Persuasion*, p. 223. As a measure of how intense the fighting was, Annet himself nearly lost his life in the campaign when his car was strafed by British planes. See CAOM, Affaires Politiques 2046, Telegram 2858, Oct. 7, 1942.

46. Armand Annet has no qualms in admitting that "many among the functionaries, the military and even the colons seemed quite favorable towards the National Revolution." Annet, *Aux heures troublées de l'Afrique française*, p. 85.

47. Paxton, *Vichy France*, p. 147.

48. CAOM, Madagascar, Agence FOM, 401, dossier 1bis/1.

49. Charles Mauban, "L'Homme de la Révolution Nationale," *Idées, Revue mensuelle* 10–11 (Sept. 1942): p. 24.

50. Gouvernement Général de Madagascar et dépendances, *Bulletin d'information et de documentation* (Feb. 1, 1942), p. 9.

51. Lydie Villars, "Madagascar, l'île de la lune," *L'Oeuvre,* May 13, 1942, p. 4.

52. Frantz Fanon, *Peau noire masques blancs* (Paris: Éditions du Seuil, 1952), p. 134.

53. Villars, "Madagascar, l'île de la lune," p. 4. Regarding the imagined "perfidy" of the Merina, see Chantal Valensky, "Madagascar inventé," in Pascal Blan-

chard et al., eds., *L'Autre et nous: "scènes et types"* (Paris: Syros/ACHAC, 1995), p. 67.

54. CAOM, Madagascar, 3B 155; and Gouvernement Général de Madagascar et dépendances, *Bulletin d'information et de documentation* (July 15, 1941), p. 5.

55. Gouvernement Général de Madagascar et dépendances, *Bulletin d'information et de documentation* (Sept. 1, 1941), p. 1.

56. See chapter 1, note 85.

57. Albert Memmi, *Portrait du colonisé* (Utrecht: Jean-Jacques Pauvert, 1966), p. 103.

58. ARDM, D 130, folder "fédération des sociétés des sports athlétiques de Madagascar."

59. Gouvernement Général de Madagascar et dépendances, *Bulletin d'information et de documentation* (June 15, 1941), p. 8.

60. Ibid. (Feb. 15, 1942), p. 11.

61. Ibid. (June 15, 1941), p. 8.

62. CAOM, Madagascar 2D 198, Rapport Politique Tamatave 1941 (also covers the "insolence" of schoolteachers).

63. CAOM, Agence FOM, Carton 401, dossier 1bis/1.

64. ARDM, 4D 45, folder "Colonisation 1941, district d'Arivonimamo."

65. Olivier Leroy, *Raisons et bases de l'Union des Français de l'Empire* (Tananarive: Imprimerie officielle, 1942), pp. 3, 7.

66. N.A., *L'Empire, notre meilleure chance* (Lyon: Audin, 1942), p. 12. Also see "Vocations coloniales," *Quinzaine impériale* (Roanne: Imprimerie Sauzet, 1942); and Jacques Marseille, "L'Empire," in Jean-Pierre Azéma and François Bédarida, eds., *La France des années noires,* vol. 1 (Paris: Le Seuil, 1993), p. 278.

67. For the original quotation on Algeria, see Jacques Soustelle, *Envers et contre tout,* vol. 1, "De Londres à Alger, 1940–1942" (Paris: Robert Laffont, 1947), p. 419.

68. Jean-Paul Cointet, *La Légion Française des Combattants, 1940–1944: la tentation fasciste* (Paris: Albin Michel, 1995), pp. 47–88.

69. CAOM, Affaires Politiques 888, dossier 1. Télégramme 3663, Nov. 17, 1941.

70. Gérard Miller, *Les Pousse-au-jouir du Maréchal Pétain* (Paris: Éditions du Seuil, 1975), p. 60.

71. CAOM, Madagascar, 3B 526, Nov. 29, 1941, #3263cf.

72. Philippe Boegner. *Carnets du Pasteur Boegner, 1940–1945* (Paris: Fayard, 1992), p. 138.

73. Gouvernement Général de Madagascar et dépendances, *Bulletin d'information et de documentation* (Jan. 15, 1942), p. 11.

74. AN 3 W 48 (Annet trial), cotes 179, 181.

75. Dower, *Into Madagascar,* p. 32.

76. CAOM, Affaires Politiques 882 dossier 2, Cayla à Amirauté française, Sept. 10, 1940.

77. *Le Journal de Madagascar,* Tuesday, Nov. 5, 1940, p. 1.

78. CAOM, Madagascar, 6 (2) D 48, dossier 1.

79. Archives Nationales, 3W128 (Procès Cayla), 3, dossier 43.

80. Dower, *Into Madagascar,* p. 89.

81. CAOM, Madagascar 3A 26 Circulaire du Gouvernement Général, Service de Documentation, Information et Propagande. CAOM, Madagascar DS 422.

82. Maunier, *Les Lois de l'empire*, p. 67.

83. CAOM, Affaires Politiques 889, dossier 3, Vallat to Platon, June 24, 1941, in response to Platon's letter to Vallat dated June 20, 1941.

84. CAOM, Affaires Politiques 889, dossier 4, Vallat to Platon, Dec. 31, 1941.

85. Regarding the census of Jews in metropolitan France, see Marrus and Paxton, *Vichy France and the Jews*, p. 100; and Dominique Rémy, *Les Lois de Vichy* (Paris: Romillat, 1992), p. 123.

86. *Servir, hebdomadaire chrétien et national, Madagascar*, 29 août 1941, p. 6.

87. CAOM, Madagascar 4D 45.

88. CAOM, Madagascar PM 128.

89. ARDM, D 736, folder "Commission permanente des délégations économiques et financières," anonymous letter to the chef de la région de Tananarive, June 9, 1942.

90. Ibid., order from June 13, 1942, "Note pour le Commissaire central de police, Tananarive."

91. The polarization of European society in Madagascar is illustrated by a Betsileo woman's questioning of the local administrator, Hubert Deschamps, in 1933: "Are you Catholic? ... then Protestant? then Freemason? ... None?" Deschamps, *Roi de la brousse*, p. 144. On Freemasonry in Madagascar, see also Pascal Chaigneau, "Politique et Franc-maçonnerie dans le tiers-monde: l'exemple révélateur de Madagascar," *L'Afrique et l'Asie modernes* 145 (summer 1985): 14; and Adriano Marchetti, "Jean Paulhan et les Hain-Teny ou les incertitudes de la poésie," *Francofonia* 39 (fall 2000): 4.

92. Quoted in Miller, *Les Pousse-au-jouir du Maréchal Pétain*, p. 168.

93. CAOM, Madagascar 3B 534.

94. On the Légion in the metropole, see Cointet, *La Légion Française des Combattants*.

95. CAOM, Madagascar PM 125. Of course, "democracy" had in reality been completely foreign to the French colonial domination of Madagascar.

96. CAOM, Affaires Politiques 885, dossier 1.

97. Ibid., dossier 2.

98. CAOM, Madagascar 3B 155, Report on the Legion (#412), Apr. 22, 1942.

99. Gouvernement Général de Madagascar et dépendances, *Bulletin d'information et de documentation* (Jan. 15, 1942), p. 4.

100. Ibid., Sept. 15, 1941.

101. Corporatism in France under Vichy is thus defined by Robert Paxton: "Corporatism proposed that all levels of the economically active population—employers, managers, workmen—be organized into natural economic groups (by branch of industry or profession) and that these natural "corporations" govern themselves and society." Paxton, *Vichy France,* p. 210; Also see Jean-Pierre Le Crom, *Syndicats nous voilà! Vichy et le corporatisme* (Paris: Les Éditions Ouvrières, 1995). On Vichy "fantasies" of corporatizing West Africa, see Cooper, *Decolonization and African Society*, pp. 142–43.

102. CAOM, Madagascar 6(2)D 49.

103. Gallieni had set an important precedent in this respect by reinventing the *fokonolona* after the French conquest. See Yvan-Georges Paillard, "Domination coloniale et récupération des traditions autochtones: le cas de Madagascar de 1896 à 1914," *Revue d'histoire moderne et contemporaine* 38 (Jan. 1991): 73–104; and Wright, *The Politics of Design*, p. 253.

104. Sinophobia was nothing new to Tamatave's chamber of commerce. In 1939, it had already called for a freeze of Chinese immigration. Leon Slawecki, *French Policy towards the Chinese in Madagascar* (Hamden: Shoestring Press, 1971), pp. 158–59.

105. CAOM, Madagascar 6(2)D 49.

106. Ibid.

107. Of course, Pétain also believed in a hierarchy of races, but the Malagasy never entered this picture.

108. CAOM, Madagascar 6(5)D 19.

109. Archives Nationales, AN 3W48, Annet trial, cote 146.

110. Ibid., and Armand Annet, op. cit., pp. 113–17.

111. *Servir, hebdomadaire chrétien*, Sept. 11, 1942.

112. CAOM, Madagascar, 6 (2) D49.

113. See Lynn Hunt, *The Family Romance of the French Revolution* (Berkeley: University of California Press, 1992), pp. 124–50.

114. CAOM, Madagascar, 6 (2) D49.

115. On this topic, see Luise White, *Speaking with Vampires: Rumor and History in Colonial Africa* (Berkeley: University of California Press, 2000).

116. Regarding the *mpakafou,* see Louis Molet, *La Conception malgache du monde, du surnaturel et de l'homme en Imerina,* tome 2, "Anthropologie" (Paris: L'Harmattan, 1979), pp. 222–28; and Maurice Bloch, *Placing the Dead: Tombs, Ancestral Villages and Kinship Organization in Madagascar* (London: Seminar Press, 1971), pp. 31–32.

117. On this particular reading of the *mpakafou,* see Monique Ratrimoarivony-Rakotoanosy, "Pouvoir colonial et laïcisation: la franc-maçonnerie et la question scolaire sur les Hautes-terres centrales de 1905 à 1910," *Omaly sy Anio* 29–32 (1989–90): 364, note 33.

118. CAOM, Madagascar, DS 511.

119. De Gaulle, *Discours et messages,* p. 329. Speech, Oct. 8, 1943.

120. CAOM, Madagascar, 4D 45, Rapport politique, p. 3.

121. CAOM, Madagascar PM 277, 1943.

122. For the last three incidents, see CAOM, Madagascar PM 154.

Chapter 3: Travail, Famille, Patrie

1. CAOM, Madagascar 4D 45, rapport politique.

2. Francis Koerner, *Histoire de l'enseignement privé et officiel à Madagascar* (Paris: L'Harmattan, 1999), p. 236.

3. Solofo Ranrianja, *Le Parti Communiste de la région de Madagascar* (Antananarivo: Foi et justice, 1989), p. 160.

4. Jacques Tronchon, *L'Insurrection malgache de 1947* (Paris: Karthala, 1986), pp. 131–32; and Martin Shipway, "Madagascar on the Eve of Insurrection, 1944–1947: The Impasse of a Liberal Colonial Policy," *Journal of Imperial and Commonwealth History* 24, no. 1 (Jan. 1996): 72–100. On 1947 in Madagascar, also see Janine Harovelo, *La SFIO et Madagascar* (Paris: L'Harmattan, 1995). On the memory of the 1947 insurrection, see the very interesting pieces by Françoise Raison-Jourde, "Une Rébellion en quête de statut: 1947 à Madagascar," *Revue de la Bibliothèque nationale* 34 (1989): 24–32; and Jennifer Cole, *Forget Colonialism? Sacrifice and the Art of Memory in Madagascar* (Berkeley: University of California Press, 2001).

5. For general English-language overviews of Malagasy history, see Mervyn Brown, *Madagascar Rediscovered* (London: Damien Tunnacliffe, 1978); Raymond Kent, *From Madagascar to the Malagasy Republic* (New York: Praeger, 1962); and the relevant sections of Gwendolyn Wright's *The Politics of Design*, pp. 235–301. In French, see Hubert Deschamps, *Histoire de Madagascar* (Paris: Editions Berger-Levrault, 1961); Pierre Boiteau, *Contribution à l'histoire de la nation malgache* (Paris: Editions sociales, 1958); Edouard Ralaimihoatra, *Histoire de Madagascar* (Antananarivo: E. Ralaimihoatra, 1966); Koerner, *Madagascar*; and Vérin, *Madagascar*.

6. See Yvan-Georges Paillard, "Marianne et l'indigène: les premiers 14 juillet coloniaux à Madagascar," *L'Information historique* 45 (1983): 112–14.

7. Laure Adler, *Marguerite Duras* (Paris: Gallimard, 1998), pp. 135–39; Pierre Assouline, "Duras, l'Indochinoise," *L'Histoire* 203 (Oct. 1996): 47.

8. Marguerite Donnadieu (alias Duras) and Philippe Roques, *L'Empire français* (Paris: Gallimard, 1940), p. 100.

9. Memmi, *Portrait du colonisé*, p. 161.

10. See S. Randrianja, "Aux origines du MDRM," in Francis Arzalier and Jean Suret-Canale, eds., *Madagascar 1947: la tragédie oubliée* (Paris: Le Temps des cerises, 1999), pp. 65–66.

11. On associationism in the interwar period, see Wright, *The Politics of Design*, pp. 73–84; Conklin, "'Democracy' Revisited," pp. 59–84; and Betts, *Assimilation and Association*, pp. 106–32. For the opinion that association sometimes amounted to "paternal authoritarianism," see Cohen, *Rulers of Empire*.

12. Koerner, *Madagascar*, p. 192.

13. Raoul Allier, *L'Enseignement primaire des indigènes à Madagascar* (Paris: Cahiers de la quinzaine, 1904), p. 65. Also see Brown, *Madagascar Rediscovered*, p. 259.

14. Cohen, *Rulers of Empire*, p. 72.

15. See Conklin, "'Democracy' Revisited," p. 79. See also Wright, *The Politics of Design*, pp. 73–84, 297–300.

16. CAOM, Madagascar PM 319. On the Popular Front's failure to conduct thorough and lasting colonial reforms, see William B. Cohen, "The Colonial Policy of the Popular Front," *French Historical Studies* 7, no. 2 (spring 1972): 368–93.

17. Koerner, *Madagascar*, p. 199.

18. CAOM, Agence FOM, 401, 2bis, 1.

19. On parallels with earlier discourses of "civilization" in French West Africa, see Conklin, *A Mission to Civilize*, pp. 139–40.

20. OSS State Department Intelligence and Research reports, part XIII (Africa), reel 8, p. 262.

21. See Christian Faure, *Le Projet culturel de Vichy* (Lyon: CNRS, 1989), p. 123; and Eric Jennings, "Reinventing *Jeanne*: The Iconology of Joan of Arc in Vichy Schoolbooks, 1940–1944," *Journal of Contemporary History* 29, no. 4 (Oct. 1994): 711–34.

22. These constructions were potentially problematic, for Andrianampoini-merina like Joan of Arc could also stand as a referent for national liberation.

23. CAOM, Madagascar PT 143.

24. Ibid.

25. Ibid.: 1941 annual report Soavinandriana.

26. Ibid.

27. Ibid.

28. Ibid.

29. Gouvernement Général de Madagascar et dépendances, *Bulletin d'information et de documentation,* Aug. 1, 1941, p. 9.

30. See Eric Jennings, "Vichy à Madagascar: la Révolution Nationale, l'enseignement et la jeunesse, 1940–1942," *Revue d'histoire moderne et contemporaine* 46, no. 4 (Dec. 1999): 727–44.

31. CAOM, Madagascar 2D 107, rapport politique 1941, p. 5.

32. For an interesting interpretation, according to which the phrase "our ancestors the Gauls" represents nothing more than a myth employed by detractors of French assimilationism, see Denise Bouche, "Autrefois, notre pays s'appelait la Gaule," *Cahiers d'études africaines* 29 (1968): 110–22.

33. CAOM, Madagascar 2D 169.

34. See Jennings, "Vichy à Madagascar."

35. On the "return to the soil" in metropolitan France, see Paxton, *Vichy France,* pp. 200–209.

36. Gouvernement Général de Madagascar et dépendances, *Bulletin d'information et de documentation,* June 15, 1942, p. 18.

37. CAOM, Madagascar 3B 153.

38. Leroy, *Raisons et bases de l'Union des Français de l'Empire,* p. 7.

39. CAOM, Affaires Politiques 2046, CAOM, Madagascar 3B 153 and 4D 45.

40. CAOM, Madagascar 4D 45, p. 10.

41. *Journal officiel de l'Etat français,* June 13 1942, law 474 dated Apr. 17 1942, p. 2058. This law further stipulated that the denaturalized "native" was to be "replaced into the indigenous status which he held prior to his admission as a citizen." See also CAOM, Cabinet 4, dossier 21; CAOM, Affaires Politiques 2555, dossier 6.

42. CAOM, Affaires Politiques 3619, July 21, 1942, Brévié to Garde des Sceaux, and CAOM, Madagascar 6(2)D 101.

43. Marrus and Paxton, *Vichy France and the Jews,* p. 367.

44. Paxton, *Vichy France,* pp. 174–75.

45. Memmi, *Portrait du colonisé,* pp. 100–101.

46. Wright, *The Politics of Design,* p. 300.

47. Brown, *Madagascar Rediscovered,* p. 128.

48. F. H. Lem, "Une Institution malgache traditionelle," *France: revue de l'Etat nouveau* (Apr. 20, 1944): 87.

49. Ibid.: 82.

50. Ibid.: 85.

51. CAOM, Madagascar 3B 153.

52. CAOM, Madagascar 2D 136, rapport annuel 1941.

53. CAOM, Madagascar 3B 525.

54. Gouvernement Général de Madagascar et dépendances, *Bulletin d'information et de documentation*, Jan. 15, 1942, p. 9.

55. CAOM, Madagascar 2D 81, rapport 1940, p. 5.

56. The description offered by the head of the region of Tamatave was sent to the far corners of Madagascar, with instructions "not to let this comparison escape your attention. ... It is to be developed whenever possible during *kabary* (speeches) to the natives." CAOM, Madagascar 3B 525, and CAOM, Madagascar PM 124.

57. CAOM, Madagascar 2D 81, "rapport politique région de Diego-Suarez," 1940, p. 5.

58. CAOM, Madagascar 2D 176, "rapport politique région de Morondava," 1941, p. 4.

59. CAOM, Madagascar PM 124.

60. CAOM, Madagascar 2D 107, "rapport politique région de Fort-Dauphin," 1941, p. 2.

61. Arthur Herman, Jr., "The Language of Fidelity in Early Modern France," *Journal of Modern History* 67, no. 1 (Mar. 1995): 8.

62. Gerald Berg, "Royal Authority and the Protector System in Nineteenth-century Imerina," in Conrad Kottak et al., eds., *Madagascar: Society and History* (Durham: Carolina Academic Press, 1986), p. 185.

63. CAOM, Madagascar 3B 154, report of Feb. 2, 1942.

64. CAOM PM 124. The head of the Soalala district in Majunga's propaganda directives, Feb. 16, 1942.

65. Ibid., 124. Barat to Gauche, Majunga.

66. ARDM, 4D 60, folder "Province de Tuléar, District Ambovombe, Distinctions honorifiques," Annet circular note #54P, Aug. 14, 1942.

67. CAOM, Madagascar 3A 27, Mar. 23, 1942 (circulaire 28 AP).

68. CAOM, Madagascar 3B 535. Police reports, Tananarive, Feb. 10, 1942.

69. CAOM, Madagascar PM 124, District of Soalala, report to Gauche, Majunga, July 1, 1942.

70. CAOM, Madagascar 2D 3 (3), rapport annuel district d'Ambato-Boéni, Région de Majunga, 1941.

71. *Lumière,* Jan. 26, 1942. During this Quinzaine impériale alone, fifteen million francs were raised in Madagascar for the metropole (see ibid., Feb. 20, 1942).

72. CAOM, Cabinet 2, dossier 18, May 15, 1942.

73. Laurent Gervereau and Denis Peschanski, eds. *La Propagande sous Vichy* (Paris: BDIC, 1990), pp. 276, 279.

74. CAOM, Madagascar 3B 157.

75. CAOM, Madagascar CF 3, dossier 14.

76. On February 16, 1942, the head of the Soalala district in Majunga ordered his subordinates to tell the Malagasy in even the remotest villages: "The new state's motto is Work, Family, Fatherland. You must therefore respect the family, and care for it. ... Everyone must work, for the more you work the better you can

clothe and nourish yourselves. ... Finally ... we must remain united around our leaders. You know that a family where discord reigns finishes in misery, whereas one which is united prospers." CAOM PM 124.

77. CAOM, Affaires Politiques 2520, dossier 9, and CAOM, Madagascar 3B 151, Annet to Platon, Oct. 22, 1941.

78. CAOM, Madagascar 2D 198.

79. Gillian Feeley-Harnik, "Ritual and Work in Madagascar," in Kottak et al., *Madagascar*, p. 162.

80. Ibid., p. 163.

81. *Le Cri des nègres*, Nov.–Dec. 1933: 1, "Madagascar, pays d'esclavage"; July–Aug. 1933, p. 1.

82. Ratrematsialonina, "Madagascar pendant la deuxième guerre mondiale," vol. 2, pp., 180, 184, 185.

83. CAOM, Madagascar 2D 126, rapport annuel Mahabo.

84. CAOM, Madagascar PT 145.

85. CAOM, Madagascar 6 (2) D 20.

86. *Servir, hebdomadaire chrétien*, Oct. 31, 1941, p. 3.

87. CAOM, Madagascar 2D 136.

88. CAOM, Madagascar 3B 151, Annet to Platon, Oct. 22, 1941.

89. CAOM PM 139, circulaire du 30 mars 1942.

90. *Servir, hebdomadaire chrétien*, Oct. 31, 1941, p. 3.

91. CAOM, Madagascar 3D 331 rapports, Tuléar et Fort Dauphin, inspection des 9 et 10 septembre 1941, District de Vangaindrano, p. 19.

92. On Vichy's exaltation of the peasant and the artisan, see Faure, *Le Projet culturel de Vichy*, pp. 105–25.

93. CAOM, Madagascar 3A 27, Circulaire 20AE, Mar. 8, 1942.

94. Gillian Feeley-Harnik, "Ritual and Work in Madagascar," pp. 162–63; Wright, *The Politics of Design*, pp. 298–300.

95. Lucile Rabearimanana, "Le District de Manjakanandian," 435.

96. AN 3W 48, Annet trial, Feb. 1942. The original name of the organization is Jeunesse Volontaire Malgache de la Révolution Nationale.

97. Gouvernement Général de Madagascar et dépendances, *Bulletin d'information et de documentation,* June 1, 1942, pp. 18–19.

98. CAOM, Madagascar 6(2) D48, Rapport d'indicateur, Oct. 15, 1940.

99. The head of the region of Tamatave reported in 1941: "The native says openly that with the new *fanjaka* (regime) we have the right to pray." CAOM, Madagascar 2D 198, rapport politique Tamatave, 1941.

100. CAOM, Madagascar PM 124.

101. AN 3W 48, London, Nov. 24, 1942.

102. VVS stands for *Vy, Vato, Sakelika,* or iron, stone, ramification.

103. Brown, *Madagascar Rediscovered*, p. 262.

104. CAOM, Madagascar 3B 529, Tananarive, Mar. 6, 1942.

105. CAOM, Madagascar 4D 45.

106. CAOM, Madagascar PT 144.

107. CAOM, Madagascar 3B 518, note de renseignements, Tamatave, Mar. 3, 1941.

108. Similar claims have been made regarding metropolitan France, some historians arguing that the advent of the Service du Travail Obligatoire, which sent French workers to Germany in February 1943, served as the most important catalyst for the French Resistance.

109. CAOM, Madagascar PM 124, Dec. 1941 report; telegram from Befandriana to Majunga, July 29, 1942.

110. Ibid., Soalala to Majunga, Oct. 1, 1941.

111. CAOM, Madagascar 3D 330, inspection report for the region of Fianarantsoa, Dec. 1941.

112. ARDM, D 697, "Revendications de l'Amicale des citoyens français d'origine malgache," petition of Oct. 6, 1943.

113. Cooper, *Decolonization and African Society*, pp. 187–89.

114. CAOM, Madagascar 3B 534.

115. Tronchon, *L'Insurrection malgache de 1947*, pp. 131–32.

116. CAOM, Madagascar 3B 517, Police report, Feb. 20, 1941.

117. CAOM, Madagascar 3B 534. Police report.

118. CAOM, Madagascar 3B 535, Police report, Feb. 9, 1942.

119. CAOM, Madagascar 3B 534. Police report.

120. Shipway, Madagascar on the Eve of Insurrection," p. 85; Tronchon, *L'Insurrection malgache de 1947*, p. 131. Tronchon argues that the term "Parti National Socialiste Malgache" was intentionally borrowed from the Nazis in an effort to combat the French.

121. ARDM, D 867, folder "Surveillance de Jacques Rabemananjara," report of Oct. 27, 1946, on the meeting of the MDRM that same day.

122. CAOM, Madagascar 3B 516, note de renseignements.

123. CAOM, Madagascar PM 150, renseignements de la police, 1941.

124. CAOM, Madagascar DS 227, Compte-rendu du premier anniversaire de la Légion.

125. On the use of jokes, pranks, and Rabelaisian humor as oppositional practices, see Susanna Barrows, "Popular Culture and French Republicanism in the Early Third Republic," paper kindly made available to me by its author, pp. 3–5, 16.

126. CAOM, Affaires Politiques 2413, dossier 7. Note dated June 20, 1944.

Chapter 4: Suppressing the Republic in Guadeloupe

1. USNA Record Group 59, Box 5197, document 851B.4016/1—Malige to Cordell Hull.

2. For Guadeloupe's population and its institutions on the eve of the Vichy era, see Ministère des Colonies, service intercolonial d'information et de documentation, *La Guadeloupe* (1940), p. 2.

3. Jacques Adélaïde-Merlande, *Histoire générale des Antilles et des Guyanes* (Paris: Editions Caribéennes, 1994), pp. 251–52.

4. On assimilation in Guadeloupe, see Josette Fallope, "La Politique d'assimilation et ses résistances," in Henriette Levillain, ed., *La Guadeloupe, 1875–1914: les soubresauts d'une société pluri-ethnique ou les ambiguïtés de l'assimilation* (Paris: Autrement, 1994), pp. 34–47.

5. Memmi, *Portrait du colonisé*, p. 182.

6. Eliane Sempaire, *La Guadeloupe en tan Sorin, 1940–1943* (Paris: Edition et diffusion de la Culture antillaise, 1984), p. 40.

7. Eric Jennings, "Monuments to Frenchness? The Memory of the Great War and the Politics of Guadeloupe's Identity, 1914–1945," *French Historical Studies* 21, no. 4 (fall 1998): 561–92.

8. Jacques Adélaïde-Merlande, "Va-t-on céder les Antilles françaises aux Etats-Unis?" in Maurice Burac, ed., *Guadeloupe, Martinique et Guyane dans le monde américain* (Paris: Karthala, 1994), pp. 161–65.

9. Jean-Pierre Sainton, *Rosan Girard, Chronique d'une vie politique en Guadeloupe* (Paris: Jasor/Karthala, 1993), pp. 79–82.

10. On the 1930 strikes, see ibid., pp. 80–91.

11. F. Fabre and G. Stehle, "Le Cyclone de 1928 à la Pointe-à-Pitre," *Bulletin de la société d'histoire de la Guadeloupe* 91–94 (1992): 41–73; Lucien-René Abenon, *Petite histoire de la Guadeloupe* (Paris: L'Harmattan, 1992), pp. 173–75.

12. *Le Cri des nègres*, July–Aug. 1933, p. 3.

13. Philippe Cherdieu, "L'Échec d'un socialisme colonial: la Guadeloupe, 1891–1914," *Revue d'histoire moderne et contemporaine* 31 (Apr.–June 1984): 315.

14. Brian Weinstein, *Eboué* (New York: Oxford University Press, 1972), pp. 178–96.

15. See Julien Mérion, "La France et ses Antilles: vers la citoyenneté intégrale," in Henriette Levillain, ed., *La Guadeloupe, 1875–1914*, pp. 48–75.

16. See, for instance, "Comment on vote aux Colonies," *Le Nouvelliste de la Guadeloupe*, Nov. 29, 1924, p. 2.

17. USNA Record Group 59, document 851B.918/1.

18. Service Historique de la Marine, Vincennes, France, TTE 32, Robert to Sorin, July 1, 1941.

19. On Sorin's wife being Jewish, see Dr. René Schneyder, "L'Amiral [Robert], homme-lige du Maréchal," in Elisabeth Antébi, ed., *Histoire des Antilles et de la Guyane* (Fort-de-France: Arawak, 1978), p. 287; and Laurent Farrugia, "L'Époque de Vichy," in Roland Suvelor, ed., *L'Historial Antillais*, vol. V (Fort-de-France: Société Dajani, 1980), p. 3.

20. ADG, Série Continue 4101, telegram #248, June 18, 1940.

21. Michel, "Les Ralliements à la France Libre en 1940." I wish to thank Marc Michel for making available to me the following unpublished manuscript, "The *Ralliements* of the French Colonies to Free France," which reads: "The natives were actually put aside and their reactions totally ignored."

22. Adolphe Roberts, *Les Français aux Indes Occidentales* (Montréal: Editions variétés, 1945), pp. 342–43.

23. See Schneyder, "'La Seconde guerre mondiale," p. 291.

24. Allen Cronenberg, "The French West Indies during World War II," *Proceedings of the Annual Meeting of the Western Society for French History* 18 (1991): 524.

25. AN 3W331, cote 2312.

26. CAOM, Affaires Politiques 767, dossier 1, Rouyer report, pp. 1–8.

27. Sainton, *Rosan Girard*, p. 127.

28. On police brutality and torture, see ADG 4mi 411, letter of protest from M. Roger Fortuné, Aug. 1941; and Jean-Charles Timoléon, *Chronique du temps passé* (Basse-Terre: OMCS, 1987), p. 13.

29. Guadeloupe et dépendances, *Délibérations du Conseil Général, Session extraordinaire du 1er juillet 1940* (Basse-Terre, 1940), pp. 5–10.

30. CAOM, Affaires Politiques 767, dossier 1, report by Lorée, chef de la Sureté de la Guadeloupe, Jan. 17, 1941.

31. CAOM, Affaires Politiques 2520, dossier 9, Report Number 5 (Oct. 1940), "Suspension des Conseils Généraux des colonies."

32. CAOM, Indochine Nouveau Fonds 2767 offers a summary of such anti-democratic legislation.

33. CAOM, Affaires Politiques 888, dossier 2, "Sorin au Ministre des Colonies Vichy," Nov. 29, 1940.

34. CAOM, Télégrammes 807, Sorin au Ministre des Colonies, Vichy, Nov. 11, 1941.

35. Ibid., Devouton to Ministre des Colonies, Vichy, Aug. 23, 1941.

36. Guadeloupe et dépendances, *Délibérations du Conseil Général, Session extraordinaire du 1er juillet 1940* (Basse-Terre, 1940), p. 9.

37. ADG, Série Continue 3974, 178 Cab. Transmission de directives du Secrétaire d'Etat aux Colonies, Feb. 18, 1941.

38. Ibid.

39. CAOM, Affaires Politiques 767, dossier 1, Rouyer report, p. 11.

40. Ibid.

41. CAOM, Affaires Politiques 768, Devouton to Platon, report dated Sept. 30, 1941.

42. CAOM, 2APOM 11 (Papiers d'agents), dossier Devouton.

43. Jean Cazenave de la Roche, "Tension in the French West Indies," *Foreign Affairs* 21, no. 3 (Apr. 1943): 564.

44. AN 3W 331, cotes 2310 and 2312.

45. ADG, SC 3995, Sorin to all mayors, circular number 75, Sept. 16, 1941.

46. Paxton, *Vichy France*, p. 20.

47. See "Suspension du Conseil Général," *La Démocratie sociale* Nov. 9, 1940: 1.

48. Timoléon, *Chronique du temps passé*, p. 12.

49. USNA, Record Group 59, Box 5193, document 851B.00/52, copy of Admiral Robert's radio broadcast.

50. CAOM, Télégrammes 700. Telegram number 43, Jan. 22, 1941, Vichy to Fort-de-France, Basse-Terre and St. Denis.

51. Ibid.

52. Paxton, *Vichy France*, p. 197.

53. CAOM, Affaires Politiques 768, notice relating to the law of April 11, 1941.

54. CAOM, 2APOM 11, dossier Devouton.

55. CAOM, Affaires Politiques 767, dossier 1, Sorin to Platon, Jan. 10, 1942.

56. Ibid., Sorin to Ministry of Colonies, Vichy, Jan. 18, 1941.

57. ADG, Série Continue 6206, "liste des maires de la Guadeloupe et Dépendances."

58. CAOM, Affaires Politiques 768, Carcassonne to Platon, Dec. 20, 1941.

59. Dominique Chathuant, "La Guadeloupe dans l'obédience de Vichy, 1940–1943," *Bulletin de la société d'histoire de la Guadeloupe* 91–94 (1992): 21–26.

60. CAOM, Affaires Politiques 898 bis, Guadeloupe, sous-dossier 10, noms de rues.

61. "Loi du 25 septembre 1942," *Journal officiel de la Martinique* 41, Oct. 3, 1942; and CAOM, Indochine Nouveau Fonds 2767, "Institution de conseils locaux aux Antilles."

62. USNA, Record Group 59, Box 5198, document 851C.01/12, Malige to Secretary of State, Oct. 6, 1942.

63. Ibid.

64. Letter reproduced in CAOM, Indochine Nouveau Fonds, 2767.

65. Claude Lévi-Strauss, *Tristes tropiques* (Paris: Plon, 1955), p. 29.

66. CAOM, Télégrammes 688, Sorin to Colonies Vichy, N531, Dec. 19, 1940.

67. CAOM, Affaires Politiques 3503, Réforme judiciaire, report drafted by the Procureur Général de la Guadeloupe, Viennet.

68. Ibid.

69. Ibid., cited in Platon report.

70. "Let us not forget that the jury system is expensive." Ibid., Réforme judiciaire, report drafted by the procureur général de la Guadeloupe, Viennet.

71. Ibid., Report by Dumoulin, Chef du Service Judiciaire.

72. Ibid., Platon to Robert, Feb. 6, 1941.

73. Ibid.

74. Ibid., Devouton to Platon, Mar. 26, 1941, and exposé accompanying note of Feb. 1, 1941.

75. CAOM, Affaires Politiques 2520, dossier 9, Report #12, June to Oct. 1941.

76. ADG, Série Continue 4105, numéro 43, Sorin à tous les maires, Jan. 12, 1942.

77. ADG, Série Continue 4087, Maire Gourbeyre to Basse-Terre, Jan. 17, 1942; Maire Port-Louis to Sorin, Jan. 17, 1942; Maire Baie-Mahaut to Sorin, Jan. 16, 1942; Maire Basse-Terre to Sorin, Jan. 16, 1942.

78. ADG, Série Continue 3995, Basse-Terre, Jan. 28, 1942, Sorin à tous les maires, numéro 12.

79. Ibid.

80. CAOM, Affaires Politiques 767, dossier 1. Rouyer report, p. 8: "Application de la Loi du 2 juin 1941."

81. ADG, Série Continue 4087, Telegram, Aug. 12, 1941, Sorin to all functionaries.

82. ADG, Série Continue 6201, X to Sorin, Oct. 11, 1941, and Sorin to Rivier, head of Guadeloupe's Legion, Oct. 25, 1941.

83. CAOM, Affaires Politiques 768, letter from Ministry of the Interior to Platon, Nov. 29, 1940.

84. Ibid.

85. Ibid., Robert's position is cited in Platon's response to the Interior Ministry, Jan. 8, 1941.

86. CAOM, Série Télégrammes 807, Telegram number 61, Mar. 19, 1941, signed Sorin.

87. Marrus and Paxton, *Vichy France and the Jews*, pp. 112–14, 161–64.

88. Ibid., p. 164.

89. "Arrêté portant promulgation à la Guadeloupe de la loi du 18 août 1941," *Journal officiel de la Guadeloupe*, Aug. 23, 1941, pp. 974–75.

90. "Circulaire invitant tous les fonctionnaires … à souscrire une déclaration." *Journal officiel de la Guadeloupe*, Oct. 7, 1941, p. 1171. Copies of both declaration forms were forwarded to the U.S. State Department by the American consul to the French West Indies. One read: "I the undersigned, declare under oath, having never belonged in any capacity to any of the following societies: Grand Orient de France, Grande Loge de France, Grande Loge Nationale Indépendante, Ordre Mixte International du Droit Humain, Société Théosophique, Grand Prieuré des Gaules … or to any other association targeted by the law of August 13, 1940, and hereby give my word of honor that I shall never become a member of one in future, should they ever be reinstituted." The second document asked, among other queries: "Were your paternal … and maternal … grandfathers members of the Jewish race or belonging to the Jewish religion?" After posing the same question regarding grandmothers, the form went on to ask, "Is your spouse Jewish?" USNA Record Group 84, French West Indies Security Segregated General Records (1942) box 3, section 800.

91. See Sempaire, *La Dissidence an tan Sorin*, pp. 57–58.

92. CAOM, AP 3619, letter from the secretary of state to the colonies, Vichy, to Monseigneur Chappoulie, Maison du Missionnaire, Vichy, Aug. 20, 1942.

93. CAOM, Affaires Politiques 888, dossier 1, Platon to Robert, Oct. 1, 1941.

94. ADG, SC 19, dossier 2, Pierre to Ministre des Colonies, Nov. 15, 1945.

95. *Journal officiel de l'Etat français*, Oct. 27, 1940, law on Travail Féminin, Oct. 11, 1940.

96. ADG, SC 19, dossier 2, Platon to Sorin, Nov. 14, 1940, C 84 R.

97. Ibid., Relevé numérique des agents expéditionnaires et pourcentage du personnel féminin.

98. Ibid., Basse-Terre, Jan. 10, 1942, Sorin confidential circular to all chefs de service.

99. Ibid., Sorin telegram number 56, Apr. 16, 1941, to "chef de la mission d'inspection."

100. Ibid., Sorin to Platon, Dec. 14, 1940.

101. On the status of metropolitan women under the National Revolution, see Miranda Pollard, *Reign of Virtue: Mobilizing Gender in Vichy France* (Chicago: University of Chicago Press, 1998).

102. Gérard Miller, *Les Pousse-au-jouir du Maréchal Pétain* (Paris: Editions du Seuil, 1975), p. 159.

103. ADG, SC 19, dossier 2, decree dated Basse-Terre, May 19, 1943, "reintroducing Mrs. X … to her position in primary education."

104. Ibid., tableau A.

105. AN 3W331, cote 2575, Devouton to Platon, June 16, 1941, number 96C.

106. ADG, SC 19, dossier 2, excerpts from a letter by Inspector Carcassonne.

107. Ibid., letter from Governor Pierre to the Minister of Colonies, Nov. 15, 1945.

108. ADG, SC 3995, Sorin to Robert, Apr. 10, 1942, #173.

109. Archives du Ministère des Affaires Etrangères (Quai d'Orsay), Guerre 1939–1945, Vichy—Afrique, dossier 89, "adjudications publiques en Afrique Occidentale Française."

110. "Premier anniversaire de la Légion; allocution de M. Cabre," *L'Hebdomadaire de la Guadeloupe,* Sept. 13, 1941, p. 1.

111. CAOM, Affaires Politiques 768, sous-dossier: "Télégrammes Amirauté," Allocution de Sorin à l'occasion du 11 novembre 1940.

112. Ibid.

113. Ibid.

114. ADG, SC 3995, Sorin to Robert, Jan. 12, 1942.

115. ADG, SC 6201, Telegram #135 from Sorin to Robert, May 21, 1941.

116. Ibid., speech by Cabre, Oct. 1941.

117. ADG, SC 4105, Sorin to all mayors, #941, Nov. 30, 1942.

118. One prominent example involves the seemingly unresolvable conflicts between Vichy's educational authority, Jacques Grandjouan, and the island's bishop, Msgr. Genoud. One source reveals that "Grandjouan entered into personal conflict with almost the entire ecclesiastical profession," AN 3W 311; and CAOM, Affaires Politiques 769, Robert to Platon, Oct. 21, 1941.

119. ADG, "Cérémonie de prestation de serment des Légionnaires, dimanche 3 août 1941." This entire ceremony is recorded in the aforementioned document recently uncovered by Mme. Ghislaine Bouchet, head of Guadeloupe's Archives. Although it has not yet been assigned a call number, Mme. Bouchet was kind enough to bring the document to my attention.

120. AN 3W331, cote 2572, note on the Corporatist Regime.

121. Ibid.

122. ADG, SC 3974, Nov. 15, 1941, #1064 AEI.

123. CAOM, Cabinet 7, dossier 25, Minister of the Colonies Brévié to Fort-de-France, Sept. 19, 1942.

124. Ibid., Declaration signed by Thevenin de Reynal, relayed by note of Apr. 9, 1942, #171.

125. ADG, SC 6194, Pointe-à-Pitre, Feb. 24, 1941, speeches by Constant Sorin and Mr. Zamia before the city's Chamber of Agriculture.

126. ADG, SC 3995, Basse-Terre, Jan. 12, 1942.

127. ADG, SC 3996, Basse-Terre, Mar. 26, 1943.

Chapter 5: Guadeloupean Society under Vichy

1. Maryse Condé, *Tree of Life (La Vie scélérate)* (New York: Random House, 1992), p. 119.

2. Sempaire, *La Guadeloupe en tan Sorin,* p. 21.

3. Farrugia, "L'Époque de Vichy," p. 5.

4. See Ibid., pp. 81–82; 86; Sempaire describes on p. 96, how, almost by mira-

cle, "an entire people went to work [to generate the Effort Guadeloupéen]." On page 158 she writes: "The battle was won ... but the war continued ... against all forms of exploitation, against all forms of assistance. It continued against cultural alienation, and against a dated economic system which forced Guadeloupe to import constantly more, she who had been self-sufficient from 1940 to 1943." Sempaire, *La Guadeloupe en tan Sorin*.

5. USNA, Record Group 84, French West Indies 1941, Box 5, document 885.91, Jan. 30, 1941.

6. USNA, Record Group 59, box 5198, document 851C.00/21, July 13, 1940; U.S. Consulate Martinique to War Department.

7. Sempaire, *La Guadeloupe en tan Sorin*, p. 113.

8. Francisque Gay, *Comment se nourrir au temps des restrictions* (Paris: Blond et Gay, 1941), pp. 38; 146–47.

9. "Du pain ... pays," *Le Bulletin de France: organe des comités d'information des Antilles*, Mar. 16, 1943, p. 4.

10. Jean Juraver and Michel Eclar, *Anse-Bertrand, une commune de Guadeloupe, hier, aujourd'hui, demain* (Paris: Karthala, 1992), pp. 45–46.

11. "Dans la maison du voisin," *Le Bulletin de France: organe des comités d'information des Antilles*, Mar. 16, 1943, p. 4.

12. This stems from an interview Mr. Guy Cornély kindly accorded to me at his home in Guadeloupe on May 3, 1997.

13. ADG, SC 6206, Sorin to mayors, Feb. 23, 1942.

14. USNA, Record Group 59, box 5193, document 851.01/73 3/10 May 13, 1943, Struble (Navy) to State Department.

15. USNA, Record Group 59, document 851B.00.33, U.S. Report from vice consul to Foreign Service, Mar. 13, 1941.

16. "Allocution adressée à la jeunesse de la Guadeloupe par Constant Sorin," *La Démocracie sociale* (Basse-Terre), July 26, 1941, p. 1.

17. CAOM, Affaires Politiques 2521, Telegram 1736, Dec. 15, 1942.

18. "La Fête de la canne," *La Démocracie sociale* (Basse-Terre), Feb. 1, 1941.

19. *La Raison*, Oct. 15, 1941, p. 2.

20. "Le Premier mai, fête du Travail et de la Paix sociale," *La Démocratie sociale*, Apr. 1941.

21. Raphaël Confiant, *Le Nègre et l'amiral* (Paris: Grasset, 1988), p. 265.

22. ADG, SC 4101, Sorin to Robert, #224, July 8, 1941.

23. ADG, SC 6194, "Dimanche 11 janvier 1942, journée de la jeunesse."

24. *La Raison*, Oct. 15, 1941, p. 2.

25. ADG, SC 3995, Basse-Terre circulaire 24 SG2, Feb. 21, 1941.

26. Timoléon, *Chronique du temps passé*, p. 12.

27. AN F60 315.

28. ADG, 2mi 105 (R 226), Platon (signed Fatou) to Sorin, Feb. 26, 1941.

29. Ibid., cited in Platon to Sorin, Mar. 3, 1941.

30. "La Semaine pédagogique," *La Démocratie sociale*, Mar. 8, 1941.

31. See ADG SC 3995, Sorin au Commandant supérieur des troupes aux Antilles, Mar. 26, 1942; and SC 3996, Sorin to Robert, #76, Apr. 3, 1943.

32. Platon appended the following handwritten note to a telegram on the pos-

sibility of introducing the Chantiers to Guadeloupe: "The Governor of Guadeloupe does not have sufficient personnel for the Chantiers to operate under good
conditions, and without evoking fears of forced labor." CAOM, Affaires Politiques
767, dossier 2: handwritten note clipped to Platon telegram to Robert, 20 décembre 1941.

33. Ibid., 769, Robert to Platon, Oct. 21, 1941.

34. ADG, 4mi 411 "Gourbeyre, en avant!"

35. Ibid.

36. Ibid.

37. Hoover Archives, Stanford University. France, Commissariat Général à la
Famille: "Before 1939, France won a record ... the record of alcoholics"; and
"Young Frenchman, think of your family responsibilities."

38. CAOM, Affaires Politiques 898, dossier 4, Admiral Decoux to Vichy, Nov.
8, 1940.

39. *Journal officiel de la Guadeloupe*, Jan. 18, 1941, p. 61.

40. Ibid., p. 63.

41. See Barrows, "Popular Culture and French Republicanism in the Early
Third Republic."

42. CAOM, Affaires Politiques 898, dossier 4.

43. ADG, SC 3995, Circulaire 17 SG2, Feb. 12, 1941, to all mayors.

44. Ibid., Circulaire 14 SG2, Feb. 10, 1941; and ibid., letter on alcoholism, May
17, 1941.

45. Sempaire, *La Guadeloupe en tan Sorin*, p. 127; and Juraver and Eclar, *Anse-
Bertrand, une commune de Guadeloupe*, p. 50.

46. Wright, *The Politics of Design*, pp. 53–84; Paul Rabinow, *French Modern:
Norms and Forms of the Social Environment* (Chicago: University of Chicago Press,
1995), pp. 285–89.

47. G. Robert, *Les Travaux publics de la Guadeloupe* (Paris: Librairie militaire
Fournier, 1935), p. 265.

48. Laurence Bertrand Dorléac, *L'Art de la défaite, 1940–1944* (Paris: Editions
du Seuil, 1993), pp. 181–82.

49. ADG SC 3995, Basse-Terre, circulaire N 35 to all mayors, Apr. 3, 1941.

50. Ibid.

51. ADG SC 4087, Sorin to mayor of Basse-Terre, Aug. 23, 1941.

52. ADG SC 4101, Circulaire to all mayors #1322, Oct. 15, 1941.

53. ADG SC 4087, Sorin to mayor of Pointe-à-Pitre, Number 1130, Aug. 23,
1941.

54. Jean-Luc Bonniol, "De l'architecture créole: tradition et créativité dans
l'habitat rural martiniquais et guadeloupéen," *Etudes Créoles* 1–2 (1982): 77.

55. ADG SC 4101, Circulaire 570, June 26, 1941.

56. Laurence Bertrand Dorléac, "La Question artistique et le régime de Vichy,"
in Jean-Pierre Rioux, ed., *La Vie culturelle sous Vichy* (Bruxelles: Editions Complexe, 1990), pp. 144–45: "[In] order to prolong what seemed to be vanishing
every day, the regime dwelled upon the persistence and the grandeur of traditions
and crafts ... which were seen as incarnating the spiritual values of man."

57. "Monsieur le Gouverneur Sorin s'adresse à la jeunesse guadeloupéenne," *L'Hebdomadaire de la Guadeloupe,* Dec. 5, 1941.

58. Bonniol, De l'architecture créole, 78.

59. See Rabinow, *French Modern,* p. 1.

60. Le Corbusier, "Le Problème du logis," *L'Hebdomadaire de la Guadeloupe,* Apr. 18, 1942.

61. On Le Corbusier and Vichy, see Mary McLeod, "Urbanism and Utopia: Le Corbusier from Regional Syndicalism to Vichy," Ph.D. dissertation, Princeton University, 1985; William Curtis, *Le Corbusier, Ideas and Forms* (Oxford: Phaidon, 1986), p. 128; and Dorléac, *L'Art de la défaite,* p. 93.

62. Rabinow, *French Modern,* p. 338.

63. ADG, SC 3995, Basse-Terre, Apr. 3, 1941, Circulaire à tous les maires.

64. Ibid.

65. Ibid.

66. Sorin declared to Guadeloupean youngsters in December 1941: "Your village is your own. In the small cemetery lie those who left you, those of whom you keep a pious memory. ... Love your village well. Surround it with affection. Take good care of it. ... Form ... teams of volunteer workers to clean and beautify houses, squares and streets. ... Do not allow our beautiful Guadeloupe to be sullied." "Le Gouverneur Sorin s'adresse à la jeunesse guadeloupéenne," *L'Hebdomadaire de la Guadeloupe,* Dec. 5, 1941.

67. "Donnons à nos villes et bourgs un cachet moderne," *Le Nouvelliste de la Guadeloupe,* Sept. 15, 1943.

68. Ibid.

69. Ibid.

70. Burton, "Vichysme et Vichyistes à la Martinique."

71. USNA Record Group 59, box 5192, document 851B.00/16, Fort-de-France, Aug. 21, 1940.

72. "Gratien Candace, Conseiller National," *La Démocratie sociale,* Feb. 22, 1941.

73. CAOM, Télégrammes 700, Telegram from Gratien Candace #88, Feb. 8, 1941.

74. The tiny half-British, half-French New Hebrides islands in the Pacific Ocean were actually the first to side with de Gaulle, on July 23, 1940.

75. Confiant, *Le Nègre et l'amiral,* pp. 129–30.

76. Timoléon, *Chronique du temps passé,* p. 13.

77. Henry Thomasset, "Guadeloupe and Martinique," *Royal Bank Magazine* (Apr.–May 1936): 3–18.

78. USNA Record Group 59, box 5195, document 851B.20/288, Mar. 31, 1943.

79. Ibid.

80. Ibid.

81. Schneyder, "La Seconde guerre mondiale," p. 287.

82. Georges Robert, *La France aux Antilles, 1939–1943* (Paris: Plon, 1950), p. 169. The last suggestion in this passage was not too far-fetched, for an island neighboring Guadeloupe already bore the colorful name of "La Désirade."

83. Farrugia, "L'Époque de Vichy," p. 399; Sempaire, *La Guadeloupe en tan Sorin*, p. 137.

84. Cornély interview.

85. Ibid.

86. Charles de Gaulle, *Mémoires de Guerre*, vol. 1, "l'Appel" (Paris: Plon, 1954), p. 167.

87. CAOM, Agence FOM 112, "dossier Robert," press release from the Agence France Presse, Mar. 12, 1947.

88. Testimony by Omer Kromwell, in a television documentary, France 3, "La France libérée," episode "Libérateurs venus d'outre-mer" by Benjamin Stora and Jim Damour. Series by Jean-Pierre Azéma and François Bédarida.

89. See for instance, "Le Racisme et la France, ou la question de couleur," *L'Hebdomadaire de la Guadeloupe*, Aug. 1, 1942.

90. CAOM, Affaires Politiques 767, dossier 1, Rouyer report, p. 7.

91. Timoléon, *Chronique du temps passé*, p. 26.

92. Burton, "Vichysme et Vichyistes à la Martinique."

93. ADG SC 4105, Quoted in Sorin's circular to all mayors, #907, Nov. 20, 1942.

94. Ibid., Circular #938, Nov. 28, 1942.

95. ADG SC 6201, "Session communale de Pointe-à-Pitre."

96. USNA, Record Group 59, box 5192, document 851B.00/18, report from Martinique consulate, Sept. 3, 1940.

97. Ibid.

98. Ibid.

99. Ibid.

100. Sempaire, *La Guadeloupe en tan Sorin*, p. 139.

101. Cornély interview.

102. Jean Massip, "La 'Résistance' aux Antilles," *Revue de Paris* (May 1945): 4–5.

103. Ibid., p. 2. For a comparison between resistance in Martinique and Guadeloupe, see Eric Jennings, "La Dissidence aux Antilles, 1940–1943," *Vingtième siècle, revue d'histoire* 68 (Oct.–Dec. 2000): 55–71.

104. ADG SC 4088, Telegram, Apr. 30, 1943.

105. ADG SC 3995, Circulaire #51, "Appel aux maires," Basse-Terre, May 18, 1942.

106. Cornély interview; also related in Sempaire, *La Dissidence an tan Sorin*, p. 83.

107. Sempaire, *La Dissidence an tan Sorin*, p. 83.

108. Massip, "La 'Résistance' aux Antilles," p. 2.

109. ADG SC 3995, Sorin to all mayors, Feb. 24, 1941.

110. USNA Record Group 59, box 5193, document 851B.00/110, U.S. Navy, signed P. G. Hale, Mar. 23, 1943.

111. On the peaceful protests that led to the rallying of French Guiana, see Alexandre, *La Guyane sous Vichy*, pp. 47–49.

112. ADG 4Mi 411, "Événements de 1943."

113. Ibid.

114. Farrugia, "L'Époque de Vichy," p. 399.

115. Ibid., and ADG 4Mi 411, "Evénements de 1943."

116. ADG 4Mi 411, "Evénements de 1943."

117. ADG SC 6194, Fédération sportive de la Guadeloupe, année 1943.

118. Massip. "La 'Résistance' aux Antilles," pp. 4–5; and Farrugia, "L'Époque de Vichy," p. 398.

119. Ibid.

120. Ibid.

121. USNA Record Group 59, box 5193, document 851B/01/79.

122. ADG 4Mi 411, "Evénements de 1943."

123. CAOM, Affaires Politiques 2293, dossier 14, Giacobbi to the president of the CNR, July 21, 1945.

124. Ibid.

125. Sempaire, *La Guadeloupe en tan Sorin*, p. 22.

126. "Collaborationistes," *l'Homme enchaîné*, Sept. 21, 1944.

127. *Journal officiel de la Guadeloupe*, July 24, 1943, p. 379.

128. Lilien Legone, "Naissance de la France du grand large," *Le Monde*, Mar. 17–18, 1996, p. 10. Departmentalization was undoubtedly also partly a political re-action to the direct American condemnation of French imperialism voiced a year earlier at the first meeting of the United Nations in San Francisco.

129. ADG, 4mi 411, reel 3, p. 5.

130. Farrugia, "L'Époque de Vichy," p. 5.

131. Some Guadeloupean intellectuals have been indulgent with Sorin and Robert—arguing as others have for the metropole, that he spared Guadeloupe from the "worst." Interestingly, to one author at least, the "worst" in this instance meant American annexation. Lucien-René Abenon and John Dickinson, *Les Français en Amérique* (Lyon: Presses Universitaires de Lyon, 1993), p. 189.

Chapter 6: Adapting the National Revolution to Indochina

1. Jean Decoux, *A la barre de l'Indochine: Histoire de mon gouvernement général 1940–1945*. (Paris: Plon, 1949), p. 360.

2. William Hoisington, Jr., "Politics and Postage Stamps: The Postal Issues of the French State and Empire, 1940–1944," *French Historical Studies* 7, no. 3 (spring 1972): 365.

3. Stein Tønnesson, *The Vietnamese Revolution of 1945: Roosevelt, Ho Chi Minh and de Gaulle in a World at War* (London: Sage Publications, 1991), p. 47.

4. See, for instance, Martin Shipway, *The Road to War, France and Vietnam, 1944–1947* (Oxford: Berghahn Books, 1996).

5. David Marr's encyclopedic *Vietnam 1945* does tend to draw a teleological line-age culminating in the "glorious" August 1945 Revolution. David Marr, *Vietnam 1945: The Quest for Power* (Berkeley: University of California Press, 1995).

6. See for example, Kiyoko Nitz, "Independence without Nationalists? The Japanese and Vietnamese Nationalism during the Japanese Period, 1940–1945," *Journal of Southeast Asian Studies* 15, no. 1 (Mar. 1984): 108–33; and Ralph B. Smith, "The Japanese Period in Indochina and the Coup of 9 March 1945," *Journal of Southeast Asian Studies* 9 (Sept. 1978): 268–301.

7. On most of these issues, see Tønnesson, *The Vietnamese Revolution of 1945*. On U.S. perceptions specifically, see Patricia Lane, "Eléments sur la mise en oeuvre de la politique américaine envers l'Indochine, 1940–1945," *Les Cahiers de l'IHTP* numéro spécial, "les Guerres d'Indochine de 1945 à 1975" 34 (June 1996): 19–34. For English–Free French relations and Indochina, see Martin Thomas, "Free France, the British Government and the Future of French Indochina, 1940–45," *Journal of Southeast Asian Studies* 28 (1997). On Free French perceptions from Algiers, see Institut Charles de Gaulle, *Le Général de Gaulle et l'Indochine, 1940–1946* (Paris: Plon, 1982). On the British outlook, see Nicholas Tarling, "The British and the First Japanese Move into Indochina," *Journal of Southeast Asian Studies* 21 (Mar. 1990): 35–65.

8. *Office of National Intelligence Weekly*, Jan. 24, 1945, p. 303.

9. See, for example, Jacques Valette, *Indochine, 1940–1945: Français contre Japonais* (Paris: Sedes, 1993); Alfred McCoy, ed., *Southeast Asia under Japanese Occupation* (Yale University, Southeast Asia Studies, Monograph 22, 1981); Tran My-Van, "Japan and Vietnam's Caodaists: A Wartime Relationship, 1939–1945," *Journal of Southeast Asian Studies* 27, no. 1 (Mar. 1996): 179–93; Kiyoko Nitz, "Japanese Military Policy towards French Indochina during the Second World War: The Road to the Meigo Sakusen (9 March 1945)," *Journal of Southeast Asian Studies* 14, no. 2 (Sept. 1983): 328–53; Motoo Furuta and Takashi Shiraishi, eds. *Indochina in the 1940's and 1950's: Translation of Contemporary Japanese Scholarship on Southeast Asia* (Ithaca: Cornell University Southeast Asia Program, 1992); Shiraishi Masaya, "La Présence japonaise en Indochine, 1940–1945," in Paul Isoart, ed., *L'Indochine française 1940–1945* (Paris: PUF, 1982); Murakami Sachiko, "Japan's Thrust into French Indochina, 1940–1945," Ph.D. dissertation, New York University, 1981; John Dreifort, "Japan's Advance into Indochina, 1940: The French Response," *Journal of Southeast Asian Studies* 13 (Sept. 1982): 279–95; A. Benabi, "Les Français, les Japonais et le mouvement national vietnamien (1940–1945)," Ph.D. dissertation, Université de Paris I, 1988. An important (and underutilized) collection of archival sources in Aix-en-Provence, under the heading "Gouvernement Général de l'Indochine, Cabinet Militaire," contains a gold mine of information on the Japanese occupation of Indochina.

10. Panivong Norindr, *Phantasmatic Indochina: French Colonial Ideology in Architecture, Film and Literature* (Durham: Duke University Press, 1996), p. 155.

11. "Adresse du Vice-Amiral d'Escadre Decoux, Gouverneur Général de l'Indochine," *La Tribune indochinoise*, July 22, 1940, p. 1.

12. "Le Retour à la campagne," *La Tribune indochinoise*, Mar. 9, 1942, p. 3.

13. Wright, *The Politics of Design*, pp. 188–93.

14. *Discours prononcé le 28 octobre 1930 par M. Pasquier, Gouverneur Général de l'Indochine* (Hanoi: Imprimerie d'Extrême-Orient, 1930), p. 17.

15. Gilles de Gantès, "Protectorate, Association, Reformism: The Roots of the Republican Policy Pursued by the Popular Front in Indochina," in Tony Chafer and Amanda Sackur, eds., *French Colonial Empire and the Popular Front: Hope and Disillusion* (London: St. Martin's Press, 1999), pp. 109–10.

16. See Pierre Brocheux and Daniel Hémery, *Indochine: la colonisation ambiguë, 1858–1954* (Paris: La Découverte, 1995), p. 310.

17. Huynh Kim Khánh, *Vietnamese Communism, 1925–1945* (Ithaca: Cornell University Press, 1982), pp. 36–38.

18. Patrice Morlat, *La Répression coloniale au Vietnam, 1908–1940* (Paris: L'Harmattan, 1990), p. 137.

19. Bruce Lockhart, *The End of the Vietnamese Monarchy* (New Haven: Council on Southeast Asian Studies, 1993), pp. 47–48.

20. Milton Osborne, *Southeast Asia* (Sydney: Allen and Unwin, 1988), p. 124.

21. Georges Grandjean (Jan. 1931), quoted in Brocheux and Hémery, *Indochine: la colonisation ambiguë*, p. 323.

22. Morlat, *La Répression coloniale au Vietnam*, pp. 232–33.

23. On the Popular Front in Indochina, see Norindr, "The Popular Front's Colonial Policies in Indochina," p. 230. On the limits of the Popular Front's colonial reforms in general, see Cohen, "The Colonial Policy of the Popular Front," 368–93.

24. Morlat, *La Répression coloniale au Vietnam*, p. 232.

25. Decoux was technically a rear-admiral at the time of his nomination, only to be promoted to admiral a few years later.

26. For the lowest figure, see Vu Ngu Chieu, "Political and Social Change in Vietnam between 1940 and 1946," Ph.D. dissertation, University of Wisconsin, Madison, 1984, p. 67. For the highest, see David Marr, *Vietnam, 1945*, p. 73. Perhaps the most reliable figure is that of 34,000 white French out of a total population of 22,655,000 in 1940. Brocheux and Hémery, *Indochine: la colonisation ambiguë*, p. 175.

27. For a detailed study of Hanoi's European community, see Michael Vann's dissertation: "White City on the Red River: Race, Power and Culture in French Colonial Hanoi, 1872–1954," Ph.D. dissertation, University of California, Santa Cruz, 1999.

28. Wright, *The Politics of Design*, p. 162.

29. See Marianne Boucheret, "Le Triomphe du caoutchouc," *L'Histoire*, numéro spécial, "L'Indochine au temps des Français" 203 (Oct. 1996): 39.

30. See Charles Meyer, *Les Français en Indochine, 1860–1910* (Paris: Hachette, 1985), pp. 78, 85, 94, 234, 239, 248.

31. Vu Ngu Chieu, "Political and Social Change in Vietnam between 1940 and 1946," p. 101.

32. For the opinion that the *Croix de Feu* was more fascist than is commonly allowed, see William Irvine, "Fascism in France and the Strange Case of the Croix de Feu," *Journal of Modern History* 63 (1991): 271–95.

33. I am grateful to Michael Vann for bringing to my attention this material on the *Croix de Feu* in Indochina. CAOM, GGI 64200, Tonkin, août 1936.

34. Henri Lerner, *Catroux* (Paris: Albin Michel, 1990), pp. 132–142.

35. AMB, Fonds Decoux, untitled box bearing the title "Maréchal Pétain," letter from the *Association pour défendre le Maréchal Pétain*, Jan. 10, 1956.

36. In Japan, the crux of the debate revolved around the imperial army's practice of presenting Tokyo with military faits accomplis, as it had done years before by invading Manchuria. David Marr, *Vietnam, 1945*, p. 20.

37. Paul Baudoin, *The Private Diaries of Paul Baudoin, March 1940 to January 1941* (London: Eyre and Spottiswoode, 1948), p. 201.

38. Ibid., pp. 199, 203.

39. Unbeknownst to them, however, Tokyo's agenda of protecting its own Rubicon from the hawkish general of its South China Army proved the decisive factor in concluding a peaceful accord. Marr, *Vietnam, 1945*, pp. 20–21.

40. Baudoin, *The Private Diaries of Paul Baudoin*, p. 203.

41. Marr, *Vietnam, 1945*, pp. 20–21.

42. In the words of a Vichy internal report: "Indochina is completely incapable of resisting on its own to Japanese military might. ... The Lang Son affair opened the eyes of even the most optimistic. ... The worst is, for any attempt at resistance would involve mostly bluff, that the Japanese have no illusions [about our weakness]. On January 3, one could read in the *Züricher Zeitung*: "[T]he Japanese have a very low opinion of the capacity to resist on the part of the French military in the colony." CAOM, Affaires Politiques 2520, dossier 9. Report #12, Oct. 1941.

43. CAOM, Indochine Nouveau Fonds (Hereafter INF) 1198, report on Lang Son.

44. Baudoin, *The Private Diaries of Paul Baudoin*, p. 239.

45. USNA, document 851G.00/11–844, Baudoin report, "La Crise franco-japonaise de l'été 1940," pp. 14, 16.

46. On the view that the Japanese imperial regime was also motivated by political affinities with Vichy, and that it intended to utilize Indochina as a "commissary line" in Southeast Asia, see Nitz, "Japanese Military Policy towards French Indochina," pp. 347–48.

47. USNA, document 851G.00/11–844, Baudoin report, p. 7.

48. Georges Sabattier, *Le Destin de l'Indochine: souvenirs et documents, 1941–1951* (Paris: Plon, 1952), p. 52.

49. See Georges Gautier, *La Fin de l'Indochine Française* (Paris: Société de production littéraire, 1978), pp. 52–53.

50. Ibid., p. 70. On food cards, see CAOM, Agence FOM 272, dossier 451. See also André Angladette "La Vie quotidienne en Indochine de 1939 à 1946," CRA-SOM [*Académie des Sciences Outre-mer,* "Mondes et cultures"] 31, no. 3 (June 1979): 467–98.

51. CAOM, RSTNF 6282, "Situation politique."

52. Msgr. François Chaize, "Au Tonkin: une mission dans la tourmente, 1940–1945," *Revue des deux mondes* (July 1, 1948): 45.

53. Marr, *Vietnam, 1945*, p. 104.

54. Nguyen Khac Vien, "Vietnam during World War II," *Vietnamese Studies* 24 (1970): 121.

55. Ho Chi Minh, *Selected Writings, 1920–1969* (Hanoi: Foreign Language Publishing House, 1973), p. 44.

56. CAOM, Affaires Politiques 928, dossier 4, "Note."

57. CAOM, Télégrammes 807, Marine Saigon to Platon. New Caledonia had been one of the first colonies to fall into Free French hands, on September 29, 1940. On New Caledonia during the Second World War, see Kim Munholland,

"The Trials of the Free French in New Caledonia," *French Historical Studies* 14 (1986): 547–99.

58. SHAT 10 H 81, Telegram #807, Vichy Jan. 26, 1942.

59. For the third anniversary of the Legion on August 30, 1943, massive rallies were held throughout Indochina. Decoux described the ceremony as follows: "Next to the Legion, formations of youths paraded with flags and banners while singing '*Maréchal, nous Voilà!*'" CAOM, Agence FOM, carton 272, dossier 451, Hanoi, Aug. 31, 1943.

60. Sabattier, *Le Destin de l'Indochine*, p. 39.

61. AMB, Fonds Decoux, Box 2, telegrams, Hanoi, Apr. 21, 1942, to Vichy.

62. "Paroles du Maréchal," *L'Echo annamite* (Saigon), Apr. 22, 1941.

63. For Saigon cathedral, see *Indochine, hebdomadaire illustré*, Jan. 8, 1942, p. 8. On Dalat's waterfall, see Gilbert David, *Chroniques secrètes de l'Indochine, 1928–1946* (Paris: L'Harmattan, 1994), vol. 1, pp. 18, 150. Please note that some doubts have arisen on the authenticity of Gilbert David's book, which purports to recount Masonic and Cao Dai activities in Indochina.

64. AN F60 316, Apr. 19, 1941, Decoux to Présidence du Conseil.

65. CAOM, Télégrammes 725, Decoux to Vichy, Apr. 2, 1941.

66. "L'Acte de naissance du Maréchal Pétain," *Le Courrier d'Haiphong*, Mar. 10, 1941, p. 1.

67. Thierry Maulnier, *Révolution Nationale: l'avenir de la France* (Hanoi: Publication du Gouvernement Général de l'Indochine, 1942), p. 71.

68. S. Lehnebach, *Pour mieux comprendre la Révolution Nationale* (Saigon: Éditions du service local de l'IPP, 1943), quoted in *Indochine, hebdomadaire Illustré*, Sept. 2, 1943, p. 2.

69. Lehnebach, *Pour mieux comprendre la Révolution Nationale*, p. 1.

70. Georges Taboulet, *Le Retour à la tradition: ou la cité reconstruite* (Hanoi: Editions du Gouvernement Général de l'Indochine, 1941), p. 7.

71. On Taboulet's public speaking appearances, see "Conférence sur le Maréchal Pétain," *La Tribune indochinoise*, Jan. 7, 1942, p. 1.

72. CAOM, RSTNF 6282, p. 1.

73. Ibid.

74. Nguyen Tien Lang, *Pages françaises: études sur la littérature française*, 2d ed. (Hanoi: Huong-Son, 1943), preface.

75. Ibid., p. 10.

76. CAOM, INF 337, dossier 2699, anonymous report, p. 5.

77. CAOM, INF 2586.

78. Ibid.

79. Philippe DeVillers, *Histoire du Vietnam de 1940 à 1952* (Paris: Editions du Seuil, 1952), p. 86.

80. N.A., *Les Réalisations de la Révolution Nationale en Indochine* (Hanoi: Gouvernement Général de l'Indochine, 1942), p. 21.

81. VNNA, Résidence Supérieure du Tonkin, D62, #79.891, folder #1, p. 43.

82. Ibid., p. 44; also see folder #3 of this same box.

83. On Vietnamese members of Masonic lodges, see Jacques Dalloz, "Les Viet-

namiens dans la franc-maçonnerie coloniale," *Revue française d'histoire d'outre-mer* 85, no. 320 (1998): 103–18; and David, *Chroniques secrètes*, vol. 1, pp. 86, 115–16.

84. VNNA, Résidence Supérieure du Tonkin, D62, #79.891, folder #2.

85. VNNA, Résidence Supérieure du Tonkin, D62 F9 #79.890, "Statut des Juifs."

86. VNNA, Résidence Supérieure du Tonkin, D62, #79.891, folder #1, note #132, from Résident Supérieur du Tonkin. Note: This document on the Jewish Statute somehow made its way into a box on anti-Masonic legislation.

87. VNNA, Résidence Supérieure du Tonkin, D62 F9 #79.890, document #34 "Mayor of Hanoi to the Résident Supérieur du Tonkin, March 3, 1943."

88. Ibid., D62 F9 #79.890, document #56, "Decoux to Résident Supérieur du Tonkin, Oct. 7, 1941."

89. F. R. Giraud and Bui Ngo Hien, *Livret de l'étudiant indochinois* (Hanoi: Direction de l'instruction publique, 1943), pp. 227–28.

90. CAOM, RSTNF 2044, "Statut des Juifs."

91. Ibid.

92. On the Japanese treatment of Jews in the Shanghai ghetto, see Ernest Heppner, *Shanghai Refuge: A Memoir of the World War II Jewish Ghetto* (Lincoln: University of Nebraska Press, 1993); David Kranzler, *Japanese, Nazis and Jews: The Jewish Refugee Community of Shanghai, 1938–1945* (New York: Yeshiva University Press, 1976); and David Goodman, *Jews in the Japanese Mind: The History and Uses of a Cultural Stereotype* (New York: Free Press, 1995).

93. CAOM, Affaires Politiques 889, dossier 1, "mise sous séquestre des biens Juifs," Decoux to Vichy, Aug. 8, 1942.

94. Ibid.

95. Ibid.

96. SHAT 10 H 81, Decoux to Ministry of the Colonies, Vichy. Telegram 772, Oct. 24, 1942.

97. CAOM, INF, 1198, Rothé to Pétain, letter dated Feb. 9, 1941.

98. Sabattier, *Le Destin de l'Indochine*, p. 56.

99. *Indochine, hebdomadaire illustré*, July 20, 1944, interview with Jean Decoux, p. 3.

100. Maurice Ducoroy, *Ma trahison en Indochine* (Paris: Editions internationales, 1949), p. 25.

101. Sabattier, *Le Destin de l'Indochine*, p. 37.

102. Decoux, *A la barre de l'Indochine*, p. 141. In January 1941, after suffering a major setback on land, Vichy forces won a decisive naval battle over the Siamese at Koh-Changh on January 17, 1941. The victory would be short-lived, for in a matter of days, Japan brokered a treaty that proved extremely favorable to Siam.

103. Morgan Sportès, *Tonkinoise* (Paris: Le Seuil, 1995), p. 52.

104. On the Legion in Indochina, see Pierre Lamant, "La Révolution Nationale dans l'Indochine de l'Amiral Decoux," *Revue d'histoire de la deuxième guerre mondiale et des conflits contemporains* 138 (Apr. 1985): 27–30.

105. "Le Serment des Légionnaires," *Indochine, hebdomadaire illustré*, July 3, 1941, p. 2.

106. "Une Grande journée légionnaire à Hanoi," *L'Action*, May 2, 1942, p. 1.

107. "Discours de M. P. Delsalle," *L'Action*, May 2, 1942, p. 1.

108. "Avis aux légionnaires," *Tribune indochinoise*, Apr. 15, 1942, p. 4.

109. CAOM, Affaires Politiques 886, dossier 2, Decoux to Platon, Oct. 23, 1942.

110. Ibid., Vichy to Decoux, Nov. 10, 1942.

111. CAOM, Affaires Politiques 2047, Brevié to Decoux, May 22, 1942.

112. Decoux, *A la barre de l'Indochine*, p. 365.

113. CAOM, Haut Commissariat Indochine, dossier 623.

114. CAOM, INF 1226; and Affaires Politiques 885, dossier 1, Decoux to Vichy, June 14, 1943.

115. *La Légion, Bulletin Trimestriel de l'Union Cochinchinoise de la Légion Française des Combattants*, n.d., p. 16, "Présidents des Unions locales."

116. A. Lohenet, "Traditions annamites et rénovation française," *Indochine, hebdomadaire illustré*, Aug. 2, 1941, p. 11.

117. Pierre Brocheux, "La Question de l'indépendance dans l'opinion vietnamienne de 1939 à 1945," in Charles-Robert Ageron, ed., *Les Chemins de la décolonisation de l'empire français, 1936–1956* (Paris: Editions du CNRS, 1986), p. 202.

118. CAOM, Affaires Politiques 884, Decoux to Vichy, July 10, 1941.

119. CAOM, GGI 65415, dossier 57.

120. Ibid.

121. Lohenet, "Traditions annamites et Rénovation française," p. 11.

122. Ton That Binh, Nguyen-Manh-Tuong, et al., "Patrie Française et patrie Annamite," in *Témoignages* (Hanoi: Imprimerie Taupin et Cie., 1941), pp. 5–8.

123. Nam Dong, "Les Annamites et la Révolution Nationale," *L'Action, organe de collaboration franco-indochinoise*, Apr. 24, 1942, p. 1.

124. Viet-Nam was in fact originally a slightly derogatory term coined by the Chinese, signifying "the South of Viet." The name had since been appropriated by the Vietnamese, who had previously preferred Nam-Viet, or "Southern Viet." Benedict Anderson, *Imagined Communities* (London: Verso, 1996), pp. 157–58.

125. Nguyen Viet-Nam, "Le Travail, La Famille, La Patrie," *Indochine, hebdomadaire illustré*, Nov. 21, 1940, p. 14.

126. Edward Said, *Orientalism* (New York: Vintage Books, 1979), p. 114.

127. A. Agard, "Réflexions sur les paroles du Maréchal et l'enseignement moral de Confucius," *Bulletin général de l'instruction publique* (Jan. 1943): pp. 108–12.

128. Jean François and Nguyen Viet-Nam. *Câu Dôi Pháp Nam: Sentences parallèles franco-annamites.* (Hanoi: Presses du Gouvernement Général, 1942), pp. 2–3.

129. Ibid., pp. 16–17.

130. Ibid., pp. 64–65.

131. Ibid., pp. 2–25.

132. "Coincidence Franco-indochinoise," *L'Echo annamite*, Apr. 25, 1941, p. 1.

133. Nguyen Tien Lang, "Révolution Nationale et Culture Indochinoise," part 3, *Indochine, hebdomadaire illustré*, May 27, 1943, p. 4.

134. Nam Dong, "Les Annamites et la Révolution Nationale," p. 1.

135. Nguyen Tien Lang, "Révolution Nationale et Culture indochinoise," part 1, *Indochine, hebdomadaire illustré*, May 13, 1943, p. 5.

136. The Trung sisters had ousted the Chinese from the Red River Delta during the first century A.D. On Decoux's call for a dual celebration of Joan and the Trung, see CAOM, Affaires Politiques 2196, dossier 7, Decoux to Platon, May 12, 1941.

137. David Marr, *Vietnamese Tradition on Trial, 1920–1945* (Berkeley: University of California Press, 1981), p. 200.

138. N.A., *Hymnes et pavillons d'Indochine* (Hanoi: Imprimerie d'Extrême-Orient, 1941).

139. Ibid.

140. See Arundhati Virmani, "National Symbols under Colonial Domination: The Nationalization of the Indian Flag, March–August 1923," *Past and Present* 164 (Aug. 1999): 169–87.

141. Ton That Binh, "Patrie Française et patrie Annamite," *Indochine, hebdomadaire illustré*, Aug. 2, 1941, p. 5.

142. Nguyen Manh Tuong, "Rencontre," in *Témoignages*, pp. 20–21.

143. Jean François and Nguyen Viet-Nam, *Cau Doi Phap Nam, Sentences parallèles franco-annamites*, preface p. 1.

144. Ibid., preface p. 2.

145. "Marche des Etudiants, Chant fédéral de l'Université indochinoise," *La Tribune indochinoise*, July 1, 1942, pp. 1–2.

146. Tao-Trang, "Reconstruction," *L'Annam nouveau*, Dec. 15, 1940, 1.

147. "Le Maréchal Pétain et les Annamites," *L'Annam nouveau*, Sept. 21, 1941, 1.

148. On Pham Quynh's fascination with Charles Maurras, see Lamant, "La Révolution Nationale dans l'Indochine de l'Amiral Decoux," p. 34; and Trinh Van Thao, *Vietnam du Confucianisme au Communisme* (Paris: L'Harmattan, 1990), 214–17; 318. On Pham Quynh's activities in the 1930s, see Christopher Goscha, "L'Indochine repensée par les Indochinois: Pham Quynh et les deux débats de 1931 sur l'immigration, le fédéralisme et la réalité de l'Indochine," *Revue française d'histoire d'outre-mer* 82 (1995): 421–53; and Bernard Le Calloc'h, "Le Rôle de Pham-Quynh dans la promotion du quôc-ngu et de la littérature vietnamienne moderne," *Revue française d'histoire d'outre-mer* 72, no. 3 (1985): 309–20.

149. Marr, *Vietnamese Tradition on Trial*, p. 18.

150. "Redressement français et restauration annamite," *L'Annam nouveau*, Oct. 26, 1941.

151. Vu Ngoc Lien, "Chanson et musique annamites," *L'Annam nouveau*, Nov. 7, 1940.

152. Marr, *Vietnam, 1945*, p. 93.

153. CAOM, Affaires Politiques 2520, dossier 9. Report #11, Apr. 11, 1941, p. 20.

154. "La Sagesse populaire de France et d'Annam," *L'Action*, Apr. 14, 1942, p. 2.

155. Lohenet, "Traditions annamites et Rénovation française," p. 11. In italics is Pétain's famous phrase, *La terre qui, elle, ne ment pas*.

156. Yves Chaeys, "Théâtres indigènes," *Indochine, hebdomadaire illustré*, Jan. 9, 1941, p. 2.

157. Frances Gouda, *Colonial Practices in the Netherland Indies, 1900–1942* (Amsterdam: Amsterdam University Press, 1995), pp. 119–20.

158. D. Antomarchi, "Le Bi Duê, recueil des coutumes rhadées," *Indochine, hebdomadaire illustré*, Feb. 20, 1941, p. 7.

159. Nguyen Tien Lang, "Révolution Nationale et culture Indochinoise," *Indochine, hebdomadaire illustré*, May 27, 1943, p. 4.

160. Bibliothèque Nationale, Paris. Hoang Van Co, "La Rénovation de l'économie indigène: le paysannat et l'artisanat d'outre-mer," lecture at the Université de Clermont-Ferrand, Tuesday Feb. 12, 1942. (Service Général d'information et de propagande).

161. Ibid.

162. Marr, *Vietnam, 1945*, p. 93.

163. Huynh Kim Khánh, *Vietnamese Communism, 1925–1945*, pp. 232–65.

164. Ho Chi Minh, *Selected Writings*, pp. 44–45.

165. SHAT 10 H 78, Rapport sur la vie politique en Indochine de 1940 à 1950.

166. Gautier, *La Fin de l'Indochine Française*, pp. 71–72.

167. Ibid.

168. Herman Lebovics, *True France: The Wars over Cultural Identity, 1900–1945* (Ithaca: Cornell University Press, 1992), p. 119. Gail Paradise Kelly, *Franco-Vietnamese Schools, 1918–1938: Regional Development and Implications for National Integration* (Wisconsin Papers on Southeast Asia, Apr. 1982).

169. Ageron, *La Décolonisation française*, p. 65.

170. Ho Chi Minh, *Selected Writings*, p. 44.

Chapter 7: Toward a New Indochina

1. Kim Lefevre, *Métisse blanche* (Paris: Bernard Barrault, 1989), p. 19.

2. Sportès, *Tonkinoise*, pp. 125–26.

3. Ageron, *La Décolonisation française*, p. 65. It should be noted that former members of Decoux's entourage later emerged as his most vociferous postwar apologists, precisely on the basis of his allegedly "liberal" indigenous policies. Claude de Boisanger, "L'Amiral Decoux, un sujet d'étude pour les historiens," *La Revue des deux mondes*, Aug. 15, 1968, p. 490–95; Claude de Boisanger, *On pouvait éviter la guerre d'Indochine: Souvenirs, 1941–1945* (Paris: Maisonneuve, 1977), pp. 119–21.

4. AMB, Fonds Decoux, Box 10, "doubles de télégrammes," telegram from Decoux in Hanoi, Dec. 15, 1941.

5. Huynh Kim Khánh, *Vietnamese Communism, 1925–1945*, p. 254.

6. CAOM, INF 1096, Platon to Decoux, July 31, 1941.

7. Ibid., Gaston Joseph, note dated May 10, 1941.

8. Admiral Darlan's veritable declaration of war on Communism, intended for "all Ministers and Secretaries of State," is enclosed in CAOM, Affaires Politiques 818, dossier 2.

9. CAOM, INF 1096, quoted in Platon to Decoux, July 31, 1941.

10. Ibid., Decoux to Platon, Aug. 19, 1941.

11. Paul Isoart, "Aux origines d'une guerre: L'Indochine française, 1940–1945," in Paul Isoart et al. *L'Indochine française, 1940–1945* (Paris: PUF, 1982), p. 15.

12. N.A., "La France a pratiqué en Indochine, depuis 1939, une politique très libérale d'association." *Marchés coloniaux du monde*, May 8, 1948.

13. David, *Chroniques secrètes*, vol. 1, p. 138.

14. CAOM, INF 696 (dossier 2) Nguyen Trong Tan, "En vue d'une collaboration totale entre Français et Annamites, de l'unification du patriotisme annamite avec l'amour de la France."

15. CAOM, INF 133 CAOM, INF (dossier 1200) Telegram 4625, Joseph, dated Aug. 8, 1941.

16. CAOM, 14PA 50, Platon to Decoux, Oct. 9, 1941.

17. AMB, Fonds Decoux, Box 2, Decoux to Ministry of Colonies, Vichy, Feb. 9, 1942.

18. CAOM, Télégrammes 807, télégrammes 5143 to 5146, Oct. 20, 1941.

19. Ibid., télégrammes 6430 to 6438, Oct. 27, 1941.

20. Ibid., télégramme 5371, Oct. 29, 1941.

21. CAOM, Affaires Politiques 2555, dossier 6.

22. Cao Van Chieu, "Accès des Annamites dans la haute administration indochinoise: le sens d'une réforme," *France-Annam*, Aug. 18, 1944, p. 1.

23. N.A., *Les Réalisations de la Révolution Nationale en Indochine* (Hanoi: Gouvernement Général de l'Indochine, 1942), p. 9.

24. "Urgence des réformes communales," *La Lutte*, June 12, 1938, p. 1.

25. Pasquier, *Discours prononcé le 28 octobre 1930*, p. 17.

26. CAOM, Affaires Politiques 888, dossier 2, under dossier "Port des insignes aux colonies," Decoux to Platon, Jan. 25, 1941.

27. AN F60 316, law relating to the wearing of certain decorations in Indochina.

28. Martin Stuart-Fox, *A History of Laos* (Cambridge: Cambridge University Press, 1997), pp. 54–55.

29. Jean Decoux and Pham Quynh, *Mission du Mandarinat:* discours prononcés le 24 décembre 1941 à l'occasion de la proclamation des résultats du concours de Tri-Huyên (CAOM Library), p. 14.

30. Ibid.

31. Ibid., p. 15.

32. CAOM, Agence FOM, carton 261, dossier 403. Telegram dated Sept. 29, 1943, Decoux to Ministry of Colonies, entitled: "Les mandarins d'autorité dans l'Indochine nouvelle."

33. Ibid.

34. CAOM, GGI 65339. Circulaire, Saigon, Oct. 13, 1941.

35. CAOM, Agence FOM, carton 261, dossier 403. Telegram dated Sept. 29, 1943, Decoux to Ministry of Colonies, entitled: "Les mandarins d'autorité dans l'Indochine nouvelle."

36. N.A., *Souverains et notabilités d'Indochine* (Hanoi: Editions du Gouvernement Général de l'Indochine, 1943), p. 89.

37. Philippe Devillers, however, is persuaded that this constituency was "pro-Japanese and anti-French," a contention that I would dispute. See Devillers's comments in Ageron, *Les Chemins de la décolonisation de l'empire français*, p. 289.

38. Hue Tam Ho Tai, *Radicalism and the Origins of the Vietnamese Revolution* (Cambridge: Harvard University Press, 1992), pp. 258–63.

39. Pierre-Richard Féray, *Le Vietnam au 20ème siècle* (Paris: Presses Universitaires de France, 1979), p. 172.

40. On Pham Quynh's death, see Marr, *Vietnam, 1945,* p. 453.

41. "Retour à la terre," *L'Echo annamite,* June 6–7, 1941, p. 1.

42. Cochinchinese reforms are detailed in CAOM, GGI 56341.

43. CAOM, Agence FOM, 251, dossier 375, "Le Village annamite," Aug. 16, 1939.

44. CAOM, GGI 65343, "Politique rurale en Cochinchine."

45. Ibid.

46. CAOM, GGI 65339, "Note sur la commune annamite en Cochinchine," Oct. 31, 1941.

47. VNNA, Gouv. Gen. 1305, p. 5.

48. Le Dinh Chan, "Commune annamite et Révolution Nationale," *L'Action,* July 17, 1942, p. 2.

49. "Une Réforme capitale: réorganisation de la commune annamite au Tonkin," *Indochine, Hebdomadaire illustré,* June 19, 1941, p. 3.

50. Le Dinh Chan, "Commune annamite et Révolution Nationale," *L'Action,* July 17, 1942, p. 2.

51. "Une Réforme capitale," p. 3.

52. Le Dinh Chan, "Commune annamite et Révolution Nationale," part 2, *L'Action,* July 18, 1942, p. 3.

53. Paxton, *Vichy France,* pp. 268–73; Richard Kuisel, *Capitalism and the State in Modern France* (Cambridge: Cambridge University Press, 1981), pp. 128–56.

54. CAOM, INF, carton 343, dossier 2749, "Programme d'action sociale et culturelle, 1944."

55. Ibid.

56. Ibid.

57. Peyrouton, *Du Service public à la prison commune,* p. 123.

58. Christopher Goscha, *Vietnam or Indochina? Contesting Concepts of Space in Vietnamese Nationalism, 1887–1954* (Copenhagen: NIAS, 1995), pp. 79–80. On this issue, see also Benabi, "Les Français, les Japonais et le mouvement national vietnamien," p. 278.

59. Devillers, *Histoire du Vietnam de 1940 à 1952,* p. 83.

60. "La Région," *Indochine, hebdomadaire illustré,* Apr. 29, 1943, p. 2.

61. "Il y a trois ans, le 20 juillet 1940, l'Amiral Decoux prenait en main les destinées de l'Indochine," *Indochine, hebdomadaire illustré,* July 22, 1943, p. 4.

62. Library of Congress. Paul Boudet, *L'Indochine dans le passé: Exposition de documents historiques organisée par la direction des archives et des bibliothèques à l'occasion de la Foire-Exposition de Hanoi* (Hanoi: Société de Géographie de Hanoi, 1941), pp. 2–3.

63. Goscha, *Vietnam or Indochina?,* p. 80.

64. Hoa Ng Van To, "L'Indochine dans le passé," *L'Annam nouveau* Jan. 25, 1942, p. 1.

65. According to Said, Chateaubriand, in particular, envisioned the Arab as "a civilized man fallen again into a savage state." Said, *Orientalism*, pp. 170–72.

66. Georges Taboulet, *Histoire de France à l'usage des élèves français d'Indochine* (Hanoi: Direction de l'instruction publique, 1944), p. 66.

67. CAOM, 56 APOM 5, "note personnelle," June 8, 1940.

68. CAOM, GGI 65322.

69. Ibid.

70. AN F30 316, decree of July 22, 1943, relating to the status of Franco-Asian métis functionaries with respect to salaries.

71. AMB, Fonds Decoux, Box 10, "doubles de télégrammes," telegram from Decoux in Dalat, to all local administrative leaders, Sept. 14, 1943.

72. AN F30 316, decree #535 of Mar. 16, 1943, relating to the salary scales of Asian functionaries serving in Indochina.

73. AMB, Fonds Decoux, Box 10, doubles de télégrammes, telegram from Decoux in Dalat, to all local administrative leaders, Sept. 14, 1943; and, in the same box, "Note postale ciruclaire #72 S-P/I, Hanoi, Nov. 17, 1943, Decoux to heads of local administrations, "Bases de la determination de l'origine."

74. Ann Laura Stoler, "Sexual Affronts and Racial Frontiers: European Identities and the Cultural Politics of Exclusion in Colonial Southeast Asia," in Frederick Cooper and Ann Laura Stoler, eds., *Tensions of Empire: Colonial Cultures in a Bourgeois World* (Berkeley: University of California Press, 1997), p. 200.

75. Ibid., p. 225.

76. CAOM, Residence Supérieur de Tonkin, Nouveau Fonds, 6282, p. 2.

77. *Annuaire statistique de l'Indochine*, 1941–42, p. 25, and 1943–46, p. 32.

78. VNNA, Gouv. Gen. 6564, pp. 34–48.

79. See pp. 62–63 of this book.

80. VNNA, Gouv. Gen. 6564, pp. 36–47.

81. Ibid., p. 48.

82. CAOM, Agence FOM, Carton 251, dossier 375, télégramme 4338, dated Oct. 7, 1943.

83. David, *Chroniques secrètes*, vol. 1, pp. 138–42.

84. "A la recherche d'une politique coloniale," *L'Echo annamite* (Saigon), Sept. 12–13, 1941, p. 1.

85. Nguyen Khac Vien, "Vietnam during World War II," p. 120.

86. VNNA, Gouv. Gen. 1309, "Question de la réforme des assemblées et création de nouveaux conseils," p. 1.

87. For the law of November 8, 1940, see CAOM, INF 2762.

88. USNA, Record Group 59, box 5200, document 851G.031/1.

89. CAOM, GGI carton 313, dossier 1612, Saigon May 10, 1940, signed Catroux.

90. CAOM, INF 2762, "Textes gouvernant les Assemblées locales élues des colonies depuis juin 1940," p. 2.

91. CAOM, Télégrammes 787, télégramme 2730, Apr. 29, 1943, Decoux to Ministry of Colonies, Vichy.

92. CAOM, INF 2762, "note sur la création d'un conseil fédéral indochinois."

93. "Les Conseillers fédéraux, Cochinchine," *Indochine, hebdomadaire illustré,* Aug. 21, 1941, p. 9.

94. Ibid.

95. "Les Conseillers fédéraux, Tonkin," *Indochine, hebdomadaire illustré,* Sept. 18, 1941, p. 6.

96. CAOM, INF 2762, "note sur la création d'un conseil fédéral indochinois."

97. AMB, Fonds Decoux, Box 2, "Lettre d'un jeune révolutionnaire annamite à son Excellence le Ministre des Affaires de la Grand'Asie, novembre 1943," p. 4.

98. CAOM, INF 2762, Bléhaut to Decoux, Apr. 29, 1943.

99. Ibid., Decoux to Bléhaut, May 9, 1943.

100. CAOM, Indochine Résidence Supérieure du Cambodge 349. "Rapport de province," Mar. 11, 1942.

101. CAOM, INF 1130, "extrait d'un rapport du Sous-lieutenant Esnault."

102. CAOM, INF 1198, "Lettre de M. Bui Luang Chien," Apr. 25, 1941.

103. Ibid.

104. CAOM, INF 2762, Decoux to Ministry of Colonies, Vichy, Nov. 19, 1941.

105. VNNA, Gouv. Gen. 7032, Information from the Commission du Contrôle Postal de l'Indochine, 1942–1944, p. 42.

106. Ibid., p. 94.

107. VNNA, Gouv. Gen. F74, #50, pp. 17–26.

108. Ibid.

109. Ibid., p. 27.

110. *Bulletin général de l'instruction publique* (Sept. 1942), p. 12.

111. For a comparison with Vichy's regimentation of youth in Madagascar, see Jennings, "Vichy à Madagascar."

112. CAOM, Agence FOM, carton 244, dossier 332. Decoux to Ministry of Colonies, Aug. 12, 1943.

113. This figure was found in CAOM, Agence FOM, carton 272, dossier 451, Decoux to Ministry of Colonies, Feb. 13, 1944.

114. Marr, *Vietnamese Tradition on Trial,* p. 79.

115. CAOM, RSTNF 6050.

116. "Conférence de M. Pham Xuan Do," *L'Action,* Dec. 4, 1942, p. 2.

117. Decoux, *A la barre de l'Indochine,* pp. 285–87.

118. J. Desjardins, "A l'ombre de la Révolution Nationale: le Cambodge et sa jeunesse," *Indochine, hebdomadaire illustré,* Aug. 17, 1944, pp. 4, 6.

119. Ibid., p. 5.

120. Ibid.

121. Ibid.

122. Ibid., pp. 5, 9.

123. Ibid., p. 6.

124. CAOM, INF 2435, Decoux to Ministry of Colonies, Feb. 10, 1944.

125. Ducoroy, *Ma trahison,* p. 151; CAOM, Agence FOM, carton 244, dossier 332. "Telegram #1822 from Decoux to Ministry of Colonies." On Uriage, see John Hellman, *The Knight-Monks of Vichy France: Uriage, 1940–1945* (Kingston: McGill University Press, 1997).

126. Ducoroy, *Ma trahison*, p. 151.

127. AMB, Fonds Decoux, Box entitled "ouvrages," *Foire Exposition de Saigon, 1942–1943; Album Souvenir*, p. 106.

128. Ducoroy, *Ma trahison*, p. 157.

129. Maurice Ducoroy, "La Leçon Hébert d'éducation physique," *Indochine, hebdomadaire illustré*, July 17, 1941, pp. 8–10.

130. CAOM, Agence Fom, carton 244, dossier 332. "Telegram #1822 from Decoux to Ministry of Colonies."

131. Ducoroy, *Ma trahison*, p. 157.

132. Ibid., p. 165.

133. Though pelote basque has now found a following in Florida and Central America under the name of *jai alai*, it has hardly become a global sport.

134. VNNA, Gouv. Gen. 1310, "Conseil Fédéral Indochinois: Education physique de la jeunesse indochinoise," p. 3.

135. AMB, Fonds Decoux, Box entitled "ouvrages," *Foire Exposition de Saigon, 1942–1943; Album Souvenir*, p. 106.

136. Ducoroy, *Ma trahison*, p. 103.

137. CAOM, Agence Fom, carton 244, dossier 332. "Telegram #1822 from Decoux to Ministry of Colonies."

138. Ibid.

139. Commissariat général à l'éducation physique, aux sports, et à la jeunesse [en Indochine], *Premières tâches du chef de jeunesse provincial* (Jan. 1943), p. 7.

140. AMB, Fonds Decoux, Box 2, "L'Indochine au Travail," pp. 7–10.

141. AMB, Fonds Decoux, Box 3, "En l'honneur de la visite de l'Amiral Decoux à l'Ecole Supérieure des Cadres de Jeunesse de l'Indochine."

142. Anderson, *Imagined Communities*, pp. 131–32. On the subject of the emergence of Cambodian, Vietnamese, and Lao identities, see Christopher Goscha, *Vietnam or Indochina?*; and David Henley, "Ethnogeographic Integration and Exclusion in Anticolonial Nationalism: Indonesia and Indochina," *Comparative Studies in Society and History* 37 (April 1995): 286–324.

143. CAOM, Agence FOM, carton 272, dossier 451, Decoux to Ministry of Colonies, Feb. 13, 1944.

144. Ibid., p. 12.

145. See Ducoroy, *Ma trahison*, p. 16.

146. Ibid.

147. "Foot-ball, Annam-Tonkin," *L'Action*, Dec. 4, 1942, p. 2.

148. "L'Oeuvre du Commissariat Général à l'Education Physique, aux Sports et à la Jeunesse en Indochine," *Indochine, hebdomadaire illustré*, July 22, 1944, p. 20.

149. Ducoroy, *Ma trahison*, pp. 147–48.

150. Ibid., p. 147.

151. Ibid., pp. 166–89.

152. Bao Dai, *Le Dragon d'Annam*, p. 97.

153. *Premières tâches du chef de jeunesse provincial* (Jan. 1943), p. 8.

154. "Un Camp de chefs à Sam-Son," *L'Action*, Sept. 3, 1942, p. 3.

155. Ibid.

156. "Une Belle réalisation: les camps de jeunesse du Mont-Bavi," *Le Légionnaire*, Dec. 1942, p. 3; "Notre-Dame du Ba-Vi," *L'Action*, July 31, 1942, p. 2.

157. J. de Lacourt, "Avec ceux du camp de jeunesse Notre-Dame du Ba-vi," *Indochine, hebdomadaire illustré*, Aug. 14, 1941.

158. On hill stations as the seats of colonial power, see Dane Kennedy, *The Magic Mountains: Hill Stations and the British Raj* (Berkeley: University of California Press, 1996), pp. 147–74.

159. J. de Lacourt, "Avec ceux du camp de jeunesse Notre-Dame du Ba-vi," *Indochine, hebdomadaire illustré*, Aug. 14, 1941.

160. VNNA, Gouv. Gen. 1293, "Rapport sur la formation morale de la jeunesse," p. 9.

161. Ibid., pp. 7–8.

162. Naturally, Ducoroy insists that the salute he introduced to Indochina was strictly Olympic and not fascist.

163. VNNA, Gouv. Gen. 1293, "Rapport sur la formation morale de la jeunesse," p. 12.

164. Ibid., p. 3.

165. Ibid., pp. 3–4.

166. VNNA, Gouv. Gen. 1310, "Arrêté du 22 février 1942," p. 2.

167. "La Femme au foyer," *L'Annam nouveau*, Dec. 21, 1941, p. 1.

168. On Lehnebach's closeness with Decoux, see AMB, Fonds Decoux, Carton 3, seating arrangements and guest lists.

169. Lehnebach, *Pour mieux comprendre la Révolution Nationale*, p. 33.

170. Meyer, *Les Français en Indochine*, p. 209. This liberation from domestic chores was often presented as a burden of its own, leading only to terrible "boredom" and "idleness."

171. VNNA, Gouv. Gen. 1310, p. 1.

172. "Baptême de la première promotion de l'école des monitrices à Dalat," *l'Action*, June 2, 1942, p. 2.

173. "La Jeunesse féminine à Dalat," *Indochine, hebdomadaire illustré*, May 6, 1943.

174. VNNA, Gouv. Gen. 1293, p. 3.

175. Ducoroy, *Ma trahison*, pp. 88–89.

176. *Bao Moi*, Jan. 3, 1942, reproduced in *Indochine, hebdomadaire illustré*, Jan. 8, 1942, p. 12.

177. VNNA, Gouv. Gen. 1310, "Education physique de la jeunesse indochinoise," p. 1.

178. Marr, *Vietnam 1945*, p. 119; and Trinh Dinh Khai, *Décolonisation du Viêt Nam: un avocat témoigne* (Paris: L'Harmattan, 1994), p. 64.

179. Benabi, "Les Français, les Japonais et le mouvement national vietnamien," p. 265.

180. SHAT, 10 H 78, Rapport sur la vie politique en Indochine de 1940 à 1950, p. 13.

181. Jean-Michel Pedrazzani, *La France en Indochine de Catroux à Sainteny* (Paris: Arthaud, 1972), p. 111.

Chapter 8: The Pétainist Festival

1. Confiant, *Le Nègre et l'amiral*, p. 132.

2. For the Antilles, See Richard Burton, *La Famille coloniale: La Martinique et la mère patrie, 1789–1992* (Paris: L'Harmattan, 1994), pp. 138–46; and Laurent Farrugia, "Le Tricentenaire," in Roland Suvelor, ed., *L'Historial Antillais* (Fort-de-France: Dajani, 1980), vol. V, p. 304. For Algeria, see Jacques Cantier, "Les Gouverneurs Viollette et Bordes et la politique algérienne de la France à la fin des années 20," *Revue française d'histoire d'outre-mer* 84, no. 1 (1997): 25–49.

3. See Paillard, "Marianne et l'indigène," pp. 107–20; and Marc Michel, "'Mémoire officielle,' discours et pratique coloniale. Le 14 juillet et le 11 novembre au Sénégal entre les deux guerres," *Revue française d'histoire d'outre-mer* 287 (1990): 145–58.

4. See, for instance, Lebovics, *True France*, pp. 51–97; Charles-Robert Ageron, "L'Exposition coloniale de 1931: mythe républicain ou mythe impérial," in Pierre Nora, ed., *Les Lieux de mémoire*, vol. 1, *La République* (Paris: Gallimard, 1984), pp. 561–91; Jacques Marseille, *L'Age d'or de la France coloniale* (Paris: Albin Michel, 1986); Elizabeth Ezra, "The Colonial Look: Exhibiting Empire in the 1930's," *Contemporary French Civilization* 19, no. 1 (winter 1995): 33–47; Yael Simpson-Fletcher, "Capital of the Colonies ... ," in Driver and Gilbert, *Imperial Cities*, pp. 135–54; Norindr, *Phantasmatic Indochina*, pp. 21–30.

5. On the notion of a battle over a true France, see Lebovics, *True France*, pp. 162–88. The Free French, who were not yet a force to contend with in the metropole, were already very much perceived as a colonial threat in 1940.

6. CAOM, Affaires Politiques 883 dossier 20, note sur la propagande et l'information aux colonies.

7. Ibid., dossier 21, rapport à L'Amiral Platon sur le fonctionnement du SIID au cours de l'année 1941, p. 9.

8. ADG 6198, dossier 5; Charles Robert Ageron, although conceding that under Vichy "propaganda in the colonies reached a heretofore unparalleled intensity," nonetheless contends that Vichy also devoted considerable energy to colonial propaganda in the metropole as part of a "compensatory myth." Charles-Robert Ageron, "Vichy, les Français et l'empire," in Jean-Pierre Azéma and François Bédarida, eds., *Le Régime de Vichy et les Français* (Paris: Fayard, 1992), pp. 126–32.

9. Pascal Blanchard and Gilles Boëtsch, "La Révolution impériale: apothéose coloniale et idéologie raciale," in Nicolas Bancel et al., eds., *Images et colonies: iconographie et propagande coloniale sur l'Afrique française de 1880 à 1962* (Paris: BDIC, 1993), pp. 203–4.

10. Lynn Hunt, preface to Mona Ozouf, *Festivals and the French Revolution* (Cambridge: Harvard University Press, 1988), p. xi.

11. H. R. Kedward, *Occupied France: Collaboration and Resistance, 1940–1944* (Oxford: Basil Blackwell, 1987), p. 46.

12. CAOM, Affaires Politiques 350, dossier "Politique coloniale du régime de Vichy."

13. Ibid., Platon to governors, Nov. 7, 1941.

14. ADG, SC 4101, Telegram #221, July 8, 1941.

15. Matthew Truesdell, *Spectacular Politics: Louis-Napoleon Bonaparte and the Fête Impériale, 1849–1870* (Oxford: Oxford University Press, 1997), p. 188.

16. Avner Ben Amos, "La Commémoration sous le régime de Vichy: les limites de la maîtrise du passé," in Chrisophe Charle et al., eds., *La France démocratique, mélanges offerts à Maurice Agulhon* (Paris: Publications de la Sorbonne, 1998), 397–408.

17. Alceo Riosa, "Alcuni appunti per una storia della festa del lavoro durante il regime fascista," in Alceo Riosa, ed., *Le Metamorfosi del I Maggio: La festa del lavoro in Europa tra le due guerre* (Venice: Marsilio editori, 1990), p. 74.

18. Maurice Dommanget, *Histoire du premier mai* (Paris: Editions de la tête de feuilles, 1972), p. 321.

19. Ibid., p. 323.

20. CAOM, Slotfom III, 150, report on May 1, 1930.

21. See Brocheux and Hémery, *Indochine, la colonisation ambiguë*, p. 321.

22. CAOM, GGI 64 199, Nov. and May 1935.

23. As George Mosse points out, the early street protests of May day had actually been demonstrations, rather than festivals. Vichy, fearing the ritual "conquest of the streets" of May 1, preferred to annex the celebration by shifting it to the stadium, whose influence had been all the more regulating since the introduction of *hébertisme* under Vichy. See George Mosse, *The Nationalization of the Masses: Political Symbolism and Mass Movements in Germany from the Napoleonic Wars through the Third Reich* (Cornell: Cornell University Press, 1991), pp. 168–69.

24. CAOM, Affaires Politiques 350, dossier "Politique coloniale du régime de Vichy."

25. Ibid., Platon to Decoux, Apr. 28, 1941.

26. Ibid., Decoux to Platon, May 3, 1941.

27. CAOM, Télégrammes, Tel 725, Indochine, Decoux to Platon, May 4, 1941.

28. On May 1, 1942, in Hanoi, see *Le Légionnaire* (Hanoi), May 15, 1942, p. 1, "Compte-rendu de la Fête Nationale du 1er mai à Hanoi," and *L'Action* (Hanoi), May 1, 1942, p. 3, "programme du rassemblement du 1er mai."

29. Emilio Gentile, "Fascism as a Political Religion," *Journal of Contemporary History* 25, no. 2 (May–June 1990): 229–51; Emilio Gentile, *The Sacralization of Politics in Fascist Italy* (Cambridge: Harvard University Press, 1996); George Mosse, *The Nationalization of the Masses*, p. 207; George Mosse, "Fascist Aesthetics and Society: Some Considerations," *Journal of Contemporary History* 31, no. 2 (Apr. 1996): 245.

30. CAOM, Affaires Politiques 2196, dossier 7, Decoux to Vichy, May 5, 1942.

31. Claudio Fogu, "Fascism and Historic Representation: The 1932 Garibaldian Celebrations," *Journal of Contemporary History* 31, no. 2 (Apr. 1996): 337.

32. CAOM, Télégrammes, Tel 787, Indochine, Decoux to Vichy, May 4, 1943.

33. "La Vie indochinoise," *Indochine, hebdomadaire illustré*, May 6, 1943.

34. CAOM, Agence FOM, dossier 451, Indochine, Decoux to Vichy, May 24, 1944.

35. *Le Prolétariat Malgache*, Apr. 30, 1937; May 6, 1938.

36. *Le Prolétariat Malgache*, May 19, 1939, p. 1.

37. *Le Journal de Madagascar*, May 3, 1941.

38. AN, 3W 48, Annet Trial, cote 236, Telegram 239 cfc, Tananarive, Apr. 26, 1941.

39. Ibid.

40. CAOM, Affaires Politiques 2196, dossier 7, Jules Brévié aux Gouverneurs, Circulaire 146, Apr. 23, 1942.

41. Gouvernement de Madagascar et dépendances, *Bulletin d'information et de documentation*, June 1, 1942, p. 17.

42. Paxton, *Vichy France*, 219–20.

43. Gouvernement de Madagascar et dépendances, *Bulletin d'information et de documentation*, June 1, 1942, pp. 17–18.

44. Ibid., p. 16.

45. *La Petite patrie*, June 9, 1920. "In view of reinstituting ... a tradition, interrupted during the war, of rewarding compatriots who distinguish themselves through their labor."

46. See *Le Nouvelliste de la Guadeloupe*, May 9, 1934, and May 1, 1937, p. 1.

47. ADG SC 4101 telegram 317 to all mayors, Apr. 24, 1941.

48. CAOM, Télégrammes, Tel 722 Guadeloupe, Sorin to Platon, May 2, 1941.

49. ADG SC 4101 telegram 317 to all mayors, Apr. 24, 1941.

50. ADG 2mi 247, *La Démocratie sociale*, Apr. 1941.

51. CAOM, Affaires Politiques 350, dossier "Politique coloniale du régime de Vichy," Sorin to Vichy, Apr. 17, 1942.

52. CAOM, Affaires Politiques 2196, dossier 7, Sorin to Vichy, May 5, 1942. For a detailed list of the 186 workers, see ADG SC 6198, dossier 6.

53. ADG SC 4088.

54. ADG, 4 Mi 111, reel 1.

55. CAOM, Affaires Politiques 2047, Vichy to Decoux, July 22, 1942.

56. On fascist historical representation and the notion of "making" history, see Claudio Fogu, "*Il Duce Taumaturgo*: Modernist Rhetorics in Fascist Representations of History," *Representations* 57 (winter 1997): 39–44.

57. Robert Paxton mentions it in passing, although with relation to anti-Italian sentiment in Nice. See Robert Paxton, *Parades and Politics at Vichy: The French Officer Corps under Marshal Pétain* (Princeton: Princeton University Press, 1966), p. 115.

58. ADG, SC 6201, Platon to Sorin, Aug. 28, 1941, Telegram 563.

59. Eric Hobsbawm, "Inventing Traditions," in *The Invention of Tradition* (Cambridge: Cambridge University Press, 1983), p. 1.

60. Ibid., p. 9.

61. The novelist Raphaël Confiant implies as much in his brilliant description of Legion Day 1942 in Martinique. Confiant, *Le Nègre et l'amiral*, pp. 132–34.

62. Gergovie had not constituted an *haut lieu* of republican memory, and may at first seem a peculiar choice for a Vichy festival. Admittedly Paris, Chartres, St. Denis, Rouen, Orléans, and Reims were all ruled out, for they lay in the occupied zone—but why had Vichy not turned to such medieval landmarks as Aigues Mortes, Carcassonne, or even a site of a victory over the English such as Toulon? The answer might well lie in the fact that Vichy sought to break from the recent

past, and although eminently pro-Catholic, also found resonance in a pagan genealogy.

63. Burton, *La Famille coloniale*, p. 151.

64. CAOM, Madagascar 6(2) D49, "Cérémonie du 30 août 1942."

65. Faure, *Le Projet culturel de Vichy*, pp. 199–237.

66. On consensus building through festivals and commemorations under a fascist regime, see Marla Stone, "Staging Fascism: The Exhibition of the Fascist Revolution," *Journal of Contemporary History* 28, no. 1 (Apr. 1993): 215–44.

67. Mosse, *The Nationalization of the Masses*, p. 207. The work of Pascal Blanchard, although at times overly schematic, does tend to confirm the birth of a new imperial identity under Vichy, one considerably more uniform and less diverse than the republic's. Pascal Blanchard et Stéphane Blanchoin, "Les 'Races' dans l'imaginaire colonial français," in Pascal Blanchard et al., eds., *L'Autre et nous: "scènes et types"* (Paris: Syros/ACHAC, 1995), pp. 232–33. See also Pascal Blanchard and Gilles Boëtsch, "La France de Pétain et l'Afrique: images et propagandes coloniales," *Canadian Journal of African Studies* 28, no. 1 (1994): 20.

68. *L'Action, Journal d'information politique et littéraire, organe de collaboration franco-indochinoise Hanoi*, Aug. 25, 1942, p. 1.

69. Known today as Fort Delgrès or Fort Saint Charles.

70. ADG, SC 6201, Chef de la Légion, Guadeloupe to Sorin, Aug. 11, 1942.

71. CAOM, Affaires Politiques 3619, Jules Brévié to head of Legion, #4886, Aug. 18, 1942.

72. Marc Bloch, *The Royal Touch: Sacred Monarchy and Scrofula in England and France* (London: Routledge, 1973), p. 228.

73. Ibid.

74. Fogu, *"Il Duce Taumaturgo,"* p. 24.

75. CAOM, Affaires Politiques 3619, July 31, 1942, Gaston Joseph to Directeur de la Légion.

76. CAOM, Affaires Politiques 886, dossier 1, Decoux to Platon, sent to Legion on Sept. 15, 1942.

77. CAOM, Agence FOM 272, dossier 451, Aug. 31, 1943.

78. *Le Légionnaire* (Hanoi), Aug. 30, 1944, p. 1.

79. *Le Réveil de Madagascar*, May 18, 1934, p. 1. "La fête de Jeanne d'Arc."

80. *Le Miroir de la Guadeloupe*, May 18, 1939, p. 3, "La Brillante fête de Jeanne d'Arc": "Joan of Arc Day was celebrated in Pointe-à-Pitre, as throughout the rest of Guadeloupe, with unusual *éclat.*"

81. Gerd Krumeich, "The Cult of Joan of Arc under the Vichy Régime," in Gerhard Hirschfeld and Patrick Marsh, eds., *Collaboration in France: Politics and Culture during the Nazi Occupation, 1940–1944* (Oxford: Berg, 1989), p. 102.

82. See, respectively, Jennings, *"Reinventing Jeanne,"* pp. 711–34; and Michel Winock, "Jeanne d'Arc et les Juifs," in Michel Winock, *Edouard Drumont et cie: Antisémitisme et fascisme en France* (Paris: Le Seuil, 1982), pp. 67–79.

83. CAOM, Affaires Politiques 2196, dossier 7. Platon's directives on Joan Day 1941, dated May 7, 1941.

84. ADG 2Mi 105 R 226 (Depêches Ministérielles). Platon aux Gouverneurs des Colonies, Mar. 6, 1941.

85. Ibid., enclosed circular from Georges Lamirand.

86. Ibid.

87. Ibid.

88. CAOM, Affaires Politiques 2196, dossier 7, Decoux to Platon, May 17, 1941.

89. Ibid.

90. Ibid., Decoux to Platon, May 12, 1941.

91. Thanks to David Del Testa for bringing this source to my attention. National Library of Vietnam, #M 15377, "Fête de Jeanne d'Arc" (Hanoi: Imprimerie G Taupin et Cie., 1942).

92. CAOM, Affaires Politiques 2196, dossier 7, Decoux to Platon, May 12, 1941.

93. Ibid., Sorin to Platon, May 14, 1941.

94. ADG SC 4101, Sorin à tous les maires, May 3, 1941.

95. CAOM, Affaires Politiques 2196, dossier 7, Sorin to Platon, May 14, 1941.

96. On First World War monuments as pedagogical tools teaching abnegation and devotion to the dead in metropolitan France, see Antoine Prost, "Les Monuments aux morts," in Pierre Nora, ed., *Les Lieux de mémoire*, vol. 1, *La République* (Paris: Gallimard, 1984), p. 215.

97. Confiant, *Le Nègre et l'amiral*, pp. 110–12.

98. CAOM, Madagascar, PT 141.

99. Ibid.

100. CAOM, Cabinet 2, dossier 18, Brévié to Tananarive, Dakar, Hanoi, Fort-de-France, St. Denis, Djibouti, May 8, 1942.

101. National Library of Vietnam, #M 15377, "Fête de Jeanne d'Arc."

102. Ibid.

103. CAOM, Cabinet 2, dossier 18, Brévié to Annet, May 9, 1942.

104. CAOM, Madagascar, 6(2) D49, Cérémonie du 30 août 1942.

105. ADG SC 4105, Sorin à tous maires, #371, May 8, 1942.

106. CAOM, Affaires Politiques 884, Sorin to Brévié, May 13, 1942, #575.

107. Ducoroy, *Ma trahison*, p. 130.

108. Ibid.

109. CAOM, Madagascar CF 3, dossier 9, poster for "La fête nationale du 11 novembre."

110. ADG 4mi 111 (Guadeloupe), Dr. Gabriel François Julien, "Espoir et Certitude."

111. *Justice*, Hebdomadaire du Parti Communiste, Fort-de-France, Martinique, 29 avril 1944.

112. CAOM, Madagascar, CF 3, dossier 9, Poster: "Ville de Tananarive, fête de la victoire … et fête de Jeanne d'Arc."

113. On the interaction of "invented traditions" and national identities, see John Gillis, "Memory and Identity: The History of a Relationship," in *Commemorations: The Politics of National Identity* (Princeton: Princeton University Press, 1994), pp. 3–24.

114. On revolutionary festivals, see Ozouf, *Festivals and the French Revolution*.

115. Cohen, *Rulers of Empire*, pp. 161–62.

116. See Blanchard et Blanchoin, "Les 'Races,'" 232–33; and Blanchard et Boëtsch, "La France de Pétain et l'Afrique," 20.

117. Ducoroy, *Ma trahison,* p. 129.

Conclusion

1. Maunier, *Les Lois de l'empire,* p. 58.

2. Anderson, *Imagined Communities,* p. 158.

Bibliography and Sources

I. Archival Sources

1) Archives Nationales, Centre des Archives d'Outre-mer d'Aix-en-Provence (CAOM)

Affaires Politiques, all dossiers on World War II, from Affaires Politiques 210 to Affaires Politiques 3619. (*Important collection emanating from the Direction des Affaires Politiques du Secrétariat d'Etat aux Colonies, Vichy, and pertaining to all colonies.*)

MADAGASCAR

3A Circulars
1B Correspondence to and from the governors, 1940–42
3B Correspondence to and from the governors, 1940–42
2D Administrative reports from the provinces
3D Inspection reports
4D General reports
6D Direction des Affaires Politiques

CF Régie des Chemins de Fer

Fonds des Provinces
    DS Diego-Suarez
    PM Province de Majunga
    PT Province de Tananarive

INDOCHINE

Fonds des Amiraux et Gouverneurs (GGi)
Fonds du Conseiller Politique
Fonds du Haut Commissaire
Indochine Nouveau Fonds
Résidence Supérieure du Cambodge
Résidence Supérieure du Tonkin, Nouveau Fonds

AGENCE FOM
   (Agence Economique de la France d'Outre-mer)

SÉRIE TÉLÉGRAMMES

CABINETS MINISTÉRIELS
Secrétariat d'Etat aux Colonies, Vichy, 1942–43

PAPIERS D'AGENTS

2) Archives Nationales, Paris (AN)

Fonds 3W Haute Cour de Justice
Fonds F60 Présidence du Conseil

3) Archives Départementales de la Guadeloupe (ADG)

Série Continue (SC) (emanating from Governor's offices)
3N 154 *Conseil Général,* deliberations, 1940 and 1943
2mi 105, Dépêches ministérielles
2mi 247 Newspapers from the Vichy period

4) National Archives of Vietnam, Colonial Period (Archives #1), Hanoi (VNNA)

Gouvernement Général
Résidence Supérieure du Tonkin

5) National Archives of Madagascar, Antananarivo, Madagascar (ARDM)

6) Service Historique de l'Armée de Terre, Vincennes, France (SHAT)

7) Service Historique de la Marine, Vincennes, France

8) Archives Municipales de Bordeaux, Bordeaux, France (AMB)

Fonds Jean Decoux (NB: when I consulted this collection in 1999, it had yet to
   be sorted in any way. As a result, current box and file locations may change.)

9) National Archives #2, Washington, College Park (USNA)

State Department Consular files:
   Record Group 59
   Record Group 84

10) Bibliothèque de Documentation Internationale Contemporaine (BDIC), Nanterre

11) Public Record Office, London, UK

12) Archives du Ministère des Affaires Etrangères (Quai d'Orsay)

13) Hoover Archives, Stanford, Calif.

14) National Archives of Canada, Ottawa

II. Printed Sources: Newspapers and Serials

METROPOLITAN FRENCH

Le Cri des nègres   *Les Nouveaux temps*
France: Revue de l'Etat nouveau   *L'Oeuvre*
Journal officiel de l'Etat français   *Le Temps*

MADAGASCAR

Bulletin d'information et de documenta-
*   tion*
Le Journal de Madagascar
Journal officiel de Madagascar
Lumière

Le Prolétariat Malgache
Le Réveil de Madagascar
Servir, hebdomadaire chrétien et na-
*   tional, Madagascar*

GUADELOUPE

Le Bulletin de France: organe des comités
*   d'information des Antilles*
La Démocratie sociale
L'Hebdomadaire de la Guadeloupe
l'Homme enchaîné
Journal officiel de la Guadeloupe

Journal officiel de la Martinique
Le Miroir de la Guadeloupe
Nouvelliste de la Guadeloupe
La Petite patrie
La Raison

INDOCHINA

L'Action, organe de collaboration franco-
*   indochinoise*
L'Annam nouveau
Annuaire statistique de l'Indochine
Bulletin général de l'instruction publique
l'Echo annamite
France-Annam

Indochine, hebdomadaire illustré
La Légion
Le Légionnaire
La Lutte
Le Nouveau Laos
La Tribune Indochinoise

III. Printed Primary Sources: Contemporaneous Materials and Memoirs

Allier, Raoul. *L'Enseignement primaire des indigènes à Madagascar*. Paris: Cahiers de la Quinzaine, 1904.

Annet, Armand. *Aux heures troublées de l'Afrique française*. Paris: Editions du conquistador, 1952.

Augagneur, Victor. *Erreurs et brutalités coloniales*. Paris: Librairie Montaigne, 1927.

Bao Dai. *Le Dragon d'Annam*. Paris: Plon, 1980.

Baudoin, Paul. *The Private Diaries of Paul Baudoin, March 1940 to January 1941*. Translated by Sir Charles Petrie. London: Eyre and Spottiswoode, 1948.

Bléhaut, Bernard. *Pas de Clairon pour l'Amiral: Henri Bléhaut, 1889–1962*. Paris: Editions Jean Picollec, 1991.

Boegner, Philippe. *Carnets du Pasteur Boegner, 1940–1945*. Paris: Fayard, 1992.

Boisson, Paul. "Trois directives de colonisation africaine," Dakar, 21 aout 1941.

Boudet, Paul. *L'Indochine dans le passé: exposition de documents historiques organisée par la Direction des Archives et des bibliothèques à l'occasion de la Foire-Exposition de Hanoi*. Hanoi: Société de Géographie de Hanoi, 1941.

Brasillach, Robert. *La Conquérante, roman colonial*. Paris: Plon, 1943.

Buhrer, Jules (général X). *Aux heures tragiques de l'empire*. Paris: Office colonial d'édition, 1947.

Carle, Michel ed. *Au pays des lambas blancs: Documents pour servir à l'histoire du missionnariat québecois dans la première moitié du XXème siècle*. Ottawa: University of Ottawa Press, 1995.

Cazenave de la Roche, Jean. "Tension in the French West Indies," *Foreign Affairs* 21, no. 3 (April 1943): 560–65.

Chaize, Msgr. François. "Au Tonkin: une mission dans la tourmente, 1940–1945," *Revue des deux mondes* (July 1 and 15, 1948): 42–58; 307–19.

Comité d'action anti-Bolchevique. "Le Parti Communiste et les colonies" (July 1940).

Comité France-Empire. *Les Empires en Marche*. Lyon: 1942.

Commissariat général à l'éducation physique, aux sports, et à la jeunesse de l'Indochine. *Premières tâches du Chef de jeunesse provincial* (October 1942).

David, Gilbert. *Chroniques secrètes de l'Indochine, 1928–1946*. Paris: L'Harmattan, 1994.

De Boisanger, Claude. *On pouvait éviter la guerre d'Indochine: souvenirs, 1941–1945*. Paris: Librairie Maisonneuve, 1977.

Decoux, Jean. *A la barre de l'Indochine: histoire de mon gouvernement général 1940–1945*. Paris: Plon, 1949.

Decoux, Jean, and Pham Quynh. *Mission du Mandarinat: discours prononcés le 24 décembre 1941 à l'occasion de la proclamation des résultats du concours de Tri-Huyên* (CAOM Library).

De Gaulle, Charles. *Discours et messages pendant la guerre, 1940–1946*. Paris: Plon, 1970.

————. *Mémoires de Guerre*. Paris: Plon, 1954.

De Saussure. Léopold. *Psychologie de la colonisation français dans ses rapports avec les sociétés indigènes*. Paris: Librairie Germer Baillière, 1899.

Deschamps, Hubert. *Roi de la brousse: mémoires d'autres mondes*. Paris: Berger-Levrault, 1975.

Donnadieu, Marguerite (Marguerite Duras), and Philippe Roques. *L'Empire français*. Paris: Gallimard, 1940.

Dower, K. C. Gandar. *Into Madagascar*. Harmondsworth: Penguin Books, 1943.

Duboscq, André, ed. *Les Empires en marche*. Lyon: Comité France-Empire, 1942.

Ducoroy, Maurice. *Ma trahison en Indochine*. Paris: Les Éditions internationales, 1949.

Du Moulin de Labarthète, Henri. *Le Temps des illusions: souvenirs, juillet 1940–avril 1942*. Geneva: Editions du cheval ailé, 1948.

Esmérian, Paul. *Journal d'Etrême-Orient*. Paris: Editions entente, 1980.

François, Jean, and Nguyen Viet-Nam. *Cau Doi Phap Nam: Sentences parallèles franco-annamites*. Hanoi: Presses du Gouvernement Général, 1942.

Gautier, Georges. *La Fin de l'Indochine Française*. Paris: Société de production littéraire, 1978.

Girault, Arthur. *Principes de la colonisation et de législation coloniale*. Paris: Libraire Recueil Sirey, 1929.

Giraud, F. R., and Bui-Ngo-Hien. *Livret de l'étudiant indochinois*. Hanoi: Direction de l'instruction publique, 1943.

Grapin, Henri J. M. *Madagascar, 1942*. Paris: La Pensée universelle, 1993.

Guadeloupe et Dépendances. "Délibérations du Conseil général, session extraordinaire du 1er juillet 1940." Basse-Terre, 1940.

Guéhenno, Jean. *Journal des années noires*. Paris: Gallimard, 1947.

Guèye, Lamine. *Itinéraire africain*. Paris: Présence africaine, 1966.

Hoang Van Co. "La Rénovation de l'économie indigène: le paysannat et l'artisanat d'outre-mer." Paper, Université de Clermont-Ferrant, February 12, 1942 (CAOM Library).

Ho Chi Minh. *Selected Writings, 1920–1969*. Hanoi: Foreign Language Publishing House, 1973.

Honorien, E. *Le Ralliement des Antilles à la France Combattante*. Martinique, 1945.

Lapierre, Jacques. "Souvenir: le 9 mars 1945, les Japonais attaquaient par surprise les troupes françaises en Indochine," *Le Figaro* March 11–12, 2000.

Leblond, Marius. "L'Empire et la France de Pétain." In *France 1941: la Révolution Nationale constructive, un bilan et un programme*. Paris: Editions Alsatia, 1941.

Le Bourgeois, Jacques. *Ici Radio Saigon, 1939–1945*. Paris: Editions France-Empire, 1985.

Lefevre, Kim. *Métisse blanche*. Paris: Bernard Barrault, 1989.

Lehnebach, S. *Pour mieux comprendre la Révolution Nationale*. Saigon: Editions de l'IPP, 1943.

Lémery, Henry. *D'une république a l'autre: souvenirs de la mêlée politique, 1894–1944*. Paris: Table ronde, 1964.

Leroy, Olivier. *Raisons et bases de l'Union des Français de l'Empire*. Tananarive: Imprimerie officielle, 1942.

Lévi-Strauss, Claude. *Tristes tropiques*. Paris: Plon, 1955.

Lyautey, Pierre. *Pour l'empire français: action et doctrine*. Vichy: Comité de la France d'Outre-mer, 1940.

Madagascar et dépendances: direction des douanes. *Rapport annuel* (1941).

Martial, René. *Les Métis*. Paris: Flammarion, 1942.

Massip, Jean. "La 'Résistance' aux Antilles," *Revue de Paris* (May 1945).

Mauban, Charles. "L'Homme de la Révolution Nationale," *Idées, Revue mensuelle* 10–11 (September 1942).

Maulnier, Thierry. *Révolution Nationale: l'avenir de la France*. Hanoi: Publication du Gouvernement Général de l'Indochine, 1942.

Maunier, René. *Des comptoirs aux empires: histoire universelle des colonies*. Paris: Librairie du recueil Sirey, 1942.

———. *L'Empire français: propos et projets*. Paris: Librairies du recueil Sirey, 1943.

———. *Les Lois de l'empire, 1940–1942*. Paris: Domat-Montchrestien, 1942.

———. *Sociologie coloniale*. Vol. 3. Paris: Editions Dumat-Montchrestien, 1942.

Maunier, René, ed. *Elements d'économie coloniale*. Paris: Librairie du recueil Sirey, 1943.

Maurras, Charles. *La seule France*. Lyon: Lardanchet, 1941.

Ministère des Colonies, service intercolonial d'information et de documentation, *La Guadeloupe* (1940).

Mordant, Eugène. *Au service de la France en Indochine, 1941–1945*. Saigon, 1950.

N.A. *L'Empire, notre meilleure chance*. Lyon: Audin, 1942.

N.A. "Fête de Jeanne d'Arc." Hanoi: Imprimerie G Taupin et Cie., 1942.

N.A. *Hymnes et pavillons d'Indochine*. Hanoi: Imprimerie d'Extrême-Orient, 1941.

N.A. *Les Réalisations de la Révolution Nationale en Indochine*. Saigon: 1942.

N.A. *Souverains et notabilités d'Indochine*. Hanoi: Editions du Gouvernement Général de l'Indochine, 1943.

Nguyen Tien Lang. *Pages françaises: études sur la littérature française*. Saigon: Huong-Son, 1943.

Nguyen Van Huyen. *La Civilisation annamite*. Hanoi: Direction de l'instruction publique, 1944.

OSS State Department Intelligence and Research reports, part XIII (Africa), reel 8.

Paillard, Jean. *L'Empire français de demain*. Institut d'études corporatives et sociales, 1943.

———. *La Fin des Français en Afrique noire*. Paris: Les Oeuvres francaises, 1935.

———. *1940–1944: la révolution corporative spontanée*. Paris: Editions du Vivarais, 1979.

Pasquier, Pierre. *Discours prononcé le 28 octobre 1930 par M. Pasquier, gouverneur général de l'Indochine*. Hanoi: Imprimerie d'Extrême-Orient, 1930.

Peyrouton, Marcel. *Du service public à la prison commune: souvenirs*. Paris: Plon, 1950.

Pollacchi, Paul. *Atlas colonial français*. Paris: L'Illustration, 1929.

Réalisations de la France combattante à Madagascar et la Réunion. Ministère de l'Information, 1945.

Ricord, Maurice. *Au service de l'empire, 1939–1945*. Paris: Société des éditions coloniales et métropolitaines, 1946.

Robert, G. *Les Travaux publics de la Guadeloupe*. Paris: Librairie militaire Fournier, 1935.

Robert, Georges. *La France aux Antilles, 1939–1943*. Paris: Plon, 1950.

Roberts, Adolphe. *Les Français aux Indes occidentales*. Montréal: Editions variétés, 1945.

Ruscio, Alain, ed. *Ho Chi Minh: Textes, 1914–1969*. Paris: L'Harmattan, 1990.

Sabattier, Georges. *Le Destin de l'Indochine: souvenirs et documents, 1941–1951*. Paris: Plon, 1952.

Saint-Mleux, André. "Les Japonais s'emparent de l'Indochine," *Le Monde* (March 5–6, 1995): 10.

Salan, Raoul. *Mémoires: fin d'un empire (I): le sens d'un engagement, juin 1899–septembre 1946*. Paris: Presses de la cité, 1970.

Sallé, R. M. *70,000 kilomètres d'aventures: notes de voyage Indochine-France et retour*. Hanoi: Imprimerie d'Extrême-Orient, 1942.

Soustelle, Jacques. *Envers et contre tout*. Vol. 1: *De Londres à Alger*. Paris: Robert Laffont, 1947.

Taboulet, Georges. *Histoire de France à l'usage des élèves français d'Indochine*. Hanoi: Direction de l'instruction publique, 1944.

———. *Le Retour à la tradition: ou la cité reconstruite*. Hanoi: Editions du Gouvernement Général de l'Indochine, 1941.

Timoléon, Jean-Charles. *Chronique du temps passé*. Basse-Terre: OMCS, 1987.

Ton-That Binh, Nguyen-Manh-Tuong, et al. *Témoignages*. Hanoi: Imprimerie Taupin et Cie., 1941.

Trinh Dinh Khai. *Décolonisation du Viêt Nam: un avocat témoigne*. Paris: L'Harmattan, 1994.

Union France Empire, assemblée générale du 20 mai 1942.

Viard, René. *L'Empire et nos destins*. Paris: Sorlot, 1942.

Vignon, Louis. *Un programme de politique coloniale*. Paris: Plon, 1919.

Vivier de Streel, E. "Notre future politique coloniale," *La Revue des deux mondes* (November 1 and 15, 1940).

"Vocations coloniales." *Quinzaine impériale*. Roanne: Imprimerie Sauzet, 1942.

Whitcomb, Philip, trans. *France during the German Occupation, 1940–1944: A Collection of 292 Statements on the Government of Maréchal Pétain and Pierre Laval*. Vol. II. Stanford, Calif.: Hoover Institution, 1957.

IV. Secondary Sources

Abenon, Lucien-René. *Petite histoire de la Guadeloupe*. Paris: L'Harmattan, 1992.

Abenon, Lucien-René, and John Dickinson. *Les Français en Amérique*. Lyon: Presses Universitaires de Lyon, 1993.

Abitbol, Michel. *Les Juifs d'Afrique du Nord sous Vichy*. Paris: Maisonneuve et Larose, 1983.

Adas, Michael. *Machines as the Measure of Men: Science, Technology, and Ideologies of Western Dominance*. Ithaca: Cornell University Press, 1989.

Adélaïde-Merlande, Jacques. *Histoire générale des Antilles et des Guyanes*. Paris: Editions caribéennes, 1994.

Ageron, Charles-Robert. *La Décolonisation française*. Paris: Armand Colin, 1991.

———. "L'Exposition coloniale de 1931: mythe républicain ou mythe impérial." In Pierre Nora, ed., *Les Lieux de mémoire*. Vol. 1: *La République*. Paris: Gallimard, 1984.

———. *France coloniale ou parti colonial?* Paris: PUF, 1978.

Ageron, Charles-Robert, ed. *Les Chemins de la décolonisation de l'empire français, 1936–1956*. Paris: Editions du CNRS, 1986.

Ageron, Charles-Robert, Catherine Coquery-Vidrovitch, Gilbert Meynier, and Jacques Thobie. *Histoire de la France coloniale 1914–1990*. Paris: Armand Colin, 1990.

Akpo-Vaché, Catherine. *L'Afrique occidentale française et la Seconde Guerre Mondiale*. Paris: Karthala, 1996.

Aldrich, Robert. *Greater France: A History of French Overseas Expansion*. London: Macmillan, 1996.

Alexandre, Rodolphe. *La Guyane sous Vichy*. Paris: Editions caribéennes, 1988.

Anderson, Benedict. *Imagined Communities*. London: Verso, 1991.

Andrew, Christopher, and S. Kanya Forstner. *The Climax of French Imperial Expansion, 1914–1924*. Stanford, Calif.: Stanford University Press, 1981.

Angladette, André. "La Vie quotidienne en Indochine de 1939 à 1946," CRASOM 31, no. 3 (June 1979): 467–98 [*Académie des Sciences Outre-mer,* "Mondes et cultures"].

Antébi, Elizabeth, ed., *Histoire des Antilles et de la Guyane*. Fort-de-France: Arawak, 1978.

Aouate, Yves. "La Place de l'Algérie dans le projet antijuif de Vichy," *Revue française d'histoire d'outre-mer* 301 (October 1993): 599–613.

Aron, Robert. *The Vichy Regime, 1940–44.* New York: Macmillan, 1958.

Arzalier, Francis, and Jean Suret-Canale, eds. *Madagascar 1947: la tragédie oubliée.* Paris: Le Temps des cerises, 1999.

Azéma, Jean-Pierre, and François Bédarida, eds. *La France des années noires.* Paris: Le Seuil, 1993.

———, eds. *Le Régime de Vichy et les français.* Paris: Fayard, 1992.

Baptiste, F. A. "Le Régime de Vichy à la Martinique," *Revue d'histoire de la Deuxième Guerre Mondiale* III (1978): 1–24.

Barrows, Susanna. *Distorting Mirrors: Visions of the Crowd in Late Nineteenth-Century France.* New Haven: Yale University Press, 1981.

Benabi, A. "Les Français, les Japonais et le mouvement national vietnamien (1940–1945)." Ph.D. dissertation, Université de Paris I, 1988.

Ben Amos, Avner. "La Commémoration sous le régime de Vichy: les limites de la maîtrise du passé." In Chrisophe Charle, Jacqueline Lalouette, et al., eds., *La France démocratique: mélanges offerts à Maurice Agulhon.* Paris: Publications de la Sorbonne, 1998, 397–408.

Benot, Yves. *Massacres coloniaux, 1944–1950: la IVème république et la mise au pas des colonies françaises.* Paris: Editions de la découverte, 1995.

Bergère, Marie-Claire. "L'Epuration à Shanghaï, 1945–46: L'Affaire Sarly et la fin de la concession française," *Vingtième siècle, revue d'histoire* 53 (January–March 1997): 25–31.

Bertrand Dorléac, Laurence. *L'Art de la défaite, 1940–1944.* Paris: Editions du Seuil, 1993.

Betts, Raymond. *Assimilation and Association in French Colonial Theory, 1890–1914.* New York: Columbia University Press, 1961.

———. *France and Decolonization, 1900–1960.* New York: St. Martin's Press, 1991.

———. *Tricouleur: The French Overseas Empire.* London: Gordon and Cremonesi, 1978.

Blanchard, Pascal. "La France de Pétain et l'Afrique: images et propagandes coloniales," *Canadian Journal of African Studies* 28 (1994): 1–31.

———. "Nationalisme et colonialisme: idéologie coloniale, discours sur l'Afrique et les Africains de la droite nationaliste française des années 30 à la Révolution Nationale." Ph.D. dissertation, University of Paris I, 1994.

Blanchard, Pascal, and Nicolas Bancel. *De l'indigène à l'immigré.* Paris: Gallimard, 1998.

Blanchard, Pascal, and Gilles Boëtsch. "Races et propagande coloniale sous le régime de Vichy, 1940–1944," *Africa, rivista trimestrale di studi e documentazione dell'Instituto Italo-Africano* 49 (December 1994): 531–61.

———. "La Révolution impériale: apothéose coloniale et idéologie raciale." In Nicolas Bancel et al., eds., *Images et colonies: iconographie et propagande coloniale sur l'Afrique française de 1880 à 1962.* Paris: BDIC, 1993.

Blanchard, Pascal, et al., eds. *L'Autre et nous: "scènes et types."* Paris: Syros/ACHAC, 1995.

Bloch, Marc. *The Royal Touch: Sacred Monarchy and Scrofula in England and France.* Translated by J. E. Anderson. London: Routledge, 1973.

Bloch, Maurice. *From Blessing to Violence: History and Ideology in the Circumcision Ritual of the Merina of Madagascar.* Cambridge: Cambridge University Press, 1986.

———. *Placing the Dead: Tombs, Ancestral Villages and Kinship Organization in Madagascar.* London: Seminar Press, 1971.

Boiteau, Pierre. *Contribution à l'histoire de la nation malgache.* Paris: Éditions sociales, 1958.

Bonniol, Jean-Luc. "De l'architecture créole: tradition et créativité dans l'habitat rural martiniquais et guadeloupéen," *Etudes Créoles* 1–2 (1982): 69–81.

Bouche, Denise. "Autrefois, notre pays s'appelait la Gaule," *Cahiers d'études africaines* 29 (1968): 110–22.

———. "Le Retour de l'Afrique occidentale française dans la lutte contre l'ennemi aux côtés des Alliés," *Revue d'histoire de la Deuxième Guerre Mondiale* 114 (1979): 41–68.

Boucheret, Marianne. "Le Triomphe du caoutchouc," *L'Histoire*, numéro spécial, "L'Indochine au temps des Français" 203 (October 1996): 39.

Bourderon, Roger. "Le Régime de Vichy était-il fasciste?" *Revue d'histoire de la Deuxième Guerre Mondiale* 91 (July 1973): 23–45.

Brechtken, Magnus. *"Madagaskar für die Juden": Antisemitische Idee und politische Praxi, 1885–1945.* München: Oldenbourg Verlag, 1997.

Brocheux, Pierre. "L'Implantation du mouvement communiste en Indochine: le Nge-Tinh, 1930–1931" *Revue d'histoire moderne et contemporaine* 24 (January–March 1977): 49–77.

———. "La Revue 'Thanh Nghi': un groupe d'intellectuels vietnamiens confrontés aux problèmes de leur nation, 1941–1945," *Revue d'histoire moderne et contemporaine* 34 (April–June, 1987): 317–29.

Brocheux, Pierre, and Daniel Hémery. *Indochine: la colonisation ambiguë, 1858–1954.* Paris: La Découverte, 1995.

Brown. Mervyn. *Madagascar Rediscovered.* London: Damien Tunnacliffe, 1978.

Buffet, Cyril. *La Collaboration … à gauche aussi.* Paris: Perrin, 1989.

Burac, Maurice, ed. *Guadeloupe, Martinique et Guyane dans le monde américain.* Paris: Karthala, 1994.

Burton, Richard. *La Famille coloniale: la Martinique et la mère patrie, 1789–1992.* Paris: L'Harmattan, 1994.

———. "Vichysme et Vichyistes à la Martinique, 1940–1943," *Cahiers du CERAG* 34: 1–101.

Cantier, Jacques. "1939–1945: une métropole coloniale en guerre." In "Alger, 1940–1962," *Autrement* 56 (March 1999): 16–61.

———. "Les Gouverneurs Viollette et Bordes et la politique algérienne de la France à la fin des années 20," *Revue française d'histoire d'outre-mer* 84, no. 1 (1997): 25–49.

Caron, Vicki. *Uneasy Asylum: France and the Jewish Refugee Crisis, 1933–1942.* Stanford, Calif.: Stanford University Press, 1999.

Castor, Elie. *Félix Eboué: gouverneur et philosophe*. Paris: L'Harmattan, 1984.

Çelik, Zeynep. *Urban Forms and Colonial Confrontations: Algiers under French Rule*. Berkeley: University of California Press, 1997.

Chafer, Tony, and Amanda Sackur, eds. *French Colonial Empire and the Popular Front: Hope and Disillusion*. London: St. Martin's Press, 1999.

Chaigneau, Pascal. "Politique et Franc-maçonnerie dans le tiers-monde: l'exemple révélateur de Madagascar," *L'Afrique et l'Asie modernes* 145 (summer 1985).

Chanet, Jean-François. *L'Ecole républicaine et les petites patries*. Paris: Aubier, 1996.

Chathuant, Dominique. "Dans le sillage de la marine de guerre, pouvoir et Eglise en Guadeloupe, 1940–1943," *Bulletin de la société d'histoire de la Guadeloupe* 103 (1995): 40–64.

———. "La Guadeloupe dans l'obédience de Vichy, 1940–1943," *Bulletin de la société d'histoire de la Guadeloupe* 91–94 (1992): 3–27.

Chauvet, Camille. "La Martinique pendant la deuxième guerre mondiale." Ph.D. dissertation, Université de Toulouse le Mirail, 1983.

Cherdieu, Philippe. "L'Échec d'un socialisme colonial: la Guadeloupe, 1891–1914," *Revue d'histoire moderne et contemporaine* 31 (April–June 1984): 308–33.

Christian, William. *Divided Island: Faction and Unity on St. Pierre*. Cambridge: Harvard University Press, 1969.

Clancy-Smith, Julia, and Frances Gouda. *Domesticating the Empire: Race, Gender and Family Life in French and Dutch Colonialism*. Charlottesville: University of Virginia Press, 1998.

Cohen, William B. "The Colonial Policy of the Popular Front," *French Historical Studies* 7, no. 2 (spring 1972): 368–93.

———. *Rulers of Empire: The French Colonial Service in Africa*. Stanford, Calif.: Hoover Institution Press, 1971.

Cointet, Jean-Paul. *La Légion française des combattants, 1940–1944: la tentation fasciste*. Paris: Albin Michel, 1995.

Cointet, Michèle. *Vichy capitale, 1940–1944*. Paris: Perrin, 1993.

———. *Vichy et le fascisme*. Bruxelles: Editions complexe, 1987.

Cole, Jennifer. *Forget Colonialism? Sacrifice and the Art of Memory in Madagascar*. Berkeley: University of California Press, 2001.

Condé, Maryse. *Tree of Life (La Vie scélérate)*. New York: Random House, 1992.

Confiant, Raphaël. *Le Nègre et l'amiral*. Paris: Grasset, 1988.

Conklin, Alice. "Colonialism and Human Rights, a Contradiction in Terms? The Case of France and West Africa, 1895–1914," *American Historical Review* 103, no. 2 (1998): 419–42.

———. "'Democracy' Revisited: Civilization through Association in French West Africa, 1914–1930," *Cahiers d'etudes africaines* 145 (1997): 59–84.

———. *A Mission to Civilize: The Republican Idea of Empire in France and West Africa, 1895–1930*. Stanford, Calif.: Stanford University Press, 1997.

Cooper, Frederick. *Decolonization and African Society: The Labor Question in French and British Africa*. Cambridge: Cambridge University Press, 1996.

Cooper, Frederick, and Ann Laura Stoler, eds. *Tensions of Empire: Colonial Cultures in a Bourgeois World*. Berkeley: University of California Press, 1997.

Coquery Vidrovitch, Catherine. "Vichy et l'industrialisation aux Colonies," *Revue d'Histoire de la Deuxième Guerre Mondiale* 114 (April 1979): 69–94.

Cremieux-Brilhac, Jean-Louis. *La France libre: de l'appel du 18 juin à la Libération*. Paris: Gallimard, 1996.

Cronenberg, Allen. "The French West Indies during World War II," *Proceedings of the Annual Meeting of the Western Society for French History* 18 (1991): 524–33.

Crowder, Michael. "Vichy and the Free French in West Africa during the Second World War." In M. Crowder, ed., *Colonial West Africa, Collected Essays*. London: Frank Cass, 1978, 268–82.

Cubero, José-Ramon. *Nationalistes et étrangers: le massacre d'Aigues-Mortes*. Paris: Imago, 1996.

Dalloz, Jacques. "Les Vietnamiens dans la franc-maçonnerie coloniale," *Revue française d'histoire d'outre-mer* 85, no. 320 (1998): 103–18.

De Boisanger, Claude. "L'Amiral Decoux: un sujet d'étude pour les historiens," *La Revue des deux mondes* (August 15, 1968): 490–95.

De la Gorce, Paul-Marie. *L'Empire écartelé, 1936–1962*. Paris: Denoël, 1988.

Deschamps, Hubert. *Histoire de Madagascar*. Paris: Editions Berger-Levrault, 1961.

Devillers, Philippe. *Histoire du Vietnam de 1940 à 1952*. Paris: Editions du Seuil, 1952.

Dinan, Desmond. *The Politics of Persuasion: British Policy and French African Neutrality, 1940–1942*. New York: University Press of America, 1988.

Dommanget, Maurice. *Histoire du premier mai*. Paris: Editions de la tête de feuilles, 1972.

Dreifort, John. "Japan's Advance into Indochina, 1940: The French Response," *Journal of Southeast Asian Studies* 13 (September 1982): 279–95.

Driver, Felix, and David Gilbert, eds. *Imperial Cities: Landscape, Display and Identity*. Manchester: Manchester University Press, 1999.

Echenberg, Myron. *Colonial Conscripts: The 'Tirailleurs sénégalais' in French West Africa, 1857–1960*. London: James Currey, 1991.

Ellis, Stephen. *The Rising of the Red Shawls: A Revolt in Madagascar, 1895–1899*. Cambridge: Cambridge University Press, 1985.

Esperance, Martin, JC. "L'Île de la Réunion de 1939 à 1945," DEA (master's thesis), joint: Faculté de Droit d'Aix-en-Provence and l'Université française de l'Océan Indien.

Ezra, Elizabeth. "The Colonial Look: Exhibiting Empire in the 1930's," *Contemporary French Civilization* 19, no. 1 (winter 1995): 33–47.

Fabre, F., and G. Stehle. "Le Cyclone de 1928 à la pointe-à-pitre," *Bulletin de la société d'histoire de la Guadeloupe* 91–94 (1992): 41–73.

Fallope, Josette. "La Politique d'assimilation et ses résistances." In Henriette Levillain, ed., *La Guadeloupe, 1875–1914: les soubresauts d'une société pluri-ethnique ou les ambiguités de l'assimilation*. Paris: Autrement, 1994.

Fanon, Frantz. *Peau noire masques blancs* Paris: Éditions du Seuil, 1952.

Faure, Christian. *Le Projet culturel de Vichy*. Lyon: CNRS, 1989.

Feeley-Harnik, Gillian. *A Green Estate: Restoring Independence in Madagascar*. Washington, D.C.: Smithsonian Institution Press, 1991.

Féray, Pierre-Richard. *Le Vietnam au 20ème siècle*. Paris: Presses Universitaires de France, 1979.

Ferro, Marc. *Histoire des colonisations*. Paris: Editions du Seuil, 1994.

———. *Pétain*. Paris: Fayard, 1987.

Fogu, Claudio. "Fascism and Historic Representation: The 1932 Garibaldian Celebrations," *Journal of Contemporary History* 31, no. 2 (April 1996): 317–45.

———. *"Il Duce Taumaturgo:* Modernist Rhetorics in Fascist Representations of History," *Representations* (winter 1997): 24–51.

Folin, Jacques. *Indochine 1940–1955: la fin d'un rêve*. Paris: Perrin, 1993.

Foll, J. J. "Le Togo pendant la Deuxième Guerre Mondiale," *Revue d'histoire de la Deuxième Guerre Mondiale* 115 (July 1979): 69–77.

Furuta, Motoo, and Takashi Shiraishi, eds. *Indochina in the 1940's and 1950's: Translation of Contemporary Japanese Scholarship on Southeast Asia*. Ithaca: Cornell University Southeast Asia Program, 1992.

Gay-Lescot, Jean-Louis. "La Propagande par le sport: Vichy, la politique sportive de l'Etat de Vichy dans l'empire, 1940–1944." In *L'Empire du sport*. Aix-en-Provence: AMAROM, 1992, 56–60.

Gentile, Emilio. "Fascism as a Political Religion," *Journal of Contemporary History* 25, no. 2 (May–June 1990): 229–51.

———. *The Sacralization of Politics in Fascist Italy*. Cambridge: Harvard University Press, 1996.

Gervereau, Laurent, and Denis Peschanski, eds. *La Propagande sous Vichy*. Paris: BDIC, 1990.

Giblin, James L. "A Colonial State in Crisis: Vichy Administration in French West Africa." *Africana Journal* 16 (1994): 326–40.

Gillis, John. "Memory and Identity: The History of a Relationship." In *Commemorations: The Politics of National Identity*. Princeton: Princeton University Press, 1994.

Girardet, Raoul. *L'Idée coloniale en France, de 1871 à 1962*. Paris: La Table ronde, 1972.

Gontard, Maurice. "La Premiere consultation électorale malgache: l'élection du délégué au Conseil supérieur de la France d'outre-mer en 1939," *Annales de l'Université de Madagascar, série lettres et sciences humaines* 7 (1967): 7–20.

Gordon, Bertram. *Collaborationism in France during the Second World War*. Ithaca: Cornell University Press, 1980.

Goscha, Christopher. "L'Indochine repensée par les Indochinois: Pham Quynh et les deux débats de 1931 sur l'immigration, le fédéralisme et la réalité de l'Indochine," *Revue française d'histoire d'outre-mer* 82 (1995): 421–53.

———. *Vietnam or Indochina? Contesting Concepts of Space in Vietnamese nationalism, 1887–1954*. Copenhagen: NIAS, 1995.

Gouda, Frances. *Colonial Practices in the Netherland Indies, 1900–1942*. Amsterdam: Amsterdam University Press, 1995.

Grimal, Henri. *La Décolonisation de 1919 à nos jours*. Bruxelles: Editions complexe, 1996.

Guérin du Marteray, Christian. "Une Colonie pendant la guerre ou les origines d'une révolte: Madagascar, 1939–1947." Ph.D. dissertation, Université de Nice, 1977.

Ha, Marie-Paule. "Engendering French Colonial History: The Case of Indochina," *Historical Reflections* 25, no. 1 (1999): 95–125.

Haas, Gottfried. "Französisch-Indochina zwischen den Mächten, 1940–1945." Ph.D. dissertation, Freien Universität Berlin, 1970.

Harovelo, Janine. *La SFIO et Madagascar*. Paris: L'Harmattan, 1995.

Hellman, John. *The Knight-Monks of Vichy France: Uriage, 1940–1945*. Kingston: McGill University Press, 1997.

Hémery, Daniel. *Ho Chi Minh, de l'Indochine au Vietnam*. Paris: Gallimard, 1990.

———. *Révolutionnaires vietnamiens et pouvoir colonial en Indochine de 1932 à 1937*. Paris: Maspero, 1975.

Henley, David. "Ethnogeographic Integration and Exclusion in Anticolonial Nationalism: Indonesia and Indochina," *Comparative Studies in Society and History* 37 (April 1995): 286–324.

Heppner, Ernest. *Shanghai Refuge: A Memoir of the World War II Jewish Ghetto*. Lincoln: University of Nebraska Press, 1993.

Herman, Arthur, Jr. "The Language of Fidelity in Early Modern France," *Journal of Modern History* 67, no. 1 (Mar. 1995): 8.

Hesse d'Alzon, Claude. *La Présence militaire française en Indochine, 1940–1945*. Vincennes: Publications du service historique de l'Armée de Terre, 1985.

Hobsbawm, Eric. "Inventing Traditions." In *The Invention of Tradition*. Cambridge: Cambridge University Press, 1983.

Hoisington, William, Jr. *The Cassablanca Connection: French Colonial Policy, 1936–1943*. Chapel Hill: University of North Carolina Press, 1984.

———. "Politics and Postage Stamps: The Postal Issues of the French State and Empire, 1940–1944," *French Historical Studies* 7, no. 3 (spring 1972): 349–67.

Hue Tam Ho Tai. *Radicalism and the Origins of the Vietnamese Revolution*. Cambridge: Harvard University Press, 1992.

Hunt, Lynn. *The Family Romance of the French Revolution*. Berkeley: University of California Press, 1992.

Huynh Kim Khánh. *Vietnamese Communism, 1925–1945*. Ithaca: Cornell University Press, 1982.

Institut Charles de Gaulle. *Brazzaville, janvier-février 1944: aux sources de la décolonisation*. Paris: Plon, 1988.

———. *Le Général de Gaulle et l'Indochine, 1940–1946*. Paris: Plon, 1982.

Irvine, William. "Fascism in France and the Strange Case of the Croix de Feu," *Journal of Modern History* 63 (1991): 271–95.

Isoart, Paul, ed. *L'Indochine française 1940–1945*. Paris: PUF, 1982.

Jennings, Eric. "Blacks in France and the Empire." In Bertram Gordon, ed., *Historical Dictionary of World War II France*. Westport, Conn.: Greenwood Press, 1998, 37.

———. "La Dissidence aux Antilles, 1940–1943," *Vingtième siècle, revue d'histoire* 68 (October–December 2000): 55–71.

———. "Monuments to Frenchness? The Memory of the Great War and the Politics of Guadeloupe's Identity, 1914–1945," *French Historical Studies* 21, no. 4 (fall 1998): 561–92.

———. "Reinventing *Jeanne*: The Iconology of Joan of Arc in Vichy Schoolbooks, 1940–1944," *Journal of Contemporary History* 29, no. 4 (October 1994): 711–34.

————. "Vichy à Madagascar: la Révolution Nationale, l'enseignement et la jeunesse, 1940–1942," *Revue d'histoire moderne et contemporaine* 46, no. 4 (December 1999): 727–44.

Juraver, Jean, and Michel Eclar. *Anse-Bertrand, une commune de Guadeloupe, hier, aujourd'hui, demain.* Paris: Karthala, 1992.

Kedward, H. R. *Occupied France: Collaboration and Resistance, 1940–1944.* Oxford: Basil Blackwell, 1987.

Kelly, Gail Paradise. *Franco-Vietnamese Schools, 1918–1938: Regional Development and Implications for National Integration.* Madison: Wisconsin Papers on Southeast Asia, 1982.

Kennedy, Dane. *The Magic Mountains: Hill Stations and the British Raj.* Berkeley: University of California Press, 1996.

Kent, Raymond. *From Madagascar to the Malagasy Republic.* New York: Praeger, 1962.

Klein, Martin. *Slavery and Colonial Rule in French West Africa.* Cambridge: Cambridge University Press, 1998.

Koerner, Francis. *Histoire de l'enseignement privé et officel à Madagascar.* Paris: L'Harmattan, 1999.

————. *Madagascar: colonisation française et nationalisme malgache.* Paris: l'Harmattan, 1994.

Kottak, Conrad, Jean-Aimé Rakotoarisoa, Aidan Southall, and Pierre Vérin. *Madagascar: Society and History.* Durham: Carolina Academic Press, 1986.

Kranzler, David. *Japanese, Nazis and Jews: The Jewish Refugee Community of Shanghai, 1938–1945.* New York: Yeshiva University Press, 1976.

Kuisel, Richard. *Capitalism and the State in Modern France.* Cambridge: Cambridge University Press, 1981.

————. "Vichy et les origines de la planification économique," *Mouvement social* 89 (January–March 1977): 77–101.

Lamant, Pierre Lucien. "La Révolution Nationale dans l'Indochine de l'Amiral Decoux," *Revue d'histoire de la Deuxieme Guerre Mondiale* 138 (April 1985): 21–41.

Lambeye-Boy, Pierrette. *La Guadeloupe au début de la Seconde Guerre Mondiale.* Centre départemental de documentation pédagogoque. Archives départementales de la Guadeloupe, 1987.

Lane, Patricia. "Eléments sur la mise en oeuvre de la politique américaine envers l'Indochine, 1940–1945," *Les Cahiers de l'IHTP* numéro spécial, "Les Guerres d'Indochine de 1945 à 1975" 34 (June 1996): 19–34.

Larson, Pier. "Desperately Seeking 'the Merina' (Central Madagascar): Reading Ethnonyms and Their Semantic Fields in African Identity Histories." *Journal of Southern African Studies* 22, no. 4 (1996): 541–60.

Lawler, Nancy. "The Crossing of the Gyaman to the Cross of Lorraine: Wartime Politics in West Africa, 1941–1942," *African Affairs* 96 (January 1997): 53–71.

————. *Soldiers of Misfortune: Ivoirien Tirailleurs of World War II.* Athens: Ohio University Press, 1992.

Lebovics, Herman. *True France: The Wars over Cultural Identity, 1900–1945.* Ithaca: Cornell University Press, 1992.

Le Calloc'h, Bernard. "Le Rôle de Pham-Quynh dans la promotion du quôc-ngu et de la littérature vietnamienne moderne," *Revue française d'histoire d'outre-mer* 72, no. 3 (1985): 309–20.

Le Crom, Jean-Pierre. *Syndicats nous voilà! Vichy et le corporatisme.* Paris: Les Éditions ouvrières, 1995.

Lefeuvre, Daniel. "Vichy et la modernisation de l'Algérie: intention ou réalité?" *Vingtième siècle, revue d'histoire* 42 (April–June 1994): 7–16.

Lemore, Yagil. "Jeunesse de France et d'outre-mer et la vision de l'homme nouveau dans la France de Vichy," *Guerres mondiales et conflits contemporains* 158 (1990): 93–104.

Lerner, Henri. *Catroux.* Paris: Albin Michel, 1990.

Levillain, Henriette, ed. *La Guadeloupe, 1875–1914: les soubresauts d'une société pluriethnique ou les ambiguïtés de l'assimilation.* Paris: Autrement, 1994.

Lewis, James. "The French Colonial Service and the Issues of Reform, 1944–1948," *Contemporary European History* 4 (July 1995): 153–88.

Lockhart, Bruce. *The End of the Vietnamese Monarchy.* New Haven: Council on Southeast Asian Studies, 1993.

Lorcin, Patricia. *Imperial Identities: Stereotyping, Prejudice and Race in Colonial Algeria.* London: Tauris, 1999.

Loucou, Jean-Noël. "La Deuxieme Guerre Mondiale et ses effets en Côte-d'Ivoire," *Annales de l'Université d'Abidjan*, Serie 1, tome VII histoire (1980).

Lupo-Raveloarimanana, Monique. "Soldats et travailleurs malgaches en France pendant la seconde guerre mondiale," *Omaly sy Anio (Hier et Aujourd'hui)* Université de Madagascar 28 (July–December 1988): 23–42.

MacMaster, Neil. *Colonial Migrants and Racism: Algerians in France, 1900–1962.* London: Macmillan, 1997.

Maguire, G. E. *Anglo-American Policy towards the Free French.* New York: St. Martin's Press, 1995.

Marchese, Stelio. "Il Giornale 'la Lutte' e i trotskysti di Saigon, 1934–1939," *Storia e politica* 16 (1977): 664–83.

Marchetti, Adriano. "Jean Paulhan et les Hain-Teny ou les incertitudes de la poésie," *Francofonia* 39 (fall 2000): 4.

Marr, David. *Vietnam 1945: The Quest for Power.* Berkeley: University of California Press, 1995.

———. *Vietnamese Anticolonialism, 1885–1925.* Berkeley: University of California Press, 1971.

———. *Vietnamese Tradition on Trial, 1920–1945.* Berkeley: University of California Press, 1981.

Marrus, Michael. *The Unwanted: European Refugees in the Twentieth Century.* Oxford: Oxford University Press, 1985.

Marrus, Michael, and Robert Paxton. *Vichy France and the Jews.* New York: Schocken Books, 1981.

Marseille, Jacques. *L'Age d'or de la France coloniale.* Paris: Albin Michel, 1986.

———. *Empire colonial et capitalisme français.* Paris: Albin Michel, 1984.

Marshall, Bruce. *The French Colonial Myth and Constitution-making in the Fourth Republic.* New Haven: Yale University Press, 1973.

Martin du Gard, Maurice. *La Carte impériale: histoire de la France outre-mer 1940–1945*. Paris: A. Bonne, 1949.

McCoy, Alfred, ed. *Southeast Asia under Japanese Occupation*. Yale University, Southeast Asia Studies, Monograph 22, 1981.

Memmi, Albert. *Portrait du colonisé*. Utrecht: Jean-Jacques Pauvert, 1966.

Mercier, Fabienne. *Vichy face à Chang Kai-Shek*. Paris: L'Harmattan, 1995.

Meyer, Charles. *Les Français en Indochine, 1860–1910*. Paris: Hachette, 1985.

Michel, Jacques. *La Marine française en Indochine de 1939 à 1955*. Vol. 1: 1939–1945. Paris: Service historique de la marine, 1972.

Michel, Marc. "'Mémoire officielle,' discours et pratique coloniale: le 14 juillet et le 11 novembre au Sénégal entre les deux guerres," *Revue française d'histoire d'outre-mer* 287 (1990): 145–58.

———. "Les Ralliements à la France Libre en 1940." Paper delivered at the journée d'études: "La Seconde Guerre Mondiale et son impact en Afrique," Université d'Aix-en-Provence, February 10, 1996.

Michel, Marie. "Maréchal Nous Voilà ... ou comment Vichy a détruit le prestige de la France en Indochine," *Les Etoiles* (February 1946): 1.

Miller, Gérard. *Les Pousse-au-jouir du Maréchal Pétain*. Paris: Éditions du Seuil, 1975.

Molet, Louis. *La Conception malgache du monde, du surnaturel et de l'homme en Imerina*. Paris: L'Harmattan, 1979.

Morlat, Patrice. *La Répression coloniale au Vietnam, 1908–1940*. Paris: L'Harmattan, 1990.

Mosca, Liliana. "Italian Perspectives on the Allied Campaign in Madagascar, May–November 1942," *Africana Journal* 16 (1994): 341–64.

Mosse, George. "Fascist Aesthetics and Society: Some Considerations," *Journal of Contemporary History* 31, no. 2 (April 1996): 245–52.

———. *The Nationalization of the Masses: Political Symbolism and Mass Movements in Germany from the Napoleonic Wars through the Third Reich*. Ithaca: Cornell University Press, 1991.

Munholland, Kim. "Empire." In Bertram Gordon, ed., *Historical Dictionary of World War II France*. Westport, Conn.: Greenwood Press, 1998.

———. "The Trials of the Free French in New Caledonia," *French Historical Studies* 14 (1986): 547–99.

My Van, Tran. "Japan and Vietnam's Caodaists: A Wartime Relationship, 1939–1945," *Journal of Southeast Asian Studies* 27, no. 1 (March 1996): 179–93.

N.A. "La France a pratiqué en Indochine, depuis 1939, une politique très libérale d'association," *Marchés coloniaux du monde*, May 8, 1948.

Nguyen Khac Vien, "Vietnam during World War II," *Vietnamese Studies* 24 (1970).

Nitz, Kiyoko. "Independence without Nationalists? The Japanese and Vietnamese Nationalism during the Japanese Period, 1940–1945," *Journal of Southeast Asian Studies* 15, no. 1 (March 1984): 108–33.

———. "Japanese Military Policy towards French Indochina during the Second World War: The Road to the Meigo Sakusen (9 March 1945)," *Journal of Southeast Asian Studies* 14, no. 2 (September 1983): 328–53.

Noiriel, Gérard. *Les Origines républicaines de Vichy*. Paris: Hachette, 1999.

———. *The French Melting Pot*. Minneapolis: University of Minnesota Press, 1996.

Norindr, Panivong. *Phantasmatic Indochina: French Colonial Ideology in Architecture, Film and Literature*. Durham: Duke University Press, 1996.

Osborne, Milton. *Southeast Asia*. Sydney: Allen and Unwin, 1988.

Ozouf, Mona. *Festivals and the French Revolution*. Cambridge: Harvard University Press, 1988.

Paillard, Yvan-Georges. "Domination coloniale et récupération des traditions autochtones: le cas de Madagascar de 1896 à 1914," *Revue d'histoire moderne et contemporaine* 38 (January 1991): 73–104.

———. *Les Incertitudes du colonialisme: Jean Carol à Madagascar*. Paris: L'Harmattan, 1990.

———. "Marianne et l'indigène: les premiers 14 juillet coloniaux à Madagascar," *L'Information historique* 45 (1983): 107–20.

Paxton, Robert. *Vichy France: Old Guard and New Order, 1940–1944*. New York: Columbia University Press, 1982.

Payne, Stanley. "Fascism in Western Europe." In Nathaniel Greene, ed., *Fascism: An Anthology*. New York: Thomas Crowell, 1968.

Pedrazzani, Jean-Michel. *La France en Indochine de Catroux à Sainteny*. Paris: Arthaud, 1972.

Peer, Shanny. *France on Display*. Albany: SUNY Press, 1998.

Peschanski, Denis. *Vichy, 1940–1944: contrôle et exclusion*. Bruxelles: Editions complexe, 1997.

Pollard, Miranda. *Reign of Virtue: Mobilizing Gender in Vichy France*. Chicago: University of Chicago Press, 1998.

Prochaska, David. *Making Algeria French: Colonialism in Bône, 1870–1920*. New York: Cambridge University Press, 1990.

Prost, Antoine. "Les Monuments aux morts." In Pierre Nora, ed., *Les Lieux de mémoire*. Vol. 1: *La République*. Paris: Gallimard, 1984.

Rabearimanana, Lucile. "Le District de Manjakanandiana (Province d'Antananarivo) pendant la deuxième guerre mondiale: désorganisation économique et restructuration sociale," *Omaly sy Anio* 29–32 (1989–90): 433–55.

Rabinow, Paul. *French Modern: Norms and Forms of the Social Environment*. Chicago: University of Chicago Press, 1995.

Raison-Jourde, Françoise. "Une Rébellion en quête de statut: 1947 à Madagascar," *Revue de la Bibliothèque nationale* 34 (1989): 24–32.

Rakotoanosy Ratrimoarivony, Monique. "Histoire et nature de l'enseignement à Madagascar de 1896 à 1960." Ph.D. dissertation, Université Paris IV, 1986.

Ralaimihoatra, Edouard. *Histoire de Madagascar*. Antananarivo: E. Ralaimihoatra, 1966.

Ranrianja, Solofo. *Le Parti Communiste de la région de Madagascar*. Antananarivo: Foi et justice, 1989.

Ratrematsialonina, Dox F. "Madagascar pendant la deuxième guerre mondiale: un essai d'autarcie, 1939–1943." Ph.D. dissertation, Université d'Aix-en-Provence, 1986.

Ratrimoarivony-Rakotoanosy, Monique. "Pouvoir colonial et laïcisation: la franc-maçonnerie et la question scolaire sur les Hautes-terres centrales de 1905 à 1910," *Omaly sy Anio* 29–32 (1989–90): 353–66.

Rémy, Dominique. *Les Lois de Vichy*. Paris: Romillat, 1992.

Riosa, Alceo. "Alcuni appunti per una storia della festa del lavoro durante il regime fascista." In Alceo Riosa, ed., *Le Metamorfosi del 1 Maggio: la festa del lavoro in Europa tra le due guerre*. Venice: Marsilio editori, 1990.

Rioux, Jean-Pierre, ed. *La Vie culturelle sous Vichy*. Bruxelles: Editions complexe, 1990.

Rosenberg, Clifford. "Republican Surveillance: Immigration, Citizenship and the Police in Interwar Paris." Ph.D. dissertation, Princeton University, 2000.

Rousso, Henry. *The Vichy Syndrome*. Cambridge: Harvard University Press, 1991.

Sachiko, Murakami. "Japan's Thrust into French Indochina, 1940–1945." Ph.D. dissertation, New York University, 1981.

Said, Edward. *Culture and Imperialism*. New York: Vintage Books, 1994.

———. *Orientalism*. New York: Vintage Books, 1979.

Sainton, Jean-Pierre. *Rosan Girard: chronique d'une vie politique en Guadeloupe*. Paris: Jasor/Karthala, 1993.

Schalk, David. "Reflections d'outre-mer on French Colonialism," *Journal of European Studies* 28, nos. 1–2 (March 1998): 5–23.

Sempaire, Eliane. *La Dissidence an tan Sorin, 1940–1943*. Editions Jasor, 1989.

———. *La Guadeloupe en tan Sorin, 1940–1943*. Paris: Edition et diffusion de la culture antillaise, 1984.

Sghaier, Amira Aleya. "Les Collaborationnistes français en Tunisie entre juin 1940 et mai 1943," *Les Cahiers de Tunisie* 49, no. 173 (1996): 209–21.

Sherzer, Dina. "French Colonial and Post-colonial Hybridity: condition métisse," *Journal of European Studies* 28, no. 1–2 (March 1998): 103–20.

Shipway, Martin. "Madagascar on the Eve of Insurrection, 1944–1947: The Impasse of a Liberal Colonial Policy," *Journal of Imperial and Commonwealth History* 24, no. 1 (January 1996): 72–100.

———. *The Road to War: France and Vietnam, 1944–1947*. Oxford: Berghahn Books, 1996.

Slama, Alain-Gérard. "Vichy était-il fasciste?" *Vingtième siècle, revue d'histoire* 11 (July 1983): 41–53.

Slawecki, Leon. *French Policy towards the Chinese in Madagascar*. Hamden: Shoestring Press, 1971.

Smith, Ralph. "The Japanese Period in Indochina and the Coup of March 1945," *Journal of Southeast Asian Studies* 9, no. 2 (September 1978): 268–301.

Sportès, Morgan. *Tonkinoise*. Paris: Le Seuil, 1995.

Stone, Marla. "Staging Fascism: The Exhibition of the Fascist Revolution," *Journal of Contemporary History* 28, no. 1 (April 1993): 215–44.

Stovall, Tyler. "The Color Line behind the Lines: Racial Violence in France during the Great War," *American Historical Review* 103, no. 3 (1998): 737–69.

Stuart-Fox, Martin. *A History of Laos*. Cambridge: Cambridge University Press, 1997.

Suvelor, Roland, ed. *L'Historial Antillais*. Fort-de-France: Société Dajani, 1980.

Sweets, John. *Choices in Vichy France: The French under Nazi Occupation*. New York: Oxford University Press, 1986.

Tarling, Nicholas. "The British and the First Japanese Move into Indochina," *Journal of Southeast Asian Studies* 21 (March 1990): 35–65.

Thomas, Martin. "After Mers-el-Kébir: The Armed Neutrality of the French Navy, 1940–1943," *English Historical Review* 112 (1997): 643–70.

———. "Free France, the British Government and the Future of French Indo-china, 1940–45," *Journal of Southeast Asian Studies* 28 (1997): 137–60.

———. *The French Empire at War, 1940–1945*. Manchester: Manchester University Press, 1998.

———. "Imperial Backwater or Strategic Outpost? The British Takeover of Vichy Madagascar, 1942," *Historical Journal* 39, no. 4 (December 1996): 1049–74.

Todorov, Tzvetan. *On Human Diversity: Nationalism, Racism and Exoticism in French Thought*. Cambridge: Harvard University Press, 1994.

Tønnesson, Stein. *The Vietnamese Revolution of 1945: Roosevelt, Ho Chi Minh and de Gaulle in a World at War*. London: Sage, 1991.

Trinh Van Thao. *Vietnam du Confucianisme au Communisme*. Paris: L'Harmattan, 1990.

Tronchon, Jacques. *L'Insurrection malgache de 1947*. Paris: Karthala, 1986.

Truesdell, Matthew. *Spectacular Politics: Louis-Napoleon Bonaparte and the Fête Impériale, 1849–1870*. Oxford: Oxford University Press, 1997.

Valensky, Chantal. "Soldats malgaches et culture française," *Revue française d'histoire d'outre-mer* 315 (1997): 78–83.

Valette, Jacques. "Essai bibliographique: l'Indochine de 1940 à 1945," *Revue d'histoire de la Deuxième Guerre Mondiale* 138 (1985): 137–44.

———. *Indochine, 1940–1945: Français contre Japonais*. Paris: Sedes, 1993.

Vann, Michael. "White City on the Red River: Race, Power and Culture in French Colonial Hanoi, 1872–1954." Ph.D. dissertation, University of California, Santa Cruz, 1999.

Vergès, Françoise. *Monsters and Revolutionaries: Colonial Family Romance and Métissage*. Durham: Duke University Press, 1999.

Vérin, Pierre. *Madagascar*. Paris: Karthala, 1990.

Virmani, Arundhati. "National Symbols under Colonial Domination: The Nationalization of the Indian Flag, March–August 1923," *Past and Present* 164 (August 1999): 169–87.

Von Henneberg, Krystyna. "Imperial Uncertainties: Architectural Syncretism and Improvisation in Fascist Colonial Libya," *Journal of Contemporary History* 31, no. 2 (1996): 373–95.

Vu Ngu Chieu. "Political and Social Change in Vietnam between 1940 and 1946." Ph.D. dissertation, University of Madison, Wisconsin, 1984.

Weber, Eugen. *Action française*. Stanford, Calif.: Stanford University Press, 1962.

Weinberg, Gerhard. *A World at Arms*. Cambridge: Cambridge University Press, 1994.

Weinstein, Brian. *Eboué*. New York: Oxford University Press, 1972.

White, Luise. *Speaking with Vampires: Rumor and History in Colonial Africa*. Berkeley: University of California Press, 2000.

Winock, Michel. *Edouard Drumont et Cie.: antisémitisme et fascisme en France*. Paris: Le Seuil, 1982.

Wright, Gwendolyn. *The Politics of Design in French Colonial Urbanism*. Chicago: University of Chicago Press, 1991.

Zdatny, Steven. "Collaboration or Resistance? French Hairdressers and Vichy's Labor Charter," *French Historical Studies* 20, no. 4 (fall 1997): 737–72.

Zuccarelli, François. *La Vie politique sénégalaise, 1940–1988*. Paris: Cheam, 1988.

Index

In this index an "f" after a number indicates a separate reference on the next page, and an "ff" indicates separate references on the next two pages. A continuous discussion over two or more pages is indicated by a span of page numbers, e.g., "57–59." *Passim* is used for a cluster of references in close but not consecutive sequence.

CPSIA information can be obtained
at www.ICGtesting.com
Printed in the USA
LVHW031753171218
600759LV00002B/388/P